Lucknow
Memories of a City

Lucknow
Memories of a City

Edited by
VIOLETTE GRAFF

OXFORD
UNIVERSITY PRESS

OXFORD
UNIVERSITY PRESS

YMCA Library Building, Jai Singh Road, New Delhi 110001

Oxford University Press is a department of the University of Oxford. It furthers the
University's objective of excellence in research, scholarship, and education
by publishing worldwide in

Oxford   New York
Athens   Auckland   Bangkok   Bogota   Buenos Aires   Calcutta
Cape Town   Chennai   Dar es Salaam   Delhi   Florence   Hong Kong   Istanbul
Karachi   Kuala Lumpur   Madrid   Melbourne   Mexico City   Mumbai
Nairobi   Paris   Sao Paolo   Singapore   Taipei   Tokyo   Toronto   Warsaw

with associated companies in

Berlin   Ibadan

© Oxford University Press 1997

Oxford India Paperbacks 1999

ISBN 019 564 887 0

Typeset by Guru Typograph Technology, New Delhi 110 045
Printed in India at A P Offset, Delhi 110 032
and published by Manzar Khan, Oxford University Press
YMCA Library Building, Jai Singh Road, New Delhi 110 001

To the memory of Asif Kidwai

Preface

It was the fag end of March 1989. I was leaving Lucknow with a heavy heart. Within a week two dear friends had died, and I was not sure whether I would ever want to return. Lucknow seemed empty.

It was precisely at this point when, back home in Paris, I was presented with a request which, at once, lifted my spirits. Would I participate in the launching of a series called 'Memories of Cities'? The idea was to look at places endowed with an especially meaningful past, i.e. places where, at one point of time, a major experience had taken place, leaving unending memories for one reason or the other; Florence and the Medici patronage during the Italian Renaissance, Athens and the extraordinary display of the Greek philosophy during the fifth-third centuries BC; London under the Victorians; or Barcelona during the Spanish Civil War

But all these cities were in Europe, and the French publishers were very keen to include other parts of the world, namely Asian cities and of course, among them, India's most significant places. Would I like to consider a book on Delhi, Calcutta or Madras? As the reader may guess, my immediate answer was yes, provided it was Lucknow!

And this is how this book came about, with of course a number of vicissitudes before it took shape. To start with, there was a problem of size. The number of enthusiastic replies which answered my first circular letter was so high that the publishers were compelled to back out. Financing the translation and adjustment of so many sophisticated papers for a French general readership would have been extremely costly. But why not publish the book in English? And publish it in India, of course, since its very purpose, and what bound the contributors together, was their desire to pay homage to the city of Lucknow and its people.

The next step was not easy either. How to manage a volume which would be both comprehensive and balanced, lively and readable, a faithful mirror of the feelings, hopes and commitments of our Lucknawi friends. To sum it up, how to convey understanding and feeling, without being too emotional? I for one was just that, and it may not be irrelevant to explain why. It has nothing to do, I am afraid, with the Nawabs or with my compatriot Claude Martin! It has a lot to do with my personal background and family legacies.

The first of these legacies is a deep empathy with refugees and those who have been uprooted. I shall always remember the nostalgia of my two grandmothers who hailed from Alsace, the beloved province which their parents had left after the Prussian war (1870–71). Divided families. I had always known what it meant. I could understand many a tragedy.

I have another legacy. I belong to this small French religious minority which, in India, to my delight, is still known as Huguenot—a community which has led a tormented existence, has fought fiercely for its faith, for freedom of expression and, in modern times, for a strict separation between Church and State. How could I dream of finding a better illustration of these various themes than in Lucknow, meeting the people whom I met, whose lives had so much resonance with my own?

The first of these friends is fortunately still very much alive and kicking. He is Ram Advani, a famous book-seller in Lucknow whose shop on Hazratganj is the most welcoming meeting-place that a scholar can ever hope to find. A real 'institution', that was entirely built by him. A Kshatriya from Sindh, a refugee from Lahore, he is the epitome of Hindu tolerance and ecumenical mind. If Lucknow, and Uttar Pradesh more generally, is one of the most studied parts of India, it is because Ram has made the capital city a most pleasant and stimulating place for generations of scholars from North America, Europe and Australia to work. Not only is he the most genial and enabling of hosts but he has also kept memories refreshed with phone calls, letters and books when those scholars have returned to their universities.

The second personality whom I met, and to whom this book is dedicated, was an extraordinary man, Dr Asif Kidwai. Asif, who died in 1989, had been lying on his cot for some 40 years. He was a gifted student in AMU when rheumatoid arthritis struck and slowly, but inexorably, paralysed his body. By then he had managed to study homeopathy, and become a practising doctor. His room opened directly on one of the main roads of Aminabad, in the family mansion where his dear ones were looking after him with devotion, and where he would attend to patients every day. That was not all. He had assumed full editorship of the well-known Urdu newspaper, *Azaem*. A practising Muslim, close to the Nadwat-ul-Ulema, an active translator of the books of its Rector, 'Ali Mian', he was at the same time a militant secularist. I wish I could quote here one of the many letters received from him over the years, where he managed to convey illuminating summaries of the current political situation. A magnificent human being. A guru for several of us.

A Christian family will complete the list of those people who, ever since my first visit to Lucknow in 1974, taught me to love the place. Frederic and Gladys Solomon had a small, modest flat, in Hazratganj. Dr Freddie had been a close associate and friend of a well-known Muslim politician, Dr A.J. Faridi. A dedicated PSP worker and a member of the Lucknow corporation for years, he was, above all, one of those doctors who would attend to people day and night and never care to press for fees. His clinic was always full while, upstairs, Gladys, a former YWCA worker, would always find time for me, for vivid small talk or long, sharp well-informed discussions, over a 'plain omelette without pepper', for my poor un-Indian stomach.

These were cherished breaks, and this is exactly what I was looking for when, one day, reaching Lucknow in a kind of stupor (the Urdu press had just announced the death of Asif), I was shocked beyond belief. The last prayers were being said around the body of Dr Solomon. I hope the reader will forgive me for remembering these sad hours. They were to lead to what was an extraordinary demonstration of religious fervour and harmony: the singing of a hymn at the gate of the Nishat cemetery in a way I had never heard before. The congregation was incredibly 'composite', Christians of course, but Muslims, Hindus, Sikhs in large numbers. All of them singing a well-known protestant hymn, which was also the favourite song of Gandhiji, 'Abide with me'. This was Lucknow at its best.

Acknowledgements

Many friends and colleagues had volunteered to join in this Lucknow volume. It was unfortunately not possible to accommodate all the proposals and suggestions which came. Moreover, some of them over-lapped with others while, at the same time, there were important periods or topics which were not covered as they should have been. I am, for instance, extremely sorry that we could not include chapters dealing with the traditional arts and games of Lucknow (nothing on the famous School of *Kathak* dance!), nor with the superb craftsmanship of the local artisans (*chikan* embroideries, etc.). At a different level, I would have liked to gather personal reminiscences about the 1937–47 years. It proved difficult. Scars are still vivid.

Let me now thank warmly all those whose names should have appeared in the Table of Contents, or who took a keen interest in the conception of the book, namely (in alphabetical order): Viqar Ahmad (London), Nicole Balbir (Paris), Andréine Bel (Marseille), Paul Brass (Seattle), Satish Chandra (New Delhi), Sunita Charles (Lucknow), Anees Chishti (New Delhi), Barun De (Calcutta), M.M. Dhar (Lucknow), Myriam Ghalmi (Beirut), Harold Gould (Chicago), S.M. Jaffar (Lucknow), Vijay Khan (Lucknow), Atiya Habib Kidwai (New Delhi), T.N. Madan (New Delhi), Saeed Naqvi (New Delhi) and S.K. Narain (Lucknow).

I would like also to express my gratitude to all those who, whether in Lucknow or elsewhere, opened their houses, and their files, listened patiently to my questions, gave life literally to the past, as for instance the late Major General Habibullah, who took me to the battle-fields of 1857–58, and described vividly the operations as if they had appeared yesterday. Or Suleiman, Raja of Mahmudabad, who keeps doing the rounds of the palatial mansion where one can still find, hanging on the walls, the yellowing old photos of those leaders who, in 1916, partici-pated in the Lucknow Pact. Or Sakina Hasan and Hamida Lalljee when they bring back to life their father, the Shia leader, Ali Zaheer. Or the Faridi family with their reminiscences and their warm hospitality. Or Professor S.K. Narain, who knows everything about his beloved city and would never agree to move out of his striking old mansion in Mashakganj. Or Sunita Charles, Principal of Isabella Thoburn College, with her knowledge of the local institutions and their problems. And, at a different level, how could I forget the warm welcome of Prince Anjum Qadr in Matia Burj (Calcutta) and the nostalgia emanating from the 'King of Oudh mausoleum' and its fascinating relics.

Other friends and personalities are to be thanked. Among them, Rajeswar Dayal, who was Home Secretary for UP in 1946, and T.N. Dhar, from the UP cadre, a former Principal Secretary to the Chief Minister. Among their younger colleagues, I would like to single out Rajiv R. Shah (and his wife, Smita), N.C. Saxena, and Ashok Priyadarshy. They never misconstrued my efforts to decipher the on-going politics. I am also deeply grateful to those in political circles who found the time to answer my questions, among whom Narain Dutt Tiwari, several times head of the Lucknow Government, and his late wife and Atal Behari Vajpayee, the twice elected representative of Lucknow and, at one point, the Prime Minister of India.

It is time now to thank warmly those colleagues who, over the years, have given me the unfailing support of their understanding and affection.

For the affection I received, I would single out Daniel and Alice Thorner. The only handicap of Alice is that she has no connection with Lucknow! Nevertheless, in Paris—and at times in Delhi—we have been close neighbours, and close collaborators. She has helped me to get rid of my long, French-style sentences. I hope it is for the better!

For a fresh academic look at things Indian, I am indebted to Paul Brass and Francis Robinson. Their books on UP, released simultaneously in 1974, have been my constant companions. During the last ten years, i have relied heavily on their advice and guidance. I do hope that I have not been too much of a nuisance to them.

I am afraid this is what I have proved to be for Imtiaz Ahmad. He has been a friend since 1974, when he gave me my first list of people I should look up in Lucknow. More recently he has demonstrated that he could also be my rescuer. In fact this book would never have materialized if, in 1995, after serious problems which damaged my vision, Imtiaz had not taken upon himself the thankless task of revising the copy-edited manuscript, and seen it through the press. It was a time-consuming job. My warmest thanks to him and also to the three colleagues who helped in the rescue: Muzaffar Alam, Narayani Gupta and Mushirul Hasan. My gratitude goes also to D.L. Sheth: he has always been most encouraging.

For the illustrations, I am most grateful to Jean-Marie Lafont whose help has been invaluable in identifying, obtaining and reproducing the photographs. I am greatly indebted to R.K. Laxman whose cartoons I have liberally stolen to illustrate my essay. Ajoy Bose, the Husainabad Trust and Francis Robinson also helped a lot just as Atiya Habib Kidwai supervised the maps. Shaukat Siddqi supervised the final word processing of the manuscript and helped in numerous other ways, D.L. Sachdeva word-processed the book and Kishan Gopal prepared the index. To all of them I am deeply indebted.

To conclude, on the Indian side I have to express my heartfelt thanks to the Indian Council for Social Science Research, which supported most of my visits to Delhi and Lucknow. Its staff was always most helpful and efficient.

On the French side, I must thank warmly the Maison des Sciences de l'Homme (MSH), and its successive Administrators, Clemens Heller and Maurice Aymard. I am deeply grateful as well to my Centre, the Centre d'Etudes et de Recherches Internationales (CERI), at the Fondation Nationale des Sciences Politiques (FNSP), and, for their constant encouragements, to the successive Directors of the CERI, Jean-Luc Domenach and Jean-François Leguil-Bayart. My gratitude goes also to the Centre d'Etude de l'Inde et de l'Asie du Sud (CEIAS) which provides a stimulating and congenial atmosphere. I would not like to forget Rosette de Montfalcon (MSH) and Anne Dubaquié (CERI) whose smiling efficiency has been invaluable. I must also express my gratitude to Henry Dougier, Director of the French Publishing House *Autrement*. Among many other series, he is the father of *Mémoire de villes*, a collection which, today, in France, is quite famous.

May I now remember my late parents and thank them and all those close associates in Paris who never questioned my repeated trips to India, and bore gracefully with my unceasing lectures on Lucknow? Finally, I could never have carried through the project without the solid support of Philippe, my husband, and the complicity of my children.

Contents

MAPS

Endpaper: Gentil's map of Awadh. Courtesy IOLR, British Library.

ILLUSTRATIONS (between pp. 152–3)

1. Colonel Jean-Baptiste Gentil.
   Drawing by Bourdier, engraving by Coqueret. Courtesy Jean-Marie
   Lafont.
2. Nawab Asif ud-Daullah. Courtesy Husainabad Trust.
3. The attack of Lucknow by the Sepoys, 30th July 1857. Courtesy The
   Mansell Collection.
4. Butler's Palace.
5. Kaiserbagh Palace.
6. The house of the Maharaja of Ayodhya.
7. Chattar Manzil.
8. The UP Secretariat.
9. Rickshawallahs in Hazratganj.
10. In the heart of Aminabad.
11. The University.
12. A Hindu temple in the centre of the Chowk.

Photographs 4–12, courtesy Violette Graff.

Chronology

11th century	Sheikhzadas settle on the Gomti river and build a fort, Qila Likhna.
1465	Death of the Chisti *Pir*, Shah Mina, whose *dargah* still draws crowds in Lucknow.
c. 1695	The family of Qutbuddin Shahid settle in Firangi Mahal.
1720–39	Saadat Khan (Burhan ul-Mulk) defeats the Sheikhzadas of Lucknow and two of their palaces, the Mubarak Mahal and the Panch Mahal, close to Machi Bhavan.
1739–56	Safdar Jang, nephew of Sadat Khan, although using Faizabad as his capital, buys the Mubarak and French Mahals.
1756–75	Shuja-ud-Daula looses his influence to the British at the battle of Buxar.
1775–98	Asaf-ud-Daula shifts his capital from Faizabad to Lucknow and, together with a French 'adventurer' Claude Martin (1735–1800), enlivens the City with flamboyant buildings. The main monuments are the Great Imambara, Asafi Mosque, Rumi Darwaza, old British Residency, the Chowk, and Martin's palaces: Farhat Daksh (Chattar Manzil) and Constantia.
1798–1814	Saadat Ali Khan builds Dilkusha Palace, Bailey Guard Gate, Lal Baradari, Begum Kothi and Kursheed Manzil.
1814–27	Ghazi-ud-din Haider is crowned King of Awadh by the British Governor-General, builds a canal, the tombs of his parents, and Shah Najaf.
1827–37	Nazir-ud-din Haider.
1837	English displaces Persian as the language of the Courts in British India. In NWP, Urdu prevails as the vernacular language.

1837–42	Mohammad Ali Shah builds the Husainabad Imambara and the Shahi Jumma Mosque.
1842–48	Amjad Ali Shah erects the Iron Bridge over the Gomti River.
1848	Opening of La Martinière school for boys.
1848–56	Wajid Ali Shah builds Kaiserbagh where he entertains poets and dancers with munificence. His lavishness helps Lord Dalhousie to pronounce his deposition and to keep him in exile in Calcutta (Matia Burj). The kingdom of Oudh is annexed to the British East India Company territories.
1857–58	The Mutiny uprising and the siege of the British Residency in Lucknow make news the world over. A young son of Wajid Ali Shah, Birgis Qader, is recognized by the rebels as the legitimate King of Awadh. His mother, Begum Hazrat Mahal, is regent until their flight to Nepal.
1858	Nawal Kishore starts the NK Press which will become internationally famous (closed in 1951).
1861	Birth of a British Indian Association meant for *Talukdars*. They are accommodated in the Kaiserbagh.
1862	Arrival of the Railways in Lucknow.
1868	First claims from Hindu intellectuals regarding the use of Hindi in education and administration.
1871	Isabella Thoburn, a missionary, enlarges her initial small school for girls and settles in Lal Bagh. The high school will be affiliated to Calcutta University in 1885.
1877	The province of Oudh is joined to the North-West Province to form the United Provinces of Agra and Oudh (UP). The capital of UP is Allahabad, with Chief Court for Oudh remaining in Lucknow (until 1951).
1894	Maulana Shibli Nomani founds the *Nadwat-ul-Ulema*.
1897	Pandit Madan Mohan Malaviya (one of the founders of Benares Hindu University) enters the Hindu-Urdu debate and denounces the highly persianized character of Urdu.

1900	The *Nagri* resolution comes as a shock to the Urdu well-wishers. The use of Urdu or Hindi will be optional in the Courts.
1906	Muslim leaders from all over India gather in Lucknow to discuss the memorial to be presented to the Viceroy Lord Minto, at Simla, formulating their demand for separate electorates.
1906–8	Shia-Sunni estrangement leads to rioting in Lucknow.
1910	The recently-born Muslim League elects Lucknow for its headquarters.
1913	The demolition of the lavatory of a mosque in Cawnpore, as a result of a road-widening scheme, followed by a riot in which Muslims were killed by police leads to widespread Muslim protest in India.
1915	First steps of a *Hindu Mahasabha*.
1916	The Congress and Muslim League both hold their sessions in Lucknow where they conclude the historic Lucknow Pact over constitutional reform.
1917	Opening of the Shia College.
1918	Death of Bindadin Maharaj, one of the most celebrated dancer of his time. Together with his brother Kalka, then his nephews, they made the *kathak* dance what it is today.
1918–22	Sir Harcourt Butler is Lieutenant-Governor, then Governor of UP.
1919	The principle of *diarchy* is introduced by the Montagu-Chelsmford GOI Act, and the provincial Legislative Council assumes a new importance.
1919–22	Maulana Abdul Bari, from Firangi Mahal, plays a central role in the *Khilafat* movement.
1921	Foundation stones of the Council Chamber and the University, as well as King George V Medical College and Charbagh Railway station laid. Lucknow is restored as the Capital of the province.
1924–26	Serious communal riots in UP find an echo in Lucknow.
1927	Demonstrations in Lucknow against the Simon Commission.

1935

The Government of India Act (1935) transforms the face of Indian politics. The UP Assembly will have 228 seats (140 general; 66 Muslim).

1936–37

General elections in the British provinces. In UP the performance of the Muslim League is disappointing, while the landlord party (NAP) is routed. The Congress is in a dominant position and asserts itself.

Choudhury Khaliquzzaman, formerly a Congressman, contested the Lucknow seat on a Muslim League ticket, and won.

Sajjad Zaheer, the brother of the Congress leader, Ali Zaheer, and himself a CPI activist, co-founder of the Progressive Writers Workshop, becomes Joint Secretary of the All-India Congress Socialist Party.

1937

August. G.B. Pant is sworn as Premier of UP. His government includes Rafi Ahmed Kidwai, Dr K.N. Katju, Vijayalakshmi Pandit. No agreement is reached with the Muslim League.

October. A crucial session of the Muslim League in Lucknow.

1938

The *Madhe Sahaba* quarrel leads to repeated violence between Shias and Sunnis.

The UP Tenancy Act introduces serious alterations into the agrarian system of the province.

1939

October. Following the instructions of the Congress High Command, the UP government resigns.

1942

'Quit India'. Agitation in Lucknow leads to the burning of the Alam Bagh Railway station. The Congress Socialist Party plays a major role in the movement.

The Lucknow Muslim politicians increasingly involved in the Pakistan movement, which gathers momentum.

1945–46

The new British Labour Government takes a decisive step and holds the first provincial legislative elections since 1937. In UP, the success of the Congress Party is overwhelming in the general constituencies, but it is just as impressive for the Muslim League regarding the Muslim seats (54 out of 60).

1946   *April.* A new government is formed in UP under the
                supervision of Maulana Azad, the then President of the
                Congress. G.B. Pant is Chief Minister, Rafi Ahmed
                Kidwai, Home Minister.

1947   *August.* Independence and Partition.

N.B. For the main events since 1947, see charts in Graff, pp. 258–65.

Note on Contributors

Imtiaz Ahmad is Professor at the Centre for Political Studies, Jawaharlal Nehru University, New Delhi.

Muzaffar Alam is Professor of Medieval Indian History, Centre for Historical Studies, Jawaharlal Nehru University, New Delhi.

Juan R.I. Cole is Professor in the Department of History, University of Michigan, Ann Arbor.

Michael H. Fisher is Professor in the Department of History, Oberlin College, Oberlin.

Violette Graff is Senior Researcher at the Centre d'Etudes et de Rechcerches Internationales, Paris.

Narayani Gupta is Professor of Modern History, in the Department of History, Jamia Millia Islamia, New Delhi.

Mushirul Hasan is Professor of Modern History in the Department of History, Jamia Millia Islamia, New Delhi.

James Kippen is Associate Professor of Music (ethnomusicology) in the Faculty of Music, University of Toronto.

Jean-Marie Lafont is at the Centre of Human Sciences, French Embassy, New Delhi.

Rosie Llewellyn-Jones is the Editor of *Chawkidar*, British Association for Cemeteries in South Asia, London.

Gail Minault is Associate Professor of History, at the University of Texas, Austin.

C.M. Naim is Professor in the Department of South Asian Languages and Civilizations, University of Chicago.

Veena Talwar Oldenburg is Associate Professor of History, Baruch College, New York.

Carla Petievich is Associate Professor, in the Department of History, Montclair State University, New Jersey.

Jacques Pouchpepadass is Professor of History, at the National Centre for Scientific Research, Paris.

Peter Reeves is Professor of History in the School of Social Sciences and Asian Languages, at the University of Technology, Perth, Western Australia.

Francis Robinson, is Professor and Vice Principal of the Royal Holloway College, University of London.

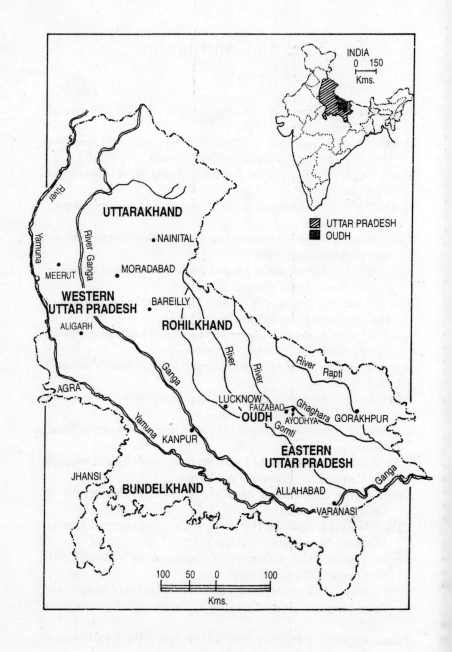

INDIA
0   150
Kms.

UTTAR PRADESH
OUDH

River Yamuna

River Ganga

UTTARAKHAND

NAINITAL

MORADABAD

MEERUT

WESTERN
UTTAR PRADESH

BAREILLY

ALIGARH

ROHILKHAND

Ganga

River

River

River Rapti

AGRA

LUCKNOW

FAIZABAD
Ghaghara

OUDH
AYODHYA
GORAKHPUR

Yamuna

Gomti

KANPUR

EASTERN
UTTAR PRADESH

JHANSI

BUNDELKHAND

ALLAHABAD

Ganga

VARANASI

100   50   0   100

Kms.

Introduction

There was a time when Lucknow was led to believe that its rulers were the emperors of the world, second to none. The glitter and the glory were not to last long: the story of the Shia Nawabs of Awadh (1722–1857) would end in disaster—but the period fascinates. It has left lingering memories in the minds of men, especially in Lucknow itself. It still has a lot to tell us, when we consider the formidable clash of cultures which characterizes the history of the province in pre-British times, the kinds of adjustment and compromise which were arrived at under the colonial rule, and the spirit of mutual tolerance and understanding which was never denied to Lakhnavis, even though outsiders would prefer to mock their debilitating, decadent culture rather than admire the deep-rooted and unfailing courtesy.

Is it surprising that in 1947 Lucknow was one of the towns where communal harmony survived the traumas of Partition? Yet the local Muslim elites had played such a role in the emergence of Pakistan that it was impossible for their people to escape the consequences. Refugees from the Punjab took the place of those who departed. It was the end of an era. A new way of life, more aggressive, more dynamic also, took over. Step by step the old cherished symbols and values were eroded, and the triumphant Congress system, because of its own internal constraints and divisions, was not especially prepared to help. It would take another forty-five years of bitter caste and communal struggles for the wheel to turn full circle. In 1775 the Shia rulers had left Faizabad-Ayodhya to settle on the Gomti. In 1991, rulers were back in Ayodhya: they now carried *trishuls* and saffron flags.

Putting together a set of articles on a theme is difficult and if the theme is an Indian town, it is doubly difficult. Indian towns have been around for centuries. Their architectural histories and morphologies, however, are often badly fractured, and many of the records and structures have disappeared. Their social history is often studied only tangentially, in terms of the histories of castes or communities, or of wider processes. Towns as prisms do reflect regional and national changes, but many of them also have social or morphological features which are uniquely specific. Indians have clear notions of the sense of place, of the charm/repulsiveness, warmth/coldness, snobbery/openness, of a particular town, but not many have written these down. Foreign travellers, in the pre-photography days, *did* describe places vividly, but often in stereotyped images, making it easier for us to study the history of *perceptions* about a town, than the town itself.

Lucknow has enjoyed more attention than most South Asian towns, except for Calcutta, the 1990 tercentenary of which inspired many books and articles. A striking example of a post-medieval town, with a considerable capital of architecture, dance, music and creative writing, enhanced by a tantalising flavour of a gracious lifestyle, Lucknow excites the imagination. The metaphor that writers employ for Lucknow is invariably that of an elusive chiaroscuro. The town glows bright when the sun of Delhi and Agra is setting; it is in turn outshone by Calcutta; after the revolt of 1857–58, the lamp flickers and sputters; in 1920, the candle burns bright when Lucknow is made the capital of the United Provinces, but with the advent of Independence and Partition in 1947 it is dimmed.

This town on the river Gomti has been in existence since the sixteenth century at least. Lucknow was a 'natural' urban site, equidistant between Gonda in the south and Ayodhya in the north, and, on a wider concentric circle, between the important centres of Gorakhpur, Varanasi and Allahabad. It was as vital a link in the eastward expansion of the Mughal Empire as Hyderabad was in the southward thrust. Under Akbar Lucknow was chosen as the capital of the *suba* of Awadh. A century later Emperor Aurangzeb gave it the status of a university town by establishing a seminary in the escheated estate of a Dutch merchant. This became known as Firangi Mahal, and played a key role in twentieth-century politics. The two provinces of Hyderabad and Awadh worked their way towards autonomy from the Mughals from the middle of the eighteenth century. The narrrative of the changing relations between the Nawabs of Awadh and the Badshahs at Delhi, and the very specific features of the nawabi regime, have been traced here and elsewhere by Alam (1986: chapter 1) and Barnett (1980). Encouraged by the increasing feebleness of the Delhi court, the Nawab, Saadat Khan (1722–39), began to treat Awadh as his family fief. His nephew and son-in-law Safdarjang (1739–50) was worsted by a rival at the Mughal court and, somewhat against his will, was cast in the role of rebel against the Emperor. He was eventually buried not in Awadh but in the beautiful mausoleum he had designed for himself in the family estate at Aliganj, equidistant between Mehrauli (the old Delhi), and the Mughal capital of Shahjahanabad, in a straight line eastward to the tomb of Emperor Humayun.

The eighteenth century saw a decline in the population of the Mughal cities of Lahore, Agra and Delhi, and the growth of towns like Lucknow and Varanasi. It was under the successors of Saadat Khan and Safdarjang that Faizabad (the twin city to Ayodhya) and Lucknow expanded into distinctive baroque capitals, celebrated in sketches and word pictures. The dynasty that built these towns was not native to Awadh. The Shia family of Saadat Khan had migrated from Nishapur, the home of Omar Khayyam, in north-eastern Iran. They were in the tradition of many individuals of talent and enterprise who had carved out niches for themselves at the courts of Delhi and Agra in the Gangetic plain, and Hyderabad and Bijapur in the Deccan. Lucknow welcomed many such immigrants during its second and more lasting spell of life as the capital of Awadh (1775–1856). Like Agra, Hyderabad and Seringapatam, Lucknow was cosmopolitan, home to a number of Europeans, who created here a part-European dilettante, part-Indian courtier life style (Lafont, chapter 4). Fisher (chapter 2) highlights the differences of culture and life-style between the rural zamindars of Awadh and the urban nobility.

Unlike Delhi, Agra and Jaipur, Lucknow was an unwalled town that expanded along the banks of the river. It had neither the formal avenues of Shahjahanabad, nor a Jama Masjid dominating the skyline. The nawabs and the Europeans raised buildings in no apparent order (Blomfield, 1992). Llewellyn-Jones (chapter 3) describes the architecture of Nawab Asaf-ud-Daula and his successors after 1775—not of marble and sandstone, but stucco and gilt, as attractive without being awesome. This 'baroque' architecture could be described as post-modern, for its catholic borrowing of styles ranged even more widely than the provenances of the various courtiers. The grand Rumi Darwaza was a copy of a gateway at Istanbul, while the façades of some palaces reminded Fanny Parks of Naples and Rome (Parks, 1850, 1: 184). Between 1775 and 1856, the successive riverside palace-complexes—the Macchi Bhawan, the Daulat Khana and the Chattar Manzil—were supplemented by a formal garden-complex (Kaiserbagh) and a ceremonial street (Hazratganj). But as early as the end of the eighteenth century, the distinctive architectural feature of Lucknow, the *imambaras* (ceremonial halls used during Mohurram) had been built. The French merchant-soldier, Claude Martin, was engaged in the construction of Constantia, the mansion which became his mausoleum (Llewellyn-Jones, 1985 and 1992). The British Residency was built as soon as the capital was moved to Lucknow, in 1775, and was located, with the Nawab's friendly acquiescence, not at a distance but very near the first palace-complex, the Machhi Bhawan (1766). In 1857 it was Indian rebels who besieged (but could not capture) the Residency, in contrast with Delhi, where it was British forces that besieged the walled city (Shahjahanabad) which was held by the rebels. The overall result of the architectural experiments was to produce a surprisingly beautiful city. Bishop Heber found Lucknow more impressive than Moscow, and William Russell found time to admire it even in the tense days of 1858, before so much of it was destroyed. The mood typically depicted was that of a city at dusk, when the lights shone out. 'We were delighted with the place and the scene altogether—the time being evening, and the streets crowded with natives' (Parks, 1850 I: 179). In Hindustani people spoke of *subah-e-Banaras, shaam-e-Awadh* and *shab-e-Malwa* (the morning light of Benaras, the evening light of Lucknow, and the beauty of night in Malwa).

The development of Lucknow as a prime centre of baroque architecture continued, remarkably unaffected by the political vicissitudes through which Awadh passed. In 1764, the East India Company's troops had defeated a coalition which included the Nawab along with the Mughal Emperor who, by a bizarre reversal of roles, had been made the Nawab's protege. From then, the East India Company made frequent demands on the Nawab. Later, in 1801, a humiliating treaty was forced on Awadh, by which the Nawab ceded still more territory and became a 'subsidiary' of the Company (Fisher, 1987; Mukherjee, 1982). The final *coup de grace* was to come in 1856, when Awadh was annexed and the Nawab deposed. In the same period, the Mughal capital, Delhi, also underwent successive crises. The Afghans defeated the Mughal-Maratha armies near Delhi in 1761. After a brief exile in Allahabad, the Mughal Emperor returned to his capital but had to rule with the Maratha chief, Scindia, standing behind his throne. In 1803 the Company's forces defeated another Mughal-Maratha army on the east bank of the Yamuna across from Delhi; the Emperor entered perforce into an alliance which put him under the control of the local British Resident. Viceroy Dalhousie intended the Mughal dynasty to come to an end when the Emperor Bahadur Shah died. Delhi would have had the same fate as Lucknow had the Revolt of 1857 not intervened.

When conditions at the court of Delhi deteriorated, poets, artists and craftsmen left for alternative centres of patronage like the relatively sheltered Lucknow, which could offer asylum and appreciation. As a result 'nawabi' Lucknow developed a distinctive culture, unforgettably delineated by the novelist Abdul Halim Sharar (1860–1926), who spent his youth in the company of the sons of Wajid Ali Shah, the last Nawab, in their exile in Calcutta (Sharar, 1975).

More than the city's compellingly beautiful appearance, it was a rich culture that made Lucknow distinctive, and gave a special meaning to the adjective *Lakhnavi*. Used pejoratively, this term suggests foppishness, fastidiousness, mannerist behaviour, reflected in costume and over-elaborate etiquette—the idle preoccupations of a powerless aristocracy with a surfeit of enforced leisure (Premchand, 1978). In today's frazzled urban landscape, there is something soothing and agreeable about this lifestyle, even if we can enjoy it only vicariously, by reading about it.

Lucknow's culture was shaped equally by men and women. In general women of aristocratic families enjoyed positions of dignity at the court. Several among them commanded great wealth, which they spent on works of charity or religious rituals. The role of the Begums of the Nawabi family in reinforcing Shia ceremonial (Juan Cole, chapter 5) anticipated Begum Hazrat Mahal, another woman of great will-power who controlled Lucknow in the difficult days of 1857–58 (Mukherjee, 1984). The courtesans too shaped much of the culture of Lucknow. The term is particularly appropriate since it was the connection with the *court* which enabled them to develop their skills in music and dance, while their counterparts in Orissa and Tamilnad refined techniques of dance under the auspices of the temples. The Lucknow *tawaif* survived with some difficulty the onslaught of Victorian morality in the later nineteenth century (Oldenburg, chapter 8). Carefully trained in social graces and confident in their ability to set fashions in dress and accessories, they helped to develop music and dance forms, and even influenced the spoken language. The quarter known as the Chowk was associated with them, and they owned considerable properties. They served as a link between town and country, and were able to build bridges between Hindus and Muslims, between the Awadhi and Urdu languages, and between the *bhakti* cults (particularly that of Krishna) and Shi'ism. Unlike the aristocratic Begums of the court, the courtesans were usually girls who had beeen kidnapped from the countryside and brought to Lucknow (Ruswa, 1961). Their training supplemented the skills of the innumerable musicgroups the rulers patronised, ranging from minstrels to those who sang in the Tansen tradition, from *kathaks* to classical musicians (Kippen, chapter 11; Neuman, 1980, and Wajid Ali Shah's own plays and writings on music). The formative period of modern Hindustani music was the eighteenth and early nineteenth centuries. Lucknow was synonymous with music in the same way as were Dharwar and Tanjore in the south of India. The courts of these towns provided points of intersection between cultural zones as well as between urban and oral traditions. The *gharanas* of Lucknow are legendary, and first impressions of the town were as much oral as visual. 'From all parts of the old town, we heard the sound of music and the jingle of anklets' wrote Ashu Chattopadhyaya (1993), describing his arrival in Lucknow at dusk on a day in 1938.

After the Revolt of 1857 was quelled, the Nawab's family was 'deported' to Matia Burj in Calcutta, where together with their entourage, they created a vivid mini-Lucknow, replete with musical traditions (shreepantha). A bizarre side-result was that Lucknow's *khayal* and *thumri* were exported to Trinidad when some of these exiles opted for a more distant exile. Although they departed as indentured labourers, they stubbornly refused to do manual labour, since they were 'artistes' (Samaroo, forthcoming). The preoccupation of the Nawabs with music, dance and the Krishna cult exasperated officers like William Sleeman, who saw in it only 'intrigue', corruption, depravity and neglect of duty and abuse of authority (Sleeman, quoted in Pemble, 1977: 97).

Urdu, which had evolved principally in Hyderabad and Delhi, was the court language at Lucknow. In the days before printing, poetry was 'performed' for an audience. When political crises left Delhi poets bereft of patronage, they migrated to Lucknow. The unhappy Mir Taqi Mir and Sauda are the best known. Sauda went to Lucknow in 1770 and lived there till his death in 1781; Mir was invited by the Nawab in 1775 and remained in Lucknow, all the while pining for Delhi, till he died in 1810. 'The ruins of Shahjahanabad were ten times better than Lucknow/Oh that I had stayed there to die, not come to live distracted here (Haque, 1992; Russell and Islam, 1969). Like most of the Mughal rulers, the Nawabs themselves were enthusiastic amateur poets, able to commandeer the help of gifted *ustads*. Lakhnavi Urdu became a distinctive tongue (Naim and Petievich, chapter 10).

Another distinctive feature of Lucknow was its Shia culture. In number the Shias were a minority amongst Sunnis and Hindus, but they were more visible and, until 1856, dominant at the court. Shia scholars in Lucknow had close links with seminaries in Iran, thus reinforcing the early link. But this did not mean that the Shias were intolerant of others. The nawabs were cordial to Hindus and Sunnis, and the Shia ceremonials, particularly Mohurram, were shared by all communities (Hasan, chapter

7). Reminiscent of medieval *munazara* (public debates) at Baghdad and Sikri were the munazara between Christian preachers and Muslims at the court of the nawab, with the British Resident in attendance, in 1833 (Powell, 1993).

Even though the nawabs were controlled by the East India Company, Lucknow was luckier than Delhi in that it was never 'invaded' or ravaged. It was also fortunate in that it did not become a deserted town after being affected with the blight of military defeat in 1801 (as had Siraj-ud-Daula's Murshidabad and Tipu Sultan's Srirangapattanam around that time). The Revolt of 1857 took many people by surprise (Nilsson and Gupta, 1992). But soon after it began, and certainly after it was crushed, the British were quite convinced that Lucknow had brought her troubles on herself, and deserved punishment. Even over a century after the event, Pemble could write, with Old Testament severity, 'So Lucknow, Babylon of India, lay prostrate before her vanquishers, condemned to a chastisement doubly severe now that she had added the sin of defiance to those of luxury and vice' (Pemble, 1977: 230; also see Farrell, 1985). The culture of the court was described as dissolute, and the very architecture that only a few years earlier had been admired, was labelled decadent. The retribution was on a truly awful scale, wholly disproportionate to the offence. To British contemporaries, however, it seemed that justice was being done, so traumatised were they by the long drawn-out siege (Pouchepadass, chapter 6). As in Delhi and Kanpur, the people of Lucknow were to be made to realise how terrible had been their 'crime'. There were mass hangings. As in Delhi, residents watched helplessly as a great swathe was cut through their city, and the cantonment was relocated from north of the river to the southwest (Oldenburg, 1984; Gupta, 1981). Many palaces and many areas were bulldozed, and many individuals reduced to penury.

But no town can be destroyed, unless it is uprooted or levelled to the ground. The Chowk still meant a great deal to the people of Lucknow. As for music and dance, its artistes found patrons in the taluqdars who were now the new elite (Oldenburg, 1984). The town was bisected by a railway line. The plaster Indo-Saracenic Charbagh railway station was the Public Works Department's contribution to Lucknow's architectural wealth. Hazratganj became a fashionable European-style shopping precinct (see Ahmad, chapter 15, on the joys of '*gunj-ing*', akin to New Delhi's 'Going to C.P.', i.e. Connaught Place). Very similar changes occurred at the same time and for the same reasons in post-Revolt Delhi. Both towns were 'disgraced' by being officially reduced to the status of *mofussil.* Half a century later, in 1912, Delhi recovered its importance when the capital was transferred there. Lucknow replaced Allahabad as the capital of the United Provinces in 1920, thanks to energetic canvassing by Sir Harcourt Butler. While Baker and Lutyens were designing the city of New Delhi, Butler concentrated not on building another urban complex, but on planning the development of Lucknow for the next fifty years (Robinson, chapter 12). He had the privilege of receiving help from the planner Patrick Geddes, whose services at the time were in great demand in many Indian towns. In the 1920s, the Legislative Council Chamber (its architect was A.V. Lanchester, an associate of Geddes), and the Courts, as well as the University (made possible by contributions from the taluqdars) were built. One wonders whether Asaf-ud-Daula would have admired these buildings. 'New Lucknow', like 'New Delhi', created a new snobbery, but because the two areas were not separate, as in the case of Delhi, the 'nawabi' and the British areas did have considerable interaction.

In the aftermath of the Revolt of 1857 poets and writers connected with the erstwhile Awadh court had good reason to mourn the eclipse of their benefactors. Recalcitrant rajas and nawabs, some of whom had revolted against the British and were consequently humbled, bemoaned the passing of an era. The *ulama* and the *mashaikh* spent sleepless nights worrying about the future of Islamic tenets in a society dominated by Western ideas and institutions. (Such apprehensions had, in fact, led Maulvi Fazl-i-Haq Khairabadi, a reputed scholar, to take part in the 1857 revolt).

It is hard to imagine anyone in Lucknow or its environs not being influenced by colonial rule or by the effects of 'the Great Western Transmutation'. Some were haunted by the prospect of Western thought undermining the moral and spiritual basis of their society. They had no cause to celebrate Great Britain's political hegemony in an area that had broadly remained insulated from the changes taking place in parts of Eastern and Western India. But most were prepared, albeit grudgingly, to make the colonial government work, seek adjustments within existing institutions and secure benefits from the newly-created administrative and bureaucratic structures. They were inclined to arrive at a workable *modus vivendi* with the new rulers and carve out new channels of aspirations and spiritual creativity. Hence the growth of schools and colleges, the bold steps taken by some forward looking Muslim personalities

(Minault, chapter 9), the incentive to join the 'heaven born', and the clamour for a share in decision-making bodies.

The Nadwat al-ulama, founded in 1894, symbolised this spirit of compromise. Its founder, Shibli Nomani, was sensitive to the winds of change and chose Lucknow as the locale for synthesising the traditional system of learning with Western methods. The Firangi Mahal, also in Lucknow and a reputed centre of Islamic education, reflected the same spirit of compromise. The traditional ulama maintained their eclectic character and refused to be drawn into sectarian conflict (Hasan, chapter 7). Maulana Abdul Bari, heir to Firangi Mahal's lively intellectual traditions, played a crucial part in fostering a Congress-Muslim League *entente* during the Khilafat and Non-Cooperation movements.

By the turn of the century, there remained a few hard nuts to crack. But the colonial government thwarted their challenge through conciliation and compromise and a policy of balance and rule between what they conceived as the two great communities, the Hindu and the Muslim. Members of landed families and of service communities, principally Kayasthas and Kashmiri Pandits, were integrated into the extensive administrative apparatus with Lucknow as the focal point. Traders and commercial men vastly benefitted from the infrastructure created to serve imperial interests. They turned to Lucknow for inspiration and legitimacy, though the changing fortunes of Lucknow (traced by Reeves, chapter 13), culminated in its formal recognition as the state capital only in 1947.

Lucknow was, as Robinson underlines (chapter 12), a great centre of landed power. In 1900, the taluqdars numbered well over 250, controlled two-thirds of the territory of Awadh and realised one-sixth of the total revenue of the province. Their position was fortified by a series of legislative enactments. But not for long. The stormy peasant unrest in the early 1920s, organised by the Kisan Sabhas and the Congress in U.P., was a warning signal to the complacent rajas and nawabs who presided over their durbars with scant regard for the impoverished *raiyat* (peasant) and the mounting dissatisfaction in their own taluqdaris. James Meston and Harcourt Butler, chief architects of a pro-landlord policy in U.P. alerted them to the dangers. But they were unmoved and paid no heed to their warnings.

In the 1930s, the Congress movement, having accorded high priority to the agrarian agenda, systematically eroded the economic and political base of the taluqdars. The landlords' party was routed in the 1937 elections. The message embodied in the U.P. Tenancy Act of 1939 was loud and clear. The disappearancee of the zamindari system in 1951 stripped the large landlords of the bulk of their estates and awarded the land to the cultivators.

Not many shed tears over the collapse of an exploitative land system. The Awadh taluqdars, as also their counterparts in Western U.P., lost their *raison d'etre* in a society that was rapidly changing under the influence of mass politics, the gradual introduction of adult suffrage, the emergence of 'new classes' poised to stake their political and economic claims, and the political awakening in the countryside. The kisan agitations generated, often independently of the Congress, unprecedented consciousness among the peasants and sensitized them to the inequities of the system to which they were subjected. The Gandhian movements, starting with the Rowlatt Satyagraha in 1919, infused confidence in the kisan's ability to protest, agitate and eventually undermine the exploitative land system as well as the authority of its beneficiaries.

The eclipse of the taluqdars, many of whom had built their palaces, *havelis* and *imambaras* in Lucknow and flirted with the British India Association or the National Agriculturist Party, did not substantially influence the political currents in Lucknow and its neighbouring districts. Lucknow had, after all, served as the venue of important national gatherings, especially those connected with the Congress, and the centre of several critical agitations. The protest against Anthony Macdonnel's Nagri resolution (April 1900), which triggered off the Hindi-Urdu controversy in North India, was masterminded in Lucknow. The historic Congress-Muslim League session was held at Baradari in December 1916 and was hosted by the Raja of Mahmudabad, one of the early supporters of the Home Rule movement and a patron of Raja Ghulam Husain, editor of *New Era*, Syed Wazir Hasan, lawyer-politician with nationalist leanings, and Choudhrry Khaliquzzaman, an up-coming lawyer linked with the Nehru household. The Raja also played host to Annie Besant, Tej Bahadur Sapru and Motilal Nehru at Mahmudabad House in Qaiser Bagh.

Finally, the presiding genius of the pan-Islamic enterprises lived in Firangi Mahal, playing host to Gandhi, the Ali brothers and other Congress leaders and devising plans to mount pressure on the government to redress the Muslim grievances over the Khilafat and the safety of the Holy Places.

The city was, for decades, the home of prominent public figures, successful lawyers, newspaper editors, Urdu and Hindi writers and poets. Some were born and brought up in Lucknow; others had moved out of

neighbouring *qasbas* in search of a better career. They carried with them
the graces of and the refinements associated with *qasbati* living. They
read poetry and classical literature, and listened to music with friends or
in the company of the courtesans in Chowk. They moved about regardless of caste and community barriers. They shared food, customs, practices and traditions. They celebrated both *Id* and *Diwali*, and observed
Muharram with equal solemnity. There can be no doubt that this degree
of composite living imposed an unmistakable imprint on, and led to the
creation of, a composite political culture in Lucknow. Religious differences surfaced time and again, but they did not weaken the inter-
community networks. *Shuddhi* and *sangathan* sabhas and *tabliqh* and
tanzim societies imposed severe strains on secular loyalties but did not
destroy the secular underpinnings of Lucknow society. Even when most
parts of the country were rocked by Hindu-Muslim violence during the
early 1920s and on the eve of India's Partition and thereafter, Lucknow
remained an island of peace and sanity. Its record, barrring some isolated
and sporadic incidents, has not been tarnished since Independence.

Lucknow's political equilibrium was disturbed by the elections in
1937 and the controversies thereafter. The Congress and the Muslim
League fell apart over the coalition issue, with Choudhary Khaliquzzaman,
the Raja of Mahmudabad and Nawab Mohammad Ismail Khan opting
to revive the defunct Muslim League in the United Provinces. In fact the
U.P. Muslim League emerged as a political factor after and not before the
coalition impasse. The formation of the Congress Ministry also triggered
off disputes and conflicts of a wide-ranging nature. The landlords were
up in arms against the U.P. Tenancy Bills, so were the kisans who staged
demonstrations in Lucknow against the agrarian policies of the Congess
Ministry. The Shias and Sunnis fought their battles on the streets of
Lucknow; the magnificent imambaras were a mute witness to the depth
of sectarian feelings in a city that had set exemplary standards of har-
monious living for its citizens. Yet, Lucknow continued to provide the
lead, remained the main arena and the focal point of nationalist activities. It was the home of an impressive generation of Congress leaders,
who championed the cause of freedom with remarkable tenacity. They
were active in the local arena, as also in provincial and nationalist politics. Kamalapathi Tripathi, G.B. Pant, Sampurnanand, Charan Singh,
Rafi Ahmad Kidwai and H.N. Bahuguna were tutored in the political traditions of Lucknow, which bore the stamp of its history, culture and ethos. Some upheld those composite political traditions after
independence; others chose not to do so.

Independence brought joy and raised hopes of a better future, but it was, also, accompanied with the partition of the country. Lucknow society was split and fragmented; the Lakhnavi culture was bruised. Families were divided, some deciding to stay while others elected to migrate to Pakistan. Lakhnavis were tormented by the happenings around, but could do little to stem the tide of hate, anger and violence. An Abdul Halim Sharar, who took great pride in his city, would have surely bemoaned the collapse of a composite social and intellectual order that the Lakhnavis had so assiduously built since 1857. A nation was born but a nation was also divided, casting its long shadows on a wounded culture and civilisation. The civilisational rhythm of the subcontinent was broken, a fact Mir Anis, Lucknow's legendary poet, would have bemoaned in his *marsiyas* (elegies). Yet, the Lakhnavis who had lived through the vicissitudes of history and had experienced many traumatic changes were able, after Independence, to get their act together and surge ahead, along with other fellow-citizens, in their quest for a better life. Bitter memories were shrugged aside in search of a prosperous future.

Lucknow in those years was not an isolated case. The whole country was surging forward and, even in the cities which had been torn apart by the tragedies of partition, people were neither sceptical, nor disillusioned. They retained faith in their leaders. The giants of the freedom struggle were in full command. In violence-haunted Calcutta, Dr B.C. Roy had the necessary authority to lay the foundations of the truncated State of West Bengal. In the more peaceful Lucknow, G.B.Pant, the Chief Minister, was able to demonstrate that he was not only a formidable administrator but also a tough politician.

Let us recall this early period. At an All-India level, the Congress party was going through a transitory phase of adjustment. The members of its socialist wing having been forced out, two major group tendencies stood face to face, strangely enough with the exception of Sardar Patel, most of the protagonists belonged to Uttar Pradesh. Accordingly, from the very first days of Independence, Lucknow appeared as a privileged arena for national politics (Weiner, 1957; Brass, 1968).

As far as old promises regarding land ownership were concerned, there were no major differences within the leadership. In UP, contrary to what was to happen in Bihar, land reforms were pushed vigorously; they were to affect deeply the relationships in the rural areas. Peasant middle castes, now concerned with political power, emerged as a direct threat to the hegemony of the upper castes, and changed completely the fortunes of the Congress party.

The early conflicts in UP had been of a different nature. They had crystallized in 1950–51 around the personality and views of the newly elected Congress President, Purushottam Das Tandon, the spiritual heir of Pandit Madan Mohan Malawiya, the founder of Benares Hindu University, and the progressives, who appeared to have won the day. However, theirs was a short-lived victory, and later political leaders espoused progressively more reactionary Hindu views. In the 1952 general elections, a new party claiming to speak for the Hindu nation, the Bharatiya Jan Sangh (BJS), managed to secure many votes (see charts in Graff pp. 258–68). In the State Assembly, its number of seats increased steadily. It was left to Prime Minister Nehru to allay the fears of the Muslims, whose position after Partition was extremely difficult.

The Congress was to rule supreme until 1967 when, for the first time, various caste groups and also a number of Muslims, rebelled against the dominance of the ruling party and tried to assert themselves, as Dr Sampurnanand, who had warned his colleagues against 'opening the doors (of the Congress) to the backward classes', had foreseen in the fifties. There followed tumultuous years, which saw the diminishing fortunes of the Congress party and the increasing volatility of the electorate: chequered coalitions, saffron crusades, and, in the end, an entirely new political landscape (Graff, chapter 14).

How much has Lucknow itself been affected by these developments? One is tempted to say that it has simply carried on, trying to survive the successive traumas, while fighting rather feebly to retain the old cherished atmosphere. The result is a strange mixture. True, the city still has the graces that an industrial town like Kanpur lacks, but it has not remained unaffected by the passing of time, the carelessness of the municipal corporation, the lack of funds, the indifferent behaviour of the new elites whose culture, in the judgement of old Lakhnavis, is 'no culture', and the huge increase in population. Is it then surprising that old Lakhnavis remember with nostalgia the Lucknow that was. Fortunately there are places where it is possible to reconcile the past and Chattar Manzil, the palace of nawabi fame, shelters today one of the most famous institutes of modern India. Claude Martin can rest in peace in the vault of La Martiniere.

Violette Graff
Narayani Gupta
Mushirul Hasan

REFERENCES

Alam, Muzaffar (1986), *The Crisis of Empire in Mughal North India: Awadh and the Punjab 1707–48*, Delhi, Oxford University Press.

Barnett, Richard B. (1980), *North India Between Empires: Awadh, the Mughals and the British*, Berkeley, University of California.

Blomfield, David (ed., 1992), *Lahore to Lucknow: The Indian Mutiny Journal of Arthur Lang*, London, Leo Cooper.

Brass, Paul R. (1968), 'Uttar Pradesh' in Myron Weiner (ed.), *State Politics in India*, Princeton, Princeton University Press.

Chattopadhyaya, Ashu (1993), *Kallol Yuger Poray* (Bengali), Calcutta, Papyrus.

Farrell, J.G. (1985), *Siege of Krishnapur*, London, Weidenfeld and Nicholson.

Fisher, Michael H. (1987), *Clash of Cultures: Awadh, the British and the Mughals*, Delhi, Manohar Book Service.

Gupta, Narayani (1981), *Delhi Between Two Empires 1803–1931*, Delhi, Oxford University Press.

Haque, Ishrat (1992), *Glimpses of Mughal Society and Culture*, Delhi, Concept Publishing House.

Llewellyn-Jones, Rosie (1985), *A Fatal Friendship: The Nawabs, the British and the City of Lucknow*, Delhi, Oxford University Press.

————— (1992), *A Very Ingenious Man: Claude Martin in Early Colonial India*. Delhi, Oxford University Press.

Mukherjee, Rudrangshu (1982), 'Trade and Empire in Awadh, 1765–1804', *Past and Present*, 94 (February).

—————, (1984), *Awadh in Revolt 1857–1858: A Study of Popular Resistance*, Delhi, Oxford University Press.

Neuman, Daniel M. (1980), *Life of Music in North India*, Delhi, Manohar Book Service.

Nilsson, Sten and Narayani Gupta (1992), *The Painter's Eye—Egron Lundgren and India*, Stockholm,

Oldenburg, Veena Talwar (1984), *The Making of Colonial Lucknow 1856–1877*, Princeton, Princeton University Press.

Parks, Fanny (1850), *Wanderings of a Pilgrim in Search of the Picturesque*, reprint 1975, Karachi, Oxford University Press.

Pemble, John (1977), *The Raj, the Mutiny and the Kingdom of Oudh 1801–59*, Hassocks, The Harvester Press.

Powell, Avril A. (1993), *Muslims and Missionaries in Pre-Mutiny India*, London, Curzon Press.

Prem Chand, Munshi (1978), *The Chess Players*, Delhi, Orient Paperbacks.

Russel, Ralph and Khurshidul Islam (1969), *Three Urdu Poets: Mir, Sauda, Mir Hasan*, London, George Allen and Unwin.

Ruswa, Mirza M.H. (1961), *Umrao Jan Ada* (*Courtesans of Lucknow*), Khushwant Singh and M.A. Husaini (trans.), Calcutta, Orient Longman.

Samaroo, Brinsley (forthcoming), *Across the Dark Water*, London, Macmillan.

Sharar, Abdul Halim (1975), *Lucknow: Last Phase of an Oriental Culture*, E.S. Harcourt and Fakhir Hussain (trans. and eds.), London, Paul Elek.

'Shreepantha' (Nikhil Sarkar) (1993), *Matia Burujer Nawab* (Bengali), Calcutta, Ananda.

Weiner, Myron (1957), *Party Politics in India: The Development of a Multi-Party System*, Princeton, Princeton University Press.

1

The Awadh Regime, the Mughals and the Countryside

MUZAFFAR ALAM

The Awadh regime (1722–1857) encountered phases of brilliant triumphs as well as days of doom and dismal failure. The founders of the dynasty built and cemented the base of their power by bringing the turbulent countryside under control, through a series of armed confrontations and tactful alliances. Later, their successors, who saw themselves as the 'Emperors of the Age', asserted the cultural superiority of their capital. During these years they manoeuvred to maintain and consolidate their power with reference to the Mughals and, in varying degrees, against the ambitions of the local elite, and then against the heavy demands of the British. In the realm of culture, their achievements were often unmatched. They generously patronised almost all forms of art and culture—architecture, dance, music, painting, poetry—as also religious scholarship. Their greatest achievement was the promotion and reinforcement of a political norm which co-ordinated, in large measure, the conflicting claims of the diverse groups and communities within the province.

The political glory of this regime was, however, short-lived, to fade off much before its evident decline. I present here a brief account of the vicissitudes of the first phase of the history of this regime (c. 1722–64). At centrestage were the Awadh rulers, initially mere governors of the Mughals in the province, struggling for additional powers and autonomy in the face of the power of Delhi. Even as they virtually rejected the authority of Delhi, they acceded to the symbolic 'paramount' position of the Mughal emperor. There were other actors also. Most of the local magnates were willing—they had also been moulded in the days of the Great Mughals—to act on the norms of the new court culture, but many adhered to their own world views. The Awadh rulers were reasonably successful in resolving this difficulty by resilience and by making compromises.[1] But compromise was of no avail against increasingly assertive Shiism of Lucknow and the East India Company's aggressive claims over the province. It would thus appear that the history of Lucknow and Awadh was not confined to the boundaries of the city and the province; it moved much beyond, to incorporate into it the history of the Mughals and of the British and their encounters with the peoples and the realities of the subcontinent.

Early Histoy and Tradition

Awadh first acquired its social and political distinction in approximately the eighth century BC as Kosala, one of the sixteen *mahajanapadas* of the later Vedic period. Over time, this region continued its cultural identity as Kosala and Madhyadesha, even as it merged into one or other of the states of northern India such as the Gupta (*c.* AD 320–510), the realm of Harshvardhana (606–47), the Pratihara (816–1090), and the kingdom of the Gahadavalas of Kanauj (*c.* 1104–94).

The details of the founding of Lucknow are uncertain. The earliest definite references to the city come from the medieval period, but local traditions trace its origins back to the hero of the *Ramayana*: Rama built Lucknow for his brother, Lakshman, naming it Lakshmanpur after him (Sharar, 1975: 36). Thus the inhabitants of this city made the same etiological appeal for legitimation as many of the leading Rajput clans of Awadh, who claimed biological descent—and therefore political authority—from Raja Rama.

Lucknow city developed as a centre of a distinct political and cultural region. Together with the city of Ayodhya in the east, Lucknow anchored the historically persistent cultural region defined by the Awadh dialect. Rural Awadh remained dominated by largely Hindu Rajput landholders. For example, Baiswara, a region historically controlled by Bais Rajput landholders, lay to the south of Lucknow. While many Rajput landholding families traced their genealogies back to Raja Rama, others asserted that their rights over their estates came from another deity, or from conquest over indigenous peoples living in jungle land. Brahmins and other Hindu castes, and many Muslim clans like Saiyids, Shaikhs and Afghans also held considerable land in Awadh. (Alam, 1986: 94–5; Fisher, 1987: 41–9) With the coming of Islam to India, especially after the establishment of the Delhi Sultanate (1206–1526), a number of established landholding families as well as significant numbers of the peasantry converted to the religion of north India's new rulers. Further, many Muslim individuals and clans entered India from Afghanistan, Central Asia, Iran, or Arabia, and settled in Awadh.

As the Delhi Sultanate asserted its power across north India, Lucknow served it as one of its several administrative seats in the Gangetic plain. The city stood as the established centre of its local region after the coming of the Mughals as well (1526). The Mughals incorporated the city into their sophisticated administrative structure, and made it the headquarters of one of Awadh province's five sub-provincial administrative units (*sarkars*). The Mughals also stationed in Lucknow one of the eight military and police commandants (*faujdars*) of the province of Awadh. Additionally, they established a mint for copper and silver coinage in the city. Often, the governor (*subadar*) of the province made it his main centre of operations in the region. All this reinforced Lucknow's prominence.

The Province and the Problems of Governance

As the eighteenth century opened, Awadh posed a problem for the Mughal emperors. On one hand, Awadh stood as a prosperous and strategic region for the empire. Over the preceding century of relative peace and political stability in north India, it had registered unmistakable economic growth. Intraregional as well as interregional trade throughout the empire in local goods, artifacts, minerals, and food grains sustained a network of towns and monetised markets of varying sizes. Economic developments in Awadh resulted not only in a rise in Mughal revenue collections but also in the emergence and affluence of a number of towns (*qasbas*), with a chain of routes to link them to long distance trade. Lucknow itself produced calico, other cotton cloth, embroidery, and archery bows, and was a sugar collection point (Habib, 1982). The agricultural prosperity of the region was to the obvious advantage of the local landholders (*zamindars*) who enjoyed a dominance in rural production.

The Mughals also valued Awadh for strategic reasons. It lay in close proximity to Delhi, and at the gateway to the eastern imperial provinces. The main route eastward, to the north of the Ganges River, went through Lucknow city where it split: one branch leading on to Ayodhya-Faizabad, the other to Varanasi. In the wake of various regional assertions (such as the Maratha and Bundela uprisings), these trade and administrative-cum-military routes through Lucknow acquired special importance for the Mughals.[2] Moreover, a large number of the smaller office-holders (*mansabdars*) in the Mughal administration, petty commanders of the imperial troopers, and associates of Mughal courtiers came from the

towns of Awadh. Mughal imperial control over the province was therefore vital to the future of the empire and Lucknow—even after the
foundation of Faizabad by the Awadh ruler in the early eighteenth century—was in turn the key to the control over the region.

At the same time, Awadh remained notoriously difficult to govern.
Local officials faced stiff resistance from landholders and peasants in the
exercise of imperial control. Typically, a landholder in Awadh based his
local control and military power on links of kinship and service with
kinsmen in the villages on his estate (Fox, 1981). Rural pressure often
took the form of a landholder mobilising his kinsfolk and armed retinue
in a rural uprising, even in a few cases to the extent of besieging an imperial fortress. Resistance to imperial authority rested on local level
linkages between the landholders and their tenants.

In the area around Lucknow city in particular, a clan putatively descended from a courtier of the Mughal Emperor Akbar, named Shaikh
'Abd-al Rahman, came to predominate as landholders; they together
with many other Shaikhs and Saiyids of the province, were collectively
known as Shaikhzadas (descendants of the Shaikh). Several Afghan clans
had also settled in the areas south and east of Lucknow city. Even when
the Mughal empire was at its height many of these landholders—especially Rajputs and Shaikhzadas—asserted some degree of local autonomy
in Awadh.

These landholders had earlier allied with the Mughals and accepted
a subordinate position either in the face of invincible Mughal armies or
to avail of imperial support to protect and promote their own individual
interests against those of others within the region. Since the Mughal
centre declined during the final years of Aurangzeb's reign (1659–1707)
and under his largely powerless successors, these rural notables now
found themselves strong enough to rise up in arms.[3] The annual revenue
collection process usually consisted of a recurrent conflict between the
landholder and the collection agent of the provincial administration.
The quantity of revenue extracted, the degree of local control exercised
by each, and the point of intersection between the authority of the
landholder and that of the district administration, remained constantly
subject to abrasive negotiation. Often these issues were decided annually
on the basis of armed struggle. The larger landholders, (in Awadh called
ta'alluqadars, landholders who paid revenue for themselves and other
zamindars), could from their villagers muster military support comparable in size to that of the administrator charged with revenue collection.
A concentrated effort by the provincial administration could dislodge

even the largest landholder. Nevertheless, the short campaign season due to the climate, the need to collect revenues just after the harvest, and the almost uniform opposition of the landholders (protected by their sturdy mud forts in the midst of impenetrable bamboo groves, and supported by the neighbouring villagers), all meant that only a few 'examples' could be made each year by the administration.

The bulk of the landholders thus escaped direct coercion, and could negotiate their payments from a position of strength. As a whole, the landholders maintained an adversarial relationship with the district administration, even as they recognised the *de jure* sovereignty of the Mughal emperor and the authority of his appointed governor. Nevertheless, the goals of these landholders were limited, narrow, and locally oriented. They relied upon support from their peasants and smaller landholders of their own caste. The scale of their mobilisation against imperial power could not transcend divisions of caste and community and failed to incorporate the interests of other regional groups. In many cases their interest remained limited to their kinfolk in their villages; townspeople and traders, like the revenue collecting agents of the administration, could become their victims.

Nevertheless, these revolts corroded the basis of Mughal imperial authority, sometimes through linkages with imperial court politics. In the emerging political situation, service and loyalty to the imperial authority ceased to count, for it was not the Emperor but the provincial governor and powerful nobles at the imperial court who began to dictate state action. Thus, the imperial assistance available to provincial nobles and local officials for coping with local problems depended more on their individual influence with powerful nobles at the centre, and less on their loyalty to the Emperor. In addition, increasing regional prosperity generated conflict amongst the local groups, as each tried to maximise its gains at the expense of the others.

In particular, two classes of people receiving temporary land revenue assignments from the Emperor sought to entrench themselves in this rich region. *Madad-i ma'ash*-holders (revenue-grantees) made a bid to turn their grants into permanent estates, without forfeiting their existing privileges and perquisites. [4] *Jagir*-holders also aspired to permanency; within the Mughal empire, an office-holder received a transferable assignment of land revenue (a jagir) from a specified area. This assigned land normatively lay in a region outside the administrative authority of that office-holder, and within the authority of a different official. By rotating these assignments frequently, the Emperors tried to prevent the entrenchment of any official in his jagir and keep each office-holder dependent for his income on the Emperor. From the late seventeenth century, however, the quantity of revenue-producing lands available in the Mughal empire fell below the income demands of the imperial establishment; further, the officially rated income from many lands far exceeded its actual revenues. In consequence, officials in possession of productive assignments resisted transfer to less productive ones, seeking to build their own permanent base out of what was suposed to be a very temporary assignment of land revenues. Additionally, by conspiring with the local administrators, jagir-holders sought to exclude the governor's influence. Some jagir-holders even managed to obtain administrative authority over the areas containing their own jagirs, thus controlling the coercive power to extract whatever revenues they could. This drive by some Mughal officials to establish themselves permanently in their jagirs would prove particularly contentious for any ambitious governor who was trying to establish his own control over his province.

Another feature characteristic of the later Mughal empire, and tending toward the decentralization of power was the institution of contract tenure (*ijaradari*). By the early eighteenth century, this institution extended through much of the Mughal empire, including Awadh. An independent party would be 'contracted' to carry out the duties of an office, typically to collect land revenue. The contractor assumed the responsibilities and authorities to extract the revenue, and often kept any excess over the agreed upon amount. Such contract relationships were varied and extensive. Indeed, a number of merchants and money-lenders contracted offices and landholdings on behalf of the officials as financial speculations. They ran them as business ventures with their own employees carrying out the functions of the official. In effect, many governors of the eighteenth century, including Sa'adat Khan, the founder of the Awadh dynasty, held their provinces on this basis. The overall effect was the diminution of central control and the increasing autonomy of individual office-holders.

Thus, prior to 1722 Awadh stood as a particularly important yet troublesome province for the Mughal empire. Lucknow, as the site of one level of Mughal imperial administration, remained an interface betwen the imperial administration and the surrounding countryside. As an economic centre as well, the city drew upon its hinterland for various kinds of agricultural produce, while at the same time linking Awadh to the larger world of interregional trade. Following the arrival of Sa'adat Khan as governor in 1722, the province would begin a new phase of its history, one of a growing regional identity over and against that of both the Mughal empire and the rest of north India as well.

The Founding of the Awadh Dynasty within the Mughal Empire

Sa'adat Khan, an Iranian who was later given the title *Burhan al Mulk*, stepped into a complex administrative and cultural situation, in a region alien to his own cultural background. Like most Mughal provinces, Awadh contained a number of administrative units, each with an official who was supposed to be appointed directly by, and responsible to, the Mughal Emperor. As newly appointed governor in a rapidly shifting imperial context, Sa'adat Khan worked quickly to solidify his control both over the Awadh imperial administration and the local landholders and other powerful figures through a series of strategies typical of successful early eighteenth-century governors.

Sa'adat Khan had left the collapsing Safavid empire and arrived in the footsteps of his father and elder brother, in 1708 at the Mughal court. His Iranian Shia background was appreciated at the Mughal court since Iranian culture and Iranian royalty had been long established as the model for sophisticated manners and imperial ritual in India. Further, the Iranians at the Mughal court were sometimes the largest and the most powerful group among the Mughal nobility (Athar Ali, 1966). Sa'adat Khan rose rapidly in the Mughal service. After just thirteen years in India he received an appointment as governor of Agra, the second most valuable province (in terms of assessed revenue demand), as well as an extremely high rank in the Mughal service. [5] The next year, however, he failed to suppress a local uprising of landholders in Agra. He was then transferred to the governorship of Awadh. At this time, there were very few of his clansmen and associations in Awadh and Sa'adat Khan shared little with the inhabitants of the province other than participation in the Mughal empire. And so he apparently felt it particularly essential to secure for himself the resources of Awadh as quickly as possible.

Sa'adat Khan's first major task was to control the city of Lucknow, then in possession of the celebrated Shaikhzadas, who claimed to be the descendants of the first Muslim conquerors of the province. They had built fortified palaces in the city and big estates in the outlying country; they controlled several important provincial offices, often defied the governor, and would not let anyone enter the city without acknowledging their supremacy. Sa'adat Khan subdued them with arms but more so by striking tactful alliances with their rivals, e.g., the Shaikhzadas of towns like Kakori and Bilgram near by (Srivastava, 1954: 32–3; Alam, 1986: 224–37).

Submission of the rural Hindu chieftains followed the capture of Lucknow. Here, again, Sa'adat Khan's military superiority as well as his new revenue schemes ensured his success. The turbulent zamindars were not just ruthlessly subjugated; they were also wooed and won over with a new land arrangement, which guaranteed them additional privileges and profits. How Sa'adat Khan and his heirs sought and gained wide powers in the ongoing conflict over power and revenues within Awadh, is illustrated from a local tradition. Extolling the valour of the Rajputs of an Awadh district, Morawan, the legend goes that when Sa'adat Khan took charge of Awadh, he found the revenue administration of the *suba* in great disorder. He resolved to tour through the country and enquire into the state of things. When he reached Morawan, he summoned all the *qanungos*[6] of Baiswara and asked them to produce the *daul* (rent roll) of their respective *parganas*. They said 'what daul will you have?' and on being asked the meaning of their answer, they explained that there were two dauls which a qanungo could give, the 'coward's' or the 'man's'. In the first against every landowner's name was written only that sum which had been fixed at the last assessment, but in the second, rent was indicated on the basis of what it should have been, taking into account the improvement that had taken place in land. Sa'adat Khan called for the 'man's daul' and on that basis, doubled the assessment of Baiswara. Then, having summoned the representatives of all the zamindars, he placed before them on one side a heap of *pan* leaves, on the other a heap of bullets and bade them, if their masters accepted the terms, to take up pan; if not, the bullets. One after one they came forward and everyone took up the pan leaves (Elliot, 1862: 73). We can speculate that years of Mughal drive against the Rajputs had broken their strength. They thus rejected the bullets and chose the pan, the obvious symbol of a friendly stance.

The new governors or the Nawabs, thus, not only subdued the rural areas of Awadh, they were able to mobilise local social magnates around their own banner through special arrangements with Muslim urban family groups, local landholding potentates, and petty jagir-holders in the province. Further, these hereditary governors also eventually brought provincial finance and all other offices under their own control.

This centralised provincial authority was opposed to the system of checks and balances prevalent in the empire to that point. In the earlier Mughal system, the governor had held executive authority, while a separate chief fiscal officer (*diwan*) oversaw the revenue aspects, both being supported by military and police commandants (faujdars) and a range of other provincial administrators. Significantly, each official appointed to the province had been separately responsible to the imperial centre. As a result of the efforts of Sa'adat Khan (governor until his death in 1739) and his successors, however, the Awadh governors subordinated all the other officials to themselves. Eventually eliminating intervention by the imperial court in the province, Sa'adat Khan and his heir, Safdarjang (1739–56) made Awadh a stable base for their dynasty.

These developments within Awadh (and simultaneously also within many of the other provinces of the empire) were achieved almost wholly within the Mughal institutional framework. Across much of India, powerful governors continued to seek links with one or other faction at the imperial court. The social and political realities of the eighteenth century required at least a semblance of reference to the imperial centre. All sources of growth had not dried up, and no region was in a position to maintain itself in complete isolation from other areas. Despite the unfettered political and military adventurism that accompanied and followed the decline of imperial power, none of the adventurers was strong enough to be able to win the allegiance of the others and then replace the imperial power. All struggled separately to make their fortunes and threatened each other's position and achievements. But only some, like the Awadh governors, could establish their dominance temporarily over the Emperor and their rivals. It was Awadh's dynamic economic growth that supported this regional autonomy, at the cost of the Mughal centre which had earlier managed to harness such economic expansion.

The Awadh governors at various times acquired rule over several other Mughal provinces as well.[7] When they or the other power-brokers of the empire sought institutional validation of their spoils, they needed a centre to legitimise their acquisitions. The imperial court provided the surest such centre, and thus the Awadh governors had ambitions at the Mughal court and conversely, a powerful base in Awadh gave them the power to strive for control over the Emperor and therefore the empire as a whole. In this way, there was a shift within the empire from control over peripheries by the centre (the seventeenth century) to control of the centre by the provinces (the early eighteenth century).

Within the Awadh countryside those who resisted the new regime faced an overwhelming military force, and those who accepted it received reduced revenue assessments. Privileges were extended by Sa'adat Khan to the landholders in proportion to their strength and the benefits that he expected from their support. Yet, even some of the smaller landholders received appointments. Sa'adat Khan also seems to have encouraged his subordinate officials to purchase landholdings, thus consolidating his strength against the rebellious rural magnates by providing opportunities for the extension of power and influence of non-Rajput elements. This strategy, however, had limited success in the face of the entrenched Rajput clans in many parts of Awadh.

Sa'adat Khan had founded a new capital, Faizabad, near Ayodhya, which was the premier seat of provincial power and politics in the eighteenth century. The new capital, however, affected little the fortunes of Lucknow, which continued to grow in economic and cultural importance with the rise of the new regime. For example, one particularly distinguished family, the *ulama* of Firangi Mahal, had migrated to Lucknow during the late seventeenth century. Over the eighteenth century they established one of the largest and most significant centres of Islamic learning in India, with significant pedagogical influence throughout India and the entire Muslim world (Robinson, 1984).

Towards an Independent Regional State

One of Sa'adat Khan's most fundamental accomplishments in consolidating control over the province in his own hands was extending the range of his power as governor deep into the local administration. One particularly telling feature of the nawabi regime was that he appointed all the faujdars in Awadh without reference to the Mughal centre. Since these police and military commandants represented the administration in a district, Sa'adat Khan was asserting his own power over that district. Eventually, this office became such a component of the governor's administration that the office now was restyled *nazim* or *naib*, 'deputy' of the governor.

Another consequence of this assertion of the governor's power was the diminishing authority of the local Islamic judges (*qazis*). Often the members of a prominent local family were hereditary judges who had earlier decided disputes over revenue matters, thus counterbalancing the office of faujdar. By incorporating the faujdar into the administration, the newly assertive provincial centre thus reduced the power of the office of qazi.

A further arena in which Sa'adat Khan and his successors tried to assert their control over Awadh was with respect to control over jagirs. The governor asserted his own authority over these assigned lands. The jagir-holders no longer sent their own agents to collect the revenues: the local officials were to approach the governor's appointed administrators for matters relating to the revenue and their own customary perquisites. In other words, the administrative functions that some jagir-holders had established over their jagirs, namely, collection of land revenue and other authorised and unauthorised cesses, was largely taken over by the governor's appointees. Indeed, Sa'adat Khan had the lands of Awadh, including jagirs, reassessed so as to fix the official rate for the land revenue in proportion to the actual full rate of production, rather than the fictive 'book' value. All communication between the jagir-holder and the local officials was thereafter to pass through the governor's office. Even though these efforts were not uniformly successful, Sa'adat Khan gained leverage over some of the powerful nobles in Delhi holding jagirs in Awadh. While some lower level officials, holding only small jagirs and hitherto unable to assert their full rights, appreciated Sa'adat Khan's reforms, some among the larger jagir-holders regarded this as an intrusion into their own control over their holdings. Consequently, some of the latter arranged to transfer their jagirs outside of Awadh, into provinces with more cooperative governors. Such transfers effectively enabled Sa'adat Khan to exclude the influence and interests of rival notables in the Mughal administration from his province. This process of excluding assignments of jagirs in Awadh to all but his supporters was not completed until almost the middle of the eighteenth century, however.

Similarly, for madad-i ma'ash-holders, Sa'adat Khan attempted reforms. He initially tried, through surveys and confiscations, to reduce or eliminate such holdings as were no longer serving their ostensible purpose. The entrenched local position, and influence at the Mughal court, of a number of madad-i ma'ash-holders, however, forced Sa'adat Khan to compromise and in several instances madad-i-ma'ash holdings became permanent landholdings. Thus given more permanency by Sa'adat Khan, many in this influential body of the local elites shifted their influence toward him. [8]

The measure of Sa'adat Khan's entrenchment in office and in Awadh came at the time of his death. Over his tenure as governor, he had transformed Awadh from a mere province (*suba*) to his home province (*suba-i mulki*) and made his governorship much more than a mere administrative assignment conferred by the Emperor. Simultaneously, Sa'adat Khan remained fully involved at the Mughal court. At various times, he played a part as a leading member of several factions in conflicts over power with other groups. His political manoeuvrings led him occasionally into open defiance of the Emperor, as when he rejected his imperial transfer order from Awadh to Malwa in 1727. At the time of the invasion of Nadir Shah (1739), Sa'adat Khan stood among the most powerful figures in India, first fighting in vain against the invasion and then negotiating what amounted to a humiliating capitulation by the Mughal Emperor to the invader.[9] On Sa'adat Khan's death soon thereafter, his office became a disputed inheritance between two of his nephews.

As his uncle's deputy governor, Safdarjang had already worked to establish his own control over Awadh. Apparently on payment to Nadir Shah of Rs 2,00,00,000 from the Awadh treasury, this nephew, Safdarjang, emerged as the principal heir, the next governor of Awadh. The general acceptance of the Sa'adat Khan family's right to inherit the governorship of Awadh indicates both the condition of the Mughal empire at the time and the family's hold over the province. Yet the Mughal Emperor's acceptance was vital to Safdarjang and he expended considerable resources bolstering his position within the empire and at the imperial court.

Using Awadh as his base, the new governor continued to further his family's interests at the Mughal centre. Safdarjang emerged after the 1748 invasion of India by the Afghan warlord Ahmad Shah Abdali, as the Vizier (chief minister) of the Empire.[10] The critical place of Awadh in general and Lucknow in particular for Safdarjang's career is evident from his most vulnerable moment. In 1751, an army of Bangash Afghans defeated Safdarjang, invaded Awadh, and—in particular—occupied Lucknow.[11] Revealing the strong base of support which Sa'adat Khan and Safdarjang had established in Awadh, is the fact that the Shaikhzadas of Lucknow themselves resisted the Afghan invasion and remained loyal to Safdarjang. After their victory over the Bangash, the Shaikhzadas sent a petition expressing their loyalty and dedication to the Nawab. The Nawab's reply significantly reveals how they had been accommodated in the new provincial administration. Safdarjang had expected such dedication from the Shaikhzadas, for he always considered them much more than 'mere servants and *ra'iyat* [peasantry]' (Hamadani, n.d.: 34–5).

The Shaikhzadas and many other of the traditional service elite families of Awadh had thus come to see far more of a future in working for the Awadh Nawabs than for the Mughal Emperors. The tendency among local people to refrain from taking service outside Awadh, can be construed as stages of the development of a definite attitude towards the new regime in the province. This attitude found much more ruthless expression in their continued support and battle for the re-establishment of the rule of Safdarjang in Awadh even after the Emperor in Delhi had ordered the confiscation of his properties following the Nawab's own defeat at the hands of the Afghans. This implied blatant defiance of the imperial directive by a powerful section of the ruling class of the province. It also showed an active appreciation of the prevalent social and political conditions which had resulted in the new Nawabi regime in Awadh. The broad stability that the Nawabi dynasty had fostered (despite occasional setbacks), and the protection it offered against the Maratha threat, proved highly attractive to many of the elite in Awadh.

The Awadh Political Culture

The early Nawabs' considered effort and policy to satisfy the claims of all the local social groups played a most crucial part in nourishing the social base of the new regime. If, on the one hand, the Muslim Shaikhzadas defended it, even in the face of an order from Delhi to the contrary, the Nawabs found in the Rajputs some of their most trusted allies in times of crisis. Sa'adat Khan and Safdarjang could afford to spend half their time in Delhi to manoeuvre the politics to their favour at court. A large contingent of Rajput zamindars were in Safdarjang's army in the Nawab's struggle against the Jats and the Marathas. In 1765 when Safdarjang's successor Shuja-ud-Daula had been defeated by the English East India Company's troops at Buxar, he fled along the banks of the Ganga to Farrukhabad, and then Achal Singh, the ta'alluqadar of Dondia Khera in Baiswara, proved to be a valuable friend and supporter. A large number of the Bais with a quarter's revenue of Baiswara joined the crestfallen Nawab at Farrukhabad (Elliot, 1862: 76).

Further, several Hindus, Kayasthas and Khatris, held in Awadh important offices. Atma Ram, a Khatri, had been associated with Sa'adat Khan since the days of his early career at the Mughal court. He was eventually made the *diwan* of Awadh. His three sons, Har Narain, Ram Narain and Pratap Narain, all held important offices. Har Narain was Sa'adat Khan's *vakil* at the court of Delhi. Among Atma Ram's grandsons, Lachhmi Narain, Shiv Narain and Jagat Narain rose to notable positions. Lachhmi Narain also served as *vakil* of the Awadh court at Delhi. The family of Atma Ram retained an eminent position throughout the eighteenth century. Nawal Rai, a Kayastha, was a close confidant of Safdarjang, and was virtually the ruler of Awadh in the 1740s when the Nawab was busy at Delhi politics. How many of his family members and associates gained eminence under Safdarjang is not known. He is mentioned, however, by a Kayastha chronicler of the early nineteenth century as 'the promoter and supporter of his community and friends . . .'. A number of other Hindu officials' names also figure prominently in the Awadh administration. (Bhatnagar, Allahabad MS: 475a; Alam, 1986: 237–41).

By integrating the aspirations of both the dominant Rajput landholders on the one hand, and the Muslims and non-Rajput Hindu urban elites on the other, the Nawabs tried to achieve a political balance. Unlike the Mughals, the Awadh Nawabs had no Abul Fazl to give a theoretical foundation or explanation to their policy. But this did not mean that theirs was a blank pragmatic arrangement. The balance in the new political alliance received inspiration and sustenance from the prevailing religious philosophy. The emphasis in Awadh religious circles was on open and non-combative interaction and, to avoid conflict, on integration and assimilation. The Awadh or Lucknow political culture had a bearing on the religious culture of the region.

Awadh had been a traditional stronghold of the sufic doctrine of *Wahdat-al-Wujud* (Unity of Being) which had promoted belief in the essential unity of all phenomena, however diverse and irreconcilably conflicting they appear at first instance. Support for the doctrine and its associated generous accommodativeness of the local beliefs and customs continued through the Mughal period. There was a setback when the Mughal state tended to be associated with Sunni orthodoxy in the late seventeenth century, but Awadh never came under the direct influence of the revivalist ideology. The province did witness religious clashes, but even in the midst of intense community conflict, the message of Awadh *sant* and sufi retained its verve. What is of significance is the fact that early eighteenth-century Awadh saw some serious efforts at rehabilitating this ideology and its social and political implications.

A generous and liberal religious climate thus promoted non-sectarian politics, which in turn helped cement the hold of the nawabs over the province. In the building of the Awadh Muslim regime the non-Muslims of the province had no insignificant part. The third Nawab, Shuja-ud-Daula, quickly consolidated his dominance both in Awadh and at the Mughal court. Indeed, using the resources of Awadh, the new ruler asserted his guardianship over the Mughal Emperor and set about reconstructing the empire. He had inherited from his father, Safdarjang, the office of the vizier as well. He successfully staved off threats to his authority from landholders and rebel peasants in north India, from the

Marathas and Ahmad Shah Abdali. But things began to change in the 1760s, following his defeat at Buxar at the hands of the East India Company. With the English Company's victory on the battlefield, the Nawab was no longer in full control of the province or the Mughal court. Awadh entered a new phase in its history as a subordinate ally of the Company. The foundations of the erstwhile political tradition began to erode. Clashes and confrontations at all levels—between Lucknow and Delhi, between the countryside and the Lucknow court, and above all between Awadh culture and the alien British values—threatened to replace the existing political equipoise.

NOTES

1. For more extensive studies in English of the history of Awadh during this phase see Alam (1986) Barnett (1980) and Srivastava (1954 and 1961).
2. The Marathas, based in what is today Maharashtra, had formed a powerful military force largely opposed to the Mughals, from the time of their leader Shivaji (1627–80) onward. The Bundela Rajputs, based in Bundelkhand (north of the Vindhiya mountains and south of the Yamuna, to the south-west of Awadh) also proved a locally-based people resistant to Mughal imperial control.
3. Following Aurangzeb's death, a series of weak Emperors and temporarily strong king-makers followed. No less than fourteen Mughal Emperors sat on the throne during the period of our study.
4. In principle, four categories of people were eligible for such nominally temporary madad-i ma'ash grants: (1) scholars, (2) those who chose a life of seclusion and self-abnegation, (3) the destitute and poor, (4) unemployed people of noble lineage. In practice, holders of these 'charity' grants constituted a considerable and well-established social force.
5. He held *mansab* ranks of 7,000 *zat* and 7,000 *sawar* (the former a personal, the latter a military rank).
6. The qanungo was a local revenue official recording and supplying information concerning revenue receipts, area statistics, revenue-rates, and rural customs and practices.
7. The dynasty held the governorships of various provinces including: Agra (1721), Kashmir (1744), Ajmer (1748), and—more frequently—Allahabad (first acquired in 1735).
8. As we shall see below, these madad ma'ash holders, many of whom came from the families of the Shaikhzadas, remained loyal to Sa'adat Khan's dynasty even when his successor lost military control over Awadh.
9. Nadir Shah remained in India only for a few months but during that time he subdued the Mughal Emperor, looted vast wealth from the Mughal treasury, and ordered a general massacre in Delhi.

10. Ahmad Shah Abdali, an Afghan of the Durrani clan, had seized the Afghan throne in 1747 and held it until his death in 1773. He invaded India on eight occasions, with varying degrees of success.
11. The Bangash were an Afghan clan, led at that time by Ahmad Khan, who had established dominance in the Farrukhabad region to the west of Awadh. The town of Farrukhabad, named after the Mughal Emperor Farrukh Siyar (1712–19), was founded by his grandfather, Muhammad Khan Bangash in 1713.

REFERENCES

Alam, Muzaffar (1986), *The Crisis of Empire in Mughal North India: Awadh and the Punjab, 1707–1748*, Delhi, Oxford University Press.
Athar Ali, M. (1966), *The Mughal Nobility under Aurangzeb*, Bombay, Asia Publishing House.
Barnett, Richard B. (1980), *North India Between Empires: Awadh, the Mughals and the British, 1720–1801*, Berkeley, University of California Press.
Bhatnagar, Bahadur Singh, 1249/1833–34 Yadgar-i-Bahaduri, Uttar Pradesh State Archives, Allahabad, MS. No.255.
Elliott, C.A. (1862), *Chronicles of Oonao*, Allahabad, Allahabad Mission Press.
Fisher, Michael M. (1987), *A Clash of Cultures: Awadh, the British, and the Mughals*, Delhi, Manohar Book Service.
Fox, Richard G. (1981), *Kin, Clan, Raja and Rule: State Hinterland Relations in Pre-Industrial India*, Berkeley, University of California Press.
Habib, Irfan (1982), *An Atlas of the Mughal Empire*, Delhi, Oxford University Press.
Hamadani, Qasim Ali (n.d.), Tarikh-i-Shahiya Nishapuriya, Rampur, MS. No. 2148.
Robinson, Francis (1984), 'The *Ulama* of Farangi Mahal and Their *Adab*', in Barbara Metcalf (ed),*Moral Conduct and Authority: The Place of Adab in South Asian Islam*, Berkeley, University of California Press.
Sharar, Abdul Halim (1975), *Lucknow: Last Phase of an Oriental Culture*, E.S. Harcourt and Fakhir Husain (trans. and eds.), London, Paul Elek.
Srivastava, Ashirbadi Lal (1954), *The First Two Nawabs of Awadh*, Agra, Shiva Lal Agarwala.
_____(1961), *Shuja-ud-daula*, 2 vols, Delhi, Shiva Lal Agarwala.

2

Awadh and the
English East India Company

MICHAEL H. FISHER

As the Mughal Empire fragmented and the British Empire laid its own
foundations, Awadh emerged as an essential component in the most important political formulations of the day. Although the various provinces
of the Mughal Empire seemed to break away during the eighteenth and
early nineteenth century, it was not until the revolution of 1857–58 that
the Mughal edifice finally collapsed. The English East India Company
sought to hasten this Mughal decline and fastened on Awadh as one of
its prime reserves for military, political, and fiscal resources. Simultaneously, however, each of the elements in the society of Awadh had its
own plans and visions of the future. Thus, the history of Awadh up to
1858 reflects the interaction among British and Mughal imperial ambitions and the agendas of the rulers, townsmen, rural landholders, peasants, and other people of Awadh.

Not until the mid-eighteenth century did Awadh clash with the
English. From its foundation in 1600 until the 1750s, the English East
India Company confined itself largely to coastal commercial concerns,
far removed from Awadh in the central Gangetic plain. The 'factories' at
Madras (obtained by the Company in 1640), Bombay (first rented by
the Company in 1668), and Calcutta (founded 1690) were at first mere
warehouses where the Company's 'factors' (merchants) collected goods
they had purchased, prior to export in the Company's ships for sale in
London. As a joint-stock corporation, the English East India Company
had as one of its goals the payment of satisfactory dividends to its shareholders. This meant steady pressure to keep costs down and returns up.
Indeed, the Company continued to pay dividends to its shareholders at
a fixed and generous rate till 1858. Until the mid-eighteenth century,

commercial rivalries with the French East Indian Company (founded 1664) played a much larger role in the English Company's policies than did political interests within the Indian heartland where Awadh lay.

The Company's earliest political confrontations with Awadh and the other Indian states grew out of its expanding commercial interests and its rivalry with its French competitors. Political strife in Europe had echoes in India, bringing on wars between the English and the French Companies in south India—the Carnatic Wars (1746–48, 1751–54, 1756–63). In their struggles, the English and French Companies allied themselves with rival powers within the many already conflicting Indian states. The English Company thus learned that its burgeoning military wing could not only stand up to the armies of the Indian states, it could allow the Company to tap the economic resources and accumulated treasures of those states. Taking this lesson with him to Bengal, Robert Clive reversed the Company's flagging fortunes there by a combination of political manoeuvre and military force against the Nawab. The result—the Company's victory over the Bengal armies at Plassey in 1757—left the Company in possession of a vast territory, three times the size of England itself. This conquest brought the English into direct collision with the aggressive political ambitions of the current ruler of Awadh, Shuja-ud-Daula (1754–75).

As each of the provincial rulers of the Mughal Empire broke away from imperial control, each nevertheless sought to use the power of the Emperor's name to further his own ambitions. The Emperors themselves made futile efforts to harness the war-lords. A series of regional rulers elevated puppet Emperors in order to legitimise their own aggrandizements. Based strategically near the Mughal capital, the Awadh nawabs proved among the most persistent of these provincial manipulators of the Mughal imperial name.

Awadh and the Company first directly challenged each other when Shuja-ud-Daula marched his armies against the English, under the Mughal banner, in 1764. The Company crushed these armies at the battlefield of Buxar.[1] But given the vast extent of the Awadh territories, the Company shrank from attempting to assert its own direct administration—lacking the funds or manpower to garrison, the expertise or power to administer, and the inclination or authority from Parliament or its Court of Directors to annex them. Consequently, the Company sought an Indian ruler to entrust with these lands. It decided to restore Shuja-ud-Daula to authority, but as its subordinate ally, and an effective buffer against hostile forces to the south and west (Marathas or Afghan intruders). Shuja-ud-Daula had proven administrative ability and access to the resources of Awadh, both of which the Company desired to exploit.

In the Treaty of 1765, the Company selected for annexation only part of the Nawab's holdings, and the rest were restored to him on payment of Rs 50,00,000—the alleged charges for the expenses of its recent campaigns. To ensure his loyalty to the Company, it bound the Nawab by this treaty to mutual defence and trade for the Company free of duty—a continuing source of dispute (Khan, 1902: 2:579, 584; Aitchison, 1909: 2:67–9). The ease with which the Nawab paid this vast sum whetted the Company's expectations of future extractions.

The Nawab had recognised the value and advantages of European arms and military science and, like other Indian rulers of the day, now recruited European military advisers to reconstitute his army. Indeed, so successful was his policy that the Company grew concerned and, in a 1768 treaty, stipulated the maximum size of his army and prescribed that less than a third could be on the 'European model' (Aitchison, 1909: 2:70). Thereafter the Company enforced an even further reduction in the Nawab's martial capacity. In 1773, it displaced parts of his army by establishing a 'subsidiary force', troops under Company control paid for by Awadh. This gave the Company the ultimate deciding power in its later confrontations with the ruler.

The East India Company and the Nawab did not, however, have only a one-sided relationship. Shuja-ud-Daula employed his new arrangement with the Company to advance his own expansive interests in north India. Most notably, he used these subsidiary brigades in support of his own army during the Rohilla War (1774).[2] Indeed, some Company officers' complained that their troops bore the brunt of the fighting while the Awadh party gained all the spoils and subsequent advantages.[3]

To manage its relations with the ruler, the Company appointed a political agent, or Resident, at the Awadh court. Until 1772, the Company had transmitted the occasional message through an officer in its army stationed nearby. But now the Resident would supervise the Company's interests there (and in the other centres of political importance to the west as well). This Resident not only gradually moved to monopolise communications between the Nawab and the Company, he eventually intervened in virtually all aspects of the foreign and internal affairs of the state, thus establishing a system of indirect rule that would eventually extend across all of the 'princely states' of India (Fisher, 1991).

Following the death of Shuja-ud-Daula, a new set of political relations between Awadh, the Mughal court, and the Company commenc-
ed. On one hand, Awadh moved toward a regional political identity,
linked to the Mughal Empire primarily in symbolic terms. On the other,
despite the exertions of the Nawab to preserve autonomy, the Company's
Resident gradually established indirect control over Awadh. As the new
capital of Awadh, Lucknow saw many moments of drama.

Awadh under Indirect Rule

Shuja-ud-Daula's successor, Asaf-ud-Daula (1775–97), sought to inaugu-
rate a glorious new era for Awadh, centered on his magnificent court.
Under the previous two rulers, Faizabad had largely displaced Lucknow
and Ayodhya as the political centre of Awadh. Faizabad was, however,
the unplanned product of the haphazard but dynamic growth of the
court under Safdarjang (1739–54) and Shuja-ud-Daula. Asaf-ud-Daula's
mother and grandmother, with whom he could not get along, dominated its court life. Its location (near Ayodhya) on the eastern border of
the territories remaining to the Nawab, lacked the centrality he now
sought. Further, much of the support for his brother and rival, Saadat Ali
Khan, came from the Faizabad administrative, military, and court establishments. Consequently, Asaf-ud-Daula shifted his court to Lucknow,
which he began to rebuild as a capital worthy of his new reign. Lucknow
had been a prosperous regional city, known as a cultural and commercial
centre, but its political importance had faded.

Following 1775, Lucknow emerged as the first city in India of its day,
rivalling (and many would argue far surpassing) both Delhi of the
Mughals and Calcutta of the Company for the richness of its high court
culture, its striking architecture, the excellence of its crafts-people and
artisans, and the fame of its artistic, musical, poetic, and scholarly luminaries. Asaf-ud-Daula's arrival brought to Lucknow not only his personal
retinue, but the headquarters of the administration and the army. The
Resident, and various European adventurers too, shifted their homes and
patronage to Lucknow. Thus new sections of the city developed around
the court, the government, and the palace complexes of these notables.[4]
Populating the new quarters around these centres were an array of poets,
musicians, courtesans, artisans, and other purveyors of the increasingly
lavish culture that became legendary as *Lakhnavi* (Sharar, 1975).

By the end of the eighteenth century, the ruling family of Awadh had
shifted its self-perception and public image significantly. Unlike the

founders of the line, these rulers of Awadh apparently no longer considered themselves members of the Mughal service elite. While they continued to regard the Mughal Emperor as sovereign until 1819, they had
so established themselves locally as to consider their position as rulers to
be hereditary. Status based on achievement was transformed by them
into status based on birth. As a contemporary Muslim official in Awadh
noted about Asaf-ud-Daula:

The Wazir Asaf-ud-Daula expects that people will yield him allegiance on
account of the names and claims of his ancestors, will submit to these tyrannies
with perfect complacence, will wink at his evil practices, which are harder than
death to endure, and will not open their lips to complain. If anyone is foolish
enough to reproach the Wazir for these actions and shuns him, he and his place-
seekers charge him with sedition, disloyalty, and enmity to Mussulmans (Taalib,
1885: 75).

While Lucknow blossomed as a cultural centre, it did so in an increasingly isolated political environment. The East India Company incre-
mentally cut Awadh off from political events outside of that province. All
political communications into and out of Awadh had to pass through the
Resident's hands. Such political isolation proved a central element in the
establishment of indirect rule here and elsewhere.

In the internal affairs as well, the Company asserted its ultimate
political and military control through its Resident. It guaranteed the protection of the ruler from external and internal enemies, and stationed
troops in Awadh and in the surrounding territories. Further, to free the
Company's regular troops for service elsewhere, the Company organized
the 'Oudh Auxiliary Force', at the ruler's expense.

The military might of the Nawab decayed. Excluded from deploy-
ment outside of the province, his forces further rapidly lost effectiveness
for use even within Awadh. Writing in 1823, a ruler explained that his
dynasty had come to regard the degradation of the army as a test of its
loyalty to the Company: 'From the time of my late Father, . . . relying
as he did on the Honorable Company's Government for support against
all domestic and foreign enemies, he considered that the maintenance of
any troops of his own was not only unnecessary, but would have had the
appearance of a separation of interests between the two (Awadh and the
Company).' He continued that he surpassed even his father in the neglect of the army in order to prove his fidelity to the Company (Bengal
Political Consultations 3 October 1823, No. 12).

After Asaf-ud-Daula's death, the Company's role as arbiter of the
political future of Awadh manifested itself overtly. As frequently proved

the case, a succession in an Indian state was a time of internal weakness, to be exploited by the British. The Resident at first acceded to the accession of Asaf-ud-Daula's designated heir, Wazir Ali (1797–98), but the new ruler's policies conflicted with the Company's.[5] Thereupon the Company's long-time client, Saadat Ali Khan—the late ruler's brother who had lived for twenty-two years in exile as a pensioner under the protection of the Company—was installed, after signing a treaty with the Company transferring to it vast territories from his father's domain. The Company later reduced the territorial cessions but extracted a large sum of money instead.

The Company used the Resident to extract the range of resources it desired from Awadh. The Company expected the Resident to secure British control over commerce, including minerals (especially saltpetre for gunpowder), hand manufactures (such as cloth and luxury goods), and grain and other agricultural products (especially cotton and indigo for Britain's cloth industry).[6] In particular, Governors-General frequently stressed to Residents the Company's need to extract cash from the ruler. The nawabs supplied vast amounts of wealth in the forms of subsidies for the Company's troops, loans at low interest, or simply donations (officially to the Company, or unofficially to individuals working for the Company, or even to influential European adventurers). Overall, between 1764 and 1856, the Company extracted (in cash) at least Rs 60,00,000 in assorted 'penalties' (imposed on various rulers, for example, to cover the Company's 'expenses' in installing them during succession disputes), some Rs 52,00,000 in loans (from rulers to the Company at below market interest rates), and between Rs 80,000,000 and 100,000,000 in 'subsidies' (for troops).

In addition, the Company regarded Awadh as a prime recruiting ground for its army and administration. Since there was no ethnic or religious unity and no great identity between the ruler and the vast bulk of the people of Awadh, the nawab apparently did not particularly interest himself in the Company's recruitment policies. Numbers of Awadh's service elites (mainly from the scribal 'castes' with traditions of administration under the Awadh and Mughal dynasties) took employment with the Company. Members of various rural Brahmin, Rajput, and Muslim families, often with small landholdings of their own, found service in the Company's armies. Such service brought not only salaries (of a regularity and scale not locally available) but also various privileges under the Company's auspices, including judicial protection against the Awadh administration for themselves and their families. Soldiers and officers from

Awadh formed the core of the Company's Bengal armies until 1857. (During the 1857 fighting, soldiers native to Awadh formed the greatest threat to the Company (see Mukherjee, 1984).

Despite Saadat Ali Khan's history as a pensioner living under Company protection, as Nawab (1798–1814) he tried to develop policies providing some degree of autonomy to his government. He sought to transform land revenue grants that had been allocated to the Lucknow nobility by his predecessors into cash pensions, thus increasing his fiscal control over them. Land revenue grants were controlled by their holders; cash pensions depended on his whim. This the Resident opposed in several test cases, thus building a constituency among the urban elite for himself, at the cost of their loyalty to their ruler.

The somewhat independent domestic policies of Saadat Ali Khan, and the Company's renewed territorial ambitions, led to further cessions from Awadh. Governor-General Wellesley (1798–1805) put particular pressure on Awadh, urging the Resident to demand from the ruler both territory (particularly the fertile and strategically located Ganges-Jumna doab) and also administrative 'reform'. Although the ruler carefully fulfilled his obligation to pay the subsidy to the Company, he struggled to repulse the Company's intervention in his internal administration. Residents had over time attempted to determine the appointment of various officials in the Avadh administrtion, set administrative policy, and generally interfered in the state apparatus. As an ultimatum, Saadat Ali Khan vowed to resign rather than submit to further intervention. The delighted Company immediately drew up a treaty by which he would cede all of Awadh in exchange for a generous personal pension to the ruler, should he step aside. The Nawab repudiated this offer, seeing it as a sell out for his personal profit, and the Company feared to annex his state by force. Consequently, in 1801 the Governor-General settled for a cession of virtually all the Nawab's territories outside of Awadh, with annual revenues at that time of over Rs 13,000,000, as permanent payment of the subsidy for its forces charged to the state. Despite Saadat Ali Khan's fervent objections, he was eventually compelled to accede, and entrust his Shi'ite co-religionists and their religious buildings to the special protection of the Governor-General (Aitchison, 1909: 2:130–42). In exchange, he received temporary relief from intervention by the Resident in the administration of his remaining territories. Later Awadh rulers would take the same position: unable to oppose the Resident's intervention, they nevertheless refused to relinquish their cultural values, even if it meant personal material loss.

In addition to extracting commerce, wealth, manpower, and territory, the Company also tried to manipulate Awadh for ideological and
political purposes. In the eyes of many Europeans, disorder and misgovernment here were potentially dangerous (lest they spread to Company
territories), but they also allegedly confirmed the relative superiority of
British administration. The Company thus held up the Awadh administration as a negative example of the alternative to British rule. Conversely, for Indian notables and disgruntled people under direct British
administration, Awadh provided a partial escape from British rule.
Rather than revolt, many emigrated into Awadh.

The East India Company selected Ghazi-ud-din Haydar (1814–27)
as the next Nawab from among Saadat Ali Khan's potential heirs. In
exchange for his elevation, Ghazi-ud-din Haydar made numerous financial and political concessions to the Company over the course of his
reign. At the same time, Lucknow continued to express its own identity
through the developing culture of its court and city. Most notably, in
1819 Ghazi-ud-din Haydar had himself crowned, in an elaborate and
ritually complex ceremony, as 'Emperor of the Age' (Fisher, 1987: 120–
59). The events of this coronation reflected how understandings about
his status varied between the court, the British, and the people of the
province of Awadh. For the Awadh court, the coronation expressed the
unique and leading place of the dynasty in the Shi'ite political universe.
For the British, this ritual simply demonstrated the demotion of the
Mughal Emperor to the mere King of Delhi, through the secession of
one of his principal subordinates. To many of the people of Awadh, the
ceremony consisted of yet another remote and costly (to them) court
escapade. Thus, the court culture that developed in Lucknow became
increasingly ingrown and isolated from political events outside of Awadh
and from connections with the people of the province.

Given the frequent and galling restrictions which the Company's
Resident placed on the Awadh rulers, each successive ruler sought a
different means of self-expression. Nasir-ud-din Haydar (1827–37)
worked—against the efforts of the Company—to locate himself prominently within the political world of both his own traditions and those of
Britain. Since he could not act politically outside of Awadh due to the
Company's strictures, he apparently felt he had to make these assertions
symbolically. On his accession, he rejected the Resident's demands for a
new 'Deed of Engagement' which would bind him 'to act agreeably to
the advice of the Honourable Company in the affairs of Government.'
Instead he succesfully negotiated a continuation of the current treaties in

force (Bengal Political Consultations, 16 November 1827, No. 15). Nevertheless, the new ruler's proposed revisions of his, his wives', and his wazir's (chief minister's) titles in light of his self-perceived imperial status met with rejection by the Company, except for their use domestically within Awadh. Diplomatic letters from Indian rulers outside of Awadh, congratulating him on his accession were turned back by the Company. Nasir-ud-din Haydar also elaborated a series of specifically Shia rituals. Beyond more conventional religious ceremonies, he devised novel observations such as designating twelve virgins to act as the mothers of the Shia Imams, and even allegedly dressing up himself as the Imams' mothers and enacting their pregnancies and labours (Sharar, 1975: 57; Bengal Political Consultations 18 September 1829, No. 43; Foreign Political Consultations 12 September 1836, No. 73). Nasir-ud-din Haydar also sought confirmation of his status in British terms, particularly through an exchange of presents and diplomacy with Queen Victoria. The Company did allow him to receive the gifts and correspondence sent by the British monarch to his late father, which arrived posthumously. Further, the Company at first allowed his dispatch of a return mission. In London, however, it blocked the delivery of his presents and corespondence and confiscated them, thereby severing these diplomatic dealings with the empress (Short Statement, 1857; Bengal Political Consultations 31 October 1828, Nos. 15, 16 and 27 February 1828, No. 16). Nevertheless, Nasir-ud-din Haydar persisted in his efforts to gain British respect, through lavish patronage of Europeans in his retinue, wearing formal English dress, building a European-style observatory, enrolling in the British Society of Architects, studying English, and adopting a curious Persian script designed to look like English letters (Bengal Political Consultations 16 August 1833, No. 32, 2 September 1831, No. 73, and 7 January 1833, No. 2; Muhammad, 1939: 40–8; Foreign Political Consultations 27 February 1837, No. 31; India Political Consultations 7 November 1836, No. 56). Ultimately, however, the Company's intervention frustrated his ability to control even administration of his own territories (see Siddiqi, 1973).

The Resident, when reduced to a direct confrontation with the ruler, could rely on the force of the Company's troops. On Nasir-ud-din Haydar's death in 1837, the Resident decided to reject his designated heir, Faridun Bakht. In a dramatic confrontation, the Resident had his troops attack the throne room where Faridun Bakht was ascending his late father's throne against the Company's wishes (Prashad, n.d.: 363, 367–9; Foreign Secret Consultations 7 August 1837, No. 10). In his place, the Company then installed Nasir-ud-din Haydar's aging uncle, Muhammad Ali Shah (1837–42) (see Ahmad, 1971).

As the price of his unexpected accession, Muhammad Ali Shah agreed to sign whatever treaty the Company might propose. Eventually, the Company presented him with the controversial Treaty of 1837, giving the Company the right to take over the administration of Awadh (should it deem necessary) and establishing a payment of Rs 16,00,000 annually for the subsidiary forces. Since the 1801 cession of territory had already satisfied this subsidy 'in perpetuity', the Court of Directors subsequently annulled the 1837 treaty. The Governor-General, rather than admit that he had been overruled, 'inadvertently neglected' to inform the Awadh ruler (and even some of the Company's later Residents) that the Treaty had been annulled, only that the additional subsidy would not be collected (Aitchison, 1909: 1:16).

During the course of his reign, Muhammad Ali Shah made efforts to reform the Awadh administration and further glorify Lucknow through an ambitious series of building projects. Control by the Resident over the most effective military forces in Awadh, however, made enforcement of the ruler's orders problematic. These troops could be used by his administration against defaulting landholders only with the Residents' approval. This cumbersome command structure led to severe limitations on their use by the Awadh administration in collecting land revenues, the main source of income for the state. Conversely, however, these troops provided the Resident with a base for his forays into the administration. Further, the soldiers themselves—mostly born in Awadh—used the Resident to provide them and their families with immunity against the Awadh administration. Thus, only through cooperation with the Resident could the Awadh ruler implement his policies or gain the funds to pay for them.

Amjad Ali Shah (1842–47) in many ways continued the practices of his father, Muhammad Ali Shah, and their predecessors. He strove to develop the identity of his court, resisting many of the assertions of the Company, while at the same time recognizing the need to find a means of working with the Resident in order to carry out the functions of the administration. In Amjad Ali Shah's case, his court culture proved more pietistic than earlier rulers. He reduced the elaborate ceremonies and rituals of the court, channeling resources rather toward Shi'ite religious luminaries and scholars.

The cultural world of the Awadh court and that of the province it ruled shared little in background, composition, or interest. As part of the process of the development of a distinctly Lakhnavi culture, a hereditary and protected nobility developed at the Awadh capital. As the Awadh rulers made a series of massive and forced loans to the East India Company, the over Rs 25,00,000 in annual interest from these loans was largely assigned in perpetuity to specific relatives and dependents of the Awadh dynasty (Uttar Pradesh, 1964). Despite the taint of usury— forbidden in the Quran and a matter of concern to both the Awadh rulers making the loans and the recipients assigned interest from them—these permanent stipends bestowed security on their recipients. Most of these were individuals who would earlier, under the Mughal pattern, have been assigned *jagirs* and would have been required to actively serve the ruler in exchange for their income. Rarely deigning to serve in the Awadh administration, however, these Lucknow 'guaranteed pensioners' formed a leisured and protected rentier class. The East India Company guaranteed its protection over this hereditary nobility in Lucknow, even against the authority of the ruler. The dependence of such a class on the Company provided its Resident with considerable influence in Lucknow.

Scattered across Awadh lay well-established towns (*qasbas*). These market and cultural centres supported an Islamicised service and commercial elite of their own. Many of the leading scholars of Islam came from, or taught in, *madrasas* located in such towns. A number of the families with traditions of education and service to the Mughals and later the Awadh rulers, had roots in these towns. As such, they formed an essential element of the culture of Awadh not based in Lucknow.

The elite of Lucknow largely avoided the rural areas of Awadh. Except for hunting parties, the courtiers and high officials of Awadh ventured out of the capital only at peril to their lives.[7] A Resident in Lucknow observed:

The most remarkable feature about the state of Oude is the entire absence of all sympathy, and I may almost say all communication between the Court and the aristocracy of the capital, and the landed aristocracy of the provinces, or districts. They know hardly any more of each other than if they occupied separate planets . . . The aristocracy of the capital . . . would, none of them, be safe a single night beyond the capital or cantonments. They would be plundered and destroyed by the landholders (Foreign Political Consultations 21 April 1849, No. 100).

Thus the elite of the court and the people and elite of the countryside shared little.

Conversely, virtually none of the established landholding families made their way into the administration or capital. Only in a few unusual cases did landholders side consistently with the administration. Land-holders who ventured into Lucknow were held hostage for the payment of their revenue, beaten, imprisoned, and even killed when discovered in the capital. The rare landholder who did enter Lucknow tried to insure his safety through guarantees from powerful individuals at court. As a rule, the ruling house, courtiers, administrators, landholders, and peas-ants each intermarried among themselves, each group within its own class and religious community.

The lack of sympathy or shared cultural identity between the courtiers and the landholders of Awadh generally precluded regular social contact and marriage between them. The rulers, and apparently virtually all of their courtiers, shunned any marriage connections with the inhabitants of the province they ruled. Only in a few unusual cases, where the land-holder made extraordinary efforts to adopt the culture of the capital, did social contact develop. In one of these rare instances, a landholding family which had already converted to Shi'ism sought to participate in the culture of the court. The result was prolonged and destructive war-fare between the members of the two cultural worlds. For instance, the Raja of Nanpara frequented Lucknow sufficiently to take as his second wife one of the favoured courtesans of the city, a woman who had al-legedly been a former intimate of the Nawab himself. When the Raja died soon thereafter, this younger, Shia, wife gathered the support of her old companions in the city to try to take over the estate of Nanpara. The late Raja's senior wife, a Sunni, held the backing of the administration of the estate and most of the neighbouring landholders who united to exclude the forces of the junior widow. In the period of conflict which ensued, the estate was devastated. Only after a compromise, which pen-sioned off both widows and placed the estate under an infant relative of the late Raja, was peace restored (Ghoshal, 1918; India Political and Foreign Consultations 28 December 1855, No. 307).

The Awadh rulers clearly regarded the Shi'ites of their court—and of the rest of the world—as their primary constituency. While Shi'ites dominated in the administration and nobility of the capital, they made up an insignificant percentage of the population of the countryside. Excluding Shi'ites in the earlier capital of Faizabad and in Lucknow, they made up less than 0.2 per cent of the population of Awadh. [8] To the detriment of the other communities, rulers demonstrated their prefer-ence for Shias in their distribution of honour and the resources of the province. They assigned over 90 per cent of the interest paid on their loans to the Company to their relatives and dependents—almost all of whom were Shia. Most of the remainder of the annual interest went to specifically Shia institutions, like *Imambaras* (where the symbols of Shia martyrdom are housed). These sums were in addition to nearly Rs 20,00,000 which went annually in direct pensions from the ruler to his relatives. Further, large gifts were made to the institutions at the site of martyrdom in Karbala in Iraq (Uttar Pradesh 1964; India Political and Foreign Consultations 19 December 1853, No. 115; Bengal Political Consultations 16 November 1827, No. 12). Thus a significant part of the revenue was committed to those who shared their sectarian identity.

The nawabs also favoured Shi'ites with key executive posts. As an example, they considered the most prominent position in the administration, that of vizier, appropriate only for Shi'ites. Of the eleven appointments to this office made during the ninetenth century, ten were to Shi'ites. The sole Sunni minister, an official favoured by the East India Company, lasted only a few months. [9]

This nearly unbroken string of Shia appointees in this highest of offices was the result of explicit policy. When the Company suggested a candidate it considered qualified for the post, the Awadh ruler rejected him out of hand because '. . . he is a Sooni, I have not long to live, the Sheeas would desert the town, there would be a blot upon my memory' (India Political Consultations 3 August 1840, No. 71). In cases where no experienced Shi'ite was available, one was appointed wazir anyway, sometimes with a trained Sunni deputed to carry out the practical work of the office; in this way, Shia prestige was preserved and the administration's functions could continue (Khaldun 1958: 1: Chapter 3).

The political pressures on the incumbent of the office of wazir made stable tenure in that office very difficult. The demands of the East India Company on the state fell squarely on the shoulders of the wazir. The ruler on his part insisted that the chief minister remain solely dependent on his favour. In consequence, there was rapid turnover in the office of wazir. Any minister who displeased the Company, or who pleased it too much for the ruler's taste, was sacked. In at least one case, the gestures of support by the Company for an incumbent minister apparently led directly to his dismissal by a jealous ruler (Diskalar, 1937: 22).

Significantly, the only chief minister who remained in office throughout the entire reign of an Awadh ruler was bound to him by ties of marriage. After a number of unsuccessful negotiations with various of his cousins, the prince who would become the last ruler of Awadh, Wajid Ali Shah (1847–56), married the daughter of Ali Naqi Khan, a courtier and distant relation. On his accession, Wajid Ali Shah appointed his father-in-law chief minister, regardless of the man's almost total lack of administrative experience (see Bhatnagar, 1968 and Bose, n.d.). In spite of the particularly severe strains placed on this minister by the political circumstances of the day, he remained wazir through the annexation of Awadh by the Company in 1856, and even after the deposition and then the exile of the ruler.

Over the years from 1764 to 1856, the Company had on several occasions proposed the annexation of Awadh, and finally in 1856 the Directors authorised the Governor-General to annex the state on the ambiguous grounds of 'misgovernment'. In British eyes, Wajid Ali Shah had became notorious for his devotion to poetry, religion, and/or sensual pleasure rather than the affairs of state.[10] Little evidence, however, supports the British contention that conditions in Awadh had particularly changed for the worse at that moment. In fact, the Governor-General admitted that he was unable to 'find a pretext' for the ultimatum, since Wajid Ali Shah 'will take any amount of kicking without being rebellious' (Baird, 1911; 344). Indeed, at the time of annexation, the ruler had just weathered a communal crisis as Hindu and Muslim partisans fought over disputed religious ground at Hanuman Garhi in Ayodhya. Wajid Ali Shah, by sending in his troops to crush a band of Muslims marching on the site, enforced order, despite thinly veiled British desires that he fail and thus justify Company intervention to 'save' Awadh from its ruler.

Governor-General Dalhousie (1848–56) had the Resident convey to the ruler the Company's unwillingness to tolerate any further 'maladministration'. Although the legal right of the Company to so intervene was debatable, Dalhousie overrode such juridical considerations and justified his act on the theoretical grounds that the Company had to protect 'the People' of Awadh from abuse by their ruler. Rather than direct annexation, the Governor-General first proposed the Company administer Awadh in the name of the ruler. The ruler would keep his main palace and titles, and would receive an annual pension of up to Rs 18,00,000 if he would sign the authorisation for this act. To put further pressure on the ruler, the Resident was to offer the Queen Mother an additional Rs 1,00,000 annually if she would induce her son to sign.

Despite these inducements, the ruler refused to compromise his honour, as he conceived it, by collaborating in this way with the Company. The Company thus annexed Awadh into its direct rule and as his final act, the ruler paid off his army and ordered all his officials and officers to cooperate with the Company, 'on no pretense to revolt or mutiny' while he 'proceeds to Calcutta, to bring his case to the notice of the Governor-General and (then to England) to intercede with Her Most Gracious Majesty the Queen'. To no avail.[11] The final blow, however, occurred in 1857–58, after the end of the 'Mutiny'. The efforts of the Queen Mother had proved futile. Under the British Raj, Lucknow in particular, and India in general, were to enter yet another phase of their existence.

NOTES

1. For studies of relations between Awadh and the East India Company see Barnett (1980), Basu (1943), Davies (1939), Fisher (1987), and Paton (1944).

2. This war arose from the political manoeuverings of Shuja-ud-Daula and the leader of this Rohilla Afghan ethnicity, Hafiz Rahmat Khan, in the context of the military threat which the Rohilla Afghans posed to the north-western flank of Awadh. The combined Awadh and Company armies proved victorious.

3. For a first-hand account of this war and the other early British conquests by a Muslim subaltern (incidently the first book written and published in English by an Indian) see Fisher (1996).

4. For the architectural history of Lucknow up to 1857, see Llewellyn-Jones, 1985. For the city's post-1857 history, Oldenburg, 1984.

5. While this deposition and reposition went smoothly, Wazir Ali later expressed anti-British resistance: in 1799, he led an unsuccessful revolt, killing the Company's Resident in Benaras but was ultimately captured and imprisoned for life by the Company.

6. For a study of the changing economy of the Gangetic plain see Bayly (1983). There is much debate about the role of British commercial interests in the Company's policy in Awadh see Marshall (1975, 1985) and Mukherjee (1982, 1985).

7. For a colourful and probably fictionalized account of the loot of a party of nobles from Lucknow by local landholders see Knighton (1856: 76–8).

8. According to the earliest census giving such information: White, 1882. The only earlier census did not identify Shi'ites: Williams, 1869.

9. The Ruler refers to this Sunni minister's death as 'timely' and saving the Ruler's good name. India Political Consultations 3 August 1840, No. 71.

10. Some scholars have seen this as an effort to find refuge from the frustrations inherent in their condition of indirect rule (see Goetz, 1938). Nevertheless, all the Nawabs worked to preserve their own sense of their position in the world, as defined by their own cultural values.

11. This annexation generated much discord, both among policy-makers and among scholars assessing it, and among the people of Awadh and north India at the time (for example see: Bird, 1971; Irwin, 1973; Shah, 1856).

REFERENCES

Ahmad, Safi (1971), *Two Kings of Awadh: Muhammad Ali Shah and Amjad Ali Shah (1837–47)*, Aligarh, P.C. Dwadash Shreni.

Aitchison, C.U. (1909), *A Collection of Treaties, Engagements, and Sunnads*, 14 vols, Calcutta, Foreign Office Press.

Baird, J.G.A. (1911), *Private Papers of the Marquis of Dalhousie*, Edinburgh, William Blackwood.

Barnett, Richard B. (1980), *North India between Empires: Awadh, the Mughals, and the British, 1720–1801*, Berkeley, University of California Press.

Basu, Purnendu (1943), *Oudh and the East India Company, 1785–1801*, Lucknow, Maxwell.

Bayly, C.A. (1983), *Rulers, Townsmen and Bazaars: North Indian Society in the Age of British Expansion, 1770–1870*, Cambridge, Cambridge University Press.

Bhatnagar, G.D. (1968), *Awadh under Wajid Ali Shah*, Lucknow, Bharatiya Vidhya Prakashan.

Bird, Robert W. [Samuel Lucas] (1971), *Dacoitee in Excelsis or The Spoilation of Oude by The East India Company*, Lucknow, Pustak Kendra, reprint of 1857 edition.

Bose, A.C. (n.d.), *Hazrat Wajid Ali Shah, King of Oudh*, n.p., A.C. Bose.

Davies, C.C. (1939), *Warren Hastings and Oudh*, London, Oxford University Press.

Diskalar, D.B. (1937), 'Foundation of an Observatory at Lucknow', *Journal of the U.P. Historical Society*, 10, Part 1 (July): 7–32.

Fisher, Michael H. (1987), *A Clash of Cultures: Awadh, The British, and the Mughals*, Delhi, Manohar.

———— (1991), *Indirect Rule in India: Residents and the Residency System*, Delhi, Oxford University Press.

———— (1996), *The First Indian Author in English: Dean Mahomed (1759–1851)*, Delhi, Oxford University Press.

Goetz, Hermann (1938), *The Crisis of Indian Civilization in the Eighteenth and Nineteenth Centuries*, Calcutta, Calcutta University Press.

Ghoshal, Benod Chandra (1918), *Some notes on Raj Nanpara or the Tragic Story of the Premier Mohamedan Estate of Oudh*, Lucknow, Anglo-Oriental Press.

Irwin, H.C. (1973), *Garden of India or Chapters on Oudh History and Affairs*, 2 vols, Delhi, Pustak Kendra (reprint of 1880 edition).

Khaldun, Ibn (1958), *The Muqaddimah: An Introduction to History*, trans. Franz Rosenthal, Bollingen Series 43, 3 vols, New York, Pantheon Books.

Khan, Seid Gholam Hossein (1902), *Seir Mutaqherin*, trans. M. Raymond alias Haji Mustafa, 4 vols, Calcutta, T.D. Chatterjee.

Knighton, William (1856), *The Private Life of an Eastern King by a Member of the Household of His late Majesty Nussir-u-Deen, King of Oude*, New York, J.S. Redfield.

Llewellyn-Jones, Rosie (1985), *A Fatal Friendship: The Nawabs, the British, and the City of Lucknow*, Delhi, Oxford University Press.

Marshall, P.J. (1975), 'Economic and Political Expansion: The Case of Oudh', *Modern Asian Studies*, 9, 4: 465–82.

———— (1985), 'Early British Imperialism in India', *Past and Present*, 106 (February).

Muhammad, K.B. Saiyid Abu (1939), 'Some Autographs of King Nasir-ud-din Hyder', *Journal of the U.P. Historical Society* 12, 1 (July): 40–8.

Mukherjee, Rudrangshu (1982) 'Trade and Empire in Avadh, 1765–1804', *Past and Present*, 94 (February): 85–102.

———— (1984), *Awadh in Revolt 1857–1858: A Study of Popular Resistance*, Delhi, Oxford University Press.

———— (1985), 'A Rejoinder', *Past and Present*, 106 (February).

Oldenburg, Veena Talwar (1984), *The Making of Colonial Lucknow: 1856–1877*, Princeton, Princeton University Press.

Prashad, Munshi Sital (n.d.), 'Mir'at al-Auza', Persian MS. 2149, Raza Library, Rampur.

Paton, John (1944), *An Abstract of the Political Intercourse between the British Government and the Kingdom of Oudh, 1764–1835*, ed. Bisheshwar Prasad, Allahabad, Allahabad University Press.

Shah, Wajid Ali (1856), *Reply to the Charges against the King of Oude*. Calcutta, J.F. Bellamy.

Sharar, Abdul Halim (1975), *Lucknow: Last Phase of an Oriental Culture* trans. and ed. E.S. Harcourt and Fakhir Hussain, London, Paul Elek.

———— (1857), *Short Statement*, London, R. Clay.

Siddiqi, Asiya (1973), *Agrarian Change in a North Indian State: Uttar Pradesh, 1819–1833*, Oxford, Clarendon Press.

Taalib, Abu (1885), *Tafzihu'l Ghafilin*, trans. W. Hoey, Allahabad, North-Western Provinces and Oudh Government Press.

Uttar Pradesh (1964), *Union Political Pensioners in Uttar Pradesh*, Allahabad, Superintendent of Printing and Stationery.

Williams, J. Charles (1869), *The Report on the Census of Oudh*, 2 vols, Lucknow, Oudh Government Press.

White, Edmond (1882), *Report on the Census of the N.W.P. and Oudh and of the Native States of Rampur and Native Garhwal taken on the 17th February, 1881*, Allahabad, North West and Oudh Government Printing Press.

3

Lucknow, City of Dreams

ROSIE LLEWELLYN-JONES

Lucknow was indeed a city of dreams, and it sometimes seems that even today, 140 years after Nawab Wajid Ali Shah left it forever, there are almost as many different ways of interpreting it, as there were dreamers. Curiously, the city's buildings appeared to visitors to have an insubstantial, dream-like quality about them. Some found them theatrical, something of a sham, the painted backdrop for an Indian masque. 'You find, on examination', wrote a disappointed traveller, 'that the white colour of the buildings, which presented in the sunlight the effect of the purest marble, is simply whitewash. The material of the buildings themselves is stuccoed brick, and your taste is shocked by the discovery that the gilded domes, of perfect shape and apparently massive construction . . . are mere shells of wood, in many places rotten' (Beg, 1915: 7).

To Honoria Lawrence, Lucknow in spite of its imperfections and its 'bad taste and inconsistency, altogether comes nearer to anything I have seen to realise my early ideas of the Arabian Nights and Lala Rookh'. (Private Papers 1830–57 MSS Eur. F85 IOL.) Maria, Lady Nugent found one of the palaces 'certainly very pretty and truly eastern—its various courts and colonnades, the variety of birds, the style of the gardens, etc., put me very much in mind of those we see on old China cups and jars'. (Nugent, 1839: I: 323).

Those who were homesick imagined that Hazratganj, the new main street, was like the High Street at Oxford, 'in the colour of its buildings and the general form and Gothic style of the greater part of them'. (Heber, 1828: I: 386). And Lucknow 'will forcibly bring to the recollection of an Englishman those cities of his native land; the same streets, fine houses, and meadows fertilized by the Goomty'. (Anon., *Sketches of India*, 1816: 151).

Indian writers, like Abdul Halim Sharar (English edition, 1975), and

Yusuf Khan Kammelposh (see Llewellyn-Jones, 1990) employ more general terms like 'genuine splendour' and 'imposing grandeur' to portray the city. P.C. Mukherji, who published *Pictorial Lucknow* in 1883, examined both Nawabi and British buildings in greater detail than had been done before, but no one, Indian or British, seemed able to enter into the minds of the nawabs and their courtiers and to ask why they had created the extraordinary edifices that adorned Lucknow before 1856. And what indeed had the Nawabs created? An 'oriental' city, with gilded domes (albeit over a wooden frame) and minarets, or an Indian version of a European spa ?

Parallels can certainly be drawn between the nawabs, retreating into a world of make believe with their European houses, furniture and amusements, and rich men in Europe who imagined themselves masters of the seraglio, in Islamic pleasure gardens. The mad Ludwig II of Bavaria is a good example of the latter, with his Moorish interiors and theatrical designs for 'The King of Lahore' (see *Designs for the Dream King*, Victoria & Albert Museum, 1978: 30, pls. 19 & 20). While many escape at times to a dream world, few have the money and imagination to create one around them, as the nawabs did. At the same time they were anxious to promote Lucknow as an Indian centre of Shi'ism by erecting large, splendid buildings for worship and burial. This raises the question of how the nawabs wanted to be seen, and remembered. Was it as honorary Englishmen, with their Neo-classical palaces, their country houses, their Worcester dinner services, their English wives, their membership of English institutions like the Royal Institute of British Architects and many other Anglophile traits? Or as virtuous Islamic rulers in a predominantly Hindu state, paying homage, however nominal, to the Mughal Emperor?

Yet Lucknow before 1856 was not built solely of nawabi fantasies. The East India Company officials, merely a handful in 1775, had, years later, expanded sufficiently in number to create a garden suburb on the Residency Hill. Here they lived in substantial bungalows, surrounded by gardens and *pukka* roads, with a small Gothic church, a post-office, a banquering hall, and tennis court. But even this 'English' redoubt contained some curious anomalies, like the small Begum Kothi mosque, and a Muslim tomb. None of the bungalows belonged to their inhabitants either. All were leased out to Company officials, mainly by the nawabs, who owned most of the site, and it was the nawabs, too, who paid for the maintenance of these bungalows, which led to many disputes as the Company became more arrogant in its dealings with the Lucknow

Court. Then there was the Company cantonment, situated uncomfortably four miles north of the Gomti river, and too far to provide immediate aid if trouble broke out in the city. Again, this was a place where Englishmen and women could feel almost at home with a little church, a ballroom, lending library, ice-club, cricket field, bandstand, and walled cemetery.

Then there were the 'adventurers', as people liked to call them, European men attracted to the rich Lucknow Court and employed by it as mercenaries, architects, engineers, painters, musicians, *aides de camp*, and even hairdressers. These included the Frenchman Major General Claude Martin, originally employed as Superintendent of the nawabi arsenal (Llewellyn-Jones, 1992), Antoine Polier, court architect, Robert Home and George Duncan Beechey, court artists. Only Martin's extraordinary buildings remain as evidence of these independent spirits. Others chose to collect their jewels, clothes, paintings and cash and, like the notorious coiffeur George Harris Derusset, make a speedy exit (*Asiatic Journal*, 1837: 94). Martin's palace mausoleum of Constantia (La Martinière) is described as a giant folly, the observer not certain whether it was a castle, a wedding cake in brick, or a baroque fantasy.

Given the weight of all these foreign elements (and the nawabs themselves had come from Nishapur in Iran only at the beginning of the eighteenth century), can the 'real' Lucknow be said to have existed at all? Home to a largely Hindu population, with a Sunni minority, old Lucknow was built on a number of small hills south of the river Gomti. Visitors complained that 'the ground is so uneven that one cannot walk about in this city except by detours, climbing up here, going down there' (Tieffenthaler, 1786–88, I: 256).

After 1775, when the Court moved from Faizabad to Lucknow, the nawabs built almost entirely along the banks of the river, for only here was the ground level enough for their large palace complexes and extravagant vistas. There were a few buildings of note before their arrival, including the Aurangzeb mosque on Lakshman Tila, the Chowk, various *ganjes* and the oddly-named Farangi Mahal (Frankish Palace), which had first housed members of the East India Company in the middle of the seventeenth century (Llewellyn-Jones, 1985: 8–9). These early traders, in their handsome and defensible 'factory', had established themselves as exporters of locally made cloth, called 'dereabauds' and they also, for a decade or so, sent Lucknow sugar and indigo to the Company port at Surat. On their departure, the Farangi Mahal became a Muslim seminary.

Before 1775, the Macchi Bhawan fort was the only building to attract favourable European comment. It stood south of the Gomti and commanded its only crossing, the 'Stone' bridge. The fort contained a number of structures and gardens which could be partially seen over its perimeter wall, with its semi-circular bastions. Viewed from the north bank, the fort reminded William Hodges (1793: 101) 'of what I had imagined might be the style of a Baron's castle in Europe, about the twelfth century . . . the exterior of the buildings is not to be commended'. From the few surviving illustrations (the fort was blown up in 1857), it appears an eclectic mixture of defensive buildings, interspersed with insubstantial pavilions and a number of walled gardens. The only part still in existence is the Bao'li, a series of water-cooled rooms around a central tank. This was one of the grandest of the state apartments, known as the Bao'li Palace, with inlaid marble floors and walls of white *chunam* and red porphyry. Unusually, it had underfloor heating from a series of flues, so that the water from its many fountains could run warm or cold.

It was here that the fourth Nawab, Asaf-ud-Daula, first settled when he moved to Lucknow on his succession to the *masnad*. As part of a deliberate attempt to step out from the shadow of his deceased father, Shuja-ud-Daula, the young Nawab quickly began altering and improving the Macchi Bhawan. Immediately adjacent to it, so close in fact that it shared a common gateway (the Panch Mahalla entrance), he created the Bara or Asafi Imambara. (This was probably the first, and certainly the largest, of Lucknow's many fine *imambaras*—see N. Das, 1991). Although Asaf-ud-Daula and his wives were buried here, the primary function of an imambara is not that of a tomb, but a place for Shi'as to gather, particularly during Mohurram, the period of mourning for the martyrs Hussain and Hasan. The Bara Imambara is an enormous, long, low structure, supposedly at one time the largest vaulted hall in the world, with seven entrance arches in the central bay. Above it are decorative terraces of arches, topped with small domes, creating a light, almost lacy, effect when viewed from ground level. Inside, apart from the tombs, are the *mimbar* (pulpit), the *taziyas* (small replica tombs), and the *alams* (banners). Elaborate glass chandeliers and tall branched candlesticks are also part of the imambara's treasure. The building shares its grounds and handsome gateways with the adjacent Asafi mosque, another long, low building, its three onion domes dwarfed by sturdy minarets.

The adjacent Rumi Darwaza, named after a supposedly similar gateway in Istanbul, is difficult to describe. It looks like half a hollow dome, set at ground level and surrounded by wild frills of green pottery. It is believed that these pottery *guldastas* (buds) were designed as fountain heads, but never worked successfully, and somewhere within the brick walls may lie a failed hydraulic system.

In less than a decade Asaf-ud-Daula had established Lucknow as the foremost Shi'a city in India. Unfortunately there are no contemporary descriptions of its religious buildings. Europeans usually felt inhibited in describing Islamic buildings, because they could not find enough familiar points of reference although many had, of course, visited Delhi and Agra, and criticised Lucknow for not producing buildings like the Red Fort or the Taj Mahal, ignoring the fact that Awadh did not have building stone, and indeed was not the capital of the Mughal Empire.

The enormous physical changes in Lucknow during this first decade were the most obvious sign that the foreign nawabs were bringing with them new ideas, new fashions, new architecture and a new culture. Ironically, though the nawabs had been appointed *subadars* of Awadh by the Mughals, their fortunes rose as Delhi waned, attracting artists of all kinds who were looking for patronage, domestic staff with their families, craftsmen offering their wares, and the usual hangers-on. After Delhi was taken by the English in 1803 the cultural exodus to Lucknow was intensified, although those who found refuge there did not hesitiate to criticise its spurious, insubstantial glitter (see Peteivich, 1992, on the Delhi poets in Lucknow). The establishment of a very rich court led to a substantial increase in the population. I have estimated (1985: 12–13) that the population increased by about 50,000 to 3,00,000 during the last quarter of the eighteenth century, and that most of this increase took place between 1775 and 1785. Not only did the court attract newcomers, but also pilgrims who came to marvel at the Bara Imambara and to join in religious occasions. In turn these holy tourists needed lodging and sustenance, which provided a further circle of 'service industries' radiating out from the centre at the Macchi Bhawan.

For the unsophisticated visitor to Lucknow in the 1780s, all the new buildings, shining with stucco and brass in the sunlight, were objects of admiration and wonder. The untrained eye would not have differentiated between the Persian-inspired architecture of the imambaras and the European-style palaces of the nawabs. Both were foreign to the medieval Hindu city of old Lucknow. Religious and secular buildings appeared rapidly among the mango topes that lined the river bank. Thousands of trees were felled to provide timber for roofs, floors, windows and doors, as well as fuel for the lime and brick kilns, and scaffolding. Grass and bamboo were used to thatch and construct auxiliary buildings and huts for the labourers working on sites. Wild animals like the wolf and boar retreated to the jungle. On the outskirts of the city, where the Qaisar Bagh was later to stand, the European residents built a small walled cemetery, with stuccoed obelisks to commemorate those who did not return home.[1]

Although rich in timber, Awadh lacked building stone. The nearest quarries were at Chunar, on the border, and marble had to be imported from the Makrana area of Rajasthan. For this reason, Awadh, and Lucknow in particular, developed the art of mimicking stone by using small, thin *lakhori* bricks, which were then covered in fine stucco (chunam). Made from crushed shells, pulses, lime and jaggery, and polished to a sparkling finish, stucco was used both externally and internally. Pottery was also occasionally used to imitate stone, especially on balustrades, and as ornamentation at parapet level. The craftsmen of Lucknow developed this art to a high level, and only as the nawabi buildings decay and brickwork becomes visible, can one appreciate that all those glittering 'marble' facades were indeed a sham.

The first new building that Asaf-ud-Daula commissioned, six months after his father's death, was 'the plan of a house after the European taste, from an Officer of the East India Company' (Secret Index, 18 Sept. 1775, NA). At that time it was probably the first such building in Lucknow, pre-dating Claude Martin's town-house by six years. How the Nawab developed a liking for European architecture is not known. He never visited Calcutta, so he had no opportunity of seeing the great houses along Chowringhee. He can only have learnt about the European style from the French advisors at his father's court. Prominent among these was Antoine Polier, employed by Shuja-ud-Daula to superintend building at Faizabad in 1773. (At the same time Polier was working for the East India Company as a land surveyor.) The Nawab asked him to draw up plans for a banqueting house in Faizabad and a palace in Varanasi, but by the time the plans were complete, Polier's employer was dead. Asaf-ud-Daula then asked him to prepare plans, as his father had wished, for some border forts, but Polier was recalled by the Company to Calcutta before he could do so.

It was at this point that Polier may have introduced Martin, as a fellow surveyor, to the Lucknow court, and it is easy to imagine how the two friends would have impressed the young Asaf-ud-Daula with their descriptions of Europe and its treasures. The Nawab was a keen collector of everything European, and a man with a genuine love of building. While the idea of the Bara Imambara clearly came from Persia, it seems equally certain that his 'European' buildings were inspired by the Frenchmen at his father's court (Lafont, 1990). This in turn inspired his successors to create 'European' palaces in Lucknow, based not on the pedestrian buildings in the Residency for the East India Company, but on Martin's realised fantasies and Polier's lost or unidentified houses.

By 1781 Asaf-ud-Daula had a substantial example of a European house, built by a European on the heavily wooded bank of the river. Claude Martin's first identifiable building was called by him simply his Lucknow House, and occasionally as 'Luckypeera' (*Lakh-i-pera*, a lakh of trees). This would have been an extraordinary building anywhere in eighteenth century India, with its moat, drawbridge and roof kiosks, decorated with stucco swags. But its most striking feature was the use of the Gomti's waters to cool the house. A series of arches, built on piers in the river, supported the great mirrored room at first floor level, giving a watery, Venetian feeling, particularly when the Gomti rose during the monsoon. There were two basement storeys, one above the other, set into the river bank. These contained extensive rooms, cool and damp even at the height of summer, as the river fell rapidly. Their open arches were hung with *tatties* kept constantly watered by servants. Here Martin would retire during the hottest months. As the annual monsoon caused the Gomti to rise, Martin too would ascend, from the lowest basement storey to the one directly below ground level, and in turn, to the ground floor. Each year, as the waters started to fall, the underground rooms would be cleaned and redecorated, ready for the next season.

Because Martin's house has been extensively altered, and partially demolished, it is difficult to appreciate fully the technical skills involved in constructing a building which was designed to be flooded annually. Many details have been lost, and many questions are unanswered. One of the most interesting is whether the inspiration for water-cooled rooms came from the Bao'li Palace at the Macchi Bhawan, with its central tank and fountain.

The splendour of Luckypeera, in its own large grounds, provided a striking contrast to the bungalows of the East India Company on the adjacent hill. The first Resident had been appointed in 1774, when the court was still in Faizabad. In the beginning, the Company establishment was modest in the extreme, consisting only of the Resident and one secretary, but it quickly grew into an enormous army of officials, reflecting the importance of Awadh to the Company. As Martin worked over the drawing board on plans for his Lucknow house, the Resident was supervising the erection of rather humbler accommodation for himself and his clerks. (Martin owned some of the land on the Residency hill and rented out houses to Company staff. He also built a row of shops, called 'Captain Bazaar', at the foot of the site, a long, low series of white-washed open booths.)

A typical Residency bungalow of this period consisted of a single-storeyed building, surrounded by a tiled veranda, with a spiral staircase at one side that gave access to the flat roof. The Residency offices and Treasury were even more makeshift and were described by the Resident as 'Straw Buildings'. It was only when these bungalows were completely destroyed by fire in 1778 that a reappraisal was made of the very *ad hoc* nature of the area. Gold coins rescued during the fire from the 'Treasury' had to be 'guarded by Sepoys and lay in the open for many days'. (Bengal Public Consultations 28 July 1778, IOL.) When reconstruction began, priority was given to a strong brick building to house bullion and the Company records. It was near this building that other offices and residential accommodation developed, as the number of Company officials increased. Trees were felled and compounds laid out, skirting the *zenana* of a Muslim house and a Muslim burial place. The Residency complex was never a clearly defined area laid out on virgin land. Company officials, arriving at first in small numbers, as emissaries to a flourishing, rich court, had to take what they were given. By the time the Company was politically strong enough in Awadh to consider something rather grander for itself, it was too well established on the hill.

Two attempts were made to shift the complex to the outskirts of the city, both instigated by the nawabs, who desired less Company interference in court affairs. By the 1820s the hill was no longer a lonely, wooded spot, but stood surrounded by new palaces and houses that had sprung up during the last fifty years. Although Company officials found this proximity with 'native' dwellings annoying, they realised that a move to the outskirts would have isolated them. Ironically, the Residency's position proved both a blessing and a curse during its prolonged siege in the 1857 uprising. Its hill location made it easier to defend, but the adjacent Indian houses to the south provided access for snipers who could stand at their windows and pick off Europeans on the makeshift ramparts (see Farrell, 1973).

Ten years after the establishment of the court at Lucknow, Asaf-ud-Daula decided to create a new palace complex, the Daulat Khana, to the west of the city. We do not know why he chose to move, given that he had spent much time, money and effort on beautifying the Macchi Bhawan and creating the Bara Imambara next to it, but we can speculate that he now felt confident enough to leave behind his father's palace in Lucknow. We can also suggest that the Imambara, with its attached mosque and Rumi Darwaza gateway, had been so successful in attracting pilgrims and sightseers, that the area had become too congested and noisy. The nawab may also have been eager to commission more European-inspired buildings of his own. Daniel Johnson wrote that 'His Highness could never bear to hear that any person possessed anything superior to his own' (Johnson, 1827: 163), and this is quite manifest in his collections of European treasures and curiosities, so often described (Twining, 1893: 311). He had already had Mr Orr's house copied for himself, and since there were 'European' buildings in his capital, he naturally wanted the biggest and best.

In 1857 the majority of the Court records of Lucknow were lost. Isolated papers remain, usually because they were sent out from Lucknow and have been discovered in other archives, but nothing appears to survive about the nawabi building departments. Even the names of the Indian architects who built most of Lucknow are mainly unknown today, and no original plans exist. Measured drawings have been made recently of buildings which are still extant, like the Asafi Kothi, the showpiece of the Daulat Khana complex, but we can only speculate on the architect. Antoine Polier may have designed this imposing semi-European structure, but if so, he had left Lucknow for good before it was completed in the late 1780s. Claude Martin may have acted as advisor, although he did not mention it in any correspondence, and the building lacks his quirks.

The Asafi Kothi was the centre-piece of the new palace complex, standing in formal gardens, with an auxiliary private mosque, a Sheesh Mahal, and the Aina Khana, the Nawab's own museum, stuffed indiscriminately with European treasures and worthless objects. The building still stands, its fine facade with semi-circular bays in reasonably good condition. At the front was a covered veranda, where petitioners and visitors could wait in the shade, for this was the *diwan-i-am*, the public building. The large central hall—with its double storey height—is surrounded by smaller rooms on two levels, where the Nawab could retire. These private apartments were equally grand, containing decorative marble fireplaces. The entire building is a good example of true Indo-European architecture.

There are strong resemblances between the Asafi Kothi and another Indo-European palace near Lucknow, called Baronne (Barowen) or Musa Bagh. Here an imposing front facade with a great semi-circular portico conceals practical defences against the heat including a sunken courtyard cut into the hill. This was the women's quarter, with small, informal rooms. Visitors would be entertained in the larger, public rooms in the front of the building. Baronne remains, even in its ruined state, the epitome of Lucknow's hybrid architecture that married the extravagance of the court with the imagined dignity of European royalty. There are hints that Martin owned the land on which Baronne stands. Whether he designed it or not is unknown, for it was erected after his death, but there are strong architectural reasons to believe that whoever built the Asafi Kothi also built Baronne.

Martin's last building, unfinished at his death in 1800, was the great house of Constantia to the south-east of the city. Its architectural style has baffled writers for years, one in particular describing it as 'a striking monument of folly' and its ornamentation as 'the heterogeneous fancies of a diseased brain' (Anon., 1816: 151–2). The building was begun in 1793 after Martin had decided that he would remain in India, and not retire to Europe, as he had once planned. It was to be his mausoleum, a suitable resting place for the French 'nabob'. The idea of free-standing mausolea—not attached to a church, had become acceptable in eighteenth-century Europe (Curl, 1980: chapter 6). There, the newly-found interest in Roman, Etruscan and Egyptian antiquities allowed architects to use 'classical' elements to provide a dignified, yet modern response to death.

The main feature is normally a windowless or toplit central room, sometimes circular, marked by the tomb itself, or a commemorative sculpture. At Constantia the tomb was first planned to lie in the centre of the basement. Above it lies the windowless octagon with a marble bust of Martin at its centre. The exterior of the building was decorated with figures from Greek and Roman mythology, but also, interestingly, a female sphinx, which reflects both Martin's antiquarian bent and the adoption of Egyptian symbols by the Freemasons, of whom he was one.

Martin may also have been inspired by the Mughal mausolea. The same long, low-arcaded structure seen, for example, in Humayun's tomb, is present at Constantia. In both cases the actual tombs are tucked away underground. The ground floor room, which, in a *maqbara*, is marked by a 'false' tomb, is marked here by Martin's bust. Both buildings have a platform roof at first-floor level, above which rises the superstructure, with small, freestanding kiosks. The central portion, four or five storeys above the tomb, is crowned by a dome. At Constantia the 'dome' is formed from arched quadrants, springing from the octagonal towers that run the length of the buildilng.

At some point towards the end of his life, Martin decided that Constantia was to be a house for the living, as well. His tomb, which had already been constructed in the centre of the basement, and shown to visitors, was moved to a less prominent position in a small adjacent chamber. Building, which had taken a long time in this city where palaces were erected in a few months, surged forward again. Constantia is possibly the single most important European building in Lucknow, one that was to influence nawabi architecture until annexation, fifty or so years later. Echoes of it appear in the statues that adorned the Qaisar Bagh, gates with their quadrant arches, and stucco decorations on private houses.

Saadat Ali Khan, who came to the *masnad* in 1798, continued the work of beautifying Lucknow. Travellers had criticised the disgusting road along which they had to travel in the old city in order to reach new Lucknow.

The street which leads to the palace [the Daulat Khana] is upwards of five miles, more than one half of which you wade through mire and filth. During the lapse of time, the streets sink from cleaning, or by the blowing away of dust while dry, so that they are fallen in the middle to the depth of ten or twelve feet. (Tennant, 1804, II: 104).

Complaints ceased after Saadat Ali Khan laid down the new road of Hazratganj, which came in from the south-east. It was described as

a very handsome street, after the European fashion, above a mile in length, with bazars striking out at right angles, and a well-built new chowk in the centre, with a lofty gateway at each extremity, which present a Grecian front on one side and a Moorish one on the other (Hamilton, 1928, II: 131).

Hazratganj was a processional path designed to show off the new European-style houses along it, and the Chaupar Stables, built in cruciform shape. It also provided a fitting prelude to the third palace complex, the Chattar Manzil, which incorporated Martin's old house, Luckypeera, now renamed the Farhat Baksh. The house provided inspiration for other, larger buildings laid out symmetrically among gardens, so that in time the original house was dwarfed by the Bara and Chhota Chattar Manzil, the Lal Baradari, the Darshan Bilas, tanks and rose gardens.

Saadat Ali Khan took an active interest in promoting European-inspired architecture in Lucknow, and it is possible that he was responsible for designing some of the buildings of this period. In 1803 an English traveller noted that his 'chief gratification seems to be building palaces of an architecture that resembles Grecian, but as he never employs an architect the faults are numerous'(Valentia, 1809: 1:173). Ten years later he was described as 'exhibiting designs for new palaces and decoration of rooms, the execution of which, if intended, must occupy and serve to amuse him for a period of several years'(The Oudh Papers, 1808–15). Obviously someone, perhaps the Nawab, had drawn up such designs, and their execution, if indeed an architect was not employed, would have been carried out by engineers, or contractors organising a skilled workforce. One of the most interesting buildings is known only from a pencil sketch made in 1814 by Robert Smith of 'The Nawab's New House'(Album, Print and Drawings Collection, IOL). It is a detached, two storeyed, neo-classical building, with a central dome. The front (and presumably rear) elevations are flat, with Ionic pilasters at first floor level supporting a triangular pediment with an heraldic device. The side elevations contain central semi-circular bays, and the corners are turned by double height octagonal towers, crenellated at the top. A pedantic critic would argue that these towers, with their small windows, accord badly with the Grecian facades, but in fact it is a spirited and dignified building. Some of the towers certainly contained spiral staircases, for even the most 'European' of houses in Lucknow did not, for some unexplained reason, feature grand central staircases.

'The Nawab's New House' is very similar to the Khurshid Manzil (now La Martinière Girls School), finished in 1818 and may be an early drawing for it. This is one of the few buildings where the architect is known. He was the Company engineer Captain McLeod, who worked in Lucknow between 1811 and 1815. The octagonal towers from the New House are certainly here, as are the exaggerated semi-circular bays (though in the Khurshid Manzil they are only one storey high), and the rosette frieze at first floor height. The moat, now dry, was copied from the now vanished moat that ran around three sides of Martin's Luckypeera.

The copying of features from one Lucknow building to another has gradually been established, mainly by studying old photographs and drawings of demolished buildings, but occasionally from present day observations. The Dilkusha House, built for Saadat Ali Khan by Sir Gore Ousely, is a fairly exact copy of Seaton Delavel in Northumberland, with some local adaptations. The Darshan Bilas, in the Chattar Manzil complex, was also known as the Chaurukhi Kothi or House of Four Faces, because each facade was a copy of a well-known Lucknow house. The rear of the building was based on the riverside facade of old Luckypeera, the front is the main facade of the Dilkusha, itself a copied building. The two wings are both based on the rear facade of Baronne (so there are really only three 'faces', not four).

Even where entire buildings or facades were not reproduced, architectural features were eagerly copied and reinterpreted, appearing many times over. The octagonal towers of Constantia are easy to trace, through the New House, the Khurshid Manzil, to the Alambagh, a country house built by Wajid Ali Shah. The Shah Najaf, a Muslim tomb and a copy of the mausoleum at Najaf in Iraq, has stucco festoons around its pillars, which come straight from similar pillars at Baronne. There is also a hint of Chinoiserie in a few Lucknow buildings. There was a fascination in Europe, and particularly England, at this time, with 'exotic' forms from the East, and one finds 'Chinese' pavilions along the wall at Baronne, a six-storeyed pagoda in the Daulat Khana complex, and 'Chinese' roofs on the Sikandar Bagh gateway. Only the latter now exists, as an interpretation of Chinoiserie that travelled from China, via England, to India.

Europeans living in India wanted buildings that reminded them of 'Home', to make their temporary exile, as they often saw it, more bearable. Neo-classical architecture gave them, they thought, the status they needed in India, as foreign rulers. But the copying by the nawabs of buildings in Europe which they had only seen in illustrations, is harder to understand. The answer seems to be that they intended to create a 'museum' of architecture with examples from both West and East.

The Shah Najaf, mentioned above, is only one of a number of religious buildings reproduced in Lucknow from originals in Western Asia. The Kazmain, with its twin brass domes, is copied from a tomb in Iraq, and the imambaras came from Persian prototypes. The taziyas, the fulcrum for the Mohurram processions, are themselves representations of the tomb at Karbala, an impeccable antecedent for reproduction. To the nawabs, who clearly saw the copying of these buildings as an act of merit, there was nothing perjorative about imitating European buildings as well, and when an interesting house was erected, like Constantia, it was perfectly acceptable to lift features from it. Hence the derivative nature of Lucknow architecture requires that we consider religious and secular structures together.

One of the most important religious buildings, the Dargah Hazrat Abbas, was reconstructed during the time of Saadat Ali Khan. It housed the metal crest of a banner belonging to Hazrat Abbas, which was brought from Iraq. Oral tradition says that the Nawab, inspired by a dream, had the original *kuchcha* structure rebuilt in pukka materials, and an Indo-European gateway was erected in front of it. Although architecturally an undistinguished building, it is of great significance to Shi'as. It was to this dargah that the Nawab Ghazi-ud-din Haidar came in procession to offer prayers immediately before his coronation as Padshah, in 1819. (It was misleadingly described by the Resident as a 'temple', a reflection of British ignorance about the Shi'a religion). Afterwards, the procession of religious leaders, courtiers, the British Resident, and various Europeans, who had all travelled on elephants, returned for a public breakfast at the Farhat Baksh. They then proceeded to the Coronation Hall, which was the old Lal Baradari, refurbished for the occasion. The court artist, Robert Home, had designed the Padshah's coronation robes, his crown, his coat of arms, his throne and palace chairs, and probably stage-managed the whole event. It provided one of the most poignant examples of a nawab striving to maintain his position as a Shi'a ruler, but being seduced by British baubles (Fisher, 1987: 136–7).

Subsequent wealthy Lakhnavis continued to Europeanise their houses with the public, male rooms in a Western fashion, while the women's quarters retained the traditional style. The new part of Lucknow, developing eastwards along the Gomti, came more and more to resemble a great European city, reminding European visitors of St. Petersburg or Dresden. At the same time, criticism of the architecture by Europeans increased, especially as they now recognised distinct elements, but found them inappropriately used.

Of course, no native of India can well understand either the origin or motive of the various parts of our [Classical] Orders—why the entablature should be divided in architrave, frieze, and cornice—why the shafts should be a certain number of diameters in height, and so on . . . the consequence is, that between his ignorance of the principles of Classic Art on the one hand, and his knowledge of what is suited to his wants and his climate on the other, he makes a sad jumble of the Orders. But fashion supplies the Indian with those incentives to copying which we derive from association and deduction and, in the vain attempt to imitate his superiors, he has abandoned his own beautiful art to produce the strange jumble of vulgarity and bad taste we find at Lucknow and elsewhere (Fergusson, 1910: 327–8).

As the short, but glittering life of nawabi Lucknow drew to a troubled close, the British drew analogies between its 'decadent' architecture and the supposed degeneracy of its rulers. 'Brilliant and picturesque as Lucknow is, still there is a puerility and want of stability about it, characteristic enough of its monarchs' (*The Calcutta Review*, 1845:315), wrote Sir Henry Lawrence, who was to die in the Residency, during the siege (and whose grave there is carefully maintained to this day by the Archaeological Survey of India). Lucknow is perhaps the only city in the world whose buildings were anthropomorphised to the extent that they were believed to resemble the very character of their builders.

Yet there was to be one last, extravagant flourish before Wajid Ali Shah was exiled to Calcutta in 1856. The Qaisar Bagh palace complex was begun in 1848 and completed four years later. It was an extraordinary series of buildings, covering a great area to the south–west of Lucknow, incorporating other structures that had grown up on the outskirts of the city, like the tomb of Saadat Ali Khan and his wife, the small British cemetery, and the Roshan-ud-daula Kothi. Much of Qaisar Bagh was demolished by the British after their recapture of Lucknow in March 1858, but an idea of the scale and magnificence of the complex can be gained from photographs taken at that time, showing a series of terraced courtyards with free-standing buildings set in landscaped gardens.

In the neo-classical style, Qaisar Bagh resembles the much earlier conceptually Central Asian idea of a walled enclosure with separate pavilions. Fatehpur Sikri, with its great battlemented walls and delicate free-standing buildings within, has been described as a series of 'petrified tents'. This indeed seems to be what the architect of Qaisar Bagh, Chhota Mian,[2] was aiming at. Here the majority of 'walls' were, in fact, two-storeyed terraced houses, but others, more interestingly, although they looked like terraces, with regular Ionic columns, and windows, were in fact no thicker than a wall. There is an oral tradition that Chhota Mian was a keen photographer, and if this is so, it explains his virtuosity with the *trompe l'oeil* effects of Qaisar Bagh, and indeed the theatrical nature of the complex. It must have been intriguing (and for an unimaginative Victorian, maddening), to walk into what looked like a solid building, only to walk out the next minute through a doorway in a wall.

Inside the gardens there were a number of unique buildings, that have never been attempted again. There was the two-storeyed pigeon house, with Corinthian columns and triangular pediments based, loosely, on the Parthenon at Athens; the Lanka (bridge), Venetian in concept, pegged to the ground by kiosks, that crossed nothing more than grass, and the double spiral staircase, that only led the visitor back to his starting point. 'Follies' is the best word to describe these last two buildings, delightful but perfectly useless. Perhaps the architect intended them as a comment on the situation of Wajid Ali Shah, hemmed in by the increasing interference of the East India Company, who could not, indeed, go anywhere and always arrived back at the point from which he had started. There were statues everywhere (inspired by those of Constantia), in the gardens, on top of the main gateways, and on the spiral staircase. There were mermaids and mermen, developed from the ancient royal symbol of the fish, which had given its name to the Macchi Bhawan. There were also many little marble kiosks, and the more substantial marble *baradari*, which still exists. With its exaggerated sculptures, and its bright colours, the Qaisar Bagh has much in common with the Post-Modern movement in Europe today. It is tragic that so much of it was demolished by the British after 1858 and that only a hint remains of its virtuosity and spirit.

A surprisingly large amount of nawabi architecture stands, inspite of the vicissitudes suffered since 1856. The Archaeological Survey of India have been working on a programme of restoration over the last decade, although their task is immense. Much is in poor condition, the stucco flaking off to reveal small, lakhori bricks underneath. Many buildings have lost their original function, the palaces have been adapted for multi-occupation, or for workshops, some of the imambaras have been turned into offices and some large tombs into dwellings. Others, like Baronne, have been pillaged for building material, especially wooden beams, and many are simply too ruinous for habitation by anything except bats. Even so, these battered hulks carry traces of fine decoration and give the lie to criticism that nawabi Lucknow was jerry-built and pregnant with decay from its inception.

Ironically, one of the most carefully tended areas has been in ruins since 1857. The siege of the Residency complex became such a symbolic feature of the Victorian dream of Empire, that the site has never been built upon or altered, so that today the visitor can literally walk back into a part of nawabi Lucknow. Yet it is important to visit other buildings too, like the imambaras, the *baradaris*, the remaining palace buildings, and La Martinière Schools, in order to gain a true picture of this remarkable city, woven from the dreams of its disparate, but imaginative, creators.

Notes

1. There are estimated to be about 26 European Cemeteries in Lucknow, although not all are currently known. Kaisarpasand, in the heart of Qaisar Bagh, is probably one of the earliest Protestant graveyards, although records show a Catholic one established before 1803 and the cemetery for traders from the Farangi Mahal has not yet been found.
2. 'Chhota Mian' was not his name, but a term of respect. This gifted architect has not been properly identified.

REFERENCES

Anon. (1816), *Sketches of India, or Observations Descriptive of the Scenery etc. of Bengal,* London, Black, Parbury and Allen.

Beg, M.A. (1950), *The Guide to Lucknow,* Lucknow, Royal Press.

Curl, James Stevens (1980), *A Celebration of Death,* London, Constable.

Das, Neeta (1991), *The Architecture of Imambaras,* Lucknow, Mahotsava Patrika Samiti.

Farrell, J.G.(1973), *The Siege of Krishnapur,* London, Weidenfeld and Nicholson.

Fergusson, J. (1910), *History of Indian and Eastern Architecture,* London, John Murray.

Fisher, Michael H. (1987), *A Clash of Cultures: Awadh, the British, and the Mughals,* Delhi, Manohar Book Service.

Hamilton, Walter (1928), *The East-India Gazetteer Containing Descriptions of Hindostan,* London, Murray.

Heber, Bishop Reginald (1828), *Narrative of a Journey through the Upper Provinces of India from Calcutta to Bombay 1824–1825,* 3 vols., London, Murray.

Hodges, William (1793), *Travels in India during the years 1780, 1782 and 1783,* London, J. Edwards.

Johnson, Daniel (1827), *Sketches of Field Sports as Followed by the Natives of India,* London, Printed for the Author by Robert Jennings.

Kammelposh, Yusuf Khan (1898), *Ajaibat-i-Farang* (Urdu), Lucknow, Munshi Newal Kishore.

Lafont, Jean-Marie (1990), 'The Quest for Indian Manuscripts by the French in the 18th Century'. Paper presented at the Indo-French Cultural Relations Seminar, Delhi, Embassy of France.

Lawrence, Honoria (1830–57), Private Papers. Mss. Eur. India Office Library, London.

Llewellyn-Jones, Rosie (1985), *A Fatal Friendship: The Nawabs, the British and the City of Lucknow,* Delhi, Oxford University Press.

——— (1990), 'Indian Travellers in Nineteenth Century England', *Indo-British Review,* vol. 18, no. 1, Madras, pp. 137–41.

——— (1992), *A Very Ingenious Man: Claude Martin in Early Colonial India,* Delhi, Oxford University Press.

Mukherji, P.C. (1883), *Pictorial Lucknow,* Lucknow,

Nugent, Lady Maria (1839), *A Journal from the Year 1811 till the Year 1813,* 2 vols, London.

Oudh Papers (1808–15), National Archives, Delhi.

Petievich, Carla (1992), *Assembly of Rivals: Delhi, Lucknow and the Urdu Ghazals,* Delhi, Manohar.

Sharar, Abdul Halim (1975), *Lucknow: Last Phase of an Oriental Culture,* trans. and eds. E.S. Harcourt and Fakhir Hussain, London, Paul Elek.

Tennant, Rev. William (1804), *Indian Recreations,* 2 vols, Edinburgh, C. Stewart.

Tieffenthaler, Joseph (1786–88), *Description Historique et geographique de l'Inde,* Berlin, Imprimerie de Bourdeaux.

Twining, Thomas (1893), *Travels in India a Hundred Years Ago*, London, James R. Osgood, Mollvanie and Co.

Valentia, Viscount George (1809), *Voyages and Travels to India, Ceylon, the Red Sea, Abyssinia and Egypt in the Years (1802–1806)*, 3 vols., London, William Miller.

Victoria and Albert Museum, (1978), *Designs for the Dream King: The Castles and Palaces of Ludwig II of Bavaria*, Victoria and Albert Museum Catalogue, London.

4

The French in Lucknow in the Eighteenth Century

JEAN-MARIE LAFONT

Claude Martin of Lyons was a well-known figure among the Europeans of Lucknow in the second half of the eighteenth century (Hill, 1901; Llewellyn-Jones, 1992). He is also remembered for his generous legacy of the three *La Martinière* schools of Lucknow, Calcutta and Lyons. But he was only one of the amazing group of the 'French of Lucknow', whose presence in Awadh provided an enriching encounter between the France of the Enlightenment and the cultural milieu of northern India. Recent research shows this encounter to be one of the components of both the 'Oriental Renaissance' in Europe and the 'Renaissance of Bengal', the latter a subject of extensive investigation (Lafont, 1991a; 1991b; 1993: 78–84 and notes).

The French had been in north India from the beginning of the seventeenth century, pursuing the most varied careers at the court of the Mughal emperors and their important officials—ministers, generals and governors. Some accounts of travellers, Tavernier's and Manucci's for example, abound in picturesque details about these Frenchmen, though no mention is made of the reasons for emigration from Europe.

Since the sixteenth century Europeans had turned to the Orient for a number of reasons, the most important of which was the religious pressure of the orthodoxies, mainly Catholic but also Huguenot, on minds which were more inclined to intellectual liberty than dogmatic belief. The religious tolerance of the Mughals was noticed by Chardin and Tavernier, both Huguenots. In addition to the religious intolerance, there was an increasing rigidity of the hierarchical structure of the nobility, culminating in France in the 'rèaction nobiliaire' from the 1720s to the French Revolution. A number of talented commoners abandoned their native country to rebuild a life elsewhere. Moreover, several attempts to create trading companies—by François I, Coligny, Henri IV, Richelieu and Colbert—provided an incentive to people looking for good returns guaranteed by royal decree. And there had always been people with personal vocations, such as the adventurer or the missionary or the doctor in search of rich patients abroad.

The first wave of Frenchmen apparently arrived in north India during the reign of Jahangir, in whose entourage were Doctor Bernard with his miraculous cures, and Augustin Hiriart, an architect and engineer whose career is a little better known than the former's (Hiriart, 1916). The Journal of Sir Thomas Roe makes several allusions to French influence at the imperial court, but the English ambassador was not expecting to find 'in some panes copyes of the French kings . . .' in the private apartments of Jahangir, near the fountain of Hafiz Jamal (Roe, 1990: 211). Hiriart and Bernard, as well as some other Frenchmen whose traces we have picked up, had found spouses among Indian families. A hundred and fifty years later, Madec met some of their descendants in Lucknow and Agra, still in the service of the local rulers (Madec, 1983: 78–9).

The second half of the seventeenth century saw the arrival of soldiers of fortune, foot-soldiers and troopers, but also gunsmiths, gunners and gun-founders, whose presence in the Indian armies is an indication of the gap in firearm technology between Europe and India. Claude Maille and his companions in Delhi (Tavernier, 1977: I, 96–7; 228–9; 231–2), or the forty nameless gunners of Golconda, well illustrate the second wave of Frenchmen, many of whom settled in India permanently.

Finally, the creation of the Compagnie des Indes Orientales by Colbert led to the founding of the French trading post at Surat in 1668, a permanent establishment at Pondicherry in 1674, and a *comptoir* in Chandernagor between 1686–90. From Chandernagor, Boureau des Landes operated a certain number of branches in the Bengal and 'the *loge*' of Patna, in the interior. With the establishment of the Compagnie des Indes came the officials and traders of the Compagnie, soldiers and officers of the garrisons, sailors and officers of the French navy and transporting vessels, businessmen and merchants, Jesuit and Capuchin missionaries, and a large number of commoners, French, Dutch, Portuguese, or Armenian, often of mixed lineage, whom we discover in fortuitous allusions in the correspondence between Chandernagor and Pondicherry. French merchants were spread out in the hinterland much before Dupleix (Ray, 1974). As Governor of Chandernagor from 1731 to 1741, Dupleix reactivated the loge of Patna, establishing privileged links with

Delhi, and developing the commercial network of his *comptoir*. This network, it appears, was extensive.

Missionaries were in touch with most of the Catholics established in Indian territories. The Portuguese fathers of Bandel more or less specialised in arranging marriages of French soldiers and sailors with Indian women (something the Compagnie forbade in French territory except with special permission—the offenders then went out to seek their fortune in an Indian state). Thus a large number of Frenchmen established residence in India, their military or technical training coming in useful for obtaining honourable employment. Volton, or du Volton, was one such person whom Dupleix discovered in Delhi; he made use of his services for various negotiations with the Mughal court (Modave, 1971: 479–80 and notes). But most of them disappeared into the hinterland without leaving a trace.

In 1742, Dupleix took up his assignment of Governor of Pondicherry, but was unable to execute his policy—indirect government of Indian states—in the Carnatic, though it was put to remarkable use by Bussy in the Deccan from 1751 to 1758. The wars between England and France (1744–48 and 1756–63) in Europe led to conflicts between them in India too. A series of French defeats in India, from the capture of Chandernagor in 1757 to that of Pondicherry in 1761, suddenly flooded the Indian 'market' with several hundred 'French' officers and soldiers, some of whom, like the hussars, dragoons, grenadiers or gunmen, had belonged to the best military units or regiments. The term 'French', after the seven-year Anglo-French war, includes the governor of French India, Comte de Lally, an Irish Catholic, the conqueror, Lord Pigot, Governor of Madras (being Huguenot of French origin whose family emigrated after 1685), Antoine-Louis Polier, a French Huguenot settled in Switzerland, the second soldier from a family to serve the East India Company (Polier, 1947: 7–17), and German horsemen in the army. Change of flag was often a comfortable way to avoid the rigours of prison life or deportation. Claude Martin, the Lyonnais, decided to cross over to the English side after a public humiliation inflicted upon him by the intemperate Lally, in whose bodyguard he served as dragoon (Llewellyn-Jones, 1992: 16–22). We find him some time later in Lucknow in the service of Asaf-ud-Daula.

In 1757 many survivors from Chandernagor and the other French loges and trading posts of Bengal, along with the arms and cannons still in their possession, joined the Indian forces resisting the advancing English armies. Organised within the *'partis français'* like that of Law de

Lauriston, Madec or Sombre they fought on the Indian side in the battles of Raj Mahal, Elsea, Udha Nala, and Baksar. Numerically few, they were unable to stop the regular English regiments on the battlefields. But they impressed Shuja-ud-Daula with their courage, discipline and expert handling of the artillery, and daresay even more, by the perpetual insistence of the English that the Indian authorities surrender the French fighters, or at least their leaders. When his army was disbanded at Baksar, Shuja-ud-Daula had to flee from Lucknow, in fear of an English attack on the city. He promptly sent his *aide-de-camp*, colonel Gentil, to negotiate with the English general Carnac, in order to save what was retrievable from the ruins of his Principality. Gentil belonged to an old Catholic family of Geneva, who had to leave their native land for France after the Huguenot persecutions of 1570. A king's officer, Gentil arrived in India with his regiment in 1752, was trained in the Indian politics by Bussy in the Deccan, and served Mir Kasim Ali Khan in Bengal before taking service with Shuja-ud-Daula, for whom he organised a '*parti français*'. In the treaty of 1765 the independence of Awadh was recognised but the English took over two provinces as 'gifts' to the Mughal emperor Shah Alam II.

Shah Shuja's gratitude to Gentil can be measured by his opposition, till the hour of death on 26 January 1775, to English demands for his expulsion. We do not have details about Gentil's military work in Lucknow, though Modave, whose aristocratic prejudices against his fellow citizens in India can be discerned in several places in his narrative, admitted that 'Shuja-ud-Daula was the first to adopt the principles of the military discipline of the Europeans. At his death, he left behind 23 batallions of well-armed and well-trained sipayes' (Modave, 1971: 312). He also conceded that 'numerous artillery pieces were manufactured for him. The guns and bayonets manufactured in Fezabad are almost as good as the ones from the ateliers of Europe' (Modave 1971: 55). He also noted the importance of the French in the casting of cannons in the Indian armies of the time. Unfortunately, Modave does not mention the name of the Frenchman who built the fort of Faizabad for Shuja-ud-Daula: 'This fort, located in the north of the city at the bank of the river, is shaped like an equilateral hexagon. If completed to its perfection, it would be without doubt the strongest in Indoustan' (Modave, 1971: 145).

In his biography of Shuja-ud-Daula, Srivastava (II, 1945: 408) relies on the *Mémoires* of Gentil as his source-material for portraying the French officer, but does not give any more information. In 1768, for example, Gentil used the influence of a common friend to reveal to

Verelst, the English governor, how general Smith was putting his own interests before those of justice and truth by sending inflammatory reports to Calcutta about the government in Awadh (Gentil, 1822: 271–2). In 1774, he accompanied the Nawab in the war against the Rohillas. On his return from this campaign, the Nawab was afflicted with a syphilitic tumour. Gentil persuaded him to seek treatment from a French surgeon, Visage, but the Nawab gave up all treatment and died on 26 January 1775.

One would like to know more about the life of the 400 to 600 Frenchmen in Faizabad and the Principality of Awadh from 1764 to 1775, for the description given by Louis-Laurent de Féderbe, Comte de Modave, is often tainted with aristocatic disdain. Gentil himself gave the amount of his salaries: Rs 25,000 yearly from 1765 to 1768, later Rs 32,000 yearly; this does not include some ten thousand rupees in gifts per year (Gentil, 1822: 273 and note). We know nothing yet of his personal business, which must surely have been carried out by his *chargé(s) d'affaires*. The salaries of the French soldiers alone cost the Nawab about 80,000 francs a month, those of the officers are not mentioned (Gentil, 1822: 264). We do not know if these amounts came from the treasury or from *jagirs* given to Gentil, personally or in his military capacity, for financing his household and troops. Since the French troops were financed by the State, the recipients of Gentil's well-known generosity were most probably his less fortunate fellow-citizens who sought refuge in the Principality of Lucknow (Modave, 1971: 159–62). Those French thrown out by the English from Bengal were not the only ones seeking refuge in Awadh. The sacking of Delhi by Nadir Shah in 1739 was accompanied by a general massacre in which seventeen members of the Barbette family, descendants of one of 'Jahangir's Frenchmen', were slaughtered in their house (Modave, 1971: 240). A few survivors of the massacre escaped to Faizabad. On the recommendation of Shuja-ud-Daula, Madec married one of the Barbette girls amidst magnificent festivities. After Ahmed Shah Abdali occupied Delhi in 1761, more massacres took place in that city and many more refugees fled to Lucknow. Gentil was particularly interested in the daughter of a young widow of Portuguese origin. Their family had been in the service of the Mughals since the 1680s, and one of their women occupying the mysterious office of 'Juliana' in the imperial harem. Shuja-ud-Dula generously consented to grant them a pension. Gentil, who had intervened several times with the Nawab on their behalf, married the young Therese Velho, great-grand-niece of the famous Juliana, in 1772.

Gentil's marriage into a family employed for over a hundred years at the Mughal court, his close links with the Awadh nobility, and his facility in the local languages led to an intimate involvement in the extremely rich cultural milieu of Awadh. What characterised Gentil, as well as Polier and Martin some years later, was an empathy for India and its cultural heritage, its ancient monuments, and civilisation. He had served under Bussy, a fine connoisseur of Indian paintings, and was a close friend of Anquetil-Duperron, one of the best European orientalists of the 1750s. According to Modave (1971: 525) Gentil was the only French-man who could appreciate the priceless cave temples of Ellora. He took with him to Paris a magnificent collection of Persian manuscripts, donat-ing most of them to the Bibliothèque Royale (a number of these passed into the private collection of Louis XVI, while some are bound with Napoléon's arms on the cover). According to Anquetil-Duperron, hun-dred and twenty-four of the hundred and thirty-three manuscripts that he donated were new additions to the collection of the Bibliothèque Royale. For his friend, Gentil brought back a copy of the Persian translation of the Upanishad commissioned by Dara Shikoh. Modave tells us (1971: 297) that he made enquiries about the rich libraries of Benares, and he initially wanted to acquire an 'authentic copy' of each of the major works kept there, but 'on further examination, he realised that six years of work would be required to satisfy his curiosity. He abandoned the project which, moreover, would have cost him large sums of money'.

Persian manuscripts as well as albums of Indian paintings and mini-atures arrived in Awadh from Delhi as and when imperial or private libraries were dispersed. The Gentil albums at the Bibliothèque Nationale therefore contain a considerable number of early Mughal miniatures. Some display a decidedly European, and Christian, influence and one wonders if they may have been part of the collection of Madame Gentil's family (Lafont, 1991a: 14–15). Perhaps the views of the palace of Dara Shikoh in Delhi in the album of large paintings of *Indian Monuments* (Lafont, 1991a: 28–9) can also be attributed to the family's souvenirs, because in his *Mémoires sur l'Hindoustan* Gentil wrote that the palace was gifted by Aurangzeb to Juliana, and stayed with the family till it was forcibly bought by Safdar Jung (Gentil, 1822: 373). This album, drawn by an architect of Shuja-ud-Daula, contains views of Mughal monu-ments that no longer exist in Delhi, Agra or Faizabad. Besides these albums, Gentil also ordered sets of paintings from at least three different Indian artists. The magnificent *Recueil de toutes sortes de Dessins sur les Usages et Coutumes des Peuples de l'Indoustan ou Empire Mogol . . .* mentions 'several Indian painters, Nevasilal, Mounsingue, etc.' The most curious of its paintings is a view of Mecca in European perspective, the original of which, as I could establish, was a plate of the great *Atlas historique* published by Chapelain and Gueudeville in Amsterdam in 1719.

This discovery raises two interesting questions: the first is that of the books, albums and engravings that Gentil had in his library. Obviously, as the above example proves, he lent them to some Indian painters. The same questions could be asked in the case of Polier, Martin, Raymond, or even the British agents posted in Lucknow who also built up collections of Indian paintings after 1775 (Archer and Falk, 1981: 14–29). The second question pertains to the contribution of these engravings and commissioned paintings to the evolution of Indian painting at Lucknow, whose distinguishing feature was the use of the 'European' perspective, which finally established itself in the nineteenth century. Besides the introduction of a new perspective, we think this patronage also led to changes in the composition of the paintings and in the way figures, groups, landscapes or monuments were presented. These commissioned paintings also led to a gradual transformation of the artists' palette of colours. It is perhaps time to redefine the concept of Company paintings to accomodate these earlier works made under European patronage (Lafont, 1995).

Gentil also displayed a marked curiosity in certain other fields. According to his son 'he presented to M(onsieur) le Comte de Buffon, for the Cabinet du Roi, a rich collection of all sorts of Indian arms, another one of old coins, including 35 gold coins, three of which are as old as the Dariques; several silver coins including a very rare set of twelve with the zodiac signs ; twenty-one medallions in silver representing the emperors of the race of Tamerlane: about the size of an ecu of six pounds, on one side the emperor's effigy, on the other the dates of his birth, crowning, reign and death. Chevalier Gentil also gave to Monsieur de Buffon his observations about natural history, that the latter found important enough to record in his immortal books' (Gentil 1822: 422). His passion for geography has been illustrated by a superb in-folio atlas of the twenty-one provinces of the Mughal empire (Gole, 1988). Add to that his efforts to send various animals, including Kashmiri goats, to l'Ile de France (Mauritius) and France, and we get some idea of the intellect of this man, whose official role in India had only to do with war and diplomacy.

After Shuja-ud-Daula's death in January 1775, the East India Company was willing to recognise Asaf-ud-Daula as the successor only on condition that Gentil be dismissed immediately. The King of Nepal had invited Gentil to visit his kingdom some time earlier, and Emperor Shah Alam II also extended an invitation to him to settle in Delhi. But Gentil preferred to return to France with his wife and mother-in-law, bringing with him collections that some Englishmen in Bengal had offered to buy for considerable sums of money. After a cordial reception at Versailles, where he was received by Louis XVI, Gentil retired to the countryside, only to return to Versailles in 1788 as one of the royal interpreters during the reception of the ambassadors of Tipu Sultan.

With Gentil gone from Awadh, the question of his successor arose. The British wished to see a competent and trustworthy person appointed, but the new Nawab did not want to hand over the responsiblity of his arsenal to a British officer. Into this delicate situation stepped Claude Martin, the Lyonnais, who was then serving as a captain in the troops of the East India Company. Martin had participated in cartographic surveys in Awadh in 1763 and 1764, collected taxes in some districts of the *nawabie* in 1765. By September 1767, he was heading the section of the state arsenal that served the English troops stationed in the Principality. In May 1778, he was asked to unite and head the two arsenals, English and Indian.

It is possible to identify the sources of Martin's wealth and the extent of the protection he received from the highest British authorities. The foremost among them was the headship of the arsenal, with all the privileges attached to the post, including the supply of iron, saltpetre and other raw materials. In winter 1776, Martin set up a new gunpowder factory, and according to the papers discovered after his death, he possessed several buildings in the military industrial complex of Lucknow (Martin, 1800). There is many a mention in contemporary records and correspondence about the excellent quality of the firearms manufactured in Lucknow, and some pieces still exist in private collections. On the terrace of La Martinière (Lucknow), for example, there stand even today a huge bell and a splendid cannon from his foundries. Martin and the British Resident also purchased the arms and uniforms for the troops stationed in Awadh. Martin knew how to facilitate transactions by loans which were then returned to him with interest. His residence in town, 'Farid Bukhsh', was used as a safe deposit for many of the great families of Lucknow, and Martin became one of the greatest financiers and loaning agencies of the Principality at the then moderate rate of 12 per cent a year. His testament, signed in 1800, gave an impressive list of debits of sums varying from a few hundred to a few thousand rupees.

One of his debtors, the businessman Massayk, owed him the sum of Rs 2,59,709 in 1791, for which Martin had an acknowledgement of debt for Rs 3,05,394, which was never paid back.

Another important source of income for Martin was his real-estate investments. In 1776, he lived in a rented house with Lise, his favourite mistress, but by the end of his life he owned thirteen houses, of which ten were rented out. Towards the end of his life, he also possessed houses in Calcutta, Maneye, Benares, Ghazipur, Entally, Chandernagor, and a bungalow in Cawnpore. He built a long covered bazar along the River Gumti in Lucknow, known as the 'Captain's Bazar'. He rented out the shops for Rs 2000, and obtained supplies for the Bazar from not only Kabul, Kashmir and central India, but also China, England, France and other parts of the world where he had traders or correspondents. In 1786 he bought Najafgarh, a splendid house located on the banks of the Ganges upstream from Cawnpur, from his friend Polier who was leaving for Europe, changed its name to Martingarh, and transformed it into industrial units. Last on the list of his real-estate investments is the jagir of Jalesar that he took in 1794 or 1795. Located between Mathura and Agra, the jagir had been given by the Great Sindhia to de Boigne and brought an income of about Rs 50,000 yearly. In 1799, Martin's 'Properties and Land in the states of the Vizir' were estimated at about Rs 4,00,000 and his 'Properties and Land in Bengal' at Rs 1,18,000 (Martin, 1800: Accounts 1799).

A part of Martin's fortune was invested in bonds of the East India Company, which brought him an approximate yearly interest of 12 per cent. The larger part was used to finance all sorts of commercial ventures, from the export of lapis-lazuli, shawls and sugar to Europe, to commerce in textiles and industrial production of indigo. The various 'adventures' of indigo, shawls and textiles listed in the accounts of 1799 add up to Rs 10,84,420 (Martin 1800: Accounts 1799). In several enterprises, Martin's assosciate was de Boigne, a Savoyard trained in the French armies, who arrived in Lucknow in 1782 with a recommendation from Warren Hastings. From 1784 to 1795 de Boigne was Sindhia's governor in Hindustan. He formed and commanded three, and later four, 'French' brigades of ten thousand men each. With the help of his numerous 'French' officers and soldiers, he created a fine military infrastructure in the provinces. De Boigne and Martin were drawn together by a sincere friendship, and he was the intermediary and guarantor for Martin's transactions with agents in Hindustan. We also have some information about the orders de Boigne placed in British India for his troop's equipments, of which Martin was the intermediary. Moreover, Llewellyn-Jones writes of a company founded by Martin, Queiros and de Boigne, for commerce in textiles (Llewellyn-Jones, 1992: 152). Queiros, Martin's *chargé d'affaires*, was in charge of the distribution of work, advance payments to the weavers' families and the reception of the products after a quality check. Martin was responsible for the sales, either to Indian intermediaries or to the East Indian Companies who were preparing their cargos. Many of de Boigne's transfers to Europe, especially toward the end of his Indian career, were sent through Martin. From 1796 onward, Martin was also responsible for the payment of maintenance allowances to the Indian wives who had stayed back in India after de Boigne's departure. De Boigne was succeeded by Perron as governor of the Maratha provinces in Hindustan, and the accounts of Martin show, for the business year 30 April 1798 to 1 May 1799, transactions of Rs 1,01,489 in favour of Perron and Rs 1,45,474 in favour of Martin.

In 1771 Martin helped a certain James Weiss to build and establish a silk factory in Commercolly. But from about the middle of the century, the most profitable investments were in indigo. Martin transformed the Najafgarh property into an *indigoterie*. Llewellyn-Jones (1992: 163) writes that from 1791 to 1800, indigo from Najafgarh and other farms that Martin rented out formed the major part of the income of Martin and his associates, Lala Devi Das and Deverinne. At a time when there was a scarcity of silver in India, Martin managed to be paid for his indigo in silver Mexican dollars. The sum of Martin properties were estimated on 1 May 1799 to be worth Rs 37,31,105, and the recapitulation of his 'articles, pensions and sommes' bequeathed in his testament dated 1 January 1800 made a total of Rs 19,09,060.

We would like to know more about the forms this 'frontier' between Indian and 'French' took in a still independent India, especially at the level of the Indian farmers and weavers. Our research has revealed that between 1770 and 1790, the British political officers were worried not only about the powerful 'French' brigades that had appeared in some Indian states—Mysore, Hyderabad (Deccan) and Hindustan—but also about the French farmers, planters and indigo-producers whose establishments were scattered in the countryside between Delhi and Benares, in territories which were not *de jure,* and sometimes not even *de facto,* under the jurisdiction of the East India Company. Some of these 'French' settlers had probably been in the villages for many generations. Others may have made use, after the French disaster of 1757 in Bengal, of the support of a Gentil or a local sovereign to settle down in the Indian countryside. Modave mentioned one such soldier employed by a small raja to teach him the French language, which the poor fellow could hardly speak himself (Modave, 1971, 454). De Boigne, Perron and Martin obviously had a personal interest in having trustworthy people in the hinterland, but official texts say almost nothing about them.

There is a remarkable, though brief, study by Nurul Hassan (1979) of a series of unpublished documents on agricultural and commercial activities of a certain Daniel 'du Jardin', an absolute unknown otherwise, living in the Doab between Aligarh and Etah from 1778 to 1787. We hope to take up a detailed study of these documents soon, but the link between 'du Jardin' and the French of Lucknow and those in the service of the Marathas has already been established. 'Du Jardin' had taken charge, on *ijira,* of two clusters of villages, one in the north-west of Etah and the other in the north-west of Aligarh. In 'du Jardin's' accounts, we find some details on how the loans (*taqavi*) to the village community were organised and the means used for the extension of agricultures by financing irrigation canals. In this sense, 'du Jardin' was no different from any traditional *ijiradar* working for his employers, the official land-owners of the village, on lease. Among the products 'du Jardin' traded in, Nurul Hassan mentions grains, but also saltpetre and salt. These were products of everyday use, and the accounts give us a useful survey of the price fluctuation of the various cereals in the district during a period of about ten years. 'Du Jardin' also stocked the cereals in granaries, some of which have been located by Nurul Hassan. The trade in tobacco, indigo and textiles, however, was clearly geared to the new markets outside India. Nurul Hassan is surprised by the astonishing rate of growth (10 to 20 per cent per year) of the revenue of many of these villages. He relates it directly to the intensive development of indigo planting that was encouraged by 'du Jardin'. As a matter of fact, the accounts show very clearly for each village the area and the percentage of land converted to indigo planting, the time and money invested in the cultivation, the price of seeds and various other payments like irrigation, harvesting or contigency expenses including salaries of the workers and supervisors. The treatment of indigo took place in the indigo-factories located at Pora, Pilwa, Marehra and Farrukhabad, probably according to the method introduced by Elias Monnereau and widely used in Bengal. 'Du Jardin' was hired most probably because of the technical knowledge necessary for the development and industrial treatment of these new crops, knowledge that was not yet available at the local level. We are here very close to the boundary between the traditional rural world of independent India and the western industrial world which began firmly implanting itself in Bengal, with a group of Europeans acting as intermediaries in the still independent Awadh. 'Du Jardin' seems to have given up his work of ijiradar in January 1788, because of the manoeuvres of the British resident at Farukhabad. As soon as de Boigne established his head-quarters in Aligarh, Nurul Hassan points out, he helped several European indigo planters to set themselves up in the territories under his authority.

By now the reader can probably imagine the degree of intimacy that linked these 'Frenchmen' and their families to the Indian society they were living in. The extraordinary *Ensha-e A'jaz-e Arslani*, a collection of several hundred letters written in Persian by Polier during eight (1773–80) of his thirty years (1757–87) spent in India, gives us much more information about the cultural integration of a 'Frenchman' in the Indian society of Awadh and north India (Colas and Richard, 1984). Composed of 771 manuscript folios (1542 pages) bound in two volumes, this correspondence is addressed to more than two hundred and thirty-nine persons so far identified by Colas and Richard (1984: 110–23). Among his correspondents were the emperor Shah Alam II as well as Daha *Baghban*, Polier's gardener in Faizabad. Many of the letters are addressed to all sorts of administrative officers, both civil and military, *qazis, gomashtas* and various *vakils, chargés d'affaires*, managers and attorneys of important personalities in the political and financial circles of northern India. Several letters are addressed to his wives or other ladies, and several others to his sons 'Antoni Babajan Sahebzade . . . ', 'Bodi Baba and Cahuthi Baba' or more vaguely just 'sons'. Some letters, addressed to Mir Hayder Ali, 'Ustad-i-Sahibzade Baba' (his son Antoni's tutor) reveal the attentive care that Polier took for the education of his children. But the most valuable to us are the letters addressed to the Indian *literati* and artists. We find correspondence with the historian and calligrapher Nawab Morid Khan, and letters to Mir Chand 'Mosawar', the well-known artist to whom Polier wrote to acknowledge numerous paintings, and from whom he commissioned a copy of one that Gentil had in his possession.

The remarkable fluency in Persian acquired by Gentil, Polier, Martin and some of their friends—Polier sometimes wrote to Louis Perceret and 'du Jardin' in that language—explains the extraordinary 'oriental' libraries that they built up during their stay in the Principality of Awadh. We have already mentioned Gentil's collection. Spurred by a deep interest in the history and literatures of India, Polier, Martin and Raymond were some others who collected manuscripts, paintings, arms, antiquities and any other objects that excited their interest. Though we do not have the count of Raymond's manuscripts, the 'oriental' library of Claude Martin contained more than five hundred and seven titles and that of Polier numbered some six hundred to six hundred and seventy volumes. These were important collections by any standards of the time: the *Bayaz-i-Khushbuy* (late seventeenth century) listed fifty-two Arabic and Persian books to be kept in the library belonging to the most important *Umras* of the Mughal Empire (Blake, 1986: 178), and by the end of the eighteenth century one of the largest private libraries, that of a Mughal prince in Delhi, contained only 400 manuscripts (Modave, 1971: 264). The memoirs written by Gentil or Polier show that they had read the contents of their libraries. A study of their collections reveals that rigorous care had been taken to obtain complete texts having an authentic manuscript tradition and covering all the historical periods of the land.

The abundance of these manuscripts can be explained in part by the rich historiographic tradition of Islamic India. But one should not forget the matrimonial relations of the Frenchmen with either Muslim (Martin, Polier, de Boigne) or Christian families (Gentil, Madec, Perron) that had served the Mughal emperors. Apart from manuscripts, they all collected paintings and miniatures. The collections of Gentil and Polier are quite well-known. One of the first Europeans to take a real interest in Indian music and dance, Polier possessed a series of splendid *Ragamalas*, now in Berlin. One painting shows a dancer demonstrating a movement to him (Lafont, 1991b: 16). Claude Martin also collected Indian miniatures: his residence of Farid Bukhsh, for example, contained an extraordinarily rich collection of 'Hindustani' and Bhutanese, Chinese and European paintings. Unlike the Gentil and Polier collection, we cannot say which miniature paintings were ancient and which were modern pieces commissioned by the collector from local artists. However, for the oil paintings, the catalogues state in most cases whether they were Indian originals or Indian copies of a European original: '1 [landscape] copy by a native artist', '6 fancy figures by native painters', and so on. We would like to know the names of the Indian painters who worked for Martin and who began at Lucknow the remarkable syncretism between European and Indian paintings, that was to produce the 'Company paintings' of the 1800s, and the 'modern' schools of Bengal and north India (Archer, 1972, 1992, Guha-Thakurta, 1992: 11–44).

Martin is probably the best example of the presence of European Enlightenment in an 'independent' Indian state. His Indian paintings and miniatures were part of a huge collection of a few thousand European paintings and engravings. Many of them were mounted and displayed, but a larger number were conserved in cases, portfolios or albums. We have an impressive list of the books in Martin's library, covering all the fields of knowledge, from anatomy and surgery (with an instrument box for trepanation) to architecture, mathematics, physics and electricity. There are several journals published by the scholarly academies of Europe, encyclopedias of Chambers as well as Diderot and d'Alembert. Martin seems to have been interested in the experimental side of sciences as much as in the theoretical. He had ordered from Europe an astonishing number of scientific and mathematical instruments, the usage of some of which is given as 'unknown' by the appraisers who made the inventories. These inventories list three steam machines, with a number of accessories. At Farid Buksh, there were several 'electrical machines' with a number of glasses, tubes and air pumps, that were used for the experiements described in the books about electricity. There were also several books about air and aerodynamics that Martin must have used for the launch of his hot-air balloons from Lucknow, a little after the successful launch of the Montgolfier brothers in Paris in 1783. Martin, it seems, was an engineer who liked to be in the forefront of technical knowledge of his time. The manufacture of firearms and cannons was one of the advanced technologies of Europe, and it is interesting to find in the library at Constantia several recent technical treatises on these topics. But one finds them in the company of works that are more theoretical. A product of the 'Siècle des Lumières', Martin, the engineer, was also of a scholarly bent of mind.

Some Englishmen of Lucknow were also interested in Indian culture: Richard Johnson, alias Rupee Johnson (Archer, 1979: 17–20, Llewellyn-Jones, 1992: 94) built up such an enormous fortune, as well as a collection of paintings, in eighteen months, that he was recalled to Calcutta, a rare case of demonstration of public morality on the part of the East Indian Company. Apparently Gentil did not have many scholarly exchanges with his English counterparts (William Bolts, Robert Orme and a few others excepted) who, nevertheless, respected him for his knowledge of India. Polier and Martin, however, were in regular contact with William Jones and the other English scholars of Benares and Calcutta who founded the Asiatic Society of Bengal in 1784. But it is their Indian contacts that interest us more today: contacts with the Muslims, but also with Hindus, as illustrated by Polier's efforts to aquire a complete copy of the *Vedas*, the very existence of which was put in doubt by some scholars in Europe (Lafont, 1991a: 15). Another fine initiative of Polier's was to get his Sikh and Brahmin friends to explain at length passages from the *Ramayana* and *Mahabharata*: years later, the accumulated notes have come to us in two volumes entitled *La Mythologie des Indous* (Polier, 1809).

In Lucknow, the impact of the Indian culture on this French milieu is becoming clearer. Some research should be undertaken to determine the effect of the presence of these Frenchmen on the host culture. If we agree that there was a Renaissance in Bengal in the nineteenth century,· it was largely a result of the trends begun in Faizabad and Lucknow. Described as *The Last Phase of an Oriental Culture* (Sharar, 1975), Lucknow is also seen to be the locus of the *Clash of Cultures* between the Mughals and the English in Awadh (Fisher, 1987). In view of what we have written about the relations betwen 'the Indians' and 'the French' in this part of India, is it not fair to speak of a pre-Renaissance, call it 'oriental' if you will, in Awadh during the years 1757 to 1800?

[Translated by Rehana Lafont]

REFERENCES

Archer, Mildred (1972), *Company Drawings in the India Office Library*, London, HSO.
—— (1979), *India and British Portraiture 1770–1825*, London, Oxford University Press.
Archer, Mildred and Tony Falk (1981), *Indian Miniatures in the India Office Library*, London, Oxford University Press.
Blake, Stephen (1986), 'Cityscapes of an Imperial Capital: Shajahanabad in 1739', in R.E. Frykenberg (ed.), *Delhi Through the Ages: Essays in History, Culture and Society*, Delhi, Oxford University Press.
Colas, Gérard and Francis Richard (1984), 'Le Fonds Polier à la Bibliothèque nationale', *Bulletin de l'Ecole Française d'Extrême-Orient*, 73, pp. 98–123.
Fisher, Michael H. (1987), *A Clash of Cultures: Awadh, the British and the Mughals*, Delhi, Manohar Book Service.
Gentil, Jean-Baptiste (1822), *Mémoires Sur l'Hindoustan Ou Empire Mogol*, Paris, Didot.
Gole, Susan (1988), *Maps of Mughal India Drawn by Colonel Jean-Baptiste Joseph Gentil Agent for the French Government to the Court of Shuja-ud-daula at Faizabad in 1770*, Delhi, Manohar.
Guha-Thakurta, Tapti (1992), *The Making of a New Indian Art. Artists, Aesthetics and Nationalism in Bengal c. 1850–1920*, Cambridge, Cambridge University Press.
Hasan, Nurul S. (1979), 'Du Jardin Papers: A Valuable Source for the Economic History of North India', *The Indian Historical Review*, vol. 5, nos 1–2.

Hill, S.C. (1901), *The Life of Claude Martin, Major-General in the Army of the Honourable East India Company*, Calcutta, Thacker, Spink and Co.

Hiriart, Augustin, (1916), 'Four Letters of Austin de Bordeaux', *Journal of the Punjab Historical Society*, vol. 4, pp. 3–17.

Lafont, Jean-Marie (1991a), 'The Quest for Indian Manuscripts by the French in 18th Century', *Indo-French Relations: History and Perspectives*, Delhi, Embassy of France.

——— (1991b), 'Les Indes des Lumières. Regards Français sur l'Inde de 1610 'à 1849', *Passeurs d'Orient: Encounters between India and France*, Paris, Ministere des Affaires Etrangères.

——— (1993), *La Présence française dans le royaume Sikh du Punjab, 1822–1849*, Paris, EFFO.

——— (1995), 'Company Paintings' ou 'Faringhi Paintings'? Contribution française à la formation d'une école de peinture indienne au XVIII ème siècle, *Revue du Musée de la Compagnie des Indes*, Port-Louis, Lorient.

——— (1997), 'Politics and Architecture in the French Settlements', *Reminiscences: The French in India*, New Delhi, INTACH, pp. 15–49, 49 illustrations.

Llewellyn-Jones, Rosie (1992), *A Very Ingenious Man: Claude Martin in Early Colonial India*, Delhi, Oxford University Press.

Madec, René (1983), *Mémoire de René Madec, Nabab dans l'Empire Mogol, Commandant d'un parti français au Service de l'Empereur 1736–1784*, Pondichery, Alliance Française.

Mansingh, Gurbir, Gen. (Rtd) (1997), 'French Military Influence in India', *Reminiscences: The French in India*, pp. 51–87, 35 illustrations.

Martin, Claude (1800), *Testament*, Suivi de comptes divers pour les années 1795–99, Texte bilingue, anglais avec traduction francaise, publié à Lyon en 1803.

Modave, Louis-Laurent de Federbe, Comte de (1971), *Voyage en Inde du Comte de Modave 1773–76*, J. Deloche (ed.), Paris, EFEO.

Polier, Antoine-Louis (1809), *La Mythologie des Indous travaillée par Mme la Chanoinesse de Polier Sur des manuscrits authentiques apportés de l'Inde par feu M.Le Colonel de Polier*, 2 vols, Paris, F. Schoell.

——— (1947), *Shah Alam II and his Court*, Pratul C. Gupta (ed), Calcutta.

Ray, Indrani (1974), 'Dupleix's Private Trade in Chandernagor', *The Indian Historical Review*, vol. 1, no. 1–2, pp. 279–94.

INTACH (1997), *Reminiscences: The French in India*, New Delhi, INTACH.

Roe, Sir Thomas (1990), *The Embassy of Sir Thomas Roe to India*, W. Foster (ed.), Delhi, Munshiram Manoharlal.

Sharar, Abdul Halim (1975), *Lucknow: Last Phase of an Oriental Culture*, E.S. Harcourt and Fakhir Hussain (eds. and trans.), London, Paul Elek.

Srivastava, A.L. (1945), *Shuja-ud-Daula*, 2 vols, Lahore, Minerva Bookshop.

Tavernier, Jean-Baptiste (1977), *Travels in India by Jean-Baptiste Tavernier, Baron of Aubonne*, W. Crooke (ed.), V. Bali (trans.), 2 vols, Delhi, Oriental Reprint.

5

Shi'ite Noblewomen and Religious Innovation in Awadh

JUAN R.I. COLE

That women might have had any role in the evolution of so patriarchal a tradition as Shia Islam once struck historians as highly unlikely. The development of women's studies as a sub-field in Middle Eastern and South Asian studies since the late 1960s, however, has refigured the way we see everyday discursive practice in Muslim communities, and given back women a place in their history. In this study I will examine what part noblewomen in the Shia-ruled state of Awadh might have played in the evolution of ritual practice. I have several questions in mind. Was there anything distinctive about the Shia beliefs and practices of noblewomen, as opposed to those of elite males? Were women able to influence the terms of discourse or ritual life? Shi'ism was, after all, a scriptural, patriarchal religion, with a powerful corps of clergy who claimed a monopoly on spiritual authority.

Farah Azari (1983), among others, has argued that Iranian Shi'ism serves as a mechanism for the suppression of female sexuality. I am not concerned here directly with the issue of suppression, and prefer a more phenomenological approach to the study of religion to Reich's reductionism. Yet, from a Reichian perspective and others, women, as the subordinate gender, often illiterate, could easily be supposed to have contributed little of importance to Shi'ite devotions, and to have been dependent on the tutelage of their men for religious instruction. For the majority who were illiterate, would it not have even been impossible to understand the abstract Arabic philosophical terminology which male believers embedded in their Urdu god-talk? Yet in Iran, Shi'ite feminists such as Zahra Rahnavard have managed to inscribe their own concerns on Khomeinist discourse, and this should make us suspicious of a patriarchal essentialism when studying historical Muslim communities (see Yeganeh and Keddie, 1986).

There was of course no question of any sort of feminism in nineteenth century Lucknow. But it is reasonable to ask whether its Shi'ite women succeeded in elaborating a religious discursive practice that had feminine elements.

The post-Mughal successor state of Awadh, between Delhi and Bengal, and ruled by the Iranian Nishapuri dynasty, is a promising venue for such a study, since a number of relevant documents about women there survive. As I said above, I want here to offer a thematic focus on the contribution of elite women to the rich religious life of Awadh (see Cole, 1988) in the nineteenth century. The Begums, the wives and mothers of the rulers of Awadh, often played important political roles. Some involved themselves in anti-colonial struggles as well, appearing in the chronicles and even in the British consular reports as 'warrior-queens'.

The Begums were in a position to influence Shi'ite devotion in Awadh because of their vast wealth and their visible political roles. Often literate, they knew a great deal about Shi'ite law and ritual. They also had the leisure to pursue those devotions. Shi'ites were a minority in Awadh, a majority-Hindu region where Sunnism predominated even among the thirteen per cent of the population that adhered to Islam. In this context, the Shi'ite nobility, both male and female, displayed their religious practices and devotions ostentatiously, which had the effect of accentuating their elite status. The Begums' ability to leave religious endowments and bequests of large property, and their influence on the public commemoration of Shi'ite holy days, made them an important religious influence in the kingdom.

The extent of property and control over resources that some of the noblewomen exercised can hardly be exaggerated. Bahu Begum, from an Iranian family close to the Mughal court, employed her own private fortune to help her husband, the Nawab Shuja-ud-Daula, pay off his war debt after the British defeated him in 1864. In return, he decided to give into her hands all the cash offerings and surplus treasury receipts he would receive thereafter. With a fortune estimated at 2 million pounds, Bahu Begum could play power broker (Barnett, 1980: 76; Santha, 1980: 63). She left much of the fortune that remained to her in her old age to the British East India Company, but stipulated that Rs 90,000 be granted to Shi'ite clergy at the holy city of Karbala in Iraq (see Cole, 1986), and she named the specific clergymen among whom it should be divided (Resident to Sec., Govt. of India, For. Dept. Pol.

Cons., 9 Nov. 1816, no. 17, National Archives of India; see Barnett, 1980: 237–8, for the political significance of the will). These were leaders of the Usuli school, and such large gifts helped reinforce their leadership in Karbala, making substantial patronage available to them.

The nawabs and kings themselves donated even vaster sums, of course, but the religious gifts from Awadh's noblewomen made a difference to some clerical careers. An unexpected, substantial bequest from Vilayati Begum, widow of the Shia nawab of Farrukhabad near Awadh, helped make a rich man of Sayyid Muhammad Nasirabadi, the chief *mujtahid* or Shi'ite jurisprudent in Lucknow from 1820 to 1867 (Ali, 1917: 360–3). The begums of the royal family ran household establishments that included positions for Shi'ite clergy as chaplains, another manner in which noblewomen could have an influence on the clergy and on religious culture.[1] Some princesses also maintained *imambaras*, buildings on their residential grounds (Ali, 1917: 23). The structures were commemorations of the lives of the Imams, especially the martyrdom of Imam Husain.

Some women stand out for the influence they exerted over religious practices. In particular, Badshah Begum, a wife of Ghazi-ud-din Haydar Shah and daughter of the royal astronomer, introduced many new usages into Awadh Shi'ism. In Awadh custom, on the sixth day after the birth of a child, both mother and child took a bath and the family threw a feast for relatives and friends. The celebration was called the *Chhati*, 'the sixth'. Badshah Begum began celebrating the Chhati of the Twelfth Imam, Muhammad al-Mahdi, six days after the anniversary of his birth, spending great sums of money on meticulously-planned festivities every year in the month of Sha'ban (For this and the following paragraphs, see Rabit, 1977).

Badshah Begum also brought eleven pretty Sayyid girls to the palace and kept them there as symbolic brides of all the Imams save Ali, paying their families handsomely for their custody. Each bore the name of one of the historical wives of the Imams, and was called *achhuti*, that is, too pure to be touched. Fatima was considered too holy a personage to be personified in this manner, so only eleven of the imams' wives were represented. They had female attendants, and Badshah Begum attempted to arrange for one of their faces to be the first thing she saw each morning. She tried to keep the achhutis from marrying, though one got out of this bind by saying she had a dream in which the imam divorced her.

On the birthday of each of the Imams, Badshah Begum richly decorated and illumined a special room at the palace in his honour. She gave expensive clothing and jewellery to his achhuti wife. Later she distributed the furnishings of the room to the maidservants in charity. She also built an imitation tomb for each of the imams, with a small mosque attached, on the palace grounds. These were known as the *Rawzih-'i davazdah imam*, the graveyard of the twelve Imams. The Begum spent much of each day in prayer and participated in the mourning ceremonies at the death anniversies of each of the Imams. She believed that, occasionally, she was possessed by the king of the jinn. At such times she dressed up in finery and sat on her throne, listening as female musicians played for her, and moving her head in a trance. 'While in such a mood, she would give answers to the queries about the past and the future made by those who were present there' (Rabit,1977: 9–10).

In 1827, when her son (some say adopted son) Nasir-ud-din Haydar became Shah of Awadh, Badshah Begum arranged for a proclamation that mourning rites for the Imam Husain would continue until the fortieth day (*chihilum*) after his death. Only then would the replicas of the Imam's tomb that Awadh Shi'is annually set up in homes or paraded in the streets, be buried or thrown into the river (previously, the cenotaphs had been buried on the anniversary of Imam Hussain's death itself). No marriages or amusement were allowed during this extended mourning period. Hindu and Sunni pressure led the British Resident to intervene against this imposition of prolonged sobriety, and the Shah finally revoked this decree, but pledged to observe the forty-day mourning period in his own royal household.

The feminine religious imagination demonstrated by Badshah Begum greatly influenced her son, Nasir-ud-din Haydar Shah (r. 1827–37). On his accession he continued the custom of keeping achhutis as symbolic wives of the Imams, and even added some further innovations. Interestingly enough, it seemed necessary for him to adopt a female gender model in order to continue the process of inventing new rituals in imitation of his mother.

One the day of the birth of the Imams he would behave like a woman in childbed and pretended that he was suffering from the pains of childbirth. A doll studded with jewels was kept lying in the King's lap to represent the false child. The selected attendants prepared dishes used by women in childbed and served them to the king (Rabit, 1977: 11).

Other men followed the king in acting out female roles so as to make the present look like sacred time, especially those from families where Shi'ite women began claiming to be achhutis. These men 'had given up manly habits, talked and behaved like women and had adopted female costumes' (Rabit, 1977: 12). The elaboration of new rituals by Badshah Begum had involved the application of ordinary female life-cycle rituals in India to the commemoration of the lives and deaths of the twelve Shi'ite Imams. Nasir-ud-din Haydar and many other Awadh men, in order to appropriate this discourse of charismatic religious innovation, found it necessary also to resort to transvestitism and other adoptions of a female gender role.

Aristocratic women in the harem constituted throughout Awadh history one pole of potential power, through their influence on male rulers and nobles. Women's greater knowledge of the full range of folk religious discourse, both Hindu and Shi'ite, allowed them sometimes to manipulate supersitious males. In September 1850, Wajid Ali Shah, the newly installed ruler of the kingdom, fell in love with one of his mother's handmaidens. His mother, however, was attached to the girl, and was reluctant to let her go. She found a pretext in a birthmark on the nape of the girl's neck, which she interpreted as a *sampan* or snake-mark, and gravely informed her royal son that it was a sign of very bad luck. The Begum kept possession of her handmaiden by this device, but it had further, unforeseen, repercussions. Wajid Ali Shah began to worry that his huge harem, filled with temporary wives and concubines, might contain other bearers of bad luck. He had his eunuchs examine them all, and the latter found eight who appeared to be marked with the *sampan.* The Shah called his chief *mujtahid,* Sayyid Muhammad Nasirabadi, and had him preside over the divorce of all eight. Someone with the king's ear, however, then suggested that Brahmins knew more, on the whole, about snake-marks than did Shi'ite clergymen, and that a solution to the problem less drastic than divorce might be found. The Brahmins, when called, concluded that the sampans could be safely burned off, and two of the wives agreed to undergo the procedure so as to remain in the monarch's harem (Sleeman, 1850, I: 107–8).

This rich little anecdote illustrates the manner in which religious authority remained profoundly contested even at the most triumphalist period of Shi'ite ascendancy. In focusing on the manner in which the Brahmins were able to overturn a decision of the Shi'ite chief mujtahid, however, we would be forgetting that the initiator of the crisis was the Shah's mother. She first hit upon the conventions of Hindu folk culture in order to keep a favourite servant in her own household. Wajid Ali Shah could have dismissed this objection as nonsense, but the Begum was able to lend her construction of the supernatural significance of the birthmark such authority that it threw the entire harem into turmoil, led to a symbolic contest between mujtahid and Brahmin, and finally to several divorces and brandings of royal wives. Ironically, an attempt at feminine solidarity in the Beguam's mansion rebounded with unpleasant consequences for the palace harem. Women could initiate religious and supernatural discourse with a powerful effect on men, but could not control the manner in which men then appropriated it to their purposes.

The way in which men feared the power of the harem is further illustrated in the story of Mubarak Mahal's attempt to learn the Shi'ite principles of jurisprudence. One of Wajid Ali Shah's more important wives was literate and wished to study Shi'ite law. She had her physician hire Maulvi Ali Hasan Bilgrami, with whom she pursued these studies. Her co-wife, Sultan-Aliyah Begum, also began taking lessons from him from behind a veil. Bilgrami grew wealthy, and, one chronicler sniffed, 'superficially eminent' by virtue of the gifts and honours these queens bestowed on him. He also apparently employed his warm relations with several noblewomen in the harem to begin exercising political influence, not only among the king's wives, but indirectly on Wajid Ali Shah himself. The Shah's minister, Mumtazu'd Daula, grew to profoundly resent Bilgrami's increasing influence, but had to proceed cautiously against this new rival. He intrigued with the Shah and the British Resident, and on 1 June 1851 at the time of afternoon prayers, Bilgrami was banished and walked out of town in public view with an escort of royal troops, and his property confiscated. Apparently the Shah's men isolated him when he was in public, away from the palace, so that the queens could not intervene. The case, according to the chronicler, went all the way to Governor-General Dalhousie, who disapproved of his Resident's involvement. Later Mubarak Mahal managed to compensate Bilgrami for some of his losses, and the tutor to the queens retired to Simla (Mashhadi, 1896: 87–8).

The literacy and legitimate quest for religious knowledge of the women enmeshed them in a set of male intrigues, as the male chronicler tells the story. Shi'ite clergy in Awadh had a great deal of influence on politics, and were often very close to secular rulers. The Shah's first minister would have favourite clergymen, who could act through the minister to influence the Shah on religious and legal policy. By inserting themselves into the midst of this political network linking secular nobles and the Shi'ite clergy, the queens offered Bilgrami a new avenue to court influence. The anecdote illustrates that study of Shia law was, by virtue of the position of the hierocracy in Awadh, an intrinsically political act, and one available to upper-class women as well as to male nobles and notables. The teller of the tale probably underestimated the positive contribution made to policy by the queens, who may, after all, have often simply buttressed the authority of their views by taking Bilgrami's name in order to bestow on themselves a mujtahid's cachet. (In this canny reading of the story, removing Bilgrami was an attempt to deny the Begums the ability to increase the authority of their ideas by taking the name of a male religious leader, rather than simply to banish a pernicious male influence on the harem and thence the king). Even our chronicler admits, however, that Mumtazu'd Daula was for long stymied in his desire to remove Bilgrami and the rising harem influence over the Shah. It is clear that he was able to act against the queens' favourite only by achieving unanimity among the male power elite in Lucknow. Moreover, he was able to do so only in the public, male, sphere, outside the spatial reach of the queens' own authority and power.

These noblewomen made a gender-specific contribution to ritual change in Awadh Shi'ism. Badshah Begum's championing of a forty-day mourning period for commemorating the Imam Husain's martyrdom may have reflected the greater leisure available to aristocratic feminine networks for concentration on ritual activities and meetings. Certainly, the manner in which she blended elements of the local Indian female and family life-cycle rites with her celebration of events related to the lives of the Imams showed a peculiarly feminine imagination at work. Women may also have been more willing to innovate in the area of ritual than men, because they were often illiterate or in any case not bound by a strict seminary-type reading of key texts. Some men, who for one reason or another had also escaped the influence of the clergy, also took an interest in the devotions introduced by women like Badshah Begum. Just as male poets attempted to appropriate female discourse in the *rekhti* style of Urdu poetry, cast in a feminine voice, so male religious virtuosi attempted to imitate Badshah Begum's religious style by dressing in female clothing and symbolically acting out female life-cycle rituals on the plane of Shi'ite sacred history. The authority of aristocratic feminine constructions of the supernatural is further demonstrated by the stories of Wajid Ali's mother and the snake-mark, and of Mubarak Mahal's mujtahid. Women, then, mattered religiously. The embededness of the feminine in the aristocratic ritual inventiveness of the 1820s and 1830s attests, not only to the religious genius of Badshah Begum as an individual, but to that of Shi'ite women in general.

NOTE

1. For instance, Sayyid Hasan Riza Zangipuri, a mujtahid from Awadh who spent some time in Iran, gained employment on his return to Lucknow in the establishment of Mubarak Mahal, a wife of Ghazi al-Din Haydar Shah (r. 1814–27) (Nauganavi, n.d., 129–31).

REFERENCES

Ali, Mrs. Meer Hasan (1917), *Observations on the Mussalamans of India*, London, Oxford University Press.

Azari, Farah (1983), *Women of Iran: The Conflict with Fundamentalist Islam*, London, Ithaca Press.

Barnett, Richard B. (1980), *North India between Empires: Awadh, the Mughals and the British, 1720–1801*, Berkeley, University of California Press.

Cole, Juan R.I. (1986), 'Indian Money and the Shi'i Shrine Cities of Iraq, 1786–1850', *Middle Eastern Studies*, vol. 22, no. 4, pp. 461–80.

——— (1988), *Roots of North Indian Shi'ism in Iran and Iraq: Religion and State in Awadh, 1722–1859*, Berkeley, University of California Press.

Mashhadi, Kamalu'Din Haydar Husayni, (1896), *Qaysar at. tawarikh* (Urdu), Lucknow, Naval Kishore.

Nauganavi, Muhammad Husayn (n.d.), *Tazkirah-i be baha'fi Tarikh al'ulama (Urdu)*, Delhi, Jayyid Barqi Press.

Rabit, Abdu'l-Ahad (1977), *Tarikh Badshah Begum* (Urdu), Muhammad Taqi Ahmad (trans.), Delhi, Idarah-i-Adbiyat.

Santha, K.S. (1980), *Begums of Awadh*, Benares, Bharati Prakashan.

Sleeman, W.H. (1850), *A Journey through the Kingdom of Oudh in 1849–1850*, 2 vols, London, Pelhan Richardson.

Yaganeh, Nahid and Nikkie R. Keddie (1986), 'Sexuality and Shi'i Social Protest in Iran', in Juan R.I. Cole and Nikkie R. Keddie (eds), *Shi'ism and Social Protest*, New Haven, Yale University Press.

6

Lucknow Besieged (1857): Feminine Records of the Event and the Victorian Mind on India

JACQUES POUCHEPADASS

What is an event? For whom does a given historical occurrence or succession of occurrences constitute an historical event? We are accustomed to view the gradation of importance of the events of history given in standard history books as a sort of objective scale of priority or significance. Such gradations, of course, are not arbitrary. But what we miss in accepting them uncritically is the realisation that the reading of a particular occurrence as an historical event is a matter of consensus, and that consensuses are based on social values. All occurrences are not events for all men or social groups, and all recognised events do not mean the same thing to everybody. The chronologies in our history books are human discourses on history.

From this it follows that there are at least two fruitful ways to study an historical event. One is to investigate the details of the occurrences, as historians usually do. The other is to bring out what the event reveals of the dominant values and imagination of the social groups which have given it prominence, as historians also do, but rarely. The significance of an event does not lie only in its objective content and impact. An event also functions as a mirror of the social group which has given it its historical status, and a place in its collective memory.

The 'siege of Lucknow', or more properly the siege of the Residency at Lucknow in 1857, lends itself particularly well to the second type of analysis, as the constant celebration of this event in the vast literature of the 'Indian Mutiny' is clearly loaded with symbolic connotations. The Rebellion struck at the foundations of British national identity. It questioned the world supremacy of Great Britain, its cultural and racial superiority in India, and the moral legitimacy of its colonial expansion as a factor of progress. An implicit self-justifying discourse tending to the restoration of the wounded British self-image could probably be traced through most of the British literature on the Rebellion, and glorification of British behaviour during the siege of Lucknow constantly recurs in this literature.

The Lucknow Episode in the History of the Rebellion

Among the various uprisings which constitute together the Rebellion of 1857–58, the rebellion of Awadh certainly remains one of the least explored,except under a few banal aspects. The dominant British viewpoint focuses on the movements of troops, on the defence of the Residency, on the daily life of the besieged, but largely ignores the Indian side of the episode. Eminent Indian historians of this century have followed suit. (Sen, 1957: chapter 5). It took a century before two Indian historians, Chaudhuri (1957: 118–43) and (mainly) Mukherjee (1984), began to fill the lacuna. However, unbalanced as the British perspective was, it did reflect the importance played by the siege of Lucknow from the point of view of the military operations. From June 1857, after the breakdown of British administration in the Oudh districts, and when Henry Lawrence, the Chief Commissioner, decided to gather the surviving European community in the fortified Residency, Lucknow became the last stronghold of British authority in the province. A concentration of rebel forces in and around Lucknow logically followed. From then on, the main objective of the British military effort in the East was the relief of the besieged. After the fall of Delhi, Lucknow became the rallying point of the rebels, and remained the main focus of military operations until its recapture by the British in March 1858.

Lucknow for more reasons than one had an important role in the Rebellion. However, the fact that the siege and relief of the Residency became such a crucial factor in the unfolding of events is less due to strategic necessities than to compelling impulsions of the colonial psyche. During the first months of the Rebellion, from a strictly military standpoint, it would have been more rational and less costly for the British to strengthen the provinces which still remained calm (Punjab on the one side, Bengal and Bihar on the other) in order to prevent the extension of troubles, and to wait until the arrival of the reinforcements from Britain to undertake the reconquest of the rebellious areas. This point of view was of course discussed in the Governor-General's Council in 1857. But, as E. Stokes wrote (1986: 44, 47), in political terms, the rebellion had been read not only in Europe but in India as a struggle for the recovery of Delhi and Lucknow . . . It proved morally and politically impossible to leave the Lucknow garrison to its fate.

The resistance of the Residency, and the British military efforts to rescue it, turned Lucknow into a focal point of military activity, where rebel troops collected. In addition, once Delhi was lost, Lucknow became the main seat and the main symbol of the rebellion. The British commanders were well aware of the capital value of this symbol to the rebels. Outram wrote to Canning, the Governor-General, in September 1857:

The moral effect of abandoning Lucknow will be very serious against us; the many well-disposed chiefs in Oude and Rohilcund, who are now watching the turn of affairs, would regard the loss of Lucknow as the forerunner of the end of our rule.

Colin Campbell in January 1858 was of opinion that

subjugation of the province will follow the fall of Lucknow as surely as the conquest of France would follow the capture of Paris.

and would thus strike a fatal blow at the rebellion. (Mukherjee, 1984:90). He was largely justified by the subsequent turn of events.

Thus the starting point of this symbolic-military chain of events was Henry Lawrence's decision to fortify the Residency and to defend it as an islet of British valour in the wild ocean of the Rebellion. The Indian perception of the event and its memory in the local tradition (oral and written, popular and learned) remains to be studied. The narrative provided by Abdul Halim Sharar, a journalist and literary man from Lucknow, who wrote on the events of 1857–58 in the 1920s 'through having heard of them from others or having read about them in the pages of history', conveys the disillusioned view of the vanquished:

The besiegers consisted of the disreputable elements of the town and unprincipled and headstrong combatants. There was not a single man of valour among them who knew anything of the principles of war or who could combine the disunited forces and make them into an organized striking force . . . People praised the efficiency and good intentions of the Queen (Hazrat Mahal) . . . Her advisers were bad and her soldiers useless. Everyone was a slave to his own desires and no one agreed with what anyone else said. (Sharar, 1975: 66–7).

Pemble (1977: part 3) provides a copious narrative of the Lucknow episode, endeavouring to bring into light the Indian as well as the British side of the event. Mukherjee (1984: 82–103) emphasises the importance of Lucknow as a rallying point for the popular rebellion of the peasantry of Awadh after the fall of Delhi. The prudence and interested motives

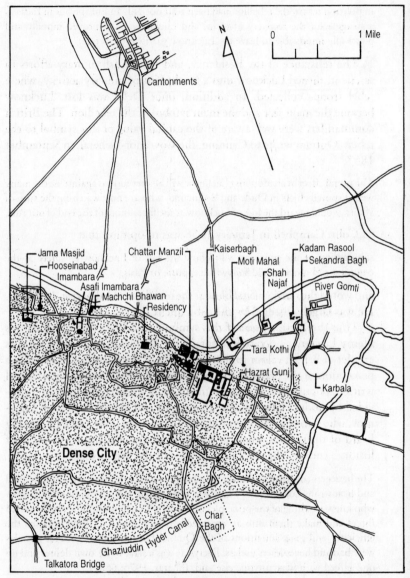

FIGURE 1 LUCKNOW IN 1856

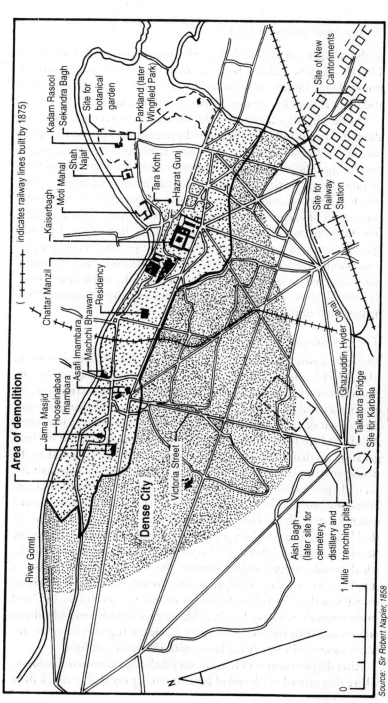

FIGURE 2 LUCKNOW IN 1858

Source: *Sir Robert Napier, 1858*

River Gomti

Area of demolition

(+++++) indicates railway lines built by 1875

Jama Masjid

Hooseinabad Imambara

Chattar Manzil

Asafi Imambara

Machchi Bhawan

Residency

Kaiserbagh

Moti Mahal

Shah Najaf

Kadam Rasool

Sekandra Bagh

Site for botanical garden

Tara Kothi

Hazrat Gunj

Parkland (later Wingfield Park)

Site of New Cantonments

Site for Railway Station

Ghaziuddin Hyder Canal

Talkatora Bridge

Site for Karbala

Aish Bagh (later site for cemetery, distillery and trenching pits)

Victoria Street

Dense City

1 Mile

0

N

of the taluqdars in the revolt are well brought out by Metcalf (1979: 174–5). All these authors, however, write on the basis of information from colonial sources. Written Indian testimonies may in fact be rare, and the oral tradition remains to be seriously explored.

On the British side, on the other hand, testimonies and narratives abound. The story of the 140 days of the siege of Lucknow has been told not only in the contemporary press and in the correspondence and reports of the officials of the time, but in a variety of literary genres, from private writings (letters and diaries) to actual literary endeavours (plays, novels and poetry), and from recollections and memoirs to more ambitious works of soldiers and analysts of the last century. There is nothing new to learn from these sources regarding the facts of the Lucknow episode, on which dozens of histories have been written. But our purpose is to examine the factors which have led to this proliferation of testimonies and commentaries by contemporaries, and the social values which lie beneath those Victorian representations and the subsequent commemoration of the event.

The Unfolding of Events

Sir Henry Lawrence had arrived at Lucknow as Chief Commissioner in March 1857, a little more than a year after the annexation of Awadh, where discontent was running high among the marginalised nobility, the expropriated landlords, the sixty thousand soldiers of the kingdom now thrown out of employment, and the peasantry subjected to new taxes. Awadh had always been one of the main recruiting grounds of the Bengal army, so that the widely scattered sepoy regiments stationed by the British government across the newly annexed territory lent a sympathetic ear to the grievances of the local population. The news of the Meerut outbreak reached Lucknow on 15 May. On the 17th, Lawrence issued orders inviting all the European women and children to gather in the Residency under guard. Preparing for the worst, he decided to fortify the Residency, an elevated site of 33 acres overlooking the Gomti river on which stood sixteen buildings besides the Residency itself. Stocks of supplies were stored in sufficient quantity to feed hundreds of people for several months. The Mutiny broke out at Lucknow on 30 May 1857 and swept across the whole of Awadh in fifteen days. British civil and military officers and their families, with other European fugitives from the districts, converged towards Lucknow until the middle of June.

After the capitulation of Kanpur, the rebels headed towards Lucknow, where they arrived at the end of June. Lawrence decided to attack them during their approach at Chinhat, in the outskirts of Lucknow, on 30 June, but his small force was routed and three hundred men were killed. Then began the siege. There were at that time in the retrenchment one thousand European officers and men, seven hundred loyal sepoys, six hundred European women and children, and seven hundred Indian servants and coolies (in all three thousand people, of whom almost half were Indian) (Joyce, 1938: 31–2). Casualties, however, reduced these figures day after day. The size of the besieging force is not known with precision, but it was initially about seven thousand strong, and was gradually reinforced by men sent from the districts by the taluqdars and who in course of time largely outnumbered the mutinied sepoys. Henry Lawrence was killed on the third day of the siege, and was succeeded by John Inglis, the colonel of one of the Lucknow regiments, whom he had just promoted to brigadier. Given the disparity of forces, the rebels should have succeeded in storming the stronghold. The lack of cohesion and efficient command prevented them from doing so. They did however repulse several attempts by General Havelock and his small force (less than two thousand men) to relieve Lucknow at the end of July and the beginning of August. Havelock had to fall back on Kanpur and wait for help, with disease decimating the remainder of his force.

The situation was worsening for the British as the Danapur garrison, from which reinforcements had been expected, now swelled the ranks of the mutineers. On 6 August, the besiegers at Lucknow announced that they had a new king, Birjis Qadr, a young son of the deposed nawab of Awadh, who was detained at Calcutta, and of one of his wives, Begum Hazrat Mahal, who assumed power in the name of her son. An increasing number of taluqdars now sent to Lucknow contingents of irregulars who, ill-trained, ill-equipped and undisciplined as they were, represented nonetheless a significant support. A rumour was also afloat that Nana Sahib himself had joined the besiegers. In the Residency, the horrors of the siege were at their maximum, with the heat, the rains, the diseases, the daily casualties caused by cannon and musket fire and snipers. Havelock at last received his reinforcements on 15 September, at the time when Nicholson was recapturing Delhi. With more than 3,000 men, he forced his way to Lucknow and into the Residency, which he reached ten days later, cutting his way through every street in the city, at considerable cost. But by so doing, he trapped himself up in the entrenchment, as he was not strong enough to break out again, encumbered with more than a thousand non-combatants including the sick and wounded. Thus the siege went on, with now seven thousand people behind the lines, including almost three thousand Europeans, eight hundred Indian troops and more than three thousand Indian camp-followers and servants.

It was only two months later that the new Commander-in-Chief, Sir Colin Campbell, was able to relieve Lucknow. He freed the Residency on 17 November. The much-weakened garrison was evacuated and the non-combatants were escorted to safety, first to Kanpur and then to Allahabad, which they reached on 7 December. Then Campbell abandoned Lucknow again and rushed to Kanpur, which was under threat of the Gwalior sepoys led by Tatya Topi. Having defeated Tatya, Campbell prepared carefully for the reconquest of Awadh. Lucknow was then the main seat and the symbol of the Rebellion, where men in arms flocked from all over North India. In January, close to one hundred thousand rebels were concentrated in the city and busy fortifying it. Campbell started out in February towards Lucknow, fought battle after battle and reached the city, which was reconquered street by street. The last resistance of the rebels was quelled on 22 March, and the city was completely sacked. A large part of the rebel force, however, had fled, and Begum Hazrat Mahal with it. The reconquest of the rest of Awadh was to take several weeks more.

Feminine Testimonies of the Siege

Most of the archives and private testimonies relating to the siege of Lucknow are matter of fact accounts which deal mainly with military matters. But one interesting particularity of the event is that it has generated a certain number of accounts by British women who were trapped in the Residency with the garrison, in the form of diaries, according to a well-established fashion. At least twenty-seven such diaries remain, most of them unpublished (see Collier, 1963: 350). Apparently many more were written or at least begun, but they disappeared either during the siege itself or in the wreck of the steamer on which the survivors had been given a free passage to England after the event (Case, 1858). These diaries deal only casually with political or military matters. They provide a straightforward expression of the moral and psychological attitude of the besieged during their long trial. A few of them were published. Their emotional impact on the British public was greater than that of the other kinds of accounts, as the Victorian woman in India was, as the phrase went, 'the soul of the race', and yet eminently vulnerable, so that her exposure to native violence was emotionally odious.

Seven published diaries have been studied here. Two were written by the wives of leading officers of the Lucknow garrison, who were comparatively comfortably installed by Henry Lawrence in the main building of the Residency, and who stayed together throughout the siege. The first lady was Julia Inglis, a daughter of the first Lord Chelmsford, who was only twenty-four then, with her baby and two boys under five years of age. Her husband was Brigadier John Inglis, who commanded the garrison after the death of Henry Lawrence until the end of the siege. The second was Adelaide Case, wife of Colonel William Case, who was killed in action at the outset during the encounter at Chinhat. Then came Maria Vincent Germon, married since 1851 to Lieutenant Charles Germon, of the 13th Bengal Native Infantry, who was then quartered at Lucknow. Emily Polehampton was the wife of Rev. Henry Polehampton, the chaplain of Lucknow. He died of an injury towards the beginning of the siege, after twelve days of agony. He was then thirty-three years old. His clerical colleague's wife, Mrs G. Harris, also wrote a diary, which she published soon after. Mrs E. Soppitt was the 18 year-old spouse of the adjutant of one of the Irregular Corps which were raised at Lucknow a few months before the beginning of the Rebellion. She settled in the Residency on the eve of the Chinhat engagement with her two year-old son, who died of cholera two days later. She was pregnant, and gave birth to her second child in November during the long march to Allahabad after the relief of the Residency (see Fitchett, 1907: 454–70). Finally, Katherine Mary Bartrum, a silversmith's daughter from Bath, was the wife of Captain Robert Bartrum, who had been sent as surgeon to Gonda. She was 23 years old, had been married three years, eight months of which she spent in Gonda, and was the mother of a 15 month-old baby. There were only five British officers and their wives at the Gonda headquarters. After the massacre of Europeans at Sitapur, K. Bartrum fled to Lucknow under the protection of loyal sepoys with her child and the other British women of Gonda, as ordered by Henry Lawrence. She reached the Residency on 9 June. Her husband, after many vicissitudes, joined the column of Havelock in September to take part in the first relief of Lucknow, and was shot dead at the gates of the Residency.

Why did these ladies write diaries during the siege, and why did a few of them afterwards decide to publish them? First of all, keeping diaries in besieged Lucknow was not a speciality of women. Julia Inglis, while preparing her journal for publication, was assisted in the treatment of the military aspects of the siege by the former aide-de-camp of her husband, who gave her the use of his own notes taken during the event. And at least one man's diary was published, that of Major Banks (see Hutchinson,

1859: 168–77). It was written in telegraphic style, and concerned almost exclusively military matters. Such writings by men were presumably mainly meant to serve later as material for memoirs or histories. The ladies' diaries, on the other hand, were initially written for purely private purposes, according to the prefaces of those which were published. They were all intended for relatives in England, and in fact represented a substitute for correspondence, which had become impossible. Harris (1858: iii–iv) wrote to her family in December 1857:

I have kept a rough sort of journal during the whole siege, often written under the greatest difficulties—part of the time with a child in my arms or asleep on my lap; but I persevered, because I knew if we survived you would like to live our siege life over in imagination, and the little details would interest you; besides the comfort of talking to you.

Some, like Mrs Soppitt, wrote not only for their families, but for themselves. 'Whilst shut up, I kept a single diary, intended for my family . . . It was kept to remind me in after years of what I had undergone in Oudh' (Fitchett, 1907: 454, 468).

The fact that some of these texts, though not written with a view to publication, were nevertheless published in England (mostly in 1858) was merely due, the authors said, to the requests of their friends, who assured them that their narratives would interest a wider public. Some of the authors also felt it their duty to bring additional information to the knowledge of their contemporaries on a subject which attracted such passionate curiosity throughout the country, and to pay homage publicly to the bravery of the men to whom they owed their survival. Yet they all warned their readers about their inexperience as writers and their inability to provide an analysis of the event, beyond the plain and sincere recital of the day-to-day occurrences and miseries which they personally witnessed or experienced. They did not want anyone to believe that they did not sneer at intellectualism and that they attempted to go beyond their part, that of Christian wives and mothers, whose competence and duties lay in the private sphere, and who left war, politics and the public domain in general to the responsibility of men. Katherine Bartrum's preface may be quoted as an example of that state of mind:

It is not the wish of the writer of this little volume, any more than it is in her power, to draw, in glowing colours, a picture of sights and scenes through which it has been her lot to pass, but merely, at the desire of her friends, to give in simple truthfulness a detail of those domestic occurrences which fell immediately under her own observations during the siege of Lucknow, to show how wonderfully she was protected in perils and dangers of no ordinary kind, and how, when called to drink deeply of the cup of human sorrow, the arm of the Lord was her stay, a 'rock of defence in the day of trouble'.

We know, however, that in the vast corpus of English diaries written by women in India, such modest acknowledgements were usually the rule, but the consciousness of writing for a public was usually there from the beginning. (Dyson, 1978: 6).

The Diaries as Parables of Victorian Fortitude

Clearly, in any case, when they yielded to the suggestions of their relatives and friends, the authors of these diaries could not be unaware that they were fulfilling a need and answering an expectation of the British public. There was more, in the public appeal of these texts, than the usual appetite for the sensational. In the context of the widespread feeling of anger and horror caused by the Rebellion in England, such writings must have been read as galvanizing testimonies of the courage and uprightness of the race, as exemplified by its women under exceptionally trying circumstances. The Victorian cult of good conduct is everywhere present behind those plain chronicles of death, pain and sorrow (Hutchins, 1967: chapter 2). Everyone puts on a brave face and copes as best he can with adversity, showing energy and industriousness, and hardly proferring a word of revolt. Just as biography,at the time, was supposed to be not only informative but morally edifying (Hutchins, 1967: 24) the Lucknow diaries were stories of suffering and noble courage written for relatives and friends with an implicit view to arousing emotion and pride. Those Victorian women, many of them in their early twenties, not having received much formal education (Thatcher, 1981) and having little knowledge and experience of India except through their husbands, were apparently ill-prepared to face so terrible an ordeal. As is well known, male preponderance in the family and in society was one of the dogmas of the Victorian social ideology, which women themselves were not the last to profess. The ideas of feminine passivity and frailness were then as deeply entrenched as that of masculine superiority. Pre–Raphaelite painting perfectly rendered the ethereal idealisation of the Victorian women, as did Coventry Patmore's celebrated collections of poems on domestic love and feminine virtues, published in London between 1854 and 1862 under the revealing general title *The Angel in the House*. Yet in Lucknow, British women brought up in this cultural context had bravely survived a five months-long siege surrounded by 'hordes' of 'bloodthirsty rebels'. First-hand narratives of their trials could not but strike a very sensitive chord in the hearts of their British readers. They also provide interesting evidence on the basic Victorian perception of the event and of India, and some clues on its symbolic significance for the British during the subsequent decades.

Living conditions in the Residency during the siege are a hackneyed topic that crops up in every account of the 'Mutiny'. A brief summary is necessary if we are to assess the conduct of the authors of the diaries and their views on the event. The six hundred European women and children were, with few exceptions, crammed into filthy, hot rooms without sanitation in the various buildings of the Residency compound. Privacy was a rare luxury. The lack of basic amenities and household equipment was especially acute for the wives and children of officers and civilians from the out-stations of Oudh, who had arrived as fugitives without servants or luggage. In very difficult conditions they had to cook their own food, draw their water, wash their own dishes and clothes and clean their own rooms. Many of them were too ill or miserable to carry out these endless menial chores, which they had never been accustomed to perform. Writes Inglis (1892: 70):

Firewood was scarce, owing to the principal stock being turned into a rampart; and I have seen ladies going out, at the risk of being shot, to pick up sticks. The palings round the Residency garden disappeared in this way.

Above all, there was the permanent proximity of violent death. Enemy fire was continuous and heavy, day and night, and women and children were also quite exposed:

Last night, while we were at prayers, a shell burst close to our door, just behind the punkah wallah . . . Not many minutes afterwards a bullet came close to the ayah, and with a tremendous clatter broke a plate, which she had beside her (Case, 1858: 133).

Besides, the dread of a successful assault by the besiegers was constant. They dug tunnels for mines under the defence-lines, attempted surprise attacks at night and stormed repeatedly the outer batteries. And possibilities of treachery within the ranks of the besieged themselves could never be ruled out.

Some of the women and children, inevitably, were hit by shot or shell. Yet disease and malnutrition were even more formidable enemies to them, the daily rations of meat and flour being gradually reduced as the siege went on, and milk, sugar and vegetables lacking almost completely.

Cholera, smallpox and scurvy (due to the lack of fresh fruit and vegetables) became very prevalent, and the mortality among children and
infants (some of whom were born during the siege) was particularly high.
In a characteristic entry of her diary, Julia Inglis wrote early in September, 'I went to see Mrs Cowper this morning, and heard from her that
five babies were buried last night'. Daily life was made even more un-
bearable by the monsoon rains pouring through the ceilings, the proliferation of rats and insects, fetid smells from imperfectly buried bodies,
and, for those in the more exposed parts of the compound, the impos-
sibility of stirring out.

Courage, devotion to others, and the upholding of self-respect, all
firmly rooted in the Christian virtues of hope and charity, were the
fundamental qualities which the authors of the diaries represented as
characteristic of their own behaviour and of that of their companions in
misfortune. The many women who had arrived without servants, or
whose servants had deserted, had no option but to roll up their sleeves
and share between themselves, in each group of refugees, the burden of
collective chores. Frivolous Maria Germon, who had insisted on taking
her piano with her when she moved into the Residency before the
beginning of the siege, wrote:

My morning duties were rather heavy, having a large number of clothes to wash;
I have always to take up all the water I require and carry it down again when
done—labour that I thought I never could have been equal to, especially in this
country.

And again

I ran down sharp to light the fire and boil the kettles—the former by far the most
difficult operation—I am very stupid at it . . . I worked really hard this morning
in the kitchen store-rooms, and it is anything but a joke this hot weather to have
to stand before the fire fanning it to make the kettle boil. I was quite tired out
before all was completed; but I am a perfect wonder to myself. I never thought
I was capable of such fatigue, or was half so accomplished as I find I am.

The very young and pregnant E. Soppitt similarly notes, 'Washed some
clothes. Hard work to one unaccustomed to such. Many a sigh heaved
during the task'.

Katharine Bartrum, packed with fifteen other women and children in
a room of the Begum Kothi ('a most uninviting looking place, so dirty,
having neither a punkah to cool the air or a scrap of furniture to set it off,
but we had to make the best of it'), reveals herself as more energetic and
resourceful than most:

I have taken upon myself to keep the room somewhat neat and clean, for most of my fellow sufferers are too ill, mentally and bodily, to care how things look; but it troubles me much to see things untidy about me, and so long as God gives me health and strength I will do my best to add to the comfort of others, even if I afford them amusement by giving them occasion to call me the servant-of-all-work. Strength is given in proportion to our day, and truly I found it so, for never did I more stand in need of an energetic and independent spirit than now, surrounded by strangers, with no husband near to look up to for protection and help, and with my little babe entirely dependent upon me.

Julia Inglis does not hesitate to write that she refused a little milk from her goats for the dying child of 'a poor woman whose husband, an overseer of roads, had been killed during the siege': this was to be understood as the sacred egoism of a mother who had her own three small children to save. But she attests that 'with few exceptions, a very kind spirit pervaded the garrison, and many noble and self-denying acts of charity were performed'.

The reference to the Christian faith is ubiquitous in the journals. Katharine Bartrum, who was escorted from Gonda to Lucknow by a few sepoys whose true dispositions were uncertain, wrote at the end of her eventful journey, 'God in His infinite wisdom softened their hearts towards us'.

Faith gave significance to the trials endured and helped the besieged to face the proximity of death and the pain of bereavement, as in the case of E. Soppitt:

My poor darling boy died of cholera yesterday, during the dreadful confusion of our troops returning pell-mell from Chinhut. Harry was two years old (my first-born). How hard, oh, how hard to bend to the Almighty's will, and say 'Thy will be done'.

Church services were held by the surviving chaplain whenever possible, and were faithfully attended.

'On Sunday, we were able, thank God, to go twice to church, which was a blessing we had scarcely dared to hope', writes Harris.

Prayer was a constant recourse against anxiety and fear for women like Case:

I read the Litany aloud, and so wonderful was the effect of that heartfelt prayer, that it is scarcely too much to say, that we rose from our knees calm, and feeling ready for whatever might await us.

The special circumstances of the siege, moreover, gave exceptional significance to the word of the Scriptures:

How intensely applicable to us are those petitions in the Litany:'From plague, pestilence, and famine, from battle, murder, and from sudden death, good Lord, deliver us'! It seems as if they never came home to one's heart before; indeed the whole of the Liturgy and the Psalms appear so wonderfully suited to our present condition, as if composed expressly for the occasion, taking in all our necessities and all our feelings. They are most comforting (Harris, 1858: 61).

Inevitably, explanations for the occurrence of the siege, and for the Indian Rebellion as a whole, were sought within the same frame of reference. There was talk among the besieged, as G. Harris reported, that the whole event was a deserved reward of the sinful conduct of the British in India:

The tribulation we are now in is a just punishment to our nation for the grasping spirit in which we have governed India; the unjust appropriation of Oude being a finishing stroke to a long course of selfish seeking our own benefit and aggrandisement. No doubt it is a judgment of God, and that we have greatly abused our power; and, as a Government, opposed the spread of Christianity; while individually, by evil example and practice, we have made our religion a reproach in the eyes of the natives. God grant that this heavy chastisement may bring all to a better mind!

One often debated question was: what course were the women to adopt if the enemy broke in? Were they to kill themselves, or to commend themselves to God's mercy? It was firmly but wrongly believed that the rebels had outraged the Englishwomen fallen into their hands at Meerut, Sitapur and elsewhere. Shortly before the beginning of the siege, the then Colonel Inglis had asked the chaplain privately whether he would be justified in killing his wife rather than let the rebels capture her. The chaplain had answered in the affirmative, adding that the allowance, however, could never apply to the children. (Collier, 1963: 104). Colonel Inglis talked at one time of blowing up the women and children with the sick and wounded of the Residency at the last minute if the worst happened. None of the women were armed. Some had poison at hand (laudanum or prussic acid), or made suicide pacts with their husbands. Others, however, held the opposite view. The dilemma was rooted in some of the unresolved contradictions of the Victorian code of good conduct, which our unfortunate heroines struggled to illustrate in their own eyes and in the eyes of others.

Middle-class Views of the Social Order

Along with the notion of proper conduct went a distinctly hierarchical view of the social order. These writers of diaries in faultless English, well-versed in the epistolary art, all belonged to the middle class. The men and women named in the journals are almost all part of the same social world, of 'gentlemen' and 'ladies'. The rest of the besieged only appear as anonymous social entities. Describing the micro-society of the Residency, Julia Inglis writes:

> The inhabitants of our court consisted principally of half-caste clerks and their families . . . On the other side of us was a square occupied by Sikhs of the 71st N.I., and some Christian drummers and their wives . . . In the next square to us lived a good many of the ladies.

Again a little later, 'our ayah to-night gave us a very melancholy account of the state of the brigade-mess, where so many of the ladies were living'.

'The ladies' were an altogether different group from 'the 32nd women' or 'the artillery women', or even that 'poor woman, Mrs Beale by name, whose husband, an overseer of roads, had been killed in the siege', and to whose dying child a little milk was refused. This is not to say that there were no gestures of generosity or good will across social barriers. Writes Mrs Case:

> Sometimes Mrs Inglis, Carry and I go down into the Ty Khana, and see the women of the regiment. Mrs Inglis never goes down empty-handed. She is kind and considerate to every one, and often takes down some pudding or soup, which may have been at dinner, to a poor sick boy. A little tea, sugar, or any old clothes we can find to take with us to them is always very gratefully received, and it cheers their spirits to talk to them a little.

After the second relief of the Residency, Emily Polehampton wrote to her brother-in-law, 'Twenty of us have become widows in the siege; this of course does not include those among the soldiers, clerks, etc.'.

W.H. Russell, The Times correspondent, who reached Calcutta in January 1858, met 'a lady who had been besieged in the Residency at Lucknow', and noted from her account that

> there was a good deal of etiquette about visiting and speaking in the garrison! Strange, whilst cannon-shot and shell were rending the walls about their ears, whilst disease was knocking at the door of every room, that those artificial rules of life still exercised their force; that petty jealousy and 'caste' reigned in the Residency. It is a pity that our admiration for the heroism of that glorious defence should be marred by such stories (quoted in Stanford, 1962: 115).

As regards the Indians, apart from the faithful servants who had followed their masters in the Residency, they appear in the diaries as components of the landscape, as in this entry of Julia Inglis' text:

In the evening, our only amusement and change was to sit outside our door, or walk up and down our court-yard filled with natives and half-castes.

The diarists give statistics of the numbers of women and children in the entrenchment at various stages of the siege, and of those that were wounded, killed or widowed, but these figures concern exclusively the Europeans. No figures are given concerning women and children among the servants, and no mention is made of the 'hundreds of men, women and children (who) were daily employed digging ditches, putting up stockades and building batteries'. The Indians, in spite of their number and proximity, remain a sort of stereotyped abstraction. They are occasionally mentioned with astonishing insensitivity:

The enemy soon retreated, having done no greater harm than cutting up about twenty grass-cutters (Polehampton, 1858: 353). I have got dear old Bustle back. Mr S. told us such a touching account of the poor dog's misery and pining . . . The order about the destruction of dogs has never been attended to, and while I see so many pariahs allowed to run about with impunity there is no reason for Bustle's exile (Harris, 1858: 65).
While we were sitting in the garden . . . the discussion was why the hanging should be stopped? There has been none in the last two days, and before that they were hanging six to eight morning and evening in front of the Muchee Bawun. (Germon, 1958: 30).

The journals betray an almost total ignorance of Indian society and culture. A few ubiquitous stereotypes on the Indian character are all the information they yield on the subject. Most prominent among these was the Victorian cliche of the untrustworthiness of Indians, which was exacerbated by the circumstances of the siege:

It was terrible to think of treachery within our walls. I said to John (Brig. Inglis) I wished we had no natives inside, but he checked me by answering, 'Do not say that; we could not hold the place without them—they outnumber us.' It was a fearful reflection.

Julia Inglis later remarks that 'one cannot trust much to native promises', and Maria Germon observes that Nana Sahib 'is a Mahratta, a notedly treacherous race'. The obsession with treason in the Residency was fueled by the frequency of desertions, against which various measures were taken. The second stereotype was native 'cowardice'. That cliche was at times expressed in more technical military terms, even more obviously borrowed from the discourse of men than the former shorter versions:

The native troops can seldom stand in open field . . . Had the enemy's cavalry behaved well, not one of our force would have returned (from Chinhat) . . . Had the enemy possessed any resolution, the place would have been theirs long ago, but they could not make up their minds to stand the British bayonets.

Finally, there was the inevitable casual remark on Indian childishness, as 'the natives are like babies—they will believe anything.'

Such platitudes, which embodied well-known Victorian preconceptions on India and the Indians (Hutchins, 1967: chapter 3), were characteristic of women

who experienced the country mainly through their husbands, who were cosseted and debarred from most real investigations of their own, who relied, by upbringing and custom, on the infallibility of the masculine judgement (Barr, 1976: 106).

Their outlook on the Rebellion was mainly emotional and moral, based on the worldview of their class, on their limited experience of India, and on hearsay. They called the rebels 'these fiends in human shape' and (most frequently) 'these wretches', but knew very little about them, and were an easy prey to the most ghastly rumours. For Harris

There was no indignity that was not inflicted on all the women the wretches got hold of. The children were murdered and thrown in a heap . . . Fancy the babies at Seetapore being dashed to the ground and bayoneted—one has no words to express one's horror and indignation.

Blazes of anger against an almost abstract enemy coexist in the texts with frequent passages expressing affection for the real Indian servants and soldiers who had followed them into the Residency and were risking and losing their lives for them. Phrases such as 'the suffering and discomfort of the poor men', 'my poor ayah', and so on are of common occurrence. But the distance from paternalistic praise to execration proved short whenever signs of disaffection appeared: '. . . their impudence is beyond bounds: they are losing even the semblance of respect. I packed off my tailor yesterday', writes Harris.

The Siege of Lucknow as Symbol

News of the Rebellion were received in England with torrents of at times hysterical passion (Salmond, 1963; Haldar, 1973). The public in London was at first rather incredulous, and the general tone of the press remained optimistic till the middle of July 1857. Then the fear of the worst began to spread as the news from India became increasingly bad. But it is towards the beginning of August that the climate of opinion suddenly turned violent, with the arrival of the first atrocity stories. Reports of British women raped or 'boiled alive in butter', of British children 'tossed on the points of bayonets', spread like wildfire, and triggered off frenzied reactions. The press cried for blood and carried floods of strident patriotism. Public meetings were held throughout the country to raise funds for the English victims of the revolt (fifty-six such meetings took place during the first week of October). The excitement went on unabated until after the news of the first relief of Lucknow arrived. It was then rapidly felt that the revolt was doomed. The supply of horror stories, moreover, had dried up since the recapture of Delhi. The tone of vituperation and the cries for revenge died down, and in the press factual military reporting gradually replaced invective. By November, India had ceased to be the main concern of British public opinion. Thus it is mainly the rumours on the fate of British women and children which triggered off the flaring of passion against the Indian rebels, and this episode of collective trance crystallized around a few highly symbolic episodes, of which the siege at Lucknow was one.

A second point relates to the social base of this current of opinion. The Times wrote that 'the great unlettered class' of Britain was only faintly aware of the events in India (Salmond, 1963: 92). The violent reaction to the Rebellion was mainly a middle- and upper-class phenomenon. There was a certain degree of homogeneity between the language of editorials and correspondence columns of the Times, or of the speeches of clergymen and retired Indian army men in the public meetings, and that of the Lucknow diaries. The rebel sepoys were everywhere called 'wretches' and 'fiends in human form'. The ideological frame of reference was identical (Christianity, the superiority of the British race, the weak and false nature of Hindu character and religion). Only the violence and unrealism of the reactions in England, compounded by distance and ignorance of the context, was much greater.

Past the first relief of Lucknow, when passions began to settle down again in England, it was gradually realised that the atrocity stories were spurious, and in particular that the wild rumours which had circulated regarding the horrors suffered by women were mostly unfounded. Sir John Lawrence (the brother of Henry Lawrence) thought that the European women in Delhi had been killed outright and not molested, and Lady Canning wrote to Queen Victoria that 'there is not a particle of credible evidence to the poor women having been 'ill-used' anywhere'. (Macmillan, 1988: 102). W.H. Russell, the correspondent of the Times, who had been sent to India with the special object of verifying the atrocity stories, and whose first dispatches reached Britain in April 1858, was convinced that nearly all the stories he heard were unauthentic and originated in Calcutta (see Michael Edwardes' preface to his edition of Russell, 1957). The evidence gathered by the Government was against the rape or torture of the victims. That a good number of women had been killed in Delhi, Kanpur, Lucknow, Sitapur and other places could not, however, be doubted, and that an even greater number had endured harrowing ordeals, notably at Lucknow, was equally obvious. Moreover, one may wonder to what extent the refutations published after the event actually reached the public at large, and whether they were successful in destroying the memory of the repulsive details which had been repeated and believed both in India and in England at the height of the event. Each of the most dramatic episodes of the 'Mutiny' became an object of social memory, one of those symbolic constructs which embody the most cherished values of a group or class, in which the identity of the group crystallizes emotionally, and which are immune to factual or historical criticism.

The siege of the Residency at Lucknow ranked foremost among these. The first relief of the Residency became

one of the set-pieces of the British Imperial Story in India: the brawny Highlanders triumphantly scooping and kissing the siege-wan children, the Lucknow ladies gazing up with brimful eyes and arms outstretched in gratitude towards their deliverers; the gruff commanders vigorously shaking hands with each other, almost too overcome to speak. And, for backdrop, the smoke of the cannon, the battered gates, the wounded begging for water and the sheer muddle of it all—camels and horses and foot soldiers and bearers, kitbags and bedding-rolls, baggage-and bullock-carts and people searching desperately for familiar faces and clamouring for news (Barr, 1976: 132).

More importantly, Lucknow, for the Victorian middle-class in England and even more in India, soon came to represent a sacred place where its women and children, the soul and future of the race, vulnerable incarnations of innocence and purity, had withstood stoically the challenge of outrage and savage death, and where a number of them had met with the ultimate sacrifice, for the cause of the Empire. The remembrance of this and other episodes was kept alive over the years by the publication of accounts by witnesses, histories and fiction. The Lucknow diaries played their role in this mythologizing alchemy of collective memory. As an eminent official who survived the siege expressed it, 'Never has the noble character of Englishwomen shone with more real brightness than during this memorable siege.' (see Macmillan, 1988: 10).

The myth-making process can be illustrated by an article published in the Calcutta Review two years after the siege. The author relates an episode of the fights at Jhansi where a young soldier and his captain, trapped in a desperate situation, were courageously helped by the soldier's 22 year-old wife, who reloaded their arms until the end. The narrative ends, 'Whether, as was first reported, the young wife fell by the hand of him who loved her best, is uncertain, but they and their infant children lie in a bloody grave'. (Calcutta Review, July–December 1859: 112).

The image is likely to last longer than the reservation on its accuracy. The author uses a similar device a few pages later when he writes:

All are not heroes or heroines who have passed through trial . . . We cannot boast that all or even most of the ladies in India are like the Christian heroines and martyrs of Cawnpore and Lucknow. (p. 116).

British society in Cawnpore and in the Residency was inevitably a mixed bag as everywhere else in India (and did include outstanding personalities as the diaries show). The artificial contrast here is only used to raise collectively on the altar of heroism and martyrdom the unfortunate victims of these accidents of history, the negative turn of the formulation and the restriction on the lesser merits of the ladies in other parts the country only serving to reinforce the glowing tribute paid globally to those whose conduct was made to symbolize the dominant values of the time. The article culminates in one concluding sentence which sums up its ideological stance:

So long as we have Christian officers as well as Christian women, we do not fear for India. (p. 126).

The battered ruins of the Residency were left standing as they were after the final reconquest of Lucknow, and turned into a memorial and museum, on which the Union Jack flew until the end of the Raj. It became a place of pilgrimage, like the memorial erected on the site of the Cawnpore massacre, and other spots to which memories of the 'Mutiny' were attached. Fifty years after the event, the Rebellion still was, as young Malcolm Darling wrote in a letter home in 1906, 'a kind of phantom standing behind official chairs' (Macmillan, 1988: 103–4).

The siege of the Residency, an object of collective memory loaded with all the values, ambitions and fears which made up British relationship with India, undoubtedly played a significant role in the symbolic economy of this phantasm of latent danger and violence. Lucknow, the pearl of the East, had for several generations become one of the sacred places of Victorian idealism and pride.

REFERENCES

Barr, P. (1976), *The Memsahibs: The Women of Victorian India*, London, Secker and Warburg.

Bartrum, Katherine Mary (1858), *A Widow's Reminiscences of the Siege of Lucknow*, London, J. Nisbet.

Case, Adelaide (1858), *Day by Day at Lucknow: A Journal of the Siege of Lucknow*, London, Richard Bentley.

Chaudhuri, S.B. (1957), *Civil Rebellion in the Indian Mutinies (1857–1859)*, Calcutta, World Press.

Collier, R. (1963), *The Sound of Fury: An Account of the Indian Mutiny*, London, Collins.

Dyson, K.K. (1978), *A Various Universe: A Study of the Journals and Memoirs of British Men and Women in the Indian Subcontinent*, Delhi, Oxford University Press.

'Englishwomen in the Rebellion', *Calcutta Review*, 33, July–December 1859.

Fitchett, W.H. (1907), *The Tale of the Great Mutiny*, London, Smith, Elder & Co.

Germon, Maria Vincent (1958), *Journal of the Siege of Lucknow*, Michael Edwardes (ed.), London, Constable.

Haldar, S.K. (1973), 'How London Reacted to the "Sepoy Mutiny"', *Bengal Past and Present*, vol. 92, no. 1., January-June.

Harris, G. (1858), *A Lady's Diary of the Siege of Lucknow: Written for the Perusal of Friends at Home*, London, John Murray.

Hutchins, F.G. (1967), *The Illusion of Permanence: British Imperialism in India*, Princeton, Princeton University Press.

Hutchinson, Captain G. (1859), *Narrative of the Mutinies in Oudh*, London, Smith, Elder.

Inglis, Julia Selina (1892), *The Siege of Lucknow: A Diary*, London, Osgood, McIlvaine & Co.

Joyce, M. (1938), *Ordeal at Lucknow: The Defence of the Residency*, London, John Murray.

Macmillan, M. (1988), *Women of the Raj*, London, Thames & Hudson.

Metcalf, Thomas R. (1979), *Land, Landlords and the British Raj*, Berkeley, University of California Press.

Mukerjee, Rudrangshu (1984), *Awadh in Revolt*, Delhi, Oxford University Press.

Pemble, J. (1977), *The Raj, the Indian Mutiny and the Kingdom of Oudh*, London, Harvester Press.

Polehampton, H.S. (1858), *A Memoir, Letters and Diary of the Reverend Henry S. Polehampton, Chaplain of Lucknow*, London.

Russell, W.H. (1860), *My Indian Mutiny Diary*, London, Cassel.

Salmond, J.A. (1963), 'The Frantic Roars of the London Times', *Bengal Past and Present*, vol. 2, no. 2, July-December.

Sen, S.N. (1957), *Eighteen Fifty Seven*, Delhi, Publications Division, Ministry of Information and Broadcasting, Government of India.

Sharar, Abdul Halim (1975), *Lucknow: Last Phase of an Oriental Culture*, London, Paul Elek.

Stanford, J.K. (1962), *Ladies in the Sun: The Memsahib's India 1790–1860,* London, Gallay Press.

Stokes, E. (1986), *The Peasant Armed: The Indian Rebellion of 1857,* C.A. Bayly (ed.), Oxford, Clarendon Press.

Thatcher, M. (1981), 'British Women in India", Paper presented at the Seventh European Conference on Modern South Asian Studies, School of Oriental and African Studies, London.

7

Traditional Rites and Contested Meanings: Sectarian Strife in Colonial Lucknow

MUSHIRUL HASAN

The truth is that in those days the whole year was spent waiting for Muharram . . . After the goat sacrifices of Baqr Id the preparations for Muharram began. Dadda, my father's mother, started to softly chant elegies about the martyrs. Mother set about sewing black clothes for all of us; and my sister took out the notebooks of laments . . . and began to practice them. I don't know about Lucknow—I don't even know about Ghazipur—but I certainly do know that among the Saiyid families of Gangauli, Muharram was nothing less than a spiritual celebration (Rahi Masoom Raza, 1994: 9–10)

In Lucknow the deafening sound of crackers from Nakhaas and the loud and clear call for prayers from Shah Najaf mark the beginning of the holy month of Mohurram. Lakhnavis observe the next ten days with solemnity. They renew and reaffirm their unflinching devotion to those Islamic principles for which Imam Husain, grandson of the Prophet of Islam, and his seventy-two companions, laid down their lives on the banks of the river Euphrates in AD 680. Once more they would, in their imagination, rally round those gallant men at Karbala and share in their *karb* (pain) and *bala* (trial).

Come day one of Mohurram and life in Lucknow comes to a standstill. Perfume and tobacco shops wear a deserted look. Trade is no longer brisk. The busy and noisy bazaars of Aminabad and Nakhaas are subdued. The city is robbed of its buoyancy. Mrs Meer Hasan Ali (1982: 30), an English lady married to a Shia and living in Lucknow in the 1820s, contrasted the profound stillness of an extensively populated city with the incessant bustle usual at all other times.

The change is manifested in several different ways. Women, including the newly-wed, remove their jewellery, their bangles and flashy clothes:

The hair is unloosed . . . and allowed to flow in disorder about the person; the coloured pyjamaahs (loose trousers) and deputtahs (long scarf) are removed, with every other article of their usual costume, for a suit that, with them, constitutes mourning—some choose black, others grey, slate, or green (Ali: 46).

Comfort, luxury and convenience are set aside. The *pallung*, the *charpoy* and the *musnad* are removed. Instead, women of all classes use a date-palm mat or simply sleep on a matted floor (Ali: 43). Men are equally abstemious, sporting white *angarkhas* (a combination of the *jama*, a collarless shirt and *bslabar*) or *achkans* in dark shades. Poets, accustomed to regaling large audiences with *ghazals*, switch to writing *marsiyas* (elegies) and *soz* (dirges). Their chief patrons, the rajas and nawabs, abandon their favourite pastimes to lead a pious and abstemious life. Their palaces, *havelis* and forts bear a sombre look during Mohurram.

Courtesans and their retinues in Chowk put away their musical instruments, their *ghungrus, payals*, and the *tabla* (a musical instrument). Umrao Jan Ada's *Khanum* commemorated Husain's martyrdom on a more elaborate scale than any other courtesan in Lucknow, decorating the place of mourning with banners, buntings, chandeliers, globes. Umrao Jan was herself an accomplished *soz-khwan* (reciter of dirges). The most celebrated professionals dare not perform in her presence. Her account finds resonances in Attia Hosain's description (1992: 64) of her visit down 'the forbidden street whose balconies during the first days of Muharram were empty of painted, bejewelled women when visitors climbed the narrow stairs only to hear religious songs of mourning'. There was the glass *tazia*, the miniature domed tomb, shining, gleaming, reflecting the light of many crystal lamps.

The city's black-clad men and women set aside their daily chores to sorrow for the martyred Imam. They marched through the lanes and bylanes of Lucknow in fervent lamentation, chanting 'Ya-Husain', 'Ya-Husain', rhythmically beating their chest, self-flagellating, carrying replicas (tazia) of Husain's tomb, his coffin (*taboot*), his standards and insignia (*alam* and *panja*) and his horse (*dul-dul*). One of the most impressive religious spectacles, commented William Crooke (1975: 263), was the long procession of tazias and flags streaming along the streets with a vast crowd of mourners, who 'scream out their lamentations and beat their breasts till the blood flows, or they sink fainting in an ecstasy of sorrow'. Notice, too, the following description:

The sun was high above the church steeple when we heard the distant chanting, 'Hasan! Husain! Hasan! Husain! Haider!' It came nearer and the measured sound of bare hands striking bare breasts, the monotonous beat of drums and cymbals made my heart beat with a strange excitement. Then the barefooted, bareheaded men came in view following *tazias* carried shoulder-high. There were *tazias* of peacock's feathers, of glass, of sugar, of bright-coloured paper, intricate, beautiful, arched, domed, some as high as telegraph poles, others from poor homes so small that they could be held on one man's head, all hurrying to join the main procession at the allotted time, for burial or consecration (Hosain, 1992: 72).

Such demonstrative acts in public were a small part of Mohurram ceremonies. The *imambaras*, many of which were symbolic of Lucknow's Shia past and present, served as the central organising spaces as well as physical statements uniting the populace of the city (Cole, 1988: 98; Freitag, 1990: 237). They also served as symbols of communitarian solidarity, and as platforms for articulating individual and collective experiences. Here the gatherings (*majlis*) were structured, adhering to a pattern laid down by the Shia Nawabs of Awadh. Beginning with soz-khwani (recitation without the aid of musical instruments), a majlis would be followed by either a sermon or *marsiya-khwani* (reading of elegy), a style of rendering inspired by the legendary Lucknow poet, Mir Anis (1802–75). It would normally conclude with the rendering of short dirges. As soon as the impressive and heart-rending notes of dirges were chanted by Mir Ali Hasan and Mir Bandey Hasan, wrote the essayist-novelist Abdul Halim Sharar (1975: 149):

Hundreds of men from elite families began to sing them, and then the women of noble Shia families also intoned them with their matchless voices . . . Matters have now reached the stage that during Muharram and on most days of mourning, heartrending sounds of lamentation and the melodious chanting of dirges can be heard from every house in every lane in old Lucknow. In every alley one will hear beautiful voices and melodies which one will never forget.

The sermon is at the heart of Mohurram rites. It is, in large part, an elegiac account of the episodes in the Karbala story, a moving narrative of the pain, anguish and agony of Husain and his companions. Year after year, speakers detail the same sequence of events, retaining the order in which members of Husain's family were killed. This is done to correlate the chain of events traditionally recorded with the leading martyrs. The commemorations are fashioned accordingly. Thus the sixth day of Mohurram is connected with Husain's young nephew, the seventh with his eighteen-year old son, the eighth with the brave and loyal brother

Abbas, the ninth with the six-month old son Ali Asghar and the tenth with Iman Husain's own martyrdom. Qasim, Ali Akbar, Abbas, Ali Asghar and Husain himself exemplified the enormity of the tragedy; so that days linked with their martyrdom convey deep meanings, special attachments and associations. Their sufferings, narrated by the man on the pulpit, move audiences (*azadar*) to mourn, wail and lament, beat their chests (*matam*) and participate in the sufferings of the martyrs by self-deprivation and mortification. Attia Hosain (1992: 68) captures the mood in Lucknow:

It was the ninth night of Muharram. On the horizon there was a glow as of a forgetful sun rising before moonset. The glow of a million lamps from the illuminated Imambaras where *tazias* and banners were laid to rest, lit the sky, and the city was alive, crowds forgetful in that bright beauty of the month of mourning . . . When he (Asad) read of the agonies of thirst of the children of the Prophet, cut off from the river by their enemies, the women sobbed softly. Ustaniji began beating her breast, saying 'Husain' softly, with a slow rhythm. Ramzano stared at her strangely and joined in. The others still sobbed softly.

Ten days of mourning ceremonies culmimate on *yaum-i ashura* with the *Majlis-i-Sham-i Ghariban* at the famous Ghuframaab Imambara, the final mournful tribute to the *Sayyid-ash-Shuhada* (Lord of the Martyrs). The final curtain is drawn on *Chehlum*, the fortieth day. Sharar describes (149–50) his visit to the Talkatora Karbala in Lucknow on that day. He witnessed a procession of women approaching carrying tazias. All were bare-headed and their hair hung loose. In the centre a woman carried a candle. By its light a beautiful, delicately formed girl read from some sheets of paper. She chanted a dirge along with other women. He was moved by the 'stillness, the moonlight, those bare-headed beauties and the soul-rending notes of their sad melody'. As the group passed through the gates of the shrine, he heard the following lament:

When the caravan of Medina, having lost all
Arrived in captivity in the vicinity of Sham
Foremost came the head of Husain, borne aloft on a spear
And in its wake, a band of women, with heads bared.

II

Mohurram, Husain and Karbala signified different things to different sections of Lucknow society. There was the potential for political mobilisation: the Khilafat leadership in India could thus employ the paradigm

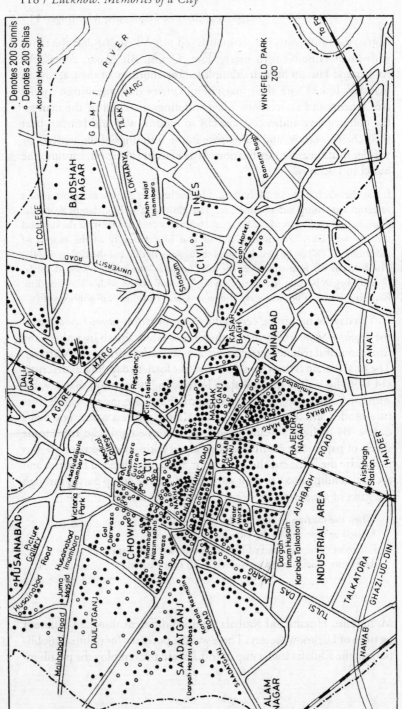

LUCKNOW CITY (1960) SHIA AND SUNNI POPULATION

Source: Census of India, 1961. (Monograph No. 3, Moharram in two cities, Lucknow and Delhi).

of Karbala and harness the most evocative themes of Shi'ism to provide depth to their movement (Mushirul Hasan, 1991). At another level, Husain's martyrdom served, to the Shias of all times and in all places, as an everlasting exhortation to guard their separate identity and to brave their numerical inferiority in the face of firmly established and some-times oppressive majorities. It made sense, according to Hamid Enayat (1982: 20), on two other levels: first, in terms of a soteriology not dis-similar from the one invoked in the case of Christ's crucifixion: just as Christ sacrificed himself on the altar of the cross to redeem humanity, so did Husain allow himself to be killed on the plains of Karbala to purify the Muslim community of sins; and second, as an active factor vindicat-ing the Shia cause, contributing to its ultimate triumph. When one adds to all this the cathartic effect of weeping as a means of releasing pent-up grief over not only personal misfortune, but also the agonies of a long-suffering minority, the reasons for the popular appeal of Mohurram cere-monies become apparent.

Husain stirred the passions and sensitivities of several groups in India. On the ninth night of Mohurram, groups of women, mostly Hindus, moved about the villages wailing and reciting *dohas*, mostly improvised lyrics on the epic tragedy. Urban and rural Hindus venerated Husain and incorporated his cult into their rituals (Cole, 1988: 116–17). They offer-ed flowers and sweets at local 'Karbalas', participated in processions, decorated and kept tazias and sought Husain's intercession in disease and calamity. The Imam's trials and tribulations inspired faith in a universal nemesis ensuring justice for oppressed souls. In popular belief he was Ram of Ayodhya carrying his crusade into the wilderness; his brother Abbas personified Lakshman, devoted, energetic and brave; his sister Zainab and wife Um-i Kulsoom were cast in the image of Sita, caring, dutiful and spirited. Yazid, the Umayyad ruler and Husain's persecutor, was Ravan, greedy, corrupt, ambitious, cruel and ruthless.

W.H. Sleeman found Hindu princes in central and southern India, 'even of the brahmin caste', commemorating Mohurram with 'illumina-tions and processions brilliant and costly'. In Gwalior, a Hindu State, Mohurram was observed with pomp, as in Baroda, where the ruler sent an exquisite prayer carpet of pearls to Mecca (Reeves, 1971: 158–9; Lawrence, 1928: 292–3; Fuller, 1910: 125–6; Blunt, 1909: 72). Hindus clothed themselves in green garments and assumed the guise of *faqirs* (Frietag, 1990: 237; Shurreef, 1863: 123; Khalidi, 1992). A Hindi news-paper reported in July 1895 that Mohurram had passed off peacefully in Banaras: 'When it is Hindus who mostly celebrate (*sic*) this festival, what fear can there be?' In Lucknow 'thousands of Hindus' chanted *nohas* along with the Shias and Sunnis (Sharar, 1975: 149).

This was not all. Munshi Faizuddin's reminiscences, published in 1885 (pp. 63–6), described Mohurram rites in the court of the last two Mughal Emperors. So does Syed Ahmad Dehlawi's (b. 1946) *Rusum-i Dehli* (Rituals and Traditions of Delhi—pp. 178–80). The Sunni raja of Nanpara had Shia *ulama* read to him elegies for Husain (Cole, 1988: 105). Rural Muslims in 1897, Crooke (1975: 263) declared, joined in the Mohurram observances 'almost without distinction of sect'. In a small north Indian princely state, a British civil servant found that every Muslim guild—the painters, the masons, the carpenters, the weavers—had their own tazias and their own troupes of actors and mourners who reproduced scenes of the struggle at Karbala (Moon, 1943: 86–7). Here and elsewhere, Shia-Sunni relations were not structured around sectarian lines. Some people nursed sectarian prejudices, but most consciously resisted attempts to create fissures in the broadly unified and consensual model of social and cultural living. Regardless of the polemics of the ulama, and the itinerant preachers, bonds of friendship and understanding remained intact because Shias and Sunnis of all classes shared a language and literature and a cultural heritage. That is probably why Sharar declared (1975: 74–5) that no one in Lucknow ever noticed who was a Sunni and who a Shia.

Lucknow was, both before and during Nawabi rule, relatively free of religious insularity or sectarian bigotry. The Shia Nawabs took their cue from their Sunni overlords in Delhi and created a broad-based polity and a cosmopolitan cultural and intellectual ethos. They adhered to the policy of *sulh-i kul* (peace with all), pioneered by Akbar. Wajid Ali Shah is reported to have said that 'of my two eyes, one is a Shia and the other is a Sunni'. Sunni officials occupied important positions in the middle and lower echelons of government departments, and in Wajid Ali Shah's court the Vazir and Paymaster were Sunnis. Sunni officers also managed the Sibtainabad Imambara and the *Baitul Buka* (House of Lamentation).

Shia-Sunni controversies did not plague most rulers of princely States. Several Shia families from Awadh, such as the Syeds of Bilgram, sought and secured lucrative positions in Hyderabad. There were several Shia-Sunni marriages, and literary and political associations. Sunnis and Shias acted in unison during the Urdu agitation against the April 1900 Nagri resolution of the government in the United Provinces. They shared the Muslim League platform. They were one in agitating over the

Kanpur mosque, the Aligarh Muslim University issue, and, much to everybody's surprise, on the Khilafat question.

So too with Urdu prose and poetry, the writings of Syed Ahmad Khan (1817–98), Altaf Husain Hali (1837–1914), Shibli Nomani (1857–1914), Maulvi Zakaullah (1832–1910), Maulvi Nazir Ahmad (1836–1912) and Abdul Halim Sharar were free of sectarian claptrap. In 1889, Sharar wrote *Hasan aur Anjalina*; Shia-Sunni relations was its theme. The great Urdu poet Asadullah Khan Ghalib (1797–1869) wore no sectarian badge, no sectarian colour. He was 'a pure Unitarian and a true believer'; suspected by some to be a Shia and by others as a *tafazili* (one who, acknowledges the pre-eminence of Ali), Ghalib revelled in the ambivalence. In fact at his death there was some confusion as to whether his funeral rites should follow Shia or Sunni rituals.

Dakhni and modern Urdu poetry were both rich in *manqabat*, poems in praise of Ali, and in marsiyas, authored by both Shias and Sunnis. Husain is everybody's hero, the embodiment of Islamic virtues of piety, courage and commitment. He laid down his life but did not compromise with a bloody-minded tyrant presiding over a degenerate political and social order. His exemplary courage inspired Mohamed Ali (1878–1931), the volatile Khilafat leader. He believed that Yazid won on the bank of Euphrates, but Husain 'reigned and still reigns over the hearts of a faith of God's human creation, while the soul of humankind in its entirety applauds the victory and final truimph of the victims of Karbala and shall continue to do so . . .' (see Hasan ed., 1985: 301).

> *Qatl-i Husain asl me marg-i Yazid hai*
> *Islam zinda hota hai har Karbala ke baad*

Husain's assasination, in reality, symbolises the death of Yazid.
Islam is, after all, rejuvenated with such tragedies

Mohammad Iqbal (1876–1938) echoed similar sentiments:

> *Nikal kar khanqahon se ada kar rasm-i Shabbiri*

Emerge from the confines of the *khanqahs* and, re-enact the example set by Husain.

Yet by the end of the nineteenth century such representations of unity gradually gave way to symbols of discord. They served, in the hands of the politician-priest combine, to heighten sectarian consciousness, assert judicial and political rights and widen areas of competition and disharmony. Each side came to nurse profound grievances about the other based on mutually exclusive interpretations of history.

The first ominous sign surfaced around 1906 when some Sunni zealots constructed their own local Karbala at Phoolkatora on the north-eastern edge of Lucknow, opposite the existing Karbala in Talkatora. The fires of sectarian unrest were then stoked by the public praise (*Madhe-Sahaba*) of the three Khulafa (plural of Khalifa/Caliph)—Abu Bakr, Umar and Usman, whom the Shias regarded as 'usurpers' of Ali's claim as successor to the Prophet. They retaliated with a villification (*tabarra*) campaign. Sunni preachers went a step further. Mohurram observances were declared as acts of heresy. People were exhorted to avoid them scrupulously (selections from Native Newspaper Reports, UP, 1936–37). Zafarul Mulk, secretary of the Lucknow Madhe-Sahaba committee, struck a sharp note by declaring *taziadaari* 'deleterious to the spiritual and temporal well-being of the Muslims' (Zafarul Mulk, n.d.: 1). The nature of the Shia-Sunni engagement inevitably led to the appropriation of certain symbols and the rejection of others. Mohurram was no longer a common symbol of veneration but an exclusively Shia concern not only in Lucknow but also in Bombay (Masselos, 1982) and Banaras (Kumar, 1988: 216). A powerful symbol of unity turned into a potent vehicle for sectarian mobilisation. In this way sectarian strife became much more common in north Indian towns than Hindu-Muslim riots.

Shia-Sunni disturbances were sparked off in Lucknow in the 1880s, 1890s and in 1907–8. 'The feeling of tension between the Sunnis and Shias of Lucknow has reached its climax', reported the *Gauhar-i Shahwar* in April 1907. Allahabad, Banaras, and Jaunpur witnessed widespread violence. What began as small-scale skirmishes in the last quarter of the nineteenth century (many of which went unnoticed in official despatches because of their listing in the category of 'Native Societies and Religious and Social Matters' in the *Selections from the Native Newspapers*) escalated into bloody feuds involving scores of people and turning Lucknow and its adjoining districts into a cauldron of sectarian animus.

The lines of cleavage were sharply demarcated by the mushroom growth of sectarian organisations, such as the Anjuman-i Sadr-us Sudoor, floated by Maulana Syed Agha Husain in 1901, and the Anjuman-i Jafariya, established by the Syeds of Barha four years later. A Shia Conference was set up in October-December 1907, some months after the Muslim League came into being. There was much talk of 'Shias of light' leading the way, mitigating the economic and educational backwardness of their community. Some were keen to take their grievances to the Viceroy (*Surma-i Rozgar*, 1 February 1907).

The depth of sectarian feeling was apparent at the first Shia Conference. Delegates delivered fiery and intemperate speeches against the
Sunnis. The atmosphere was so vitiated that Ghulam-us Saqlain (1870–
1915), editor of *Asr-i Jadid*, left the meeting in disgust. The hardliners
seized the initiative in renaming the organisation as the 'Shia Political
Conference', petitioned the government in December 1909 to enumer-
ate the Shia population separately in the census, and insisted on the
separate and distinct identity of the Shias. The conference, initially
formed to foster cultural and educational goals, turned into a platform
for articulating sectional political aims.

In the mid-1930s the Shia Political Conference, now under the firm
control of Syed Wazir Hasan (1874–1947), the architect of the Congress-League scheme of December 1916, rallied round the Congress and
supported the Muslim Mass Contact campaign, Jawaharlal Nehru's
brainchild. At the same time, it continued to clamour for separate representation in the legislative councils, a demand spurred by the defeat
of two Shia candidates in the 1937 elections. The *Sarfaraz*, a Shia weekly
from Lucknow, attributed their defeat (6, 7, 13 May 1939) to 'venom-
ous' Sunni propaganda and called for safeguarding the Shia 'national and
political rights'. The Anjuman-i Tanzimul Muminin had no faith in the
Muslim League, a body controlled by the 'Sunni Junta'. Neither did
Syed Ali of the Shia Student's Conference. The Majlis-i Ulama, held at
Lucknow on 5 July 1945, reiterated the memorandum sent by Hosseinbhoy A. Laljee to Wavell as well as the Congress High Command.
The Shia Federation threatened to organise strikes, boycotts and demonstrations if its demands were not fulfilled.

These were empty threats. The Congress was not prepared to compli-
cate the scenario by introducing the 'Shia case' in negotiating with the
British and the League. Likewise, the government did not recognise the
Shias as a major political force. 'We cannot give them special help' was
how an official reacted. 'We cannot contemplate', commented a senior
member in the Home Department, 'treating a religious sub-division of
Muslims as a new minority'. Inevitably, the future editors of the *Transfer
of Power* documents ignored Shia petitions in their compilation. 'Not
wanted: I don't think we need bother at all with those cables from the
Shias'.[1]

III

Lucknow was the scene of violent Shia-Sunni riots in 1938–39. These
were a sequel to a protest movement, launched in May 1935 against an

official suggestion to forbid Madhe Sahaba on certain days. The agitation gained intensity a year later. It turned violent in May–June 1937, when frenzied mobs in Lucknow and Ghazipur went on a rampage. Trouble in Ghazipur was instigated by a party of Sunnis from Jaunpur. Enraged mobs burnt and looted property, and killed at will. Sectarian strife, hitherto dormant, had turned into a common occurrence in the daily lives of Lakhnavis.[2]

There was more trouble during the next two years, fuelled by a committee ruling against Madhe Sahaba in Lucknow.[3] Husain Ahmad Madani (1879–1957), principal of the renowned seminary at Deoband along with other Jamiyat al-ulama leaders, now jumped into the fray. He advocated civil disobedience. Thousands paid heed to his call and courted arrest. Though a fervent advocate of secular nationalism and a principled critic of the 'two-nation theory', he stirred sectarian passions unabashedly. He spoke at a public meeting in Lucknow on 17 March 1938 sharing the platform with the firebrand Maulvi Abdul Shakoor, head of the Dar al-Muballighin, and Maulana Zafarul Mulk, chief exponent of Madhe Sahaba in Lucknow.[4] In other places, the Ahrars and the Khaksars developed common cause with the Jamiyat al-Ulama. The mercurial Khaksar leader, Allama Mashriqi, mobilised his followers from different places, though police vigilance made sure that not many sneaked into the city's municipal limits. The Ahrars, fresh from their successful agitation against the Maharaja of Kashmir, organised bands of volunteers (*jathas*) in Lucknow. They came from neighbouring Malihabad, Kanpur, Delhi, Meerut and from as far as Peshawar. By the end of March 1939, hundreds were arrested. 'Tension in the city' wrote Lucknow's deputy-commissioner, 'has increased and is now nearing breaking point'.

On 30 March, the Congress ministry allowed Madhe Sahaba on *Barawafat*, the Prophet's birthday. The Sunni leaders promptly called off civil disobedience and organised a 30,000 strong Barawafat procession to register their victory. This order, besides contravening established conventions in Lucknow, jolted Shia confidence in the Congress ministry. The *Sarfaraz* on 30 March chided Pant and his ministerial colleagues for its capitulation. An impression gained credence that the Congress had played a 'double game', sowed the seeds of Shia-Sunni dissension, stoked the fires of sectarian unrest to weaken the claim of the Muslim League to be the sole spokesman of the Muslim community. So too in an earlier period. The Muslim leadership in Allahabad, poorly integrated into both the formal and informal systems of power, had become an ob-ject of attention for political orators to exploit sectarian fissures (Bayly, 1975: 130).

The next day a large crowd of angry Shias assembled at the Asaf-ud-daula Imambara, indulged in *tabarra*, and excitedly climbed the upper stories of the gateways. Some rushed towards the nearby Tila mosque, though the police blocked their onward march. The police opened fire, dispersed the mob and imposed curfew. The scholar S. Khuda Bukhsh (b. 1842) was anguished to see a posse of police with glistening bayonets in Lucknow:

The fabric of Islam is torn by dissensions, fierce and bitter; and that nobody was trying to restore peace, concord and harmony among Muslims. What a noble sight it is to see the police officers interfere at Mohurram between the followers of the Prophet to prevent a breach of peace (Khuda Bukhsh, 1912: 273–4).

As the lieutenant governor had foreseen, Shias assembled each day at the Asafi Imambara with stiffened resolve, recited tabarra on the Husaina-bad Road and then courted arrest chanting 'Ya Ali', 'Ya Ali'. Tension mounted each day.

The Shia *mujtahid*, Maulana Nasir Husain, threatened to court arrest. So did the chairman of the All-India Shia Women's Association, the wife of Wazir Hasan. Trouble spread to other areas as well. In early April, volunteers from Agra, Kanpur, Fyzabad, Barabanki and Rampur sneaked into Lucknow to assist their beleaguered brethren. Plans were set afoot in Rae Bareli to congregate in Lucknow on Barawafat and participate in a planned Tabarra agitation. (Harper to Chief Secretary, 13 March 1939, Linlithgow Papers, Nehru Memorial Museum and Library). A batch of *burqa*-clad women from Rae Bareli turned up at Kazimain, a predominantly Shia locality, to court arrest, but the Shia mujtahid did not allow them to do so. In August, Shias of Kanpur observed hartal against police firing in Lucknow. They wore badges on their arms and black flags fluttered on their houses. Riots also broke out in Banaras.[5] A report published in August 1941 suggested that the 'attempt to find a solution of the Shia-Sunni dispute in Lucknow appears to have been abandoned'.[6]

Jawaharlal Nehru, who spent time in Lucknow to resolve the Shia-Sunni deadlock, felt that his colleagues had dealt with the dispute tactlessly. 'I fear there has been much bungling about this issue', he wrote to Maulana Abul Kalam Azad who was not consulted before the ministry executed a *volte face*. The matter was decided, he told the Maulana, 'without full consideration of the consequences' (Gopal ed., 1980: 9: 334–5). Rajendra Prasad, closely associated with some leading Shias of Bihar, was equally wary of the consequences. He observed:

I presume the Shias will continue civil disobedience and will be courting jail. . . . It must be very distressing to put nine thousand people in jail who are apparently not opposed to the Government and many amongst whom are widely respected for one reason or the other. What troubles me even more is the propaganda which is gaining ground that the Congress stands to create division amongst Musalmans and what I apprehend is that after a time both will be more united against the Congress than they have ever been before.

Rajendra Prasad added that the Shias were ardent nationalists and that the Shia Political Conference had consistently acted in unison with the Congress. For these reasons, it was imprudent for the ministry to allow anti-Congress sentiments 'to grow in any community and more so in a community sympathetically inclined' (see Choudhary ed., 1984: 3: 77).

IV

The Shias were few in number, not exceeding four per cent in any of the provinces in British India (see Tables I and II). They were most numerous in Lucknow and its satellite towns, where the imambaras and mosques stood as reminders of Shia domination under the Nawabs. Elsewhere in the United Provinces, as the district gazetteers show, they were unevenly distributed in Jaunpur where the Sharqis once held sway, in Machhlishahar, Bilgram, Allahabad, Jalali in Aligarh district (Hama- -dani, 1978), Jansath in Muzaffarnagar, Moradabad, Amroha, Sam- bhal, Badaun and Rampur areas. The rulers of Rampur and the Raja of Mahmudabad were Shias. Successful professional men were few, though some like Hamid Ali Khan, a Lucknow lawyer, Syed Raza Ali (1882– 1949), Syed Ghulam-us-Saqlain, Syed Wazir Hasan and his son, Ali Zaheer, Syed Hyder Mehdi, Congressman and chairman of the Allahabad Improvement Trust, occupied prominent positions in public life. Some achieved fame as writers and poets from the early 1940s, notably Syed Ehtesham Husain of Lucknow, Khwaja Ahmad Abbas (1914–87), a descendant of Altaf Husain Hali; Syed Sajjad Zaheer, son of Wazir Hasan and co-founder of the Progressive Writer's Movement; Ali Sardar Jafri of Balrampur State, an Aligarh student expelled from the university in the mid-1930s for his radical activities; and the poet Kaifi Azmi who spent years in Bombay in the company of socialists and communists.

Table I
Shia and Sunni Population in India

Provinces and Princely States	Muslim Population	Shias (in %)	Sunnis
Assam	22,19,947	nil	100
Baluchistan	7,73,477	1	96
Bengal	2,54,86,144	1	99
Bihar & Orissa	37,06,277	1	99
Bombay	46,60,828	3	88
CP & Berar	5,82,032	2	98
Madras	28,65,285	2	94
NWFP	20,84,123	4	95
Punjab & Delhi	1,29,55,141	2	97
Baroda	1,62,328	10	88
Kashmir	25,48,514	5	95
Rajputana & Ajmer	10,02,117	2	98

NOTE: Figures for Bombay, Baroda and Rajputana and Ajmer include Khojas, Bohras, and in some cases, even Memons.

SOURCE: *Census of India*, 1921, vol. I, p. 120.

Table II
Distribution of Shia and Sunni Population in UP, 1882

Division	Percentage of total Muslim population	
	Shias	Sunnis
Meerut	2.3	97.7
Agra	1.5	98.5
Allahabad	5.3	94.7
Rohilkhand	1.6	98.4
Banaras	2.0	98.0
Jhansi	0.8	99.2
Lucknow	10.7	89.3
Sitapur	1.7	98.3
Fyzabad	3.6	96.4
Rae Bareli	1.8	98.2

SOURCE: *Census of India*, NWFP and Oudh, 1882, vol. 1, p. 74.

Yet the success of such men was in no way illustrative of the prosperity of their Shia brethren, who were much more backward than their Sunni counterparts. Shias were few in the professions and fewer still in trade and commerce. The substantial group of poverty-stricken *wasiqadars* clung to the crumbling remains of their ancestral environs. Most lived in ghettos or in the narrow lanes and alleys of the old city of Lucknow and Allahabad. In 1913, there were 1,661 wasiqadars in Lucknow, many of whom dwelt very much in the past. Some held durbars even in the early 1920s (Ganju, 1980: 286). Their condition symbolised the decline of a class which owed its survival to nawabi patronage. They were unable to make good under the British, because they were so poorly equipped to seize the opportunities offered by newly-created administrative and bureaucratic structures.

There can be no doubt that Shia-Sunni estrangement was in some ways related to tangible material factors. The decline of the Shia aristocracy in the second half of the nineteenth century, the impoverishment of their less privileged brethren and the relative prosperity of some Sunni groups deepened Shia anxieties over their future (Ahmad, 1983; Ganju, 1980: 290–2). The British contributed insofar as they gave legal definition to the Shia-Sunni division. The approval or ban of religious commemmorations, arbitration of disputes, and regulating religious procession routes transformed latent doctrinal differences into public, political and legal issues (Hjortshoj, 1987: 291).

An even more powerful current was however at work towards the end of the nineteenth century. It appeared in the form of religio-revivalism, affecting Hindus and Muslims, Shias and Sunnis, Deobandis and Barelwis. It threatened to undermine the structure of both inter- as well as intra-community relations. The Shia-Sunni schism in Lucknow, notwithstanding its local specificity, needs to be located in the context of such countrywide trends and tendencies.

It is widely known that cow-protection societies, Hindi Pracharni Sabhas and the Arya Samaj movement were designed to homogenise Hindu society through a set of common cultural and religious paradigms. Similar currents, some in response to the intellectual and cultural hegemony of the West, but most in reaction to Hindu revitalisation campaigns, gripped Muslims as well. Towards the end of the nineteenth century, in particular, the notion of a sharply defined communitarian identity, distinct and separate from others, had acquired much greater legitimacy among the north Indian *ashraf* Muslims. In the political and educational domain, Syed Ahmad Khan plotted his trajectory within a communitarian framework. The Aligarh College, the All-India Muhammadan Educational Conference, the Urdu Defence Associations and the

Muslim League had well-defined communitarian goals. They were concerned to create a Muslim identity in Indian politics.

Such moves towards political 'separatism', exemplified in the activities of Syed Ahmad and Aligarh's 'First Generation', were matched by a concerted drive to create an ordered, unified and cohesive *religious* community within the Islamic paradigm. This was the goal of the founders of the Dar al-ulum at Deoband and the Nadwat al-ulama in Lucknow. The high priests at these institutions asserted their role as interpreters and guardians with much vigour and consistency. There was much confidence in their insistence, through sheafs of *fatawa* (religious decrees), on imposing a moral and religious code consistent with Quranic injunctions and free of accretions and interpolations. Not surprisingly, over 200 books listed in London's India Office Library Catalogue, compiled by J.M. Blumhardt in 1900, dealt with ceremonial religious observances. These included compendia of religious duties, treatises on lawful and unlawful actions, and collections on religious precepts. In a nutshell, the growth of the printing press, the proliferation of vernacular newspapers and the expanding educational networks served as powerful instruments for restructuring an *ideal* community that would conform to and reflect the Islamic ethos that prevailed during the days of the Prophet and his successors.

Initially confined to northern India, the Islamic resurgence spread to other areas rapidly. Religious revivalism, conducted under the aegis of the Faraizis, had already swept the rural Muslims in the Bengal countryside. The dominant strain of the Islamisation drive was to reject composite and syncretic tendencies and create instead a pan-Islamic or a specifically pan-Indian Muslim identity. Rafiuddin Ahmed (1981: 184) has shown how religious preachers prompted the masses to look beyond the borders of Bengal in quest of their supposesd Islamic past and attach greater importance to their 'Muslim' as opposed to their local or regional identity. This new emphasis proved crucial to the subsequent emergence of a measure of social cohesion in a diversified and even culturally polarised community.

In relation to the Hindu 'Other', the meaning of being a Muslim was translated through late nineteenth-century religious and political idioms. Shias and Sunnis, on the other hand, discovered new symbols of identification in the form of separate graveyards, separate mosques, schools, and charitable endowments (Oldenburg, 1984). These institutions defined the boundaries within which Shias and Sunnis were required to stay apart. They were to live as separate entities in a world fashioned by the religio-political leadership. Attempts to disturb the *status quo* encountered strong resistance.

Sunni Islam was just as much 'corrupted' by the incorporation of Hindu beliefs and customs as by the adoption of Shia practices. So a campaign was mounted at the turn of the nineteenth century to question shared cultural, religious and intellectual paradigms and revive those controversies that had lain dormant for long. The Madhe Sahaba processions were, for example, organised with much greater fanfare in Fatehpur and Lucknow (see Zafarul Mulk, n.d.: 11).

There was, in addition, a concerted move to discourage Shia-Sunni marriages, to portray Shias as promiscuous heretics, and traitors. Frequently singled out as traitors were Mir Sadiq, *diwan* of Tipu Sultan, Mir Alam, diwan of Hyderabad, Mir Jafar, diwan of Siraj-ud Daula, and the Bilgrami family (Khalidi, 1992: 39–40). 'Among the people classed as Muslims', observed Zafarul Mulk (n.d.: 11),

The Shias and the Ahmadis are the two sects which have basic differences with Muslims and are a constant source of internecine trouble and discord . . . *It would be a real gain to the health of the body politic of Islam if these two sects were lopped off and treated as separate minorities* (emphasis added).

Mohurram practices were the chief target of attack. The central theme, underlined years later by an *alim* of Nadwat al-ulama in Lucknow, was the impropriety of giving 'vent to one's feeling of sorrow through wailing and lamentation' and crying over a past event (Nadwi, 1974: 65). Around 1933–39, considerable polemical literature surfaced against *azadari*. The Sunni press, in particular, denounced taziadari as *bidat* and *haram*. In February 1939, the Tahaffuz-i Millat sought permission to take out small processions to dissuade Sunnis by word of mouth from taziadari. Sharar, who bemoaned Shia-Sunni differences, observed how Maulvi Abdul Shakoor perfected the art of public debates (*munazirah*) with his Shia counterparts.

The indictment of Mohurram rites was by no means a new development; the severity with which it was done in Lucknow during the 1930s was somewhat unusual and had few historical precedent. It is true that orthodox Sunni treatises were critical of and averse to the Shias. In the sixteenth century, Shaikh Ahmad Sirhindi, chief exponent of the Naqshbandi *silsilah* in India, began his careeer by writing a pamphlet against the Shias. Shah Waliullah (1702–63), one of the foremost original thinkers in the history of Indian Islam, discussed the question whether Shias were *kafirs*, apostates or just immoral. Shah Abdul Aziz (1746–1824) wrote a highly polemical book in 1889 to prevent 'Sunnis from straying away from their faith in polemics with the Shias'. Deoband's Dar al-ulum, inspired by Waliullah and his disciples, was antithetical to Shia beliefs and practices. Syed Ahmad's invitation to Deoband's founders met with an emphatic refusal: they would not associate with a college that had room for Shias (Lelyveld, 1978: 134; Rizvi, 1982: 256; Metcalf, 1982; Sharar, 1975: 95). One of its foremost alim, Husain Ahmad Madani, shared this antipathy towards the Shias, though he was at the same time a major proponent of secular nationalism. Yet the diktat of an alim here or a theologian there did not undermine those values and customs that people had shared for generations. There were other schools of thought in Sunni Islam which advocated reconciliation and rap-prochement. Many of the Shia mujtahids, including the renowned Maulvi Dildar Ali, were in fact products of the Firangi Mahal in Luck-now. And there were forces linked with Sufi Islam that cemented unity and integration.

Sectarianism in the 1930s, however, was of a distinct nature. The debates then were no longer restricted to the Khilafat. Nor were the age-old controversies confined to the learned and holy men on both sides. The energy released during the decade, spurred by newly started organisations wedded to separate Sunni and Shia world views, substan-tially altered the structure of social relations. They imposed severe strains on the overall consensus, achieved through long-standing social, cultural and economic networks.

The Shias were not far behind in fortifying their claims. They tried, first of all, to rejuvenate their educational institutions which had virtu-ally collapsed in the absensce of nawabi patronage. They regarded the M.A.O. College of Aligarh as a 'Sunni' institution, though Syed Ahmad Khan had, in recognition of Shia-Sunni differences, made a provision for teaching Shia theology. They had no theological seminary of their own. And because entry to Deoband or Nadwa was restricted to Sunni stu-dents, those Shias who aspired to become religious leaders received edu-cation not in India but in Iran and Iraq. Thus Syed Abul Qasim Rizvi (d. 1906) studied in Lucknow and Najaf in Iraq. Back in Lahore, he promoted *Usuli* Shi'ism in the second half of the nineteenth century, founding congregational prayer mosques and edifices commemorating Husain's martyrdom, and establishing an *Imami* seminary in Lahore (see Cole and Keddie, 1986: Introduction, 66–7; Cole, 1988: 288–9; Frietag,

1990: 263). Maulana Syed Ali Naqi (1903–88), a descendant of the learned Ghufranmaab family, also studied in Iraq. He returned to Lucknow in 1932 and founded the Imamia Mission and a weekly magazine *Payam-i Islam*. He wrote over 300 books. Many of his writings in the mid-1930s were in defence of azadari (Rizvi, 1988).

The establishment of the Nadwat al-ulama led to the founding of a Shia school in Lucknow. The Shia college was the brainchild of a landowner of Lahore and patronised by Nawab Hamid Ali Khan of Rampur (1875–1930) and the U.P. government. Rs 3,17,410 was raised by 1916 and the college opened in 1917.[7]

Shia societies mushroomed in every quarter of Lucknow, the hub of Shia intellectual and cultural life. Prominent amongst them were the Madrasatul-Waizeen, organised on the lines of the Shibli Academy at Azamgarh and funded by the Raja of Mahmudabad; the Imamia Mission, set up by Maulana Ali Naqi; and the Tanzimul-Muminin, the Shia answer to the Tahafuzz-i Millat, which was patronised by affluent manufacturers of tobacco and perfume. These bodies were backed by an aggressive Shia-owned press—the *Sarfaraz*, an organ of the Shia Political Conference, *Shia*, published from Lahore, *Asad, Nazzara* and the *Akhbar-i Imamia*, published fortnightly (Rizvi, 1988: Chapter 5).

With developments around the country heading towards greater Hindu-Muslim friction, sectarian competition began to resemble inter-community conflicts. Not surprisingly, the process structuring sectarian conflict paralleled that of Hindu-Muslim friction in other urban centres of the United Provinces. This was, in part, because Sunnis and Shias of Lucknow could draw on the reservoir of experiences and models developed in the subcontinent during that period. That is, the nationwide impetus to define one's community provided material that could be used by both groups of Muslims (Frietag, 1990: 249). Such tendencies were not countered by a parallel ideological crusade, though individuals like Maulana Abul Kalam Azad intervened to cement the divide, heal the wounds and keep the recalcitrant parties in check.[8]

The Congress in the United Provinces grudgingly tried to defuse the mounting sectarian tensions in Lucknow. But once Shia-Sunni riots flared up, its leaders assumed ambivalent positions. Most settled for a divide-and-rule policy, doling out concessions first to the Shias and then to the Sunnis. This strategy worked for a little while. Shia leaders, having rallied round the Congress in the past, expected to be rewarded for their loyalty. The bulk of Sunni leadership was, on the other hand, enthused by Pant's gesture on 30 March 1939. But when the Muslim

League raised new hopes and expectations in the early 1940s, the Congress base among the Shias and Sunnis was eroded.

It turned out that both the context and the reference point of Shia and Sunni leaders were rapidly eroded by the powerful Muslim League drive for a separate 'Muslim nation'. The options were suddenly diminished, because the forces of an overriding and hegemonic 'Muslim nationalism' subsumed sectarian allegiances. Shias and Sunnis undertook their long trek towards the promised *dar al-Islam* (land of Islam). The ideological conflicts were, however, carried over to the new nation, where the inconclusive debates resumed with the same intensity and fervour.

NOTES

1. Syed Ali to Jawaharlal Nehru, 6 December 1945, Jawaharlal Nehru Papers, vol. 4, Nehru Memorial Museum & Library, New Delhi; Hosseinbhoy Laljee's Cablegram to Wavell, 6 April 1945, in *Shia Muslim's Case* (Bombay: Jawahar Press, n.d.), pp. 1–2, 6–96; L/P & J/8, 693; Transfer of Power Papers, L/P&J/, 10/64, IOLR (India Office Library and Records, London). 43 18 February, 16 December 1946, 16 December 1974, ibid., L/P7/J, 10, 64.

2. Shia-Sunni riots broke out in May–June 1937. The provincial government believed that they were provoked by the Shias to indicate that any change introduced in their past practices would be resisted. See Harry Haig to Linlithgow, 7 June and 4 July, 1937, 2–4 June 1938, 10 and 23 October 1939, L/P.J/5/264–6, IOLR.

3. The government appointed the Piggot Committee in 1907 to regulate Mohurram observances. This was followed by the Justice Allsop Committee recommendations of 15 June 1937. The High Court Judge endorsed the Piggot Committee's report on Madhe Sahaba. *Government Gazette of the UP, Extraordinary*, 28 March 1938, L/P&J file no. 265, pp. 139–50. IOLR.

4. G.M. Harper to Jasbir Singh, 18 March 1939, General Administration Department (GAD), file no. 65, box no. 607, Uttar Pradesh State Archives, Lucknow. Harry Haig reported that Madani insisted that the Sunnis should be allowed to assert their right to recite Madhe-Sahaba. To Linlithgow, 23 October 1939, L/PJ/5/266.

5. *Pioneer*, 24 August 1939. Kanpur's superintendent of police reported the outbreak of a Shia-Sunni riot and the impending threat of the Ahrars to take out a Madhe Sahaba procession defying government orders. 10 June 1939, Diaries, Harold Charles Mitchell Papers, IOLR. For Banaras, see Allen (1981: 246–7).

6. L/P&J/5/272. See also, fortnightly report, 2nd half of March 1940, L/P&J/5/270. In 1943, the Sunnis in Lucknow tried to revive the Madhe Sahaba agitation and defy the ban on Barawafat procession which fell about the middle of March. This led to the externment of some Sunni leaders from Lucknow. Fortnightly report, 2nd half of January 1943, L/PJ/5/272.

7. 'Establishment of a Shia College at Lucknow', 25 October 1917, UP Government

(Education), file no. 398, 1926, UPSA; Fateh Ali Khan to Meston, 21 October 1915, file no. 136/15, Meston Papers IOLR. The Raja of Mahmudabad and Syed Wazir Hasan were the only two prominent Shias who were initially opposed to the Shia College. They believed that it would weaken the Aligarh Muslim University movement and accentuate Shia-Sunni differences.

8. Azad was deputed by the Congress High Command to resolve the impasse. His personal stature aided the process of reconciliation. The Shia ulama, in particular, agreed to suspend the Tabarra agitation at his instance.

REFRENCES

Ahmad, Imtiaz (1983), 'The Shia-Sunni Dispute in Lucknow', in Milton Israel and N.K. Wagle (eds), *Islamic Society and Cultures: Essays in Honour of Professor Aziz Ahmad*, Delhi, Manohar Book Service.

Ahmed, Rafiuddin (1981), *The Bengali Muslims 1871–1906: A Quest for Identity*, Delhi, Oxford University Press.

Ali, Mrs Meer Hasan (1982), *Observations on the Musalmans of India*, London, reprint.

Allen, Charles (ed.) (1981), *Plain Tales from the Raj*, London.

Bayly, C.A. (1975), *The Local Roots of Indian Politics—Allahabad, 1880–1920*, Oxford, Clarendon Press.

Blunt, W.S. (1909), *India Under Ripon: A Private Diary*, London.

Choudhary, Valmiki (ed.) (1984), *Dr Rajendra Prasad: Correspondence and Select Documents*, Delhi.

Cole, J.R.I. (1988), *Roots of North Indian Shi'ism in Iran and Iraq: Religion and State in Awadh 1772–1859*, Berkeley, University of California Press.

Cole, J.R.I. and Nikkie R. Keddie (1986), 'Introduction', in J.R.I. Cole and Nikkie R. Keddie (eds), *Shi'ism and Social Protest*, New Jersey, Yale University Press.

Crooke, W. (1975), *The North-Western Provinces of India: Their History, Ethnology, and Administration*, Reprint, Delhi, Munshilal Banarsidas.

Dehlavi, Saiyid Ahmad (1986), *Rasoom-i Delhi*, Delhi, Urdu Academy.

Enayat, Hamid (1982), *Modern Islamic Political Thought*, London.

Riazuddin, Munshi (1885), *Bazme-i Akhir*, Delhi, Urdu Academy.

Frietag, Sandra (1990), *Collective Action and Community: Public Arenas and the Emergence of Communalism in North India*, Delhi, Oxford University Press.

Fuller, Bamfylde (1910), *Studies on Indian Life and Sentiment*, London.

Gopal, S. (ed.) (1980), *Selected Works of Jawaharlal Nehru*, Delhi, Oxford University Press.

Gunju, Sarojini (1980), 'The Muslims of Lucknow, 1919–39', in K. Ballhatchet and J. Harrison (eds), *The City in South Asia: Pre-Modern and Modern*, London.

Hamadani, Syed Mohammad Kamaluddin Husain (1978), *Siraj-i Munir*, Garhi, Aligarh.

Hasan, Mushirul (ed.) (1985), *Mohamed Ali in Indian Politics: Select Writings 1906–1916*, Delhi, Manohar.

Hasan, Mushirul (1991), *Nationalism and Communal Politics in India, 1885–1930*, Delhi, Manohar.

Hosain, Attia (1992), *Sunlight on a Broken Column*, Delhi, Penguin Books.

Hjortshoj, Keith (1987), 'Shi'i Identity and the Significance of Muharram in Lucknow, India', in Martin Kramer (ed.), *Shi'ism Resistance and Revolution*, London.

Khalidi, Qmar (1992), 'The Shias of the Deccan: An Introduction', *Hamdard Islamics*, vol. 15, no. 4.

Khuda Baksh (1912). Essays Indian and Islamic, London.

Kumar, Nita (1988), *The Artisans of Banaras: Popular Culture and Identity*, New Jersey, Princeton University Press.

Lawrence, Walter Roper (1928), *The India We Served*, London.

Lelyveld, David (1978), *Aligarh's First Generation: Muslim Solidarity in British India*, New Jersey, Princeton University Press.

Masselos, Jim (1982), 'Change and Custom in the Format of the Bombay Muharram during the Nineteenth and Twentieth Centuries', *South Asia*, December.

Metcalf, Barbara D. (1982), *Islamic Revival in British India: Deoband, 1860–1900*, New Jersey, Princeton University Press.

Moon, Penderel (1943), *Strangers to India*, London, Faber and Faber.

Nadwi, Syed Abdul Hasan Ali (1974), *The Mussalman*, Lucknow.

Oldenberg, Veena Talwar (1984), *The Making of Colonial Lucknow 1856–1877*, New Jersey, Princeton University Press.

Raza; Rahi Masoom (1994), *The Feuding Families of Village Gangauli*, Gillian Wright (trans), Delhi, Penguin Books.

Reeves, Peter D. (ed.) (1971), *Sleeman in Oudh: An Abridgement of W.H. Sleeman's Journey Through the Kingdom of Oude in 1849–50*, Cambridge, Cambridge University Press.

Rizvi, Salamat (1982), *Syed al-ulama: Hayat aur Karnamen*, Lucknow.

Ruswa, Mirza Mohammad Hadi (1982), *Umrao Jan Ada* (Courtesan of Lucknow), Khushwant Singh and M.A. Husaini (trans.), Hyderabad, Orient Paperbacks.

Sharar, Abdul Halim (1975), *Lucknow: The Last Phase of an Oriental Culture*, E.S. Harcourt and Fakhir Hussain (trans. and eds), London, Paul Elek.

Shurreef, Jaffer (1863), *Qanoon-e-Islam*, G.A. Herklots (tran.), Madras.

Zafarul Mulk (n.d.), *Shia-Sunni Dispute: Its Causes and Cure*, Servants of Islamic Society Publication, no.3.

8

Lifestyle as Resistance: The Case of the Courtesans of Lucknow

VEENA TALWAR OLDENBURG

When, in 1976, I was doing the research for a study on the social consequences of colonial urbanization in Lucknow, I came across its famous courtesans for the first time. They appeared, surprisingly, in the civic tax ledgers of 1858–77 and in the related official correspondence preserved in the Municipal Corporation records' room (see Oldenburg: 1984, Chapter 5). They were classed under the occupational category of 'dancing and singing girls', and as if it was not surprise enough to find women in the tax records, it was even more remarkable that they were in the highest tax bracket, with the largest individual incomes of any in the city. The courtesans' names were also on lists of property (houses, orchards, manufacturing and retail establishments for food and luxury items) confiscated by British officials for their proven involvement in the siege of Lucknow and the rebellion against British rule in 1857. These women, though patently noncombatants, were penalized for their instigation of and pecuniary assistance to the rebels. On yet another list, some twenty pages long, are recorded the spoils of war seized from one set of 'female apartments' in the palace and garden complex called the Kaisar Bagh, where some of the deposed ex-King Wajid Ali Shah's three hundred or more consorts resided when it was seized by the British. It is a remarkable list, eloquently evocative of a privileged existence: gold and silver ornaments studded with precious stones, embroidered cashmere wool and brocade shawls, bejewelled caps and shoes, silver-, gold-, jade-, and amber-handled fly whisks, silver cutlery, jade goblets, plates, spitoons, hookahs, and silver utensils for serving and storing food and drink, and

valuable furnishings. The value of this part of the booty of war was estimated at nearly four million rupees.

These courtesans appeared in other British colonial records as well.
They were the subject of frequent official memorandums written in
connection with a grave medical crisis that engulfed the military establishment in Lucknow, as well as in all the major cantonments in British
India. A greater number of European casualties during 1857, it was discovered, were caused by disease rather than in combat. The shock of this
discovery was compounded by the embarrassing fact that one in every
four European soldiers was afflicted with a venereal disease. It became
clear that the battle to reduce European mortality rates would now be
joined on the hygienic front, to ensure a healthy European army for the
strategic needs of the empire. It became imperative that the courtesans
and prostitutes of Lucknow, along with those in the other 110 cantonments in India (and in several towns in Britain), where European soldiers
were stationed, be regulated, inspected, and controlled. The provisions
of Britain's Contagious Diseases Act of 1864 were incorporated into a
comprehensive piece of legislation, Act XXII of 1864 in India; it required
the registration and periodic medical examination of prostitutes in all
cantonment cities of the Indian empire (Oldenburg, 1984; also see Ballhatchet, 1980).

The British usurpation of the Kingdom of Awadh in 1856 and the
forced exile of the king and many of his courtiers had abruptly put an end
to royal patronage for the courtesans. The imposition of the contagious
diseases regulations and heavy fines and penalties on the courtesans for
their role in the rebellion signalled the gradual debasement of an esteem-
ed cultural institution into common prostitution. Women, who had
once consorted with kings and courtiers, enjoyed a fabulously opulent
living, manipulated men and means for their own social and political
ends, been the custodians of culture and the setters of fashion trends,
were left in an extremely dubious and vulnerable position under the
British. 'Singing and dancing girls' was the classification invented to
describe them in the civic tax ledgers and encapsulates one of the many
profound cultural misunderstandings of 'exotic' Indian women by colonial authorities.

These new challenges provoked these women to intensify their struggle
to keep out an intrusive civic authority that taxed their incomes and
inspected their bodies. Characteristically they responded by keeping two
sets of books on their income, bribing the local *dai*, or nurse, to avoid
bodily inspections, bribing local policemen to avoid arrests for selling

liquor to the soldiers, or publicly refusing to pay taxes even when threatened with imprisonment. The tactics were new but the spirit behind them was veteran. These methods were imaginative extensions of the ancient and subtle ways the courtesans had cultivated to contest male authority in their liaisons with men and add to a spirited defense of their own rights against colonial politics. Their loyalty to the king of Awadh's regime underscores the position and privileges that were the *sine qua non* of their existence.

In a departure from the conventional perspective on this profession, I would argue that these women, even today, are independent and consciously involved in the covert subversion of a male-dominated world; they celebrate womanhood in the privacy of their apartments by resisting and inverting the rules of gender of the larger society of which they are part. Their way of life is not complicitous with male authority; on the contrary, in their own self-perceptions, definitions, and descriptions they are engaged in ceaseless and chiefly nonconfrontational resistance to the new regulations and the resultant loss of prestige they have suffered since colonial rule began. It would be no exaggeration to say that their 'life-style' *is resistance to rather than a perpetuation of patriarchal values.*

Quite unexpectedly, another set of archival documents led me to a group of courtesans living in Lucknow in 1976, proud descendants of those who had survived first the pressures of a century of systematic harassment by the colonial authorities and then the ban placed on their activities by the government of independent India. These documents were the intercepted letters written by Wajid Ali Shah to some of his wives, whom he had been forced to abandon in 1856. I engaged a young Persian scholar, Chhote Miyan to help me decipher these Persian letters. He not only provided the entree required to visit this group of courtesans but also, quite fortuitously, the key to comprehending their world. He explained why he had only been given a pet name instead of a serious Muslim family name. He was the son of a courtesan and she had never revealed to him the identity of his father. Ironically, his own life story had all the elements of the socialization and upbringing accorded to a girl in a 'normal' household.

While I love and respect my mother and all my 'aunts' [other courtesans] and my grandmother, my misfortune is that I was born a son and not a daughter in their house. When a boy is born in the kotha [salon], the day is without moment, even one of quiet sadness. When my sister was born there was a joyous celebration that was unforgettable. Everyone received new clothes, there was singing, dancing, and feasting. My aunts went from door to door distributing sweets.

My sister is, today, a beautiful, educated, propertied woman. She will also·

inherit what my mother and grandmother own. She will have a large income from rents; she doesn't even have to work as a courtesan, if she so chooses. I am educated, but I have no money or property. Jobs are very hard to come by, so I live in a room and subsist on a small allowance that my mother gives in exchange for running errands for her and helping her deal with her lawyers. [She was trying to evict a tenant from a house she owned.] She paid for my education but a degree is pretty worthless these days. My only hope is that I may marry a good woman who has money and who gives me sons so they can look after me in my old age or find a way of getting a job in Dubai, as my cousin did. Otherwise my chances in life are pretty dim. Funny isn't it, how these women have made life so topsy-turvy?

In order to appreciate this rather remarkable inversion in a society that blatantly favours males over females, a brief sketch of the historical background of the *tawaif,* or the courtesans of Lucknow, is in order. At all Hindu and Muslim courts in the many kingdoms that made up the subcontinent before the British began to conquer them and displace their rulers, the courtesans were an influential female elite. The courtesans of Lucknow were especially reputable. They had established themselves at the Awadh court in the eighteenth century, under the lavish patronage of the chief noblemen, merchants, and the official elite of the capital city. Abdul Halim Sharar (1975: 192) tells of their compelling role in court politics.

A cultivated man like Hakim Mahdi, who later became Vazir [prime minister of Awadh], owed his initial success to a courtesan named Piyaro, who advanced her own money to enable him to make an offering to the ruler on his first appointment as Governor of the Province of Awadh. These absurdities went so far that it is said that until a person had association with courtesans he was not a polished man . . . At the present time [*c.* 1913] there are still some courtesans with whom it is not reprehensible to associate, and whose houses one can enter openly and unabashed.

While implying that the coming of the British had left these women as a beleaguered community, Sharar was strongly of the opinion that the morals, manners, and distinctiveness of Lucknow culture and society were sustained by the courtesans. Ensconced as they were in lavish apartments in the city's main Chowk Bazar, and in the Kaisar Bagh palace, they were not only recognised as preservers and performers of the high culture of the court, but they actively shaped the developments in Hindustani music and Kathak dance styles (see Manuel, 1987). Their style of entertainment was widely imitated in other Indian court cities and their enduring influence on the Hindi film is all too patent. They commanded great respect in the court and in society, and association with them bestowed prestige on those who were invited to their salons for cultural soirees. It was not uncommon for young sons of the nobility to be sent to the best-known salons for instruction in etiquette, the art of conversation and polite manners, and the appreciation of Urdu literature.

In Lucknow, the world of the tawaif was as complex and hierarchical as the society of which it was part. Courtesans were and still are usually a part of a larger establishment run by a *chaudharayan*, or chief courtesan, an older woman who has retired to the position of manager after a successful career as a tawaif. Having acquired wealth and fame, such women were able to recruit and train women who came to them, along with the more talented daughters of the household. Typically a wealthy courtier, often the king himself, began his direct association with a *kotha* by bidding for a virgin whose patron he became with the full privileges and obligations of that position. He was obliged to make regular contributions in cash and jewelry and privileged to invite his friends to soirees and enjoy an exclusive sexual relationship with a tawaif. His guests were expected to impress the management with their civilities and substance so that they would qualify as patrons of the women who were still unattached. The chaudharayan always received a fixed proportion (approximately one-third) of the earnings to maintain the apartments; hire and train other dancing girls; and attract the musicians, chefs, and special servants that such establishments employed. Many of the musicians belonged to famous lineages and much of late-nineteenth-century Hindustani music was invented and transformed in these salons, to accommodate the new urban elite who filled the patronage vacuum in the colonial period.

The household had other functionaries beyond the core group of daughters or nieces of the senior tawaif. These women, called *thakahi* and *randi*, were affiliates of a kotha but were ranked lower; their less remarkable appearance and talent restricted them to providing chiefly sexual services in rather more austere quarters downstairs. Another interesting group of women secretly associated with the establishment were *khangi*, or women who were married and observed strict purdah, but who, for financial or other reasons, came to the kotha for clandestine liaisons; the chaudharayan collected a fee from them for her hospitality. Doormen, watchmen, errand boys, tailors, palanquin carriers, and others, who lived in the lower floors of the house, or in detached servants quarters, and were also often kinsmen, screened suspicious characters at the door, acted as protectors of the house, and spied on the activities of the police and medical departments. Pimps or other male agents simply did not exist, then or later.

It is popularly believed that the chaudharayan's most common mode of recruitment has always been kidnapping; that the tawaif were linked to a large underground network of male criminals who abducted very young girls from villages and small towns and sold them to the kothas or *nishatkhanas* [literally, pleasure houses]. This belief was fuelled, if not actually generated, by Lucknow's famous poet and litterateur, Mirza Hadi Ruswa, in his *Umrao Jan Ada*. The novel first appeared in 1905, was an immediate success and was translated into English in 1961 (Ruswa, 1982). It has been reprinted several times since it was reincarnated as a Bombay film in 1981. The influence this novel has exerted on the popular imagination is enormous; it is the single most important source of information on courtesans of Lucknow, and by extension, the entire profession as it was practised in the nineteenth century, in northern India. Set in the second half of the nineteenth century, it is a melodramatic story of a tawaif, Umrao Jan, who as a beautiful child of five, is kidnapped and sold to a tawaif in Lucknow, where she trains and becomes, after a few complicated twists and turns in the plot, a renowned and much-sought-after courtesan. Ruswa uses the classic ploy of writing an introduction wherein he explains that he is merely recording the true story of Umrao Jan, told to him by the protagonist herself. His use of the first person in the 'memoir', in which the courtesan frequently addresses him by name, makes it all the more convincing.

Ruswa was a regular participant at several salons and the glimpses he provides of the rigorous training and the world view of the courtesan are quite accurate historically. What is less known is that Ruswa had a keen interest in crime and several of his translations and adaptations were of contemporary Victorian and Urdu potboilers. He published a then-popular series of *khuni* novels some of whose titles, such as *Khuni Shahzada* [The killer prince], *Khuni Joru* [The killer wife], *Khuni Ashiq* [The killer lover], betray his predilection for the sensational. One of the older courtesans I interviewed, who had known Ruswa personally, gave the book a mixed review. She commended Ruswa for understanding the mentality of the courtesan but blamed him for inventing characters such as the 'evil kidnapper' and the exploitative madame who became the stuff of later stereotypes.

The greatest harm was done to the reputation of the kotha, however, by British political propaganda. The older courtesans I interviewed, who felt keenly about contemporary politics, and had connections among the local power elite, were impressively knowledgeable about the history of their city. In their view it was official British policy to malign the courtesans and the culture of salons, in order to justify the British role as usurpers of the throne of Awadh in 1856. British high-handedness in this and other policies unleashed a widespread rebellion in north and central India in 1857, which raged for ten months in Awadh. To consolidate their rule in the Province of Awadh, the British turned their fury against the powerful elite of Lucknow, of which the tawaif were an integral part. Yet, when it came to matters such as using these women as prostitutes for the European garrison, or collecting income tax, the eminently pragmatic British set aside their high moral dudgeon. It became official policy to select the healthy and beautiful 'specimens' from among the kotha women and arbitrarily relocate them in the cantonment for the convenience of the European soldiers. This not only debased the profession, stripping it of its cultural function, but it also made sex cheap and easy for the men while exposing the women to venereal infection from the soldiers.

Kidnapping may have been (and perhaps still is) one of the methods by which girls find their way into the tawaif households, but it is certainly not the most common. From my interviews with the thirty women, who today live in the Chowk area of Lucknow, and whose ages ranged from thirty-five to seventy-eight, a very different picture emerged. In recording the life stories of these women, who spanned three generations, I found that the compelling circumstance that brought the majority of them to the various tawaif households in Lucknow was the misery they endured in either their natal or their conjugal homes. Four of these women were widowed in their early teens, two of whom hailed from the same district and had lost their husbands in a cholera epidemic; three were sold by their parents when famine conditions made feeding these girls impossible. Seven were victims of physical abuse, two of whom were sisters who were regularly beaten by their alcoholic father for not obliging him by making themselves sexually available to the toddy seller. Three were known victims of rape and therefore deemed ineligible for marriage; two had left their ill-paid jobs as municipal sweeper women, because they were tired of 'collecting other people's dirt'; two were battered wives; one had left her husband because he had a mistress; and one admitted no particular hardship, only a love for singing and dancing that was not countenanced in her orthodox Brahmin home. Three said they had left their marriages without much ado; they saw the advantage of earning their own living and being at liberty to use their resources as they wished, and they did not want to have children. Only four of them were daughters of other tawaif. Not one claimed that kidnapping had been her experience, although they had heard of such cases. This assortment of refugees from the *sharif*, or respectable, world gave a completely ironic slant to the notion of respectability. The problem, according to Saira Jan, a plump woman in her early forties, who recounted her escape from a violent, alcoholic husband at length and with humour, was that there were no obliging kidnappers in her mohalla (neighborhood). 'Had there been such *farishte* [angels] in Hasanganj I would not have had to plot and plan my own escape at great peril to my life and my friends, who helped me.'

This catalogue reflects the wide range of miserable circumstances from which these women had escaped. Desertion has been traditionally resorted to by those trapped in situations they had no other effective means of fighting or changing. Gulbadan, who was a chaudharayan from her late thirties (she claims she was born in 1900 and initiated when she was thirteen years old) had been the niece of a tawaif and was raised in the household she now managed. She spoke of the kotha as a sanctuary for both women and men; women found in it a greater peace and freedom than in the normal world; men escaped the boredom of their domestic lives. She reminded Saira that she was a miserable, underweight, frightened wretch when she had first appeared at her doorstep. 'She was thin as a stick, her complexion was blotchy, her eyes sunk in black holes, and she had less than two rupees tied to the end of her sari. Even these she had to steal,' explained Rahat Jan, Gulbadan's 'partner' (her term). 'Now look at her, we call her our *hathini* who eats milk and *jalebi* to keep her voice dulcet.'

Most women told their stories with enthusiasm. They had wanted to escape 'hell' (the word *jahannum*, the Islamic hell, was frequently used to describe their earlier homes) at any cost. Learning professional skills and earning their own money helped them develop self-esteem and value the relative independence they encountered in Rahat Jan's kotha. It may well be that some of the women exaggerated the horrors of the past, but the kernels of their stories were embedded in the reality of the gender bias in society. Here they could be women first, and Hindus and Muslims in a more mutually tolerant way, because the culture of the kotha represented elements of both and was acknowledged as a truly syncretic tradition.

There were many stories, each with its own flavour of horror, and of courage, and none that did not have a relatively happy ending. Comparable employment opportunities for women simply did not exist then and are few and far between even now. Gulbadan explained that not all women in need can make the kotha their refuge; some are not talented enough to become courtesans, and some are too anxious about their moral standing. Women, particularly from the higher strata of Hindu and Muslim society, fear violent reprisals if discovered by their families or shrink from exposure to strange men. She went on to say that 'many women flee their homes in the villages and come to the anonymity of the city to work as domestic servants, as *ayahs* [nannies] or maids or cooks. Some join road gangs run by government or private building contractors only to break bricks into small pieces with a hammer, all day in the sun, and earn in a month what we make in a few hours of passing the time in civilized company. To make ends meet they have to sleep with their employers and the *dalal*, or middlemen, who found them their jobs, and get beaten up by their husbands when they find out. Gulbadan explained that 'a woman compromises her dignity twenty-four hours of the day when she has no control over her body or her money'. This response was unanimously endorsed by the other courtesans.

The women who said that their own parents had sold them when they were unable to feed them, much less pay for a wedding and a dowry, felt that their parents were forced by circumstances to make such a hard decision. Yet they sent money home every month to take care of their impoverished families, which was gratefully received, and whatever resentment they may have felt for being abandoned as children had dissipated through understanding the limits imposed on women in this world. Gulbadan, who spoke more aphoristically than the others, explained that even fifty years ago, there was very little scope for women to change the lives they grumblingly led:

What they couldn't change they called their *qismat*, their fate. Here, in our world, even though things are not as good as they were before the British came, women changed their qismat. Even philosophers and poets will tell you that no one can change their qismat. Ask these women, who have lived and worked together for more than twenty years, whether or not they think that I taught them how to mould their own fate like clay with their own hands.

I did, and they agreed, with laughing nods, while they celebrated Janmashtami and Id on the third floor of Gulbadan's impressively large building. And this was the very essence of their world view.

Gulbadan had tossed this off as she sat on the large platform covered with an old Persian rug and velvet and brocade bolsters that propped her up. Watching her deft fingers prepare a *paan*, I felt I was in the presence of an alchemist who had transformed base fortunes into gold. She, along with her septuagenarian friends, had inherited a way of life and struggled to preserve it, quite selfishly, in the face of an increasingly hostile future. Their business was neither to exploit women, nor to transform the lot of the generality of womankind, but to liberate and empower those with whom they were associated. The high level of camaraderie, wit, teasing, and affectionate interaction that I observed and participated in on several visits to the apartments of the older women over ten years affirmed this impression repeatedly. The process of 'changing one's fate' (*qismat badalna*) is, under closer scrutiny, a psychosocial process through which the social construction of gender (and sexuality, as we shall see) is stripped bare. The chaudharayan act in several capacities, the most challenging being to inspire, in the women who come to them, a confidence in their own ability and worth, restore shattered nerves, set about undoing the socialization they had received in their natal homes. This delicate and difficult task, at one level, is not unlike the task modern psychotherapy purports to perform in Western society. The problem, according to Rasulan, was to forget the expectations inherent in the meaning of the word *aurat*, or woman, as it obtained in the larger society.

The process of rehabilitation for these women is rapid since they generally arrive young and are plunged into a welcoming environment. The self-affirming ethos of the kotha makes it possible for them to assimilate their newly revised perceptions and behavior patterns while living among a host of nurturing and supportive women and without the fear of men. Freedom from the pressure of the 'marriage market' where grooms were 'for sale' to the woman with the largest dowry, they unanimously agreed, gave them the inner courage to develop their skills and treat men as equals, or even as inferiors.

There are other therapeutic devices invented over the ages that are still in use in these salons. Novices are introduced to a secret repertoire of satirical and bawdy songs, dances, informal miming, and dramatic representations, aimed at the institution of marriage and heterosexual relations. These entertainments are privately performed only among women. These 'matinee shows' as they jokingly call them, are not only crucial for the solidarity and well-being of the group, but they also help the newcomers to discard the old and internalise the new meaning of being an aurat. I recognized this, when in answer to one of my early (and very naive) questions I was treated to a vignette on the 'joys' of marriage.

The women pointed out that those who dare to hold 'moral' objections to the life of a tawaif should first examine the thankless toil of an average housewife, including her obligation to satisfy a sometimes faithless or alcoholic or violent husband for the sake of a meager living. Such an existence is without dignity, and was not the situation of the housewife tantamount to that of a common prostitute, giving her body for money. 'It is we who are brought up to live in *sharafat* [genteel respectability] with control over our bodies and our money and they who suffer the degradation reserved for lowly [*neech*] women.'

Such vivid reversals of social perception and logic are stock idioms in the courtesan's speech and song. Male affines, particularly fathers and brothers-in-law, are caricatured in countless risque episodes enacted regularly and privately among women. They mock the repressive relationships and male sexuality in the conjugal home, even as they amuse, educate, and edify the denizens of the kotha. The routines, studded with subversive and irreverent jokes and obscence gestures, are performed like secret anti-rites which have been carefully distilled and historically transmitted from generation to generation, to form the core of their private consciousness and oral heritage.

I had also seriously questioned the courtesans' use of the *burqa*. It was, at first, inexplicable why tawaif not only used the burqa to move around when they went visiting or shopping, but actually insisted that I too should wear one as they led me to other kothas in the vicinity, because injunctions about female modesty did not apply to them. It was precisely because they were not expected to be in purdah, they reasoned, in another classic reversal of patriarchal logic, that they chose to block the gaze of men. It was an extension of the autonomy they enjoyed in their living space and their *jism* (bodies), unlike 'normal' women whose bodies were the property of their husbands and who were secluded but lacked privacy in their own homes. The latter were kept in *purdah* to maintain (and increase) *khandani izzat*, or family honour; for them to show their faces in public would bring disgrace to their families. 'Ah, but our case is just the opposite,' said Saira, 'men long to see our faces. If they could brag among their friends that they had seen Gulbadan or Amiran in the bazaar without a covering, they would go up in the esteem in which their friends hold them. We are not in the business of giving them cheap thrills. While we walk freely and anonymously in public places, looking at the world through our nets, they are deprived because we have blinkered *them*. We do not, as you know, bestow anything on men without extracting its price.' I would have disputed this had I not experienced the freedom the burqa gave me to walk along the winding alleys in a very old-fashioned and gossip-filled city, where I formerly never passed without being accosted with vulgar taunts from the idle youths who mill on the streets. These women had appropriated the power of the gaze while eluding the leer of sexually frustrated men.

A great deal has been said and is known about the rigorous training and education courtesans undergo to ultimately please and entertain their patrons. What has never received discursive treatment, because of its very nature, is their secret skill—the art of *nakhra*, or pretense, that courtesans have to master in order to spare no opportunity of coaxing money out of their patron and his friends. Their avowed and unabashed purpose is to amass a tidy fortune as early in their careers as possible, so that they can invest the surplus in income-producing properties or enterprises and retire comfortably at the age of thirty-five or so. To achieve their material ambitions, they use, in addition to their exorbitant charges, an arsenal of devious 'routines' that make up the hidden text of an evening's entertainment. These are subtly deployed to bargain, cajole, and extort extra cash or kind from their unsuspecting clients. Some of these are learned, some invented, some even improvised, but nuances are refigured with care to suit the temperament of a client, or the mood of the moment, to appear 'spontaneous'. Repeated rehearsals by the trainee are evaluated by the adept tawaif, until no trace of the pretense is discernible.

These well-practiced ploys—the feigned headache that interrupts a dance or a song, feigned anger for having been neglected, a sprained ankle, tears, a jealous rage—have beguiled generations of men to lose thousands of extra rupees or gold coins to these women. The tawaifs refusal, at a critical juncture, to complete a sexual interlude with a favorite patron is a particularly profitable device, because feigned coital injuries or painful menstrual cramps involve expensive and patient waiting on the part of the patron. Gulbadan said she often carried the game a step further by 'allying' herself with the patron against the 'offering' courtesan to set the seal of authenticity on the scene. She would scold and even slap her till the patron begged her not to be so harsh. Gulbadan was the privately acclaimed champion of these more serious confidence tricks and others cheerfully confessed to having blackmailed, stolen, lied, and cheated for material gain as soon as they acquired competence in this art. This may sound more like self-enrichment than resistance, but because society has virtually denied women control over wealth or property, it is essential to establishing a countercultural way of life.

The formula, Gulbadan confided, is to win the complete trust of the man. This they do by first mastering all the information about the man—his public reputation, his finances, his foibles and vanities, his domestic life, and the skeletons in his closet.

Not many come here openly any more because our salons are regarded as houses of ill-repute in the these modern times. Most come to drink and for sexual titillation. We know how to get a man drunk and pliant, so that we can extort whatever we want from him: money, even property, apologies, jewels, perfume, or other lavish gifts. Industrialists, government officers, other businessmen come here now; they have a lot of black money (undeclared cash) that they bring with them, sometimes without even counting it. We make sure that they leave with very little, if any. We know those who will pay large sums to insure secrecy, so we threaten them with careless gossip in the bazaar or with an anonymous note addressed to their fathers or their wives.

We do not act collectively as a rule but sometimes it may becomes necessary to do so. We once did a drama against a money lender who came and would not pay us the money he had promised for holding an exclusive soiree for him. So when a police officer who had fallen in love with me came by, we all told him tales of how the wretched man would not return jewels some of us had pawned with him. We filed a police report, he was arrested, and some of the pawned items (which the jeweler had taken from some of our recently straitened noble patrons) were made over to us by the lovelorn officer; others of his debtors sent us sweets and thanks for bringing the hated Ram Swarup to justice. But our biggest gambit of all is the game of love that makes these men come back again and again, some until they are financially ruined. They return every evening, like the flocks of homing pigeons, in the vain belief that it is *we* who are in love with *them*.

In Ruswa's 1905 novel about Lucknow's courtesans, this particular nakhra is insightfully described by the protagonist, Umrao Jan:

I am but a courtesan in whose profession love is a current coin. Whenever we want to ensnare anyone we pretend to fall in love with him. No one knows how to love more than we do: to have deep sighs; to burst into tears at the slightest pretext; to go without food for days on end; to sit dangling our legs on the parapets of wells ready to jump into them; to threaten to take arsenic. All these are parts of our game of love. But I tell you truthfully, no man ever really loved me nor did I love any man.

A discussion of the feigning of love for men (a discussion which occurred only after several visits) brought perhaps the most startling 'hidden' text to light. It was difficult to imagine that these women, even though they were economically independent, educated, and in control of their lives, would spurn the opportunity for real intimacy and emotional stability. Everyone agreed that emotional needs do not disappear with success, fame, or independence; on the contrary, they often intensify. Almost every one of the women I interviewed during these many visits claimed that their closest emotional relationships were among themselves, and eight of them admitted, when I pressed them, that their most satisfying physical involvements were with other women. They referred to themselves as *chapat baz*, or lesbians, and to *chapti*, or *chipti*, or *chapat bazi*, or lesbianism. They seemed to attach little importance to labels and made no verbal distinctions between homosexual and heterosexual relations. There was no other 'serious' or poetic term for lesbianism, so I settled for the colloquialisms. Their explanation for this was that emotions and acts of love are gender-free. 'Serious' words such as *mohabbat* or *prem* or 'love' are versatile and can be used to describe many kinds of love, such as the love of man or woman, the love for country, for siblings, parents of either sex, so there was no need to have a special term for love between two women. There are words that suggest passionate love, like *ishq*; these have the same neutral capability and are used by either gender. Although their lesbianism is a strictly private matter for them, the absence of a specialized vocabulary makes it a simple fact of life, like heterosexual love, or the less denied male homosexual love. The lack of terminology or the scrambling of pronouns may also be interpreted as the ultimate disguise for it; if something cannot be named it is easy to deny its existence. In Urdu poetry, ambiguity about gender is not uncommon, and homosexual love often passes for heterosexual love.

The frank discussions on the subject of their private sexuality left some of my informants uneasy. I had probed enough into their personal affairs, they insisted, and they were not going to satisfy my curiosity any further; they were uncomfortable with my insistence on stripping their strategic camouflage, by which they also preserved their emotional integrity. Their very diffidence to talk about their lesbianism underscores the thesis that they believe in a quiet, but profound, subversion of patriarchal values. It became clear that for many of them heterosexuality itself is the ultimate nakhra and feigned passion an occupational hallmark. My ardor for precise statistics faded as the real and theoretical implications of their silences and their disguises began to emerge. And it is to these that I now turn.

What do all these stories signify? Does the courtesans' presentation of their life-style add up to a subversion of existing gender relations in heterosexual marriage? Can their beliefs and behavior be seen as 'feminist' by modern standards, or are they just another example of that allegedly widespread affliction, 'false consciousness'? How do we reconcile the horizontal stratifications of class with the vertical divide of gender and their anomalous position in either group? Do they qualify as a sub-altern group as women or as an elite group by virtue of their power and connections? Does this life-style not signify that sexuality, including lesbianism, is indeed socially contructed? Let me begin to hack at this thicket by citing Romila Thapar's perspective on Hindu ascetics. In tak-ing ascetics (an equally unlikely-seeming group of rebels) both as indi-viduals or in organised groups, as dissenters, she sees in their rejection of the *grahasta-ashrama*, or the householder stage the essence of their rebellion.

An aging *grahasta* [householder] taking to *sannyasa* [the ascetic life] was merely conforming to the ideal vita . . . The negation of the family as a basic unit of society is evident from the opposition to the *grahasta* status and specially the insistence on celibacy. [Inherent in] the act of opting out of the existing life-style and substituting it with a distinctively different one . . . [is that] the characteris-tics of the new life-style be seen as a protest against the existing one. To this extent such movements may be regarded as movements of dissent. But the element of protest was muted by the wish, not to change society radically, but to stand aside and create an alternative system. (Thapar, 1978).

The life-style of female ascetics could ·not be reckoned as a true counterpart because, as Thapar points out, female ascetics, with few ex-ceptions, were always subordinate to the authority of males. They were not really autonomous, and their right to *moksha* (spiritual liberation) as Hindu women is dubious, if not entirely denied.

I would argue that the true female counterpart of the rebellious asce-tic, and perhaps the far more daring, is the tawaif. By listening carefully to the stories the courtesans tell, it becomes undeniable that they, too, are rebelling, all the more explicitly, against the housewifely stage, since this is the *only* 'stage of life' implicitly mandated for all women in both Hindu and Islamic cultural systems. It is in this stage that the woman must achieve total fulfillment, because she does not graduate, as the man does, to a more mature level. The informal 'student stage' for a girl used to be, and still is for the majority, the acquisition of practical experience in housework and childcare. Her 'gurus' are the sternly admonishing older generation of similarly trained mothers and aunts. Modesty, obedi-ence, and other subordinate behavior patterns are drilled into her until she comes to hold the single-minded belief that her eligibility for marriage is the only index of her worth. It is the 'normal' woman's social and sexual regimen that courtesans-in-the-making must unlearn and supplant by undergoing a radically different socialisation process and adopt the life-style that gives them the liberation they desire, without jerking the reflexive muscle of a repressive system.

Although life-styles of the male ascetic and the female courtesan are both modes of social dissent, the sexual differences, and the social prescriptions on which they are predicated, produce interestingly contrasted strategies and ideologies. The former emerges from a religious interpretation of grahasta with the *denial* of sexuality, lineage, and property ownership, as its strategic thrust to gain spiritual liberation. The latter, on the other hand, emerges from the secular and domestic context in which women's lives are enmeshed. The courtesans seek material and social liberation by reversing the constraints imposed on women's chastity and economic rights and by establishing a female lineage of selected and ascriptive members who make up their *gharana*. The male becomes celibate, renounces property and the privileges of his gender in this world of 'other-worldly' rewards; the female becomes sexually active and aggressively acquisitive, prefers autonomy to 'virtue', and seeks this-worldly 'women's liberation'.

Yet some consequences of these divergent paths are strikingly similar. Both life-styles subvert the hierarchies of caste and class, because in both groups lower caste and economically disadvantaged persons find refuge. The tawaif have created a secular meritocracy based on talent and education, accepting Hindus and Muslims alike. They too, like the ascetics, hold positions of respect by the society at large, and both counter-cultures exist by maintaining vital links to the overarching patriarchal culture, while consciously inverting or rejecting its values. Although neither group has the pretension of changing the entrenched notions of the householder stage, both serve their own personal ends by elaborate strategies of avoidance. By opting for the institutional security of a monastery or a brothel, both groups wielded political power in the past through the powerful heads of sects in ancient Hindu kingdoms in the subcontinent or through the chaudharayan in pre-colonial Lucknow and other court cities, such as Hyderabad, Rampur, Banaras, Bijapur, and Golkonda. In unfavourable historical circumstances, both groups lost political power, but their patented life-styles still remain viable modes for women and men to elude the shackles of patriarchy and seek their own brands of liberation.

During the reign of the nawabs of Awadh, these women could manipulate powerful courtiers and the nawabs themselves, and even the most powerful patron did not have any authority over the women's lives. The executive authority and managerial functions were the exclusive preserve of the chaudharayan and her appointees. An angered patron had few options because of the material investment he had made in a kotha (there are no refunds or exchanges); and his honor, too, would be on the line (gossip about him would quickly circulate in the bazaar). It is therefore not the patron who is ultimately significant but the matron, *who* creates the ethos, reputation, and the quality of life and services in her establishment.

The courtesan's position is of course much diminished by the events and reconfigurations of power in the colonial and post-colonial periods. Fully aware of this history, these women find hope in other educational and employment opportunities that have recently opened up for women, for their basic goal is to free themselves from direct economic dependence on men. They already had daughters or nieces competing for and obtaining posts in the banking system, or as pleaders in the local courts, but these professions were not, as Chhote Miyan, the Persian-speaking son of one of the courtesans and my first informant, pointed out, a way of life. Women might become financially independent but without the refuge of the kotha they would again be forced to marry and possibly suffer the degradation at the hands of unsympathetic husbands. Amiran's daughter, a banker, chose to marry. 'We were wary of this alliance,' Amiran recollected, 'and sure enough her husband took up with another woman and my daughter and granddaughter are back with us. She looks after our investments and bank work, so that she does really contribute to the household with her labor just as we all do.' In other words, they shrewdly recognized that while financial independence was important, it did not solve the central problem of the gender inequality inherent within marriage in a patriarchal society.

The courtesans have uniquely combined the elements of struggle for their material *needs* with those of an ideological struggle against patriarchal *values*, by creating and hiding behind their many masks. They live in outward harmony with male power and male sexuality, for the struggle can only be effective if their subterfuges are mistaken for compliance and their true intentions as collusion with men against *other women*. Their cooperation with some women outside the kotha, such as the khangi, or the married women to whom they rent space, so that they too can earn (undisclosed) extra money is also little known, as it would be no longer politic or possible if it were uncovered.

It is for these reasons that courtesans have had to resort to outward conformity and the 'partial transcript', as Scott calls the off-stage behavior of Sedaka peasants: 'That the poor should dissemble in the face of

1. Colonel Jean-Baptiste Gentil.

2. Nawab Asif ud-Daullah.

3. The attack of Lucknow by the Sepoys, 30th July 1857.

4. Butler's Palace.

5. Kaiserbagh Palace.

6. The house of the Maharaja of Ayodhya.

7. Chattar Manzil.

8. The UP Secretariat.

9. Rickshawallahs in Hazratganj.

10. In the heart of Aminabad.

11. The University.

12. A Hindu temple in the centre of the Chowk.

power is hardly an occasion for surprise. . . . No close account of the life of subordinate classes can fail to distinguish between what is said "backstage" and what may be safely declared openly (Scott, 1985: 9)'. If it can still be argued that no matter what the tawaif's self-perceptions, actions, goals, and ideology are, they were and are still complicitous in perpetuating patriarchal relations in society, it is to insist on the ideal instead of the possible in a struggle for power. As Gulbadan, the oldest courtesan I interviewed, responded to this question: 'I know we are blamed for enabling men to perpetuate their double moral standards and dominating women. Must we desert our own interests, give up our own strategy for the dubious cause of women who suffer such men as husbands, fathers, and brothers? Today we are silent, we are despised and the law has cracked down on us; has that helped the cause of women or only made life harder for us?' In fact, their silence is so complete that, for all official intents and purposes (such as taxation), this category of women is no longer acknowledged in post-colonial India. This for them is a mixed result. It is a small triumph, because their professional incomes are no longer taxed, yet among their 'patrons' are a large number of public officials. It is a larger defeat because officialdom can piously claim that they have banned female sexual exploitation while converting their once-proud profession into a species of 'vice'.

And finally I return to the question of sexuality, as reality and as a nakhra, because there is the larger question, that of the social construction of sexuality, that may well be illuminated by analyzing the world view of courtesans of Lucknow. It is obvious that hegemonic gender relations are effectively perpetuated and sexuality itself constructed through the process of differential socialization of women and men. I would [tentatively] argue further that by systematically reversing the socialization process for females, in order to combat the disabilities inherent in women's existing social and sexual roles, the courtesans have logically 'constructed' lesbian existence as a legitimate alternative, just as much as Indian society at large constructs and enforces, through the institution of compulsory marriage, heterosexuality as 'normative' behaviour. Heterosexual relations for most of the courtesans was work, not pleasure. Right from birth, if we recall the testimony of Chhote Miyan, the female is celebrated, empowered, cherished; those who arrive as adolescents in the kotha are methodically reeducated within the context of this parallel and exclusive society of women, and its 'women-centered' vision of power relations. Their relationships with men in the kotha are congenial but businesslike; except for kin, only very few ever become emotional bondsmen. Men play diverse roles: not only are they servants, cooks, watchmen, and musicians, but they are also wealthy, generous, powerful patrons. The latter relate on equal terms with the courtesans precisely because power is genuinely shared in that cultural setting. Arguably, it is therefore in the kotha, rather than in the 'normal' world, that female sexuality has the chance of being more fairly and fearlessly constructed by women.

REFERENCES

Ballhatchet, Kenneth A. (1980), *Race, Sex and Class under the Raj*, London, Weidenfeld and Nicholson.

Manuel, Peter (1987), 'Courtesans and Hindustani Music', *Asian Review* 1, pp. 12–17.

Oldenburg, Veena Talwar (1984), *The Making of Colonial Lucknow, 1856–1877*, Princeton, Princeton University Press.

Ruswa, Mirza Mohammad Hadi (1982), *Umrao Jan Ada*, Kushwant Singh and M.A. Husaini (trans.), Madras, Sangam Books.

Sharar, Abdul Halim (1975), *Lucknow: The Last Phase of an Oriental Culture*, E.S. Harcourt and Fakhir Hussain (trans. and eds.), London, Paul Elek.

Scott, James C. (1985), *Weapons of the Weak*, New Haven, Yale University Press.

Thapar, Romila (1978), *Ancient Indian Social History*, New Delhi, Orient Longman.

9

Sayyid Karamat Husain and Education for Women

GAIL MINAULT

Karamat Husain Girls' College in Lucknow, founded in 1912, is named after Sayyid Karamat Husain (1854–1917), an early champion of Muslim women's education in North India. Karamat Husain was one of the benefactors of the college from the time of its founding as a girls' school. It was named for him after his death and remains a monument to his memory. Who was Sayyid Karamat Husain, and how did he come to be remembered as a champion of women's education?

Sayyid Karamat Husain was in many ways a typical member of the *ashraf* service gentry of upper India, descended from immigrant Muslims who had come to India in the time of the sultans or the Mughals, seeking to serve the rulers and make their fortunes. His family were Sayyids, descendants of Shi'ite imams, with a tradition of Islamic learning. They had served the nawabs of Awadh as teachers and religious functionaries, and in return had received revenue assignments in the small towns or *qasbas* of northern India (Bayly, 1983: 189–93). Karamat Husain's family lands were in the qasba of Kantor, in Bara Banki District, not far from Lucknow. [1]

As the British established their dominance in the area, the minor service gentry gradually transformed themselves into a Muslim middle class, utilising their knowledge of local administration and law to serve the new rulers or the remaining native princes (Bayly, 1983: 354–6). Karamat Husain's grandfather, Mufti Sayyid Muhammad Quli Khan, was—as his title indicates—learned in Islamic law. His knowledge of Arabic and the Islamic sciences was respected among Shi'ite religious circles in Lucknow [Hamid Ali Khan, henceforth; HAK: 124].

Karamat Husain's father, Maulvi Sayyid Siraj Husain, too was educated in the classical languages of Arabic and Persian and in the Islamic
sciences, and he was also a scholar of mathematics. While he and his
brothers continued their father's reputation for piety and learning, Siraj
Husain became the first man in the family to learn English. He served
as a subjudge in the British administration, and later was employed in the
Bundelkhand agency that oversaw British relations with a number of
small Central Indian principalities. Karamat Husain was born in Jhansi
where his father was posted, and spent his early youth in Charkhari, a
minor princely state nearby (HAK: 14–16).

Karamat Husain was thus prepared by his family heritage and by the
circumstances of his father's employment to enter into the legal or
administrative service of the British or of some indirectly administered
princely state. But the circumstances of his life were in other ways
exceptional and some of these influences were more important to him in
the long run. Orphaned as a child and sickly, painfully shy, and bookish,
he turned for solace to such texts as the *Najhul Baligha* (The Maxims of
Ali) and the *Anwar-i-Suhali* (animal fables) (HAK: 20–1, 34, 37).

His paternal uncle, Sayyid Hamid Husain, a learned *mujtahid*, became his guardian in 1865, and took him to Lucknow to continue his
Islamic education. In the same year, his uncle decided to go on *hajj* and
invited Karamat Husain and his older brother, S. Enayat Husain, to go
along on the pilgrimage. The fifteen-month journey to Bombay and
from there to Jiddah, Mecca, and Medina, returning by way of the Shi'ite
pilgrimage sites of Najaf and Karbala, was Karamat Husain's first
experience of the outside world, and it whetted his appetite for further
education (HAK: 30–4).

He continued studying in Lucknow with his uncle and other Shi'ite
'*ulama*, mastering the Islamic curriculum, classical languages, and *fiqh*.
He was an excellent student and learned quickly, but he had not yet
mastered English (HAK: 36–8), necessary for a government job.

Karamat Husain married the granddaughter of one of his teachers,
Sultanul Ulama Sayyid Muhammad. The couple had one daughter. His
wife died young and he never remarried, preferring a solitary existence
(HAK: 39). When his elder brother also died young, in 1889, Karamat
Husain took over the support of his widow and children. He arranged
the marriage of his own daughter to one of his brother's sons, a preferred
marriage among ashraf Muslims. Even that one daughter predeceased
him (HAK: 101–2). It seems amazing that such a scholarly, lonely man

would have taken up the cause of women's education at a time when others were still opposed to it. His independence of mind and his firm grounding in the Islamic scriptures perhaps gave him the courage to do what was right and not worry about unfavourable public opinion.

Karamat Husain's entry into professional life followed the well-trodden path of family connections and personal recommendations. This form of patronage was the normal pattern followed by the British in filling the lower echelons of their administration in the early years of their domination, and it was only gradually phased out after the 1857 revolt in favour of a more impersonal system of examinations (Lelyveld, 1978: 56–68).

Sayyid Karamat Husain left Lucknow and his uncle's tutelage in 1874 in order to earn his living. He returned to Central India, where his elder brother, Enayat Husain, introduced him to Dr. Stratton, the Political Agent for Bundelkhand, who had been an old friend of their father's. Stratton offered him a job as a teacher at the school he was founding for the sons of the princes of the region, Rajkumar College, provided that he learn English. When the school opened in 1875, Karamat Husain became Head Maulvi, a position for which he needed no English. On the side, he studied English assiduously, and within two years had achieved reasonable fluency. He then started reading western science and philosophy, devouring works by Darwin, Huxley, Spencer and Mill (HAK 57–62).

After teaching at Rajkumar College of Bundelkhand for three years, Karamat Husain was appointed Mir Munshi to the Political Agent, Stratton. The position of 'chief clerk' sounds menial, but in fact, he was the head of a considerable bureaucracy and earned a reputation for efficiency and incorruptibility (HAK: 71–2). Stratton later appointed him to the post of *diwan* of the state of Narsinghgarh. While there, in the early 1880s, he remarked to an acquaintance that his ambition was to go to England and study medicine in order to help people and save lives. This conversation was reported to the Raja, who was contemplating a trip to England himself. He agreed to take Karamat Husain along and pay for his studies. Sir Lepel Griffin, then the Governor-General's Agent in Central India, modified their plan, arguing that if the Raja of Narsinghgarh used any state revenues to pay for Karamat Husain's education, then he should not study medicine, but rather something that would benefit the administration of the state—like law (HAK: 88, 93–4).

So in 1886, at the age of 32, Karamat Husain accompanied the Raja to England and stayed on there to study for the bar at the Middle Temple. He became a Barrister-at-Law in early 1889 and returned to India shortly thereafter, where he learned of his elder brother's death and his consequent increased family responsibilities. He returned briefly to Bundelkhand, but then established his barrister's practice in Allahabad, seat of the U.P. High Court (HAK: 95–7, 125).

In London, Karamat Husain had his first contact with a society in which women played an accepted social role. He rapidly came to the conclusion that the best way for India to progress was for its women to be educated. He and a number of his contemporaries in London, including Sayyid Ali Imam and Mazharul Haq, decided to form the *Anjuman-i-Ta'lim un-Niswan* (Association for Women's Education), but the organisation never got off the ground. As Ali Imam pointed out, to form such an association in London was premature; the real work had to begin after their return to India (HAK: 151–2).

Karamat Husain's devotion to the cause of women's education became clear after he had established his legal practice in Allahabad. The Muhammadan Educational Conference held its annual meeting in Allahabad in 1890, and Karamat Husain proposed to several of its leading members that they introduce a resolution in favor of women's education, but they were horrified at the suggestion (HAK: 152).

Meanwhile, however, events were conspiring to put Sayyid Karamat Husain at the leading Muslim educational center of North India, Aligarh. In 1890, Karamat Husain, as a Muslim barrister at the Allahabad High Court, had occasion to meet Justice Sayyid Mahmud, son of Sir Sayyid Ahmad Khan, the founder of Aligarh College. Mahmud had the reputation of being disdainful of Muslim lawyers, and hence Karamat Husain, ever diffident, had avoided him. Nevertheless, on Id, Karamat Husain and a number of his Muslim colleagues went to the Justice's chambers to extend their greetings. When they were introduced, Mahmud asked Karamat Husain if he knew S. Hamid Husain, and when Karamat Husain replied that Hamid Husain was his uncle and his teacher, Mahmud expressed tremendous respect and affection for the elder Husain, and consequently became another one of Karamat Husain's patrons and sympathisers. Later that year, when Aligarh College was looking for a Professor of Law, Mahmud suggested Karamat Husain for the post. Karamat Husain expressed some reservations, noting that while he was a supporter of women's education, Sir Sayyid Ahmad Khan was against it, and that difference of opinion might render him ineligible. Mahmud quieted his misgivings, saying that his father was not that narrow-minded. So Karamat Husain went to Aligarh as its first Professor of Law in 1891 (HAK: 103–6).

It so happened that the Muhammadan Educational Conference was meeting in Aligarh at the end of 1891. Sir Sayyid, then in the twilight of his long career as the leading Muslim educational reformer, asked Sayyid Karamat Husain why he was not a member of the Conference. Karamat Husain replied that he would gladly become a member if they would take up the question of Muslim women's education. Sir Sayyid urged him to become a member and attend the meeting. So Karamat Husain did, with some allies. They proposed a resolution that was adopted by the conference, that reads as follows:

This conference is of the opinion that, in the present condition of the Muslims, it is necessary to make efforts for the education of women as well as for men. Because for the overall progress of the community it is most necessary that women get religious, intellectual, and moral training so that they may be of benefit to the raising of future generations (MECP, 1905, App.: 33).

The Muhammadan Educational Conference paid lip service to the cause of women's education for several years thereafter. In the meantime, Karamat Husain resigned his professorship at Aligarh in 1896 and returned to Allahabad, where he taught law at Muir Central College and resumed his law practice at the High Court (HAK: 107). There, he and a number of other local legal practitioners and administrators—members of a growing Indian middle class, both Hindu and Muslim—started a fund to found a girls' school which they decided to name after Sir Charles Crosthwaite, the Lt. Governor of UP who had encouraged their efforts (HAK: 154–7). The school was established in Allahabad in the late 1890s, with Sayyid Karamat Husain as Secretary of the Managing Committee. The UP government eventually provided a grant-in-aid to the school that gave it financial security. Karamat Husain also served on a UP government committee for the improvement of women's education (UPED 332A/II/1905).

In 1898, Sayyid Karamat Husain was instrumental in establishing the Women's Education Section of the Muhammadan Educational Conference, which started working actively to found a Muslim Women's Normal School. The Secretaryship of the Women's Education Section was taken over in 1902 by Shaikh Muhammad Abdullah, who had been a law student of Karamat Husain's at Aligarh. The Shaikh, together with his wife, founded Aligarh Girls' School in 1906. The school ultimately became the Women's College of Aligarh University (Minault, 1983).

In 1907, when a judgeship on the Allahabad High Court fell vacant, Karamat Husain's name came up as a possible candidate. Justice Aikman, who was retiring because of ill health, mentioned him as one of the most knowledgeable of the High Court barristers, even though he had entered the profession relatively late in life. Aikman noted that this was, if anything, a recommendation—testimony to the quality and quickness of Karamat Husain's mind. Sir John Hewett, Lt. Governor of UP, liked Husain for his educational work (HAK: 113–16; Bilgrami: H-9).

His appointment to the bench was apparently clinched by Sayyid Husain Bilgrami, Nawab Imad ul-Mulk, former Education Director in the Hyderabad government, who had recently been appointed one of two Indian members of the Secretary of State's Council in London. When Lord Morley asked Imad ul-Mulk about the obscure Allahabad barrister, the Nawab recommended him highly. The Bilgramis—Sayyids and Shi'as—came from the same UP service gentry background as Karamat Husain, had a long tradition of Islamic learning, and were familiar with Karamat Husain's intellectual lineage. Further, they were active supporters and patrons of Aligarh College and its offshoot the Muhammadan Educational Conference. Having a Bilgrami at the right place to put in a good word at the right time was important for Karamat Husain's career at this juncture (HAK: 115;Robinson, 1974: 395).

Sayyid Karamat Husain was a judge on the Allahabad High Court from January 1908 until June 1912, when he retired for health reasons, in order to devote his remaining time and energies to the cause of women's education. Even while he was on the bench, he remained a moving spirit behind the Crosthwaite Girls' School, and frequently visited the school on his way home from the days' proceedings (HAK: 134).

After he retired from the bench, Sayyid Karamat Husain returned to Lucknow and founded the Muslim Girls' School. In this effort, he had the wholehearted support of the Raja of Mahmudabad, Sir Muhammad Ali Muhammad, a leading *taluqdar* of Awadh, active in Muslim political and educational causes, including the Muslim League and Aligarh College (Robinson, 1974: 380–1; Minault, 1982: 20–1, 50). In 1911, the Raja had visited Karamat Husain in Allahabad and admitted that he had been wrong in the 1890s when he had opposed founding a school for girls. Now, while he felt that Crosthwaite School was a very worthy cause, he nevertheless wanted to found a school in Lucknow that would be exclusively for Muslim girls. Karamat Husain apparently returned to Lucknow with this in mind, and they worked together to fund and staff the institution. Husain set up a *waqf* based on the income from his land, in the amount of rupees one lakh twenty-five thousand, the proceeds of which were to support the school. The Raja, in turn, assigned the revenues of several villages, amounting to Rs 600 per month, to the school (HAK: 159–61, 168).

The school was founded in November 1912 and occupied rented quarters in the city, with a boarding house for girls in purdah. It grew slowly over the next several years, and in the 1920s, moved to a building across the river in the newly developing suburbs of Lucknow. Then as now, it occupies a building that had originally been the Government Girls' High School, built on land also donated by the Raja of Mahmudabad (UPED 208/1913; 694/1922; 897/1930).

The Principal of the new Muslim Girls' School was Miss Amina [Ethel] Pope, an Englishwoman who had converted to Islam, and who had come to India in 1910 and been employed by Karamat Husain to superintend the girls' boarding house at Crosthwaite. On the founding day of the Muslim Girls' School, Miss Pope gave a graceful speech, in Urdu. She pointed out that Islam had once been the fountainhead of art and science and enlightenment, but that it had declined in recent centuries. One of the major reasons for that decline was the neglect of women's education. Echoing a standard reformist refrain, she said that no community can progress if its mothers are illiterate and unable to give adequate guidance to their children. She also addressed the question of purdah, saying that women's minds could be unveiled even while they maintained veiling in other respects. The school would make full arrangements for purdah, so that the girls' families should have no qualms about the school on that score. Religion would be taught, prayers recited regularly, and the girls would be taught to read Persian and Arabic, as well as their mother tongue (Urdu), and English (HAK: 162–3).

To tailor a curriculum that was recognised by British educational officials and at the same time addressed the cultural sensitivities of a purdah-observing society was a tall order. The prestige of Sayyid Karamat Husain's learning, position, and long devotion to the cause of women's education, and the support he received from Mahmudabad and the local government, helped. In March of 1913, for example, Lady Meston, wife of the Lt. Governor, officially inaugurated the school with a ritualistic speech about the need to train the mothers of future generations (HAK: 163–4).

Yet, among the Muslim professional class, there was opposition. One friend told Sayyid Karamat Husain that God would 'blacken his face'. Karamat Husain quipped that his face was already black in any case (his complexion was rather dark), so it could hardly get much blacker. On another occasion, he pointed out to an opponent: 'It is far better that I should be cursed and Muslim women become educated, than if I should retain my good name, but Muslim women remain in ignorance' (HAK: 166).

Sayyid Karamat Husain's approach to women's education was fully spelled out in a speech that he gave at a meeting of the Association for the Higher Education of Indian Women, held in Allahabad in December, 1915 (HAK: 173–9). In it, he defined good as that which makes human beings' lives easier and evil as that which gives them pain, or makes their lives harder. In the work of life, he went on, there is a division of labour between men and women. Among the Indian middle classes, the division of labour is as follows: The men earn the living, and the women manage the household. In managing the house, there are many tasks. The women need to be able to keep household accounts. They need to keep the house clean, look after the health of all the members of the household, care for the sick, prepare nutritious food, make and care for clothing, and so on. Furthermore, they bear the children, and in addition to feeding, clothing, and looking after them, they need to supervise their early education, their manners, and their religious and ethical upbringing. The women, in other words, have the more important job. All the men have to do is support their wives and children.

He went on to argue that since girls are not born knowing how to do all these things, they needed to learn religious and ethical principles as well as practical skills. If men wanted future generations to succeed in the world, it was just as important to educate their daughters as their sons; indeed, it was probably more important to educate the daughters. Keeping women ignorant meant that neither their sons nor their daughters would receive any basic education at home. The superstitions and useless customs that had crept into the culture would disappear with proper education and enlightenment. Opponents of women's education felt that sending girls to school would render them disrespectful--but the opposite was true. If they learned the precepts of their religion, they would be better wives, mothers, guides to their children, and better Muslims.

In addition, sending the girls to school—as opposed to instructing them at home—was much better, because a school could afford better teachers and broader curricular offerings than any home could. As a basic curriculum, he noted the need to teach reading and writing and mathematics for a basic knowledge of the world. He then listed practical subjects: health and cleanliness, household accounting and management, cooking, sewing, child care, gardening, and exercise for bodily health.

In conclusion, he emphasised that people who wished to keep women in ignorance were sinning against God's wishes. They were the worst enemies of humankind, assuring the decline of future generations. If the women of a community are backward, he concluded, the men of that community can never advance (*Pioneer*, 8 Dec. 1915, HAK: 174–9; *Leader*, 8 Dec. 1915; UPED 378/1916).

This may seem to be a very conventional kind of talk. Indeed, by 1915, many Indians—Hindu and Muslim—had already gone beyond the sentiments expressed here by Karamat Husain. Yet, for the daughters of the taluqdars of Awadh and the commercial and administrative classes—those groups in North Indian Muslim society for whom ashraf increasingly meant 'respectable' as opposed to 'noble' or 'foreign-descended', this was still strong medicine to swallow. The Muslim Girls' School of Lucknow was deemed a tremendous success in 1915 when it had only twenty-four students, seventeen of whom were boarders. In that year, the Begum of Bhopal, a ruling 'prince' and an enthusiastic patroness of women's education, visited the school and granted it Rs 1200 per year. The school was growing and had achieved some financial stability and security. By 1923, the total number of students had risen to fifty-two (HAK: 173, 181; UPED 897/1930).

Sayyid Karamat Husain died of a heart attack on 19 April 1917. He was active in the life of the girls' school till the day he died. The Raja of Mahmudabad continued his patronage of the school thereafter and was instrumental in naming the school after its founder (HAK: 248–50; UPED 897/1930).

Sayyid Karamat Husain, jurist, scholar, and crusader for women's education, lived a lonely life and fought a lonely battle. A combination of traditional and modern learning, and intellectual acceptance by religious scholars, western-educated Indians, and British administrators alike, led Karamat Husain to high judicial office, but also enabled him to champion an unpopular cause and give it the prestige of his concern and patronage. Today his ideas may not seem revolutionary, or even particularly innovative. Indeed, there were Muslim reformers before him who had battled much heavier odds and against greater criticism. But Karamat

Husain's single-minded courage and devotion to the cause, his unspectacular but solid achivements, deserve respect. He quietly inspired three major women's educational institutions in UP: in Allahabad, Aligarh, and Lucknow. The latter bears his name. It is an appropriate memorial.

NOTE

1. Most of the biographical information in this chapter is based on Hamid Ali Khan's Urdu biography of Karamat Husain, *Hayat-i-Maulana Karamat Husain*, Lucknow: al Nazir Press, n.d. Henceforth HAK.

REFERENCES

Bayly, C.A. (1983), *Rulers, Townsmen, and Bazaars*, Cambridge, Cambridge University Press.

Bilgrami, Sayyid Hussain (Nawab Imad ul-Mulk) (1907–8), Papers, Nehru Memorial Library, New Delhi. File H-9: Letters of J.P. Hewett, Lt. Gov. of UP to Bilgrami.

Khan, Hamid Ali (n.d.), *Hayat-i-Maulana Karamat Husain*, Lucknow, Al-Nazir Press.

Lelyveld, David (1978), *Aligarh's First Generation*, Princeton, Princeton University Press.

MECP (1905), *Muhammadan Educational Conference Proceedings*, Aligarh, Muslim University Library.

Minault, Gail (1982), *The Khilafat Movement*, New York, Columbia University Press.

——— (1983), 'Shaikh Abdullah, Begam Abdullah, and *Sharif*Education for Girls at Aligarh', in Imtiaz Ahmad (ed.), *Modernization and Social Change among Muslims in India*. New Delhi, Manohar.

Robinson, Francis (1974), *Separatism among Indian Muslims*, Cambridge, Cambridge University Press.

UP Education Department Records.

UP State Archives, Lucknow. Cited by File/Year.

10

Urdu in Lucknow/
Lucknow in Urdu

C.M. NAIM

CARLA PETIEVICH

The first flowering of what later came to be called Urdu poetry occurred in the kingdoms of Bijapur and Golkonda, followed by a second—
briefer—development at Aurangabad when that city became a major
outpost of the Mughal imperial power. The third phase, more sustained
and glorious (at least for Urdu ghazal), occurred at Delhi and lasted
roughly two generations. Then the scene moved to Lucknow. In histories
of Urdu literature, Lucknow and Urdu are mentioned together only after
the appearance of the independent state of Awadh and the eastward
migration of the Delhi poets. However, if the primary imperative behind
the formation of Urdu was the unavoidable interaction between the
speakers of Persian and Turkish, on the one hand, and the speakers of
various Indian vernaculars on the other, it would be safe to assume that
just as what we now call *dakini* and *gujari* were being formed south of
the Gangetic plain, so must have developed a few similar varieties of
'Urdu' in the plains too. In other words, some variety of Urdu must have
existed in the Awadh region long before the immigration from Delhi.

This assumption about many 'Urdus' helps explain why *dakini* could
have appeared as simultaneously similar and different to the people of
Delhi, whose language, in its turn, was similarly viewed in Awadh. Each
group felt akin to the other and yet also felt a need to differentiate itself
from it and to 'correct' the other. In other words, what each in turn encountered sounded not merely different but 'wrong'. No wonder Urdu
literati have always been overly concerned with notions of 'purity of

language' and 'correctness of idiom' and the concept of *ahl-e zuban,* 'people of the language'.

Like the previous two 'centres' of Urdu—Delhi and the Deccan— Lucknow became a 'centre' or *markaz* for Urdu only when it gained power and prosperity. It was only then that the local idiom came into direct contact with the idiom of Delhi and the interpenetration of the two continued the formation of what is now standard Urdu. The reasons these obvious matters should be reiterated are that (1) they are often forgotten in discussions concerning linguistic rivalry between speakers of different varieties of Urdu and (2) they underscore the fact that the history of pre-modern Urdu literature is a narrative of the rise and fall of political 'centres'—which then also came to be seen as literary centres, even as literary 'schools'.

Though a few religious poems were written in Awadh earlier, Urdu literary life in Awadh begins with the immigration of Urdu poets and scholars from Delhi, following attacks by the Irani, Afghan, Maratha and Jat armies. The newly independent state of Awadh offered generous patronage to poets, writers and scholars of Urdu and Persian. While poets like Khwaja Mir 'Dard' and his younger brother, Muhammad Mir 'Asar', remained behind, Sirajuddin Ali Khan-e-Arzu, the senior most poet in Persian and a mentor to many Urdu poets of the time, did emigrate, as did Mir Muhammad Taqi 'Mir' and Mirza Muhammad Rafi 'Sauda', two other preeminent poets in Urdu. Ali Jawad Zaidi gives a list of sixty-five such emigrant poets, including, beside Mir and Sauda, such prominent names as Soz, Fughan, Zahik, Jur'at, Insha, Rangin and Mushafi (Zaidi, 1971: 64).

It may be useful to note here that the poets who are closely identified with Delhi in literary chronicles were not necessarily originally from Delhi; many of them had come there from elsewhere to seek livelihood and left when that became extremely difficult. For example, Mir was born in Agra, moved to Delhi in his youth, spent a great deal of time in places such as Bharatpur, Kama and Digh, then permanently moved to Lucknow. Qalandar Baksh 'Jur'at' grew up in Delhi but moved to Bareili and later to Lucknow. Even Arzu had been born and raised in Gwalior, lived most of his life in Delhi, then moved to Fyzabad and died in Lucknow. In those days poetry was a profession, and its practitioners went where their profession could obtain proper patronage. In Delhi, such patronage had been provided by nobles (both Muslim and non-Muslim) more often than by the king. In Awadh, in contrast, the first three major nawabs—Shuja-ud-Daula, Asaf-ud-Daula and Saadat Ali

Khan—were themselves keen patrons of literature. A fourth and very important patron was Mirza Sulaiman Shikoh, who was himself a Delhi prince and had sought and found shelter and financial support at Lucknow in 1789.

Within the context of patrons and poets, one prominent feature of the literary milieu that emerged in Lucknow was furious public displays of rivalry between poets. Rivalry among poets was always a prominent feature of literary life in the pre-modern days. Its causes lay in the institutions of *mushaira*—etymologically, the word implies contestation—and courtly patronage as well as in the fact that pre-modern poets regarded themselves as men with a 'profession'. In Lucknow, in contrast to Delhi and the Deccan, we find such rivalry taking on the proportions of processions and street fights. Was this a matter of higher stakes, or was it some personal inclination of the patrons that encouraged the poets to display their rivalries in the streets of Lucknow? Perhaps it was a matter of both, further enhanced by a prevalent taste in public entertainment in the form of such contests or 'fights' (*larai*) as kite flying, cock fights, quail fights, and mock abusive quarrels between low-caste women.

It is beyond the scope of this paper to give a detailed review of everything produced in Urdu in Lucknow; it can only highlight the specially noteworthy developments. And the most significant of such development was in the genre of *marsiya* or elegy.

In Urdu literature, the word marsiya, unless otherwise qualified, refers to poems commemorating the martyrdom of Imam Husain, grandson of the Prophet Muhammad. Such elegies were also written in the Deccan and in Delhi, but short and modelled on the ghazal in having each couplet thematically independent of others. Also, they were apparently meant to be recited in chorus. What happened in Lucknow was that marsiyas became sustained narratives of substantial length on a particular hero or incident. Also, they came to be recited or declaimed in a distinctly dramatic fashion by the poet or by a trained reader before a gathering, or *majlis*, of believers. Certain structural features also became established, and, as if by consensus, marsiyas came to be written in the form of a *musaddas* or six-line stanzas (each stanza having the following rhyme scheme: aaaa bb). In these poems, the goal of the poet was not just to make his audience cry but also to exult in the bravery and devotion of the heroes of Karbala. Rather than being a simple lament, the new marsiya came to be a poem aiming for epic grandeur. The Shia milieu of Lucknow provided the necessary patronage to the practitioners of marsiya and encouraged them to innovate and elaborate. Remarkably, much of this was accomplished by two poets—Mir Babr Ali 'Anis' (d. 1874) and Mirza Salamat Ali 'Dabir' (d. 1875)—and the members of their families and their disciples.

The innovations made at Lucknow were readily adopted by marsiya writers elsewhere. Equally significantly, because of the cultural preeminence given to the elegies of Anis and Dabir as well as their sheer excellence, musaddas itself came to be the preferred form for any kind of serious verse requiring a sustained exposition. In 1879 Altaf Husain 'Hali' (d. 1914) chose to write his famous poem, 'The Tide and Ebb of Islam', in the musaddas form. Muhammad Iqbal (d. 1938) also wrote many of his most popular and effective poems in this form, as did any number of lesser and more recent poets. All of them owe a great deal to the art of the great marsiya writers of Lucknow.

Another development was the revival of interest in the genre of *masnavi* (a narrative poem of some length, consisting of rhyming couplets). In the Deccan, masnavi and ghazal were equally favoured by poets and patrons, and Dakini poets produced a considerable number of lengthy masnavis on different topics, romantic, epic, historical or sufistic. At least one major masnavi was written at Aurangabad. Delhi, too, produced only a couple, and much reduced in scale. But in Lucknow several poets again turned to this genre, the two most important being Mir Ghulam Hasan 'Hasan' (d.1786) and Pandit Daya Shankar 'Nasim' (d.1843). Hasan's *Sihr-ul-Bayan* ('The Magic of Narration') and Nasim's *Gulzar-e Nasim* ('The Garden of Nasim') are diametrically opposite in diction and narrative style—the former is simple and direct while the latter is markedly full of artifice—but both found great favour. Both utilised tales of magic and fantasy and took delight in the supernatural. The third great master of masnavi in Lucknow was Hakim Tasadduq Husain (Nawab Mirza) 'Shauq' (d. 1871), who took inspiration from neither of his illustrious predecessors. His masnavis are highly naturalistic in both plot and language, and are closer to those of the Delhi poets, Mir and Asar. Relatively short in length and rather licentious in places, Shauq's masnavis do contain long portions of elegant and effective verse, and his *Zahr-e Ishq* is an unquestionable masterpiece. Numerous other masnavis written in Lucknow did not gain lasting fame, including a masnavi version of the *Arabian Nights* which was begun, at the request of the famous publisher Munshi Newal Kishore, by Asghar Ali Khan 'Hasrat', perhaps the last emigrant poet from Delhi, continued by Tota Ram 'Shayan' and completed by Shadi Lal 'Chaman' in 1866.

It is hard to account for this revival of interest in masnavi in Lucknow.

Perhaps the genre required more munificent patronage than a ghazal or a panegyric (*qasida*), and such patrons were again available in Lucknow. But that is belied by the fact that neither Hasan nor Nasim received any patronage for their pains. Another speculation would be to link this fondness for the masnavi to the presence and popularity in that region of earlier Awadhi masnavis or *premakhyans* (as they are called today), such as the *Padmavat* of Jaisi and the *Madhumalti* of Manjhan. Perhaps more to the point would be to see reflected in this liking for masnavis a burgeoning fondness for literary stories in Urdu that seems to characterise Lucknow. It may be relevant to note here that while the last Persian *dastan* in India was composed around the middle of the eighteenth century in Delhi, the first tale in Urdu was written in Lucknow only a few decades later. In Delhi, Urdu poetry had come into its own from under the supremacy of Persian poetry; in Lucknow, Urdu prose did the same.

The emergence of modern Urdu prose is generally ascribed to the efforts at the College of Fort William (where Indian classics were recast in 'simpler' language for the instruction of colonial officers), the translation projects at Delhi College (where western books on science and moral philosophy were translated for the College's syllabus) and to such individual works as the Urdu letters of Ghalib. Lucknow is left out in such histories. Most prose works produced in Lucknow during the earlier part of our period are undoubtedly in the more elaborate and ornate old style. The only exception is a single, extraordinary work of Insha, *Rani Ketki Ki Kahani* ('The Story of Rani Ketki'), which is also the earliest piece of Urdu fiction in North India. It is a simple tale of fantasy but exceptional in being narrated in a language containing no word of Perso-Arabic origin. Sadly neglected in the canon of Urdu literature—even Sharar, who claimed that Urdu prose-writing originated in Lucknow, doesn't mention it—Insha's story has been celebrated by Hindi literary historians as their first prose work (Insha calls his language *hindavi*).

Storytelling was an art greatly cultivated in pre-modern Lucknow. As Sharar described it: 'The art of telling stories is divided under five headings: "War", "Pleasure", "Beauty" and "Love", and "Deception". The raconteurs of Lucknow have shown such perfection in telling tales under these headings that one must hear them in order to realise the extent of their skill. The painting of pictures with words and the ability to make a deep and lasting impression on the minds of their audience are the special skills of these people' (Sharar: 1975: 149). The storytellers worked with an established text or framework but were totally at liberty to extemporise to suit their mood and their audience's pleasure. Broadly speaking, the stories that the professionals told were of two kinds: (1) *qissa* or a not-too-long single tale of fantasy, and (2) *dastan* or a pointedly long and elaborate cycle of tales built around princely heroes battling against demons, magicians and other evil beings, eventually gaining victory over them by destroying their mind-boggling, magical constructs (*tilism*) while also winning the love of numerous fairies and princesses.

In addition to translations and retellings of earlier Persian tales, quite a few original qissas and dastans in Urdu were also written at Lucknow. Only the two most famous need to be mentioned here. The first was a qissa-like short work, *Fasana-e 'Aja'ib* ('Story of Marvels'), by Rajab Ali Beg 'Suroor' (d. 1869). It was written in 1824–25, published nineteen years later. Since then it has gone into hundreds of printings. The popularity of Suroor's work produced a number of rivals but none reached it in success or fame. Suroor himself had partially written it as a rejoinder to the claim for excellence that Mir Amman of Delhi had made for his language in his qissa, *Bagh-o-Bahar*. The latter, better known as *Qissa Chahar Darvesh* ('The Tale of Four Dervishes') was published in 1801 from the College of Fort William at Calcutta. As opposed to the diction adopted by both Insha and Mir Amman, Suroor chose to write in a style redolent of literary conceits. Perhaps it is that extreme quality which still makes it surprisingly popular, though far less than Mir Amman's masterpiece.

The other significant work is popularly known as the dastan of Amir Hamza, but there is neither a single work by that title nor is it by a single author. Woven around a historical figure—Hamza, an uncle of the Prophet Muhammad—and loosely linked to a shorter Persian dastan, *Rumuz-e Hamza*, it is an enormous cycle of tales that runs to forty-six volumes, averaging some 900 pages each. It was composed by Muhammad Husain 'Jah'; Ahmad Husain 'Qamar'; and Tasadduq Husain, who were commissioned by that intrepid publisher, Munshi Newal Kishore and who worked separately to produce 'the crowning glory of the Urdu dastan tradition' (Pritchett, 1991: 25).

The last major—and somewhat controversial—development in Urdu literature that took place in Lucknow was the emergence of *rekhti* as a distinct genre of poetry. Rekhti is a body of verse composed by men, employing a feminine voice, and dealing with matters—sexual and/or domestic—that exclusively concern women. Rekhti was by no means poetry for women: it was about women, for the entertainment and titillation of men. Sa'adat Yar Khan 'Rangin' (d.1835), an immigrant poet in the service of another immigrant, Prince Sulaiman Shikoh, claimed to have invented it. But similar poetry had already appeared in the Deccan, and it is possible that those rekhti-like verses were known in some circles in Delhi, where Rangin might have got his inspiration. In his verses, Rangin merely increased the references to women's hygiene and lesbianism and coined the term rekhti—supposedly a feminine form of *rekhta*, 'poetry'. Rangin's rekhti, however, was not a 'feminized' form of *rekhta*; if anything, it was a kind of misogynistic verse 'that aimed to entertain its male audience by making gross fun of women, its enhanced appeal lying in the fact that it also pretended to be a view from the inside, in fact, the very words of the object of ridicule' (Naim,1992). Rangin's close friend Insha (d.1817) also wrote a substantial quantity of rekhti verses. Some later poets also followed their lead, the most famous among them being Jan Sahib (d.1886). With time, however, the more salacious elements in rekhti were reduced, and eventually a certain degree of genuine concern for women's life in domestic confinement found expression. One lasting contribution of the development of rekhti was the preservation of a vast number of words, idioms, and proverbs peculiar to women's speech in the Urdu milieu.

In one sense, perhaps the most important contribution to Urdu literature and learning in the nineteenth century was not made by any poet or scholar, but by a visionary entrepreneur, Munshi Newal Kishore (d.1895), who was born in Aligarh district but settled in Lucknow after the Mutiny. With the active support and patronage of a British officer, he set up a press in 1858 and started to publish textbooks and circulars, and soon moved on to bigger things. Lucknow at the time was full of highly talented—but penniless after the Mutiny—poets, writers, calligraphers, dastan-tellers and other denizens of the book trade. Newal Kishore taking full advantage of this was soon publishing an incredible number of very important books, not only in Urdu but also in Persian, Arabic, Hindi and Sanskrit. He also started a weekly journal, *Avadh Akhbar*, which launched the career of one of the most important prose fiction writers in Urdu, Pandit Ratan Nath 'Sarshar' (d.1902). Soon there was a rival journal entitled *Avadh Punch*. Together these two Lucknow journals created and sustained a brief but deliriously rich period of humourous and satirical writings in Urdu, both in verse and in prose.

Newal Kishore's press was not the first in Lucknow: that had been set up as early as 1830 in the reign of Nasir-al-Din Haydar. It was the king's own press, the *Matba-e Sultani*, and published a number of handsome books, including a major dictionary, *Taj-ul-Lughat*, and probably translations of scientific texts that a royal translation bureau was set up to do. Soon other presses followed, among them *Matba-e Muhammadi* and *Matba-e Mustafai*. The production values at Lucknow presses were so good that the great Ghalib on one occasion raged at the presses in Delhi for what they did in comparison. In 1849, for some reason that still remains a mystery—libelous publications, personal animosity, displeasing newspapers?—a royal order gave the publishers in Lucknow the choice of either publishing under the auspices of the royal press and with its supervisor's permission, or ceasing to publish altogether. Some closed shop, others moved to Kanpur, to Company territory; eventually they had to return and function as ordered, only to be devastated in 1857 by the ravages of the Revolt. (The vacuum thus created was successfully filled by Newal Kishore with the help of his English patrons.) It must be noted that one of the consequences of the end of the nawabi rule in 1856 was the immediate flowering of Urdu journalism in Lucknow. According to Nadir Ali Khan, there were seven notable newspapers (weeklies) in Lucknow that flourished in the period between the annexation of Awadh and the beginning of the Mutiny (Khan, 1987: 414). The first among them was *Tilism-e Lakhnau*, edited and published by Mohammad Yaqub Ansari, who belonged to the Firangi Mahal family of scholars. In view of what the Nawabs had done to the press in Lucknow, it is ironic to note that the *Tilism* was forthright in presenting the worrisome conditions of inflation, loss of property, and lack of employment in Lucknow that followed the end of the nawabi rule. It was equally bold in criticising Company rule for its reckless and unrestrained use of power.

In (the study of) Urdu literature Lucknow figures most prominently in the context of a remarkable and overarching critical construct known as the Two School theory. This serves as an organising principle for surveying Urdu poetry, and it is based on an axiomatic distinction between Lucknow and Delhi. In Urdu literary histories and criticism there is much discussion of something called *Lakhnaviyyat* and its hypothesised opposite, *Dihlaviyyat*. Lakhnaviyyat evokes the excitement created by the combination of economic, political and cultural activity that this 'boomtown' saw under the patronage of some of the earliest nawabs, as mentioned above.

Abdul Lais Siddiqui described Lakhnaviyyat:

What is meant by *Lakhnaviyyat* in poetry and literature is that special quality which early poets of Lucknow adopted and established, and whose special characteristics distinguish it from traditional poetry . . . (Siddiqui, 1955: 39).

The 'special quality' is tied directly to Lucknow's wealth, which holds legendary stature in the imagination of both the British and Urdu scholars of the twentieth century:

Rivers of wealth flowed, riches rained down from the sky ... there was a proliferation of pleasure-seeking, an excess of material wealth. This state of affairs brought about licentiousness and imbalanced thoughts and actions ... The result was that poetry became a vehicle for coquetry, blandishments, coarse language and enumerations of feminine beauty (ibid.: 47).

In order to understand the force Lakhnaviyyat holds in Urdu culture, attention must be directed to two ideas expressed above. The first is that Lakhnaviyyat's special characteristics 'distinguished it from traditional poetry'; and the second is that Lucknow's prosperity resulted directly in moral and aesthetic imbalance, in 'pleasure-seeking and licentiousness'. It might seem counter-intuitive for Urdu critics to simultaneously celebrate a cultural achievement and denounce it as decadent, departing from 'traditional' aesthetics. The most compelling explanation for this puzzling construction in the critical literature involves looking at Lucknow within the dual context of an intense cultural rivalry between Delhi and Lucknow, on the one hand; and considering, on the other hand, the force of a colonial discourse generated by the British in the nineteenth century.

The cultural rivalry between Lucknow and Delhi was born with the inception of Lucknow's court culture in the 1780s: both Delhi and Lucknow were seats of culture, one ascendant in the nineteenth century and the other descendant; both, at least nominally, were also rival seats of political power, with Lucknow having more wealth, and Delhi having a longer tradition of prestige, to enhance their respective claims. Their respective partisans sought recognition for each as the markaz of a single, Mughal-oriented, Indo-Muslim elite culture. Competition between them ran unabated through the nineteenth century and the birth of a critical literature in Urdu.

On the other hand, the very factors that lie at the heart of the birth of Urdu critical literature in the nineteenth century created the Two School theory: (1) it took place in the aftermath of 1857, when Mughal political power was finally eclipsed; (2) it was largely under British colonial patronage that it began to develop; (3) the British, in order to rationalise their annexation of formerly-Mughal India, had a great stake in constructing Indo-Muslim culture as flamboyant, effeminate and decadent; and (4) most of the Urdu literati either hailed from Delhi or identified with it as the cultural heart of Mughal India. These 'Dihlavis' translated the long-established cultural rivalry between Delhi and

Lucknow into a critique which suggested that whatever problematic flamboyance, effeminacy and decadence existed in Indo-Muslim culture was really a manifestation of innovation from Lakhnaviyyat. This vilification of Lucknow satisfied the cultural chauvinism of the early (Dihlavi) critics at the same time as it negotiated a relationship with the British.

Thus the Two School theory proceeds from an understanding that the Lakhnavis established their own characteristic literary voice, and that it was fundamentally distinct from the literary voice that had been developed earlier in Delhi. Witness the opening remarks from the earliest formal declaration of the Two School, found in Abdus Salam Nadvi's *She'rul Hind*:

Although by the time of Mushafi and Insha it had become customary to practice poetry in Lucknow, still, all the poets of rank who had established a reputation had been residents of Delhi, and considered themselves separate from the people of Lucknow (Nadvi, 1926; l: 189).[1]

Once there was something called Lakhnaviyyat, the Two School theory was obliged to define and develop *Dihlaviyyat* as a critical construct, which came to embody the qualities of 'traditional' poetry as a counterpoint to Lakhnaviyyat. Nurul Hasan Hashimi, author of *Dilli ka Dabistan-i Sha'iri* ('The Delhi School of Poetry'), offers the following definition (1980: 257) of Dihlaviyyat:

Dihlaviyyat is the name of a point of view, an outlook, an intellectual simplicity, a poetic temperament, in order to comprehend which a step-by-step comparison will be made with Lakhnaviyyat. . . .

He then proceeds over the next seventy pages with his comparison. What it all amounts to is, in fact, summarised by Hashimi earlier (1980: 13) in the following words:

In comparison with Dihlaviyyat's spirituality and melancholoy (lit. 'attachment to sorrow', or *gham-pasandi*) Lucknow's superficial gaiety seems thin and cheap. Lakhnavi poets concentrated on enumerations of feminine beauty but omitted loftiness of thought. There is not that flame, that profound lamentation, that tone of longing which there is in the poetry of Delhi. . . .

Elements like spirituality, melancholy, loftiness of thought, profound lamentation and tone of longing are of course all to be found in Lakhnavi poetry—in fact, in most ghazal poetry, regardless of its place of origin. The 'traditional' *vs.* 'non-traditional' polarity between Dihlavi and Lakhnavi poetry does not originate with Siddiqi, Hashimi, or even Nadvi, who identifies an 'Intermediate Era' of Urdu literature, during which 'Lakhnavi poetry became established and Delhi's and Lucknow's two separate schools were founded' (Nadvi, 1926: 10). The importance of Nadvi's 'Intermediate Era' is that it locates the emergence of Lakhnaviyyat with poets like Nasikh and Atish, who had no experience of Delhi and for whom, therefore, Delhi need take no responsibility. Here Nadvi is making more explicit the distinctions noted in earlier works, those of Azad and Hali.

In *Ab-e Hayat* ('Water of Life'), published in 1980, Muhammad Husain Azad had treated all Lakhnavi poetry as an entity separate from the rest of Urdu poetry. Dihlavi poetry he had considered to comprise the remainder, while Lakhnavi poetry developed later than, and at variance with, earlier, more 'traditional' poetry. This distinction is clearly implicit in many of Azad's remarks, although it is nowhere articulated explicitly. It is not difficult to understand this implicit distinction as Azad giving voice to the cultural rivalry between Delhi and Lucknow, using the distinction to marginalise Lakhnavi poetry from 'traditional' literature (and, by extension, to suggest that this 'new' Lakhnavi culture altogether departed from, and was less worthy than, the Mughal tradition of which Indian Muslims were so rightly proud).

Azad's contemporary, Altaf Husain Hali, seems to have accepted this point of view, and develops it further, in his seminal work, *Muqaddma-e She'r-o-Sha'iri* ('Prolegomena to Poetics and Poetry'), first published in 1893. Hali rails against the decline of all Urdu poetry during the course of the nineteenth century, and tends to cite Lakhnavi poetry as a prime example of decline. Both critics were reformers and shared a belief that the qualities most in need of reform in Urdu poetry were to be found in the verse of Lucknow's poets. But the nature of reform envisioned by the two men differs somewhat. Azad seems to call for an *aesthetic* revisionism, a 'getting back to the basics' of the existing Perso-Arabic literary tradition, a rejection of the 'worn-out themes' that plagued the ghazal of his day and a return to the model of that inherently vigorous tradition. Hali, on the other hand, calls for literary reform as part and parcel of a widespread *moral* reform in Indian Islam. This has tied in very comfortably with the construction of Lakhnaviyyat in Urdu critical literature as essentially decadent, and, as we saw earlier, the pattern was carried forth in Abdus Salam Nadvi's *She'r-ul Hind.*

It must be observed, however, that the Two School theory is seriously flawed, and has not gone without challenge in recent years. In 1970 Ali Jawad Zaidi, in *Do Adabi Iskul* ('Two Literary Schools'), argued very persuasively that all of Nadvi's characteristics of Lakhnaviyyat were amply represented in Dihlavi literature; and that, conversely, Dihlaviyyat could be found in abundance in Lakhnavi poetry. Zaidi's close textual examination of both Dihlavi and Lakhnavi poetic texts reveals that the 'worn-out' and 'degraded' themes decried by Azad and Hali can be found everywhere in the nineteenth century Urdu ghazal.

Whoever thought of it first, the Two School theory seems to represent a remarkable collaboration between the heirs to Mughal glory and British colonial officials in the late nineteenth century. What these two parties had in common was an admiration for the Mughal empire, especially at its cultural apogee in the seventeenth century, and a certain disdain for successor states such as Awadh insofar as they might attempt to claim for themselves the stature historically enjoyed by Delhi. Dihlavis wished to retain Delhi as the locus of Mughal glory, and to continue to place themselves within its noble traditions, at least culturally; British colonialists wished to inscribe themselves within that tradition while co-opting it for themselves. Lucknow's power and prestige invited political and discursive neutralisation in order for both these goals to be achieved.

Zaidi's work is also noteworthy for its attempt to focus closely on poetic texts, and to take a 'scientific' approach. He is no more successful than any of his predecessors in defining what constituted 'traditional' poetry, but that is largely because the tradition did not identify itself in the 'scientific' terms called for by Zaidi. Indeed, the notion of tradition is ephemeral and evocative rather than concrete and easily identifiable in literary terms.

There is another argument that could be made to complement Zaidi's work, and it has to do with the structure of the ghazal itself. Because ghazal is determined by its form, metre and rhyme scheme (*zamin*) rather than by theme,[2] it makes a great deal of sense to look to how the form tends to give rise to various themes. If there were different Dihlavi and Lakhnavi approaches to poetry overall, one would expect to see Dihlaviyyat and/or Lakhnaviyyat reflected in how poets in each markaz evoked various associations suggested by the same word in *qafiya*-position (that is, in the end-rhyme). A detailed analysis (Petievich 1992: 100–43) demonstrated that in some instances a particular word in qafiya-position would tend to give rise to verse displaying more characteristics associated with Lakhnaviyyat; while certain other qafiya words tended to give rise to verses which more closely resemble what has been called Dihlaviyyat. In general, most verses were seen to manifest a mixture of both characteristics, and no particular Delhi-type or Lucknow-type patterns of choice could be identified. The reason is simply that all ghazal poets subscribe to the same essential literary values and aesthetics, and all are bound by the very tight structure of the genre itself. While choices in diction or tone are of course possible, they tend to be exercised in connection with the associations suggested by the qafiya word in conjunction with the particular whim or mood of the composing poet at the moment of composition. But an exhaustive examination of Lakhnavi and Dihlavi ghazals in the same zamin did nothing to advance the hypothesis that a poet's approach to the ghazal is determined by the markaz in which he or she resides. In other words, markaz ('centre') and *dabistan* ('school') are two distinct concepts which have been erroneously conflated in the Two School theory. As to why this conflation occurred so successfully, and refuses to be dislodged even in light of serious scholarly challenge, we must return to the discursive realm, to the realm of what poetry signifies culturally.

With the important role played by Urdu poetry in Indo-Muslim cultural identification, the role of poets and critics is also tremendously important, for they are the creators and guardians of poetry as a cultural signifier. A close look has been given elsewhere (Pritchett, 1993; Petievich, 1992) to Azad and Hali, the two pioneering critics mentioned above, and the role they played in the establishment of critical standards for Urdu literature, cannot be recounted in full here. However, it is worth reiterating that both these literary giants identified themselves as cultural Dihlavis and were employed by the British at about the time they wrote their monumental works. In both works we hear the refrain of the crisis of Indo-Muslim culture, and laments on fallen standards. Given the fact that standards and trends in both markaz are far more similar than distinct from one another if judged by examining poetic texts, we can assert with some confidence that Azad, Hali and the British all had some stake *other than literary* in isolating Lakhnaviyyat from 'traditional' Mughal culture. What were these stakes?

The Urdu elite, though co-opted to a certain extent by employment in the British colonial system, never went so far as to accept the totalising denigration of Indo-Muslim culture in which post-1857 colonial discourse engaged. Indeed, it is important to recognise the limited utility of critiquing colonial discourse, tempting though it remains as an explanation for much of what transpired in the negotiation of a post-1857 Indo-Muslim ethos. It must be remembered that Urdu literature—if not its critical tradition—has a history predating by far colonial domination of Hindustan, and it developed at a far remove from the British and their discourses. The force of the Two School theory must be understood as satisfying internal values as well as colonial. Hali surely mourned the decline of culture in his own times. But of its inherent worth he expresses no doubt at all. Similarly, Azad clung with loyalty and dignity to the notion of Delhi as a noble and worthy Mughal *markaz*, while suggesting that the move to Lucknow had been the occasion of cultural decline. Azad notes that, being timely, the 'new' Lakhnavi style had brought acclaim to newer poets, but that 'those first excellent poets of Lucknow were the destroyers of Delhi', flouting its authority, especially in the all-important realm of language usage (Azad, 1980: 339).

In other words, the success of colonial discourse may be attributed to a gratuitous, inadvertent tapping into the cultural rivalry between Delhi and Lucknow. This rivalry, in turn, remained potent for those of the cultural elite under such serious constraint to negotiate a place in British India. Members of this elite, literary critics, by acknowledging 'problems' with Urdu literature, accomplished the following purpose: they fulfilled the mandate of a colonial discourse about the moral (and, by extension, political) capacity of Indians to rule themselves. At the same time, by distinguishing the literature of Lucknow from that of Delhi, they suggested that the site of Indo-Muslim cultural decline was localised in Lucknow. This served to protect and preserve the literature (thus, by extension, the culture) of Delhi in moral and aesthetic terms while acknowledging that it had suffered political reverses for which it was not morally culpable.

Moral authority has played a significant part in literary criticism, informed equally, it might be argued, by reformist Islamic principles and those of Victorian England. Hali wished to reform Urdu literature, especially the ghazal, basing it on high moral principles (*akhlaqi mazamin*) and 'admitted' that it might be difficult to incorporate and popularise such themes in a genre whose essence was 'erotic' ('*ishqiya*'). Azad, too, offers the following lament:

It is unfortunate that our poetry has become trapped in the net of those themes such as eroticism, drunkenness, and the manufacture of fantastic fragrance in the absence of the flowers or even a flower garden . . . (Azad, 1980: 81).

Here Azad is paying dual lip service to the tenets of 'natural' poetry a la English Romanticism (all the rage in northern India in the late nineteenth century) while at the same time decrying the loss of the Urdu ghazal's essential nobility. His outlook was compatible with that of India's Victorian overlords in key respects. Both shared an emphasis on chasteness, austerity and authority. Both Victorian Englishmen and *sharif* Indian Muslims deplored sensuality and licentiousness; and both groups saw these deplorable elements in nineteenth century Urdu poetry, especially that of Lucknow. Just as the British considered Indian rulers unfit on account of their moral laxness and sensual self-indulgence, so too did they find Urdu poetry distasteful and objectionable for the eroticism and sensuality which they saw in it.

Azad's literary criticism can be seen as reflective of the Mughal ruling elite's values; reformist literary criticism of the time—such as Hali's *Muqaddama*—reflects, in turn, a changing definition of who constituted the ruling class in India a hundred years ago. The ruling elite was beginning to expand, and it was no longer necessarily the feudal elites and their retinue in whom power would be solely invested. On the contrary, the most virulent colonial discourse on Indian moral turpitude was directed toward them. Hali and Azad were obliged to defend themselves and their class against the attacks of an essentially middle-class British administration, which was more favourably inclined toward the emerging, English-educated, Indian middle-class than the former Mughal nobility with which Azad identified so greatly.

One cannot say whether the Muslims who called for thematic reforms in the ghazal found a convenient ally in Victorian morals or whether they were responding to the cries of 'Shame!' emanating from British mouths. In either case Indian Muslims who ascribed the cause for final Mughal defeat to the same morally suspect conditions that were enumerated by champions of British rule were content, even eager, to back their own opinions with the authority carried by British opinion on Indian moral decline. The characterisation of Lakhnavi poetry within this particular framework served the defensive strategies of reformist critics like Azad and Hali. If the deplored state of the Urdu ghazal could be pinned on the morally-suspect influences of the Lucknow court—a court which the British had overthrown for alleged moral laxness and administrative incompetence—then the literature of Urdu's other markaz (Delhi) could be promoted with relative impunity. The only recently-bygone Indo-Muslim tradition could then be stored and honoured with a reverence available solely to the past. The emergent middle class employed by the British could hark back to that one-generation-removed cultural glory and identify themselves with it. Meanwhile, they could reconcile themselves with the advent of a modern era where different values pertained but did not necessarily compete.

NOTES

1. Nadvi's great contribution to the Two School theory is that, in addition to formally announcing it, he attempted to define eight characteristics of distinction: (1) Lakhnavi effeminacy; Dihlavi fondness for Persian *tarakib* constructions; (3) longer ghazals in Lucknow, resulting in ridiculous qafiyas (rhymes) and degraded themes; (4) enumeration of the beloved's physical attributes by Lakhnavis instead of expression of more spiritual emotions; (5) *ri'ayat-e lafzi* (word-play) in Lucknow; (6) Lakhnavi degeneracy (*ibtizal*); (7) Lakhnavi *mu'amala-bandi* (amorous banter); (8) Lakhnavi *nazuk-khayali*, or excessive delicacy of simile and metaphor/abstruseness of thought.

2. This point is made with the caveat that, of course, the theme of the entire genre is '*ishq* (love).

REFERENCES

Azad, Muhammad Husain (1980), *Ab-i Hayat*, Allahabad, Ram Narayan Lal Beni Madhav.

Hali, Altaf Husain (1980), *Muqaddma-e She'r-o Sha'iri*, Delhi, Maktaba Jami'a.

Hashimi, Nurul Hasan (1980), *Dilli ka Dabistan-e Sha'iri*, Lucknow, U.P. Urdu Akademi.

Khan, Nadir Ali (1987), *Urdu Sahafat ki Tarikh, 1822–57*, Aligarh, Educational Book House.

Nadvi, Abdus Salam (1926), *Tazkira-e She'rul Hind*, vol. l, Azamgarh, Matba'-i Ma'arif.

Naim, C.M. (1992), 'Transvestic Words?: The Rekhti in Urdu', Paper presented to the South Asian Studies Seminar, University of Pennsylvania (unpublished).

Petievich, Carla (1992), *Assembly of Rivals, Delhi, Lucknow and the Urdu Ghazal*. Delhi. Manohar.

Pritchett, Frances W (1991), *The Romance Tradition in Urdu: Adventures from the Dastan of Amir Hamzah*, New York, Columbia University Press.

——— (1993), *Nets of Awareness: Urdu Poetry and its Critics*, Berkeley, University of California Press.

Sharar, Abdul Halim (1975), *Lucknow: The Last Phase of an Oriental Culture*, E.S. Harcourt and Fakhir Hussain (trans. and eds), London, Paul Elek.

Siddiqi, Abul Lais (1955), *Lakhna'u ka Dabistan-e Sha'iri*, Lahore, Urdu Markaz.

Zaidi, Ali Jawad (1971), *Do Adabi Iskul*, Lucknow, U.P. Urdu Akademi.

11

The Musical Evolution
of Lucknow

JAMES KIPPEN

If the crumbling remnants of the once glorious yet decadent palaces of
Lucknow could talk they would tell of a time, not so long ago, when
North India's very best musicians and dancers graced their halls to entertain the city's nobility. Time has taken its toll on Lucknow in many ways,
and now little is left of the old life. Yet the cultural legacy of Lucknow's
contribution to the development of North Indian classical music should
by no means be underestimated for it was here that many of the ideas and
innovations that helped shape the modern face of the tradition were
born. Therefore, much can be learned from a study of the musical evolution of Lucknow.

It comes as a great surprise to many to learn that Indian music as we
know it today, though rooted in the *Natyashastra*, an early treatise on the
dramatic arts, is in fact a relatively recent phenomenon. The general
principles of the melodic (*rag*) and rhythmic (*tal*) systems seem only to
have become crystallised in a form that would be recognizable to modern
scholars and musicians after the fourteenth or fifteenth century AD
(Jairazbhoy, 1971: 16), and North Indian music's most popular and
widely heard forms and instruments of today—*khayal, thumri*, the
instrumental *gat, sitar, sarod, tabla*—are actually creations of the last
three centuries (and in some cases considerably less). True, all dynamic
artistic tradition is constantly evolving, being reinterpreted and enriched
with every new generation of exponents; that is why contemporary performers sound different from their fathers and grandfathers. Nevertheless, the crucial formative period for modern Hindustani music lasted
from about 1720 to around 1860; and for much of this time one of the
most important and influential centres of patronage for the arts was the

city of Lucknow. An account of the history and development of music in Lucknow during this period is therefore a study of the modern evolution of Hindustani music in microcosm. Furthermore, the fate of music in the city after 1860 reflects a trend away from court and private patronage to public and state patronage, the greater accessibility of music, and the inexorable erosion of the traditional, rather insular, lifestyle of musician families.

Virtually nothing is known about music in Lucknow during the first half of the eighteenth century. It was Delhi that attracted musicians in search of court patronage, and which was the locus of at least three crucial innovations. First, the vocal form khayal emerged, a lighter and more florid alternative to the austere and intellectual *dhrupad* (Miner, 1981: 132–6). Second, the sitar, or at least a prototypical version of the instrument as we now know it, appeared around 1750 (Miner, 1981: 34). And third, the tabla developed as a hybrid of existing drums probably during the second quarter of the eighteenth century (Stewart, 1974: 6–7). All grew steadily in importance and influence to the extent that khayal, the sitar, and the tabla have dominated Hindustani music for about the last 150 years and are now the *sine qua non* of the tradition.

In 1764 the Nawab of Awadh, Shuja-ud-Daula, was compelled to forfeit a third of the revenue of his territory in return for which the British guaranteed Awadh's security and independence from Delhi with a strong military presence and the posting of a British Resident to oversee military and administrative cooperation. Free from the restraints of Mughal domination, and with the security of his territory assured, Shuja-ud-Daula moved to Faizabad and opted to pour money into a rebuilding scheme that would transform the fortress into a bustling, fashionable city which 'almost rivalled Delhi in magnificence; it was full of merchants from Persia, China and Europe, and money flowed like water' (Nevill, 1928: 223). Shuja-ud-Daula was also known to be fond of music and dance, and he promised to lavish his wealth on the pursuit of these passions. For example, it is reported that he regularly took musicians and courtesans with him on journeys (Sharar, 1975: 134). Thus, many courtesans, dancers, singers, and instrumentalists found this new and abundant source of patronage quite irresistible (Kippen, 1988: 2).

Whatever Shuja-ud-Daula achieved paled into insignificance in comparison with his son Asaf-ud-Daula's massive project for Lucknow, to which the capital was moved. Many of Lucknow's greatest palaces and most imposing mosques and *imambaras* (Shia religious congregational halls) date from this era, so too did the establishment of a court in which music and dance flourished to an unprecedented extent, so much so that Asaf-ud-Daula is still to this day fondly remembered by the people of Lucknow for his generosity and liberality (Oldenburg, 1984: 16). Yet it seems that much of the funding for Asaf-ud-Daula's extravagances came from increased tax burdens, and so ironically at the very time Lucknow burst into bloom there was an ugly undercurrent of poverty; in other words, whilst the palaces were magnificent, the back streets were crowded and dirty (Miner, 1981: 169).

Musicians flocked to Lucknow from Faizabad (Imam, 1959: 17), and Delhi. Prominent among these were two singers, Ghulam Rasul and Miyan Jani, who had specialised in *qavvali*, a Muslim devotional genre. However, on reaching Lucknow they began to specialise in khayal, to which they had been exposed in Delhi. Ghulam Rasul and Miyan Jani did much to popularize khayal, and they provide us with an important link between qavvali and khayal that is often denied by scholars who prefer to believe that khayal was mainly derived from dhrupad (see Miner, 1981: 169–70). Ghulam Rasul's son, Miyan Shori, continued the innovative trend by creating the vocal genre *tappa*, a light-classical form characterised by a constant stream of acrobatic flourishes and runs.

Clues to some of the musical activities of the time are drawn from contemporary accounts. It is said that Asaf-ud-Daula took dancers and musicians on hunting expeditions and spent excessively on events such as the wedding procession of his son and successor, Wazir Ali, in 1795.

On each side of the procession, in front of the line of elephants, were dancing girls richly dressed carried on platforms supported by men called bearers, who danced as we went along. All these platforms were covered with gold and silver cloths; and there were two musicians on each platform. The number of these platforms was about a hundred on each side of the procession. (Quoted in Pemble, 1977: 14–15)

Following the death of Asaf-ud-Daula in 1797 the British quickly deposed Wazir Ali within a year of his accession and instead promoted Saadat Ali Khan (1797–1814) who agreed in return to cede half the territory of Awadh. The British allowed the Nawabs to pursue their passions for architectural curiosities and the arts, and a general lifestyle of sybaritic luxury. Indeed, so long as these diversions kept the inhabitants of Lucknow and their nominal rulers from any thoughts of rebellion or designs on power, the British continued to turn a disapproving but nevertheless blind eye to what must have seemed to them a chaotic world created by 'a corrupt, effete, and degraded dynasty' (Russell, 1957:

57–8). They even went as far as to sanction in 1819 the rather bombastic and pompous request of Nawab Ghazi-ud-din Haydar (1814–27) that he be made 'King of Awadh'.

A famous story concerning Ghazi-ud-din Haydar and a celebrated singer of the day gives a taste of what things might have been like in the Lucknow of the 1820s.

Haideri Khan was a great singer who neither sang for money nor accepted the invitations of Lucknow's nobility to perform. He insisted that any rich man interested enough to hear him should visit him at his own modest house, share his own cheap smoking pipe, and sit on his own rudimentary charpoy. This eccentric behaviour had earned him the nickname 'Siri' ('Mad') Haideri Khan.

One day the King, Ghazi-ud-din Haydar, summoned Haideri Khan to perform at the court. When news of the inevitable refusal reached the King he was so outraged that he ordered the immediate execution of the singer. But the Prime Minister, Agha Mir, quickly explained the background and pointed out that it would not be in the King's best interests if posterity remembered him for killing a madman who defied an order to sing at court. Haideri Khan's life was therefore spared.

Sometime later the King was travelling through the city on a palanquin when one of his retinue recognised the distant figure of Haideri Khan. The King got down and approached the singer, inviting him to come and perform at his house. Dressed in ordinary clothes the King was not instantly recognizable to Haideri Khan, and so he agreed. However, he was soon horrified to see that they were approaching the palace, and to learn that his companion was in fact Ghazi-ud-din Haydar. He could not now go back on his word, and so Haideri Khan attended court and sang with a silver voice. Around midnight the King requested the poignant *Rag Sohini*. Soon Haideri Khan had his audience in tears. Impetuously, the King then repeated the request, but Haideri Khan refused. The King insisted that if he could not hear *Sohini* again he would have Haideri Khan beheaded! Angered but undaunted, the singer began to perform with such intensity that all present were utterly transfixed.

At the end of the sitting the King lavished praise on Haideri Khan and asked him to name his price. Haideri Khan assured the King he did not sing for reward. A second time the King asked, and a second time the singer refused. Ghazi-ud-din Haydar persisted a third time, to which the singer replied: 'But you would not give me what I want.' Hearing this, the King promised that he would indeed keep his word by honouring any request. 'Very well then,' said Haideri Khan, 'I would only ask that you never call me here again. If you die Awadh will have another King, but if I die India will have no other musician of my greatness' (see Kippen, 1988: 19; also Sharar, 1975: 135–6).

Nasir-ud-Din Haydar (1827–37) outdid his father in absurd and extravagant living. His exploits became the subject of a sensational and often amusing account written by William Knighton and published in London in 1855 under the title *The Private Life of an Eastern King*. The book was something of a bestseller in England, and did much to harden British attitudes already severely tested by the administrative incompetence of successive Nawabi courts. But it was the last and most notorious King of Awadh, Wajid Ali Shah (1847–56), who embodied all that was wrong with Nawabi Lucknow in the eyes of the British: not only did Wajid Ali Shah sing, dance and write poetry, he preferred the company of courtesans, dancers, musicians, and poets to that of his ministers and advisors. Sleeman illustrates the extent to which the King confided in, and was manipulated by, those he promoted to high office:

The most powerful favourites were two eunuchs, two fiddlers (perhaps *sarangi* players), two poetasters, and the Minister and his creatures. The Minister could not stand a moment without the eunuchs, fiddlers and poets, and he is obliged to acquiesce in all the orders given by the King for their benefit. The fiddlers have the control over administration of civil justice, public buildings, etc. The Minister has the land revenue, and all are making enormous fortunes (Quoted in Edwardes, 1960: 155).

The Minister referred to here is undoubtedly Ghulam Raza Khan, a sitar player whom we shall soon see had a prominent role to play in defining new trends in mid-nineteenth century Hindustani music.

The source for much information on music in Nawabi Lucknow comes from the *Ma'danul Moosiqui* ('The Mine of Music') of Hakim Mohammed Karam Imam, courtier of Wajid Ali Shah. A glance at the long columns of names of illustrious musicians mentioned by Imam is enough to provide convincing evidence that Lucknow had replaced Delhi as India's most important musical centre. Several significant hereditary family traditions were represented at court throughout the period, in particular the Seniyas, musicians claiming direct descent from the great sixteenth-century court musician Miyan Tansen. The Seniyas specialised in dhrupad, which still predominated as the major form. It was performed either vocally or on one of two instruments: the *bin* (i.e. the *rudra vina*, a stick zither with two large resonating gourds attached to each end) and the *rabab* (a lute with a large, round, wooden body and tapering fingerboard).

Chajju Khan Kalawant and Jivan Khan Kalawant, both dhrupad masters specialising in the rabab, left Delhi to join the Lucknow court of Asaf-ud-Daula. Imam mentions Jivan Khan as 'an accomplished exponent of both Marg (traditionally established, serious) and Desi (light, regional) Ragas' (Imam, 1959: 18). Generally speaking, the Seniyas were quite particular about retaining their knowledge of rags, compositions, and techniques within their lineages, or at best sharing it only with their most dedicated followers. Both these rabab players therefore probably restricted the instruction of their serious repertoire to their families and closest disciples whose role it was to continue the dhrupad tradition; by contrast they taught a different repertoire to their other students who went on to develop and popularise non-dhrupad instrumental music during the nineteenth century. The 'Desi' rags mentioned by Imam (*Zila, Pilu, Kafi, Gara,* etc.) were prevalent in that new repertoire (Miner, 1981: 170–1).

Chajju Khan had three sons: Basat Khan, Pyar Khan, and Jafar Khan. According to Imam (1959: 18) they were the last of the great rabab masters. Miner (1981: 228–9) suggests that the artistic climate of Lucknow before 1850 would have begun to favour lighter genres of music, and that these musicians would have been approached by many people from outside their families, in particular members of the nobility eager for a training in music. As Miner makes clear, 'In order to satisfy their patrons and maintain their own tradition, they taught non-dhrupad music on the sitar, an instrument rapidly establishing itself throughout Hindustan' (Miner, 1981: 229).

There was also experimentation with the creation of new instruments. Basat Khan is attributed with the invention of the *surshringar* (essentially the rabab was fitted with metal strings and metal fingerboard—Imam, 1959: 18), and Ghulam Ali Khan is credited with the invention of the sarod (similar additions were made to the smaller, skin-bellied Afghan rabab—Miner, 1981: 90–3). We also know that Basat Khan taught sarod to his most famous disciple, Niamatullah Khan (1816–1911). The existence of both serious and light repertoires and the appearance of new instruments support the view that the primary motive for their introduction was the circumvention of rules deterring the teaching of dhrupad to non-Seniya musicians (Solis, 1970: 34–5). The invention of the sarod towards the middle of the nineteenth century was therefore highly significant: whereas the Indian rabab and the surshringar became obsolete by the early twentieth century, and the Afghan rabab continued only to be played in Afghanistan and Kashmir, the sarod went on to grow in stature and has consequently become one of the most popular instruments of the modern era.

Binkar lineages were less prominent in Lucknow than the rabab lineages, but once again it appears that descendants of a famous Delhi Seniya family travelled to Lucknow by way of Faizabad in the late eighteenth century. By the mid-nineteenth century the most famous lineage was that of Umrao Khan, described by Imam as 'an Ustad of the highest merit' (Imam, 1959: 23).

Imam also mentions many non-dhrupad lineages, and makes it clear that besides the music of the Seniyas there was much activity in khayal and other lighter vocal forms as well as in instrumental music. Towards the end of the Nawabi period the sitar seems to have become prominent; initially it would have been used as an accompanying instrument, probably for dance, though by the mid-nineteenth century Ghulam Raza Khan, who must have been a direct beneficiary of the non-dhrupad training of the Seniyas, had managed to popularise it as a solo instrument in its own right. He was also credited with the invention of a style of instrumental composition, or gat, bearing his name: the *Raza Khani* gat. However, it is not entirely clear whether Ghulam Raza created this style of gat himself or merely popularised it; nonetheless it became the predominant form in medium or fast tempo, and instrumental repertoire is full of melodies conforming to its sixteen-beat rhythmic structure.

As for Ghulam Raza's own playing, Imam's comment is enlightening:

This style follows no tradition and is unsystematic. Its gats in Titala (tintal) are composed in the style of Thumri, Ragini and Dhun(and) are incomplete, hence I am not impressed. Undoubtedly Ghulam Raza had a sweet touch. The followers of this style are quite mad over it. . . . Ustads are averse to this style, and the connoisseurs are ashamed of it. Ghulam Raza developed this style only for the nobles of Lucknow (Imam, 1959: 23).

Obviously, Ghulam Raza was inspired by lighter forms, and the resulting compositions in his *Raza Khani* gat style, at least when compared with dhrupad, were short and incomplete and lacked the necessary scope to express the full character of serious rags. On the other hand the style was ideal for light rags, such as those created by Wajid Ali Shah which were named 'jogi, juhi, jasmine, or Shah pasand, "favourite of the King" ' (Sharar, 1975: 138). The fact that 'Ustads' were not impressed by it demonstrates a spilt between traditionally held musical values and the nobility's new and more frivolous craze for the light and superficial. It also suggests a further departure from the non-dhrupad training the Seniyas gave to students outside their families. But of course it was the nobility who were ultimately in a position to patronise music, and so their tastes helped establish and shape the new trend towards lighter music at the expense of more substantial and sophisticated classical forms such as dhrupad. Dhrupad has been in steady decline all over India ever since, and now only a handful of musicians still specialise in it, most notably the Dagar family and the Mallik family.

Adding to the atmosphere of frivolity in the Nawabi courts were the courtesans, or *Baijis* as they are popularly referred to because of the addition of 'Bai' to their names (e.g., i.e. Zohrabai or Jankibai). The Baijis were women who danced, sang, recited poetry, demonstrated social graces, and bestowed their expert sexual favours on those wealthy enough to be able to afford to retain them on what was usually a long-term basis. Members of Lucknow's nobility even sent their children to the Baijis for schooling in etiquette as well as to learn something of the arts, particularly poetry. Courtesans were an important link in the development of Hindustani music: they did not have access to the dhrupad tradition of the Seniyas, though they did receive training from these great masters, almost certainly in khayal. However, they were best noted for the semi-classical thumri, a vocal genre that also constitutes an important expressional and interpretive element in *kathak* dance, as well as the ghazal, a poetic form set to melodies loosely based on classical principles. Popular belief has it that the thumri was created by Wajid Ali Shah, though evidence suggests it had almost certainly already become an independent vocal form somewhat influenced by khayal by 1800 (Manuel, 1986: 471), becoming extremely popular and pervasive in the time of Wajid Ali Shah. Wajid Ali Shah also wrote and performed his own ghazals, some of which were noted for their inclusion of obscenities and sexually explicit references to his own private life.

One other genre that had become established in Lucknow, owing essentially to the nature of Shia Muslim practice so culturally dominant in the city, was *soz*. Soz was 'begun by Shias in India to keep fresh the memory of the martyrdom of the Prophet's family' (Sharar, 1975: 147), and was performed during the month of Mohurram. Based in serious rags and accompanied by voices giving the drone (no instruments were allowed), soz compositions were performed by many great musicians at private gatherings or in the great imambaras of Lucknow.

The compositions of dhrupad had always been accompanied by the large, barrel-shaped *pakhavaj*: an ancient instrument whose deep and powerful sounds are said to have had magical properties, and could, for example, subdue even a raging elephant. The pakhavaj is still used in dhrupad today. Although khayal and non-dhrupad instrumental music were probably initially accompanied by the *pakhavaj*, it soon became apparent that the tabla was a far more appropriate accompanying drum for these lighter forms with their new metric cycles such as the twelve-beat *ektal* (which emerged from dhrupad's *chautal*) and the sixteen-beat *tintal.* The Lucknow thumri, too, began to utilize tintal instead of shorter folk metres (Manuel, 1986: 474). Therefore the tabla grew in importance with the growth of interest in khayal, thumri and the sitar and sarod. Most prominent among the tabla players was Miyan Bakhshu Khan (Imam, 1959: 25), who founded a Lucknow tabla lineage which still continues in the city today, seven generations later, in the person of Ustad Ilmas Husain Khan. It appears that the demands of accompanying new forms in Lucknow, and in particular the kathak dance of the Baijis, resulted in a style somewhat different to that of the other main centre for tabla, Delhi. Whereas the Delhi style remained 'pure' with a limited number of refined finger strokes, the Lucknow style developed a wider range of strokes, particularly heavy ones derived from pakhavaj technique, needed to imitate the sounds of dance pieces.

Just as Lucknow's musical activity reached a peak under Wajid Ali Shah, so too did the intolerance of the British who, bitterly impatient with the King's blatant excesses and incompetent administration, opted to annex Awadh. Wajid Ali Shah was sent into exile at Matiya Burj in Calcutta, and was never to see his beloved Lucknow again. Not that he would have recognised it anyway, since what followed annexation was to change the complexion of the city and its culture forever. The sequel to 1857 was new British policies aimed at making Lucknow more easily defendable and thus governable. The large-scale demolition of vast tracts of the city was ordered, in some cases eradicating entire districts, and wide streets were forced though the crowded labyrinths facilitating the rapid movement of troops should these be required to suppress new rebellions (Oldenburg, 1984: 29–42). About a third of the population was displaced, and many palaces and aristocratic residences vanished. Musical activity came to a virtual standstill, as the tabla player Haji Vilayat Ali Khan, a disciple of the lineage of Bakhshu Khan, found on his return to the city from a pilgrimage to Mecca: 'the connoisseurs of Lucknow had ceased to hold music concerts because of fear of the new regime' (Imam, 1959: 26). The beneficiaries of Lucknow's sudden demise were other courts in more politically stable regions, particularly Rampur, Gwalior, Jaipur, Mewar, and Indore (Miner, 1981: 261ff.).

Not all Lucknow's musicians left for greener pastures. Soon, music-making had resumed under the remaining members of the aristocracy who still maintained residences in the city. In addition there was a newly emerging nobility, the local landowners and tax collectors (*zamindars* and *taluqdars*), who had been promoted by the British, some to the status of Maharaja, and who were regarded as allies in the administration of the region. Thus Lucknow regained some of its stature as a centre for the arts, but never again to the same extent as during Nawabi days. For India was changing. Under the British a middle class began to emerge that sought a European-style education but also quintessentially Indian symbols to represent the antiquity, depth, and sophistication of its own culture (Meer, 1980: 122). In this context, music was the key. However, there was a problem. Hitherto it had rarely been heard outside the courts, the houses of the nobility, and the salons of the courtesans. To the ordinary middle-class person, music was practically inaccessible. He could neither hear it nor learn it, since traditionally the *ustads* had kept their knowledge to themselves and their *gharanas*. Gharanas (musical lineages paralleling blood lineages) were necessary in the competitive world of the courts where musicians made a living from their ability to excel in some unique aspect of knowledge or style. Music was thus to be guarded vigorously by gharana members lest it fall into the wrong hands. Certainly, the gharanas served an important purpose: they propagated musical expertise through the traditional master-disciple relationship that virtually guaranteed to develop children of the lineage into highly accomplished masters. Gharanas also specialised in certain areas of musical knowledge and promoted a distinct and recognizable style; this has resulted in the great variety of rags, compositions, techniques, and approaches to the structuring of performance that we witness in today's generation of performers. Nevertheless, it is easy to see how the non-hereditary music enthusiast of the late nineteenth and early twentieth centuries could be frustrated by what to him would have appeared an underworld of secretive ustads.

Besides the inaccessibility of music there was its dishonourable reputation to consider. Few self-respecting members of the middle class would wish to be associated with an art form that had clearly fallen into disrepute because of its links with dissolute and debauched characters like Ghazi-ud-Din Haydar and Wajid Ali Shah. Then there were the courtesans whom the puritanical middle classes saw as little more than prostitues. Closely linked to, and very much dependent upon the courtesans, were tabla players and other accompanists like *sarangi* players. These low-caste musicians were branded as pariahs.

Nowadays, a great many people reminisce about two important saviours of their nation's musical heritage: Vishnu Digamber Paluskar (1872–1932) and Vishnu Narayan Bhatkhande (1860–1936). It is Bhatkhande who is the more important figure in the history of Lucknow: indeed, his stoical life and work has been elevated to almost mythical proportions by his followers, many of whom are still living and working in Lucknow today. Bhatkhande attempted to reconcile India's contemporary musical practices with ancient theory, thereby restoring to it the status of a highly-organised and deeply theoretically-based art form. To this end he studied the ancient treatises and embarked upon journeys throughout the country to collect as much information on rags and compositions as his resources permitted. Initially sceptical ustads were apparently quickly won over by his sincerity and integrity, and generously shared with him many of their treasures (Misra, 1985: 12). Bhatkhande was a prolific writer, and the most significant of his works was the *Kramika Pustaka Malika*, published in six volumes between 1917 and 1936. It contains a great deal of theoretical information as well as notations of thousands of vocal compositions from a great variety of sources. The compositions are arranged by rag, and each rag is located in a system of ten *thaths*, or parent scales, each of which takes its name from a prominent rag in the thath. This classification system is the most widely used today, and is the basis upon which the theory of Indian rag is taught in the majority of North India's music institutions. The materials contained in the *Kramika Pustaka Malika* are also used as the major source for practical training in vocal music.

Bhatkhande was also active in organizing a series of All India Music Conferences in Baroda (1916), Delhi (1917 and 1922), Benares (1918), and Lucknow (1924 and 1925). These events lasted several days at a time, and presented the greatest performers of the period to the general public in concerts that could be heard morning, afternoon, evening, and night. These occasions also allowed scholars and enthusiasts to gather together with the performers and 'confer' about music theory and practice.

With the support of a number of wealthy enthusiasts Bhatkhande also began to establish music schools during this period: in Baroda, Bombay, Gwalior, and Nagpur. But the biggest and most important school of music in the country came into being in Lucknow in July 1926. First called the Akhil Bharatiya Sangeet Mahavidyalaya, then the Morris Music College, the institution was later renamed after the figure who did most to inspire a generation, Bhatkhande (Misra, 1985: 27--8). Bhatkhande installed his best and most faithful disciple, S.N. Ratanjankar, as Principal of the College, and began enlisting the support of several great musicians of the day as music professors. Sakhawat Husain (grandson of Niamatullah Khan) taught sarod; the head of the Lucknow tabla gharana, Abid Husain, taught tabla; Hamid Husain taught sitar. In later years came Mohanrao Kalyanpurkar (kathak), V.G. Jog (violin), Yusuf Ali Khan (sitar), Rahimuddin Dagar (dhrupad vocal), and Ahmadjan

Thirakwa (tabla). The College flourished, and in its early days it helped turn out several excellent performers such as K.G. Ginde, S.C.R. Bhatt, and Dinkar Kaikini, all students of Ratanjankar. However, Pandit Ginde stated that institutional training alone is not an adequate preparation for a performing musician; besides classes at the College, Ginde, Bhatt, and Kaikini lived with Ratanjankar for training from their *guru* (Ginde, 1991). What the College unquestionably achieved was the training of an intelligent audience for music: a new generation of musically literate enthusiasts responsible for fulfilling Bhatkhande's dream that there be an easy system of music education open to all.

The advent of radio also contributed to the introduction of Hindustani music to an audience of previously inconceivable proportions. Lucknow's A.I.R. station was commissioned in 1938. Radio introduced the concept of state patronage, since each station was responsible for employing a small number of musicians on a permanent basis as 'staff artists' as well as engaging many more on a casual basis. The greatest musicians of the day were regular visitors to Lucknow where they broadcast: Faiyaz Khan and Alauddin Khan (sarod, Maihar-Seni gharana). Both also used their visits to Lucknow to spend time at the Bhatkhande College of Music giving masterclasses and concerts. All India Radio Lucknow remained one of the largest and most significant stations for many years.

Thus, in just a few decades the responsibility for supporting and promoting music had been handed 'from prince to populace' (Higgins, 1976). The reality of the new age was greater competition, and increasingly a different sort of competition. There were touring musicians, recordings, broadcasts, even published notations of repertoire. There was a steadily growing number of non-hereditary musicians, often hailing from the middle-class and from highly-educated backgrounds. No longer were the musicians of a distant court mere names: everyone could hear everyone else, everyone had access to musical knowledge, and much of the mystique had gone.

For many musicians the transition was a difficult one. It appears that in the early days of the Bhatkhande College of Music both Bhatkhande and Ratanjankar had their work cut out to maintain 'discipline' among the teaching staff (Misra, 1985: 15). Institutionalized training differed from gharana training in that classes were held at regular hours and certain academic expectations had to be met, like the learning of at least nine different rags within the first year (see Bhatkhande Sangit Vidyapith, 1981–83). The gharana approach was incompatible with this; traditional ustads were notorious for living by the whim of their moods. If they felt inclined to teach then their lessons might last for many hours, if not, they simply postponed instruction. Moreover in the old system rarely were more than one or two rags taught until a student became musically and technically quite advanced. Here the emphasis lay with the *system* or *process* of musical improvisation, not with *product* (i.e. particular compositions).

Comparatively few musicians today are hereditary occupational specialists, and most come from non-hereditary backgrounds. Even so, everyone identifies with a gharana, at least as a teaching lineage, since through this association there is still some stylistic currency to be had, not to mention a certain degree of enhanced musical status. The scholarly debate about gharanas continues: are they a good or bad thing? Some have insisted they are a plague, while others claim the survival of Hindustani music entirely depends upon their continuation (see Neuman, 1980: 145).

After Independence it became clear that in order to make a decent living a musician needed to exploit the markets of rapidly growing industrial and cultural centres such as Bombay, Calcutta, and Delhi. There was therefore something of an exodus of promising musicians from Lucknow during the 1950s.

What would the visitor to today's Lucknow expect to find in the way of musical activity? Although compared to the Nawabi era, or even to the early decades of the twentieth century, Lucknow's importance as a major centre for music has clearly waned, the city can nevertheless boast that it has a small but vibrant community of musicians and enough going on to maintain its place on the cultural map of North India.

Most significant of all is still the Bhatkhande College of Music, the largest employer of musicians in the city and a prominent force nationally as a respected institution. Most vocal and instrumental genres are taught, as well as classical and folk dance idioms, towards the equivalent of undergraduate (five years) and graduate (a further three years) degrees. The College lists about thirty musicians with teaching posts, and a further twenty-five or so accompanists. The only musician in the College's ranks with solid historical links to the city of Lucknow and its old musical lineages died recently: Ustad Ilyas Khan, Professor of sitar for many years, was the great grandson of Niamatullah Khan and the son of Sakhawat Husain. Otherwise, the College has in recent years employed its own outstanding graduates as teachers, or has attracted musicians from other centres, in particular Benares. There is also the Uttar Pradesh Sangeet Natak Akademi, with its emphasis on musical research and archiving.

The building also houses the Lucknow Kathak Kendra. All India Radio Lucknow, though not as far-reaching as it once was, still broadcasts to a sizeable portion of Uttar Pradesh, and is very much an integral part of the lives of a great many people despite the rapidly increasing reliance on television. The Lucknow Festival, held for two weeks each February, is the largest musical event in the city. Created in the 1970s to promote trade and tourism, it attracts some of India's most famous artists. Besides classical music, drama and folk theatre are represented, and there are a number of very popular evenings featuring lighter musical genres such as ghazal. In addition to the Festival a number of societies dedicated to the promotion of music are active in Lucknow, by far the most prominent being the Uttar Dakshin Cultural Organization which is responsible for the annual Tansen-Tyagaraja Festival, a week-long festival of Hindustani and Karnatak music.

The musical life of Lucknow is by no means dead, even if those glorious days of court patronage have disappeared forever.

REFERENCES

Bhatkhande Sangit Vidyapith (1981–83), Lucknow, *Prospectus and Syllabus.*

Edwardes, Michael (1960), *The Orchid House: Splendours and Miseries of the Kingdom of Oudh 1827–57,* London, Cassell.

Ginde, Pnadit K.G. (1991), Personal Communication, Toronto.

Higgins, Jon (1976), 'From Prince to Populace: Patronage as a Determinant of Culture Change in South Indian (Karnatak) Music', *Asian Music,* 7 (2).

Imam, Hakim Mohammed Karam (1959), *Ma'danul Moosiqui.* (Translated as 'Melody through the centuries', by Govind Vidyarthi). Sangeet Natak Akademic Bulletin, 11–12.

Jairazbhoy, Nazir A. (1971), *The Rags of North Indian Music,* London, Faber and Faber.

Kippen, James (1988), *The Tabla of Lucknow: A Cultural Analysis of a Musical Tradition,* Cambridge Studies in Ethnomusicology, Cambridge University Press.

Maharaj, Pandit Birju (1982), Personal Communication, Lucknow.

Manuel, Peter (1986), 'The Evolution of Modern Thumri', *Ethnomusicology,* 30, 3.

Meer, Wim van der (1980), *Hindustani Music in the Twentieth Century,* New Delhi, Allied Publishers.

Miner, Allyn Jane (1981), *Hindustni Instrumental Music in the Early Modern Period: A Study of the Sitar and Sarod in the Eighteenth and Nineteenth Centuries,* unpublished Ph.D. Thesis, Banaras Hindu University.

Misra, Susheela (1985), *Music Makers of the Bhatkhande College of Hindustani Music,* Calcutta, Sangeet Research Academy.

———— (1991), *Musical Heritage of Lucknow*, New Delhi, Harman Publishing House.

Nevill, H.R. (1928), *Fyzabad: A Gazetteer*, Allahabad, Government Printing Press.

Neuman, Daniel M. (1980), *Life of Music in North India*, Delhi, Manohar.

Oldenburg, Veena Talwar (1984), *The Making of Colonial Lucknow*, Princeton, Princeton University Press.

Pemble, John (1977), *The Raj, the Indian Mutiny and the Kingdom of Oudh 1801–1859*, Hassocks, The Harvester Press.

Russell, William (1957), *My Indian Mutiny Diary*, Michael Edwardes (ed.), London, Cassell.

Sharar, Abul Halim (1975), *Lucknow: The Last Phase of an Oriental Culture.* (Trans. and eds E.S. Harcourt and Fakhir Hussein), London, Paul Elek.

Solis, Theodore (1970), *The Sarod: Its Gat-Tora Tradition with Examples by Amir Khan and Three of his Students*, unpublished M.A. Thesis, University of Hawaii.

Stewart, Rebbeca (1974), *The Tabla in Perspective* (unpublished Ph.D. thesis), University of California, Los Angeles.

12

The Re-emergence of Lucknow as a Major Political Centre, 1899–early 1920s

FRANCIS ROBINSON

The second half of the nineteenth century saw a steady decline in the political fortunes of Lucknow. The annexation of Awadh in 1856 ended its position as the seat of India's most powerful regional polity. The uprising of 1857 and its aftermath saw the brutal imposition of British power and British preferences on the face and folkways of the city. The amalgamation of the old lands of Awadh with the North-West Provinces in 1877 saw further subordination as the office of Chief Commissioner for Awadh was merged with that of Lieutenant-governor based in Allahabad, to which city also moved the High Court and administration of the province. For the remainder of the century the citizens of Lucknow lived in fear that their one remaining special symbol of authority, the Judicial Commissioner's Court, would on the grounds of cutting down costs and commonsense also be removed to Allahabad. In consequence their city, which had by far the largest population in the combined provinces, and arguably the most glorious history, would be reduced to no better than a divisional capital, a Bareilly or a Meerut.

By the early 1920s the political fortunes of Lucknow had been transformed. It was acknowledged, even by the citizens of Allahabad, as the effective capital of the UP; here was the residence of the Governor, here was the purpose-built chamber of the Legislative Council. It formed the headquarters of the most important political organisation in India after the Congress, the All-India Muslim League. Its leading family of Sunni *ulama*, that of Farangi Mahal, was the driving force behind the early stages of the Khilafat movement, the most important mass political movement since 1857. As in the first two decades of the twentieth century the focus of all-India politics moved from the seaboard to the Indo-Gangetic heartland, Lucknow emerged, for a moment at least, as the political centre of upper India.

The reasons for this transformation lie in part in the history and position of Lucknow, in part in British policy and the vision of one British officer, and in part in the emergence of organised Muslim politics alongside those of the Congress, led first by Muslims of western education and then by the ulama.

Towards the end of the nineteenth century Lucknow, despite its demotion by the British, still retained much potential as a city of major political significance. It remained the centre of remarkable landed power and wealth. It was, too, the focus of a large concentration of Muslim service families, whose distinction could be traced back through several centuries, and whose members had often spread over much of India. The former capital of the kings of Awadh was still a great centre of Muslim high culture. Muslims from all over the subcontinent, and beyond, looked to its Sunni and Shi'a scholars for guidance; they also followed the lead of its citizens in art and fashion, Islamic scholarship, music, dance, poetry and other courtly attainments. At the same time the city was to be linked more and more closely to India's modern systems of communication.

That Lucknow was a great centre of landed power resulted directly from British policy. In 1857–58 the British had perceived the power of the *taluqdars*, landholders who usually ruled great dependencies wielding social, revenue, judicial and military powers. In consequence they made these 'barons' the basis of their settlement of the region. They were given rights of ownership and revenue collection. Many were given minor jurisdiction in criminal, civil and revenue matters. Their strength as landlords was sustained by the introduction of primogeniture and by the Oudh Encumbered Estates Act, which helped to preserve them from the results of their own extravagance. Their strength as a group was sustained by their organisation, the British Indian Association, and by their shared enjoyment of the culture of Lucknow, where many had been to school at the Colvin Taluqdars College, where many had apartments in the old Qaisarbagh palace, and where they met in the Qaisarbagh Baradari.

In 1900 the taluqdars numbered well over 250, controlled two-thirds of the territory of Awadh, and realised one-sixth of the total revenues of the UP.[1] Some were relatively poor but others were enormously wealthy. Throughout the last forty years of the nineteenth century, British policy was bound up with taluqdari interests. It was known as 'Oudh Policy'

(W.C. Bennett made its canonical exposition in the 1877 Gazetteer and Harcourt Butler was its valiant champion from the 1890s.) The wealthy taluqdars were important in any attempt to raise money, whether for some political purpose or for the further development of Lucknow. Their political importance meant that government trod carefully where their interests were concerned; taluqdari objections were the reason why the Judicial Commissioner's Court was never moved from Lucknow to Allahabad and the ultimate rationalisation of the provincial system of justice was not achieved. Indeed, it is not unreasonable to suggest that taluqdari concerns and 'Oudh Policy' kept alive Lucknow's chances of becoming provincial capital in the grim days when the fates seemed to favour Allahabad (see Reeves 1991: 41–92).

Lucknow had a remarkable concentration of Muslim zamindari and service families. The Qidvai families of Gadia and Bara Gaon, the family of Chaudhuri Khaliq-uz-Zaman and that of Farangi Mahal, lived in the city. Others dwelt in the *qasbas* and towns which encircled the city, some of which dated back to the early years of the Muslim presence in the region. The names of these settlements, many of which had become part of the names of their most distinguished sons are redolent of Muslim achievement in the arts, learning and public affairs. Among them were Amethi, Kakori and Nagram in Lucknow district, Dewa, Daryabad, Kursi, Rudauli and Satrickh in Bara Banki district, Sandila, Bilgram and Gopa Mau in Hardoi district, Mohan, Muradabad and Safipur in Unao district and Dalmau and Jais in Rae Bareli district. The old Muslim families of these towns had often produced men of distinction under the Mughals, the Nawabs of Awadh and the British. Typical of such families were the Sayyids of Bilgram, whose most notable representative in our period was Imad-ul-Mulk Sayyid Husayn Bilgrami, scholar, leading Hyderabadi civil servant, part-formulator of the 1906 Muslim address to the Viceroy, and member of the Secretary of State's Council from 1907. No less typical were the Sayyids of Mohan, whose most prominent representative in our period was Hasrat Mohani, poet, journalist and radical politician. More often than not these families had come to spread throughout India in search of work. Such was the case for the Chaudhuri and Maulvi branches of the Sayyids of Gopa Mau; such too was the case of the Abbasis and Alvis of Kakori. Indeed, Sleeman (1858, II: 10) wrote in 1849 that Kakori had 'more educated men, filling high and lucrative offices in our establishments, than any other town in India except Calcutta'. Most remarkable of families were the Qidvais, the most prominent clan of Barra Banki district. Landowners as well as professional men, they counted three leading taluqdars amongst their number, Tas-saduq Rasul Khan of Jahangirabad, Naushad Ali Khan of Mailaraiganj and Shaykh Shahid Husayn of Gadia, as well as a host of others who were to be prominent in public life, such as Mushir Husayn and Rafi Ahmad Qidvai (see Kidwai, 1987). The city was their natural meeting place, as was demonstrated when political life began to develop.

Indian Muslims looked to Lucknow for leadership in Islamic scholar-ship (see Sharar, 1975: 94). Under the Nawabs of Awadh it had become the centre of Ithna Ashari Shia scholarship. Prominent among the Shia learned men had been Sayyid Dildar Ali Ghufran Maab (1753–1820), his family and pupils. Ithna Ashari Shias from thoughout India took their lead from the Shia *mujtahids* of Lucknow (Cole, 1984). From the time of Aurangzeb Lucknow had also held the leading position in Sunni scholarship. The Farangi Mahal family of learned and holy men, who lived in the Chowk had devised and developed the Dars-e Nizami curri-culum which drew together the remarkable achievements in logic and philosphy of seventeenth- and early-eighteenth century Awadhi scholars. This curriculum had come to be used in *madrasas* all over India. Many traditionally-educated Muslims would have studied the books and com-mentaries of the Farangi Mahalis and some would have travelled to Luck-now to sit at their feet; many ulama, too, would have noted the names of Farangi Mahalis in their *ijazas*, or licences to teach a particular book. For, as the great eighteenth-century scholar, Ghulam Ali Azad Bilgrami, noted, most of the chains of learning in India stretched back to Mulla Qutb-ud-Din Sihalvi, the founder of the Farangi Mahal family (Ansari, 1973: 43; Robinson, 1984: 152–83 and 1993). By the late nineteenth century, however, many felt that Farangi Mahal, although its ulama commanded enormous respect, had failed satisfactorily to meet the chal-lenges of modernisation under British rule. They founded the Nadwat-ul-Ulama in which the learned were to take the lead in co-ordinating the education of Muslims and their representation to government. In 1898 the organisation had founded a school in Lucknow. This became the prime focus of its efforts, which culminated in attempts at educational rather than political leadership (Husayn, n.d.; Metcalf. 1982: 335–47). No other city was as well-placed as Lucknow to give a religious lead over a broad front to the Muslims of India.

As the host, but fifty years before, of a rich court and a ruling dynasty which had been generous patrons of the arts, Lucknow remained in Indian eyes the capital of Hindustani high culture. Moreover, after the terrible suppression of 1857–58 in Delhi the imperial city's cultivated world had dispersed and Lucknow became undisputed mistress of Urdu poetry. Of course, to a visitor from vibrantly commercial Bombay or up-to-date Calcutta, as Sayyid Nabiullah admitted in his welcoming address to the All-India Muslim League sessions of 1916, the Lucknow world, in which poets might sing of *gul* and *bulbul* and their patrons might conceive of life as primarily an opportunity for sensual connoisseurship, offered 'a rich and dainty feast' for their 'sense of the archaic'. (Pirzada ed., n.d., I: 363). Nevertheless, it would be a mistake to imagine that its citizens ignored the modern. Indeed, the 'modern' had been harnessed to project their culture to a wider world. For much of the later nineteenth century, for instance, Lucknow was UP's leading producer of Urdu newspapers, the most important of which were Newal Kishore's *Oudh Akbar* and Sajjad Husain's much-loved satirical journal, *Oudh Punch*. By the early twentieth century these had been joined by two important English language newspapers, the *Advocate* and the *Indian Daily Telegraph*. Lucknow had also become, thanks largely to the energy and initiative of Newal Kishore, by far the most important centre of book publishing in northern India. Sharar (1975: 108) credited Kishore with reviving eastern Islamic literature:

Lucknow benefitted in that it was able to meet all the literary demands of Central Asia, including those of Kashgar, Bukhara, Afghanistan and Persia. Consequently the Newal Kishore Press is the key to the literary trade. Without using it no one can enter the world of learning.

Evidently, there were many aspects of Lucknow's history, culture and recent development which gave it the basis for being a city of more than merely Awadhi significance. To these should be added first-class communications. The city had excellent connections with its immediate hinterland; the British continued the road-building activities of the Nawabs and metalled highways radiated from it in every direction. Lucknow had, moreover, what the 1904 Gazetteer describes as 'a very perfect railway system which affords easy communication with every part of India'.

Crucial to the emergence of Lucknow as the main political centre in the UP was the outcome of the struggle with Allahabad to be the capital city. That the battle had been won *de facto* in Lucknow's favour by 1921 was in large part due to Harcourt Butler, one of the most successful civil servants of his day, who was subsequently even considered, along with Austen Chamberlain, Winston Churchill and Lord Reading, for the post of Viceroy. Butler was infatuated with Lucknow. Listen to part of his valedictory speech to the municipal board and his autobiographical comment:

To me Lucknow has been an inspiration of youth, a support in late years, the abiding city beautiful, my Indian home. It was thirty-one years since I first saw the Residency and heard the frogs croaking in the Gumti; since I first gazed from the iron bridge on that wonderful eastern Oxford view of domes and minarets and cupolas, standing out against the golden glory of the setting sun. All that was best in me, and perhaps something more, I gave to Lucknow (Harcourt Butler Papers, 100, IOL).

His personal preference apart, Butler's concern to defend and promote the interests of Lucknow was the necessary concomitant of his identification with Oudh policy. Indeed, the second of his two pamphlets on the subject, *Oudh Policy: The Policy of Sympathy* (Allahabad, 1906), culminated with a peroration on Lucknow as the very focus of what he was trying to achieve in encouraging harmony between the ruler and the ruled. More generally the defence of taluqdari interests required that the landholders should have their own court of justice using Urdu in Lucknow, rather than to be absorbed into the workings of the High Court using English in Allahabad. The most effective use of this taluqdari 'aristocracy' as allies in the governance of the UP required that the political centre should be in Lucknow where their conservative weight would be most acutely felt. It was the UP government's policy to complete the transfer of government from Lucknow to Allahabad by shifting the Judicial Commissioner's court. The matter was brought to a head several times between 1884 and 1896 by revelations of inefficiencies in the Awadh court, but each time either the Secretary of State or the Government of India vetoed change. Sir Antony Macdonnell, lieutenant-governor 1895–1901, remained dedicated to the policy and told his Viceroy so in no uncertain terms (Curzon Papers, IOL). Butler working by informal means, as he so often did, actively opposed his boss. Through Curzon's secretary, Walter Lawrence, he succeeded, or so he claimed, in insinuating many of his Oudh Policy ideas in his speech to the Lucknow Durbar of December 1899 (Harcourt Butler Papers, 5, IOL).

Butler was determined to have the capital of the UP transferred to Lucknow. Allahabad with its Bengalis, Maharashtrians and close associations with Indian nationalism was too dangerous a location for the official political centre of the province (Harcourt Butler Papers 6 and 100, IOL). In February 1905 he announced in a private letter to his brother-in-law (ibid: 16) his plans and his methods:

Public opinion in Agra is already working up to demand Lucknow as a capital . . .
He that believeth shall not make haste. I shall not cease to work for it—it is the
one object I shall work for till I go. But many converging courses have to be set
in motion. Fortunately most of the work has to be done on lines that fall in my
department and I can work without disclosing my ulterior objective, until the
time is propitious to strike.

Butler had, in fact, already begun to work for his object by raising the
suggestion that the High Court should be moved from Allahabad to
Lucknow. For two years he worked assiduously for the idea until in the
summer of 1906 his Lieutenant-governor, LaTouche (1901–7), doubt-
less concerned at the way in which opposition to the idea from Allahabad
might encourage the growth of political extremism in the province, told
him to stop.

By this time, however, Butler was carrying forward his plans in other
ways. He had breathed fresh life into the scheme to establish a Medical
College whose siting at Lucknow he saw as an important step on the city's
road to becoming capital (Harcourt Butler Papers, 6, IOL). Moreover,
in 1906 he had become District Commissioner for Lucknow which enabled him, in harness with Ganga Prasad Varma, the editor of the *Advocate* and a most active city father, to launch a great campaign for the
development and beautification of the city 'long thought out' (Harcourt
Butler Papers, 100, IOL). He created gardens, restored monuments, improved roads, installed street-lighting. When the new Lieutenant-governor, Hewett (1907–12) showed his enthusiasm for improving the area
around Government House, he was delighted: 'it will all be for the glory
of Lucknow. The better Govt. House is made the longer L.Gs will stay
there' (Harcourt Butler Papers, 100, IOL). Certainly, when more than
a decade later the citizens of Allahabad petitioned the Viceroy over
the provincial government's failure to site the new Council chamber in
Allahabad, they pointed to the unfair advantages gained by Lucknow as
a result of the large sums from the provincial revenues spent on its beautification (Harcourt Butler Papers, 75, IOL).

In effect Butler's second term of duty in Lucknow as Lieutenant-
governor and Governor from 1918 to 1922 decided the issue. Soon after
his return, he initiated comprehensive plans to be drawn for the development of the city over the next fifty years, and reassured the taluqdars
that the Judicial Commissioner's Court would not be moved to Allahabad.
He announced to the municipal board that he was determined Lucknow
should have its own teaching university. By the time he left, the Lucknow
Improvement Trust had been established, a fine new building for the

Judicial Commissioner's Court (now the Awadh Chief Court) was under construction and he had driven the legislation establishing the University of Lucknow through both the Senate of Allahabad University and the UP Legislative Council. Moreover, 2,50,000 pounds sterling had been raised for the last project in large part from the taluqdars; Sir Edwin Lutyens had designed the building, and the foundation stone had been laid. Thus Butler continued his earlier policies of building up Lucknow's claim to be the premier city of the province.

The devolution of power in the Montague-Chelmsford reforms, much of which he disapproved, gave Butler the chance to play a decisive card in bringing the capital to Lucknow. The larger and more active Legislative Council would need a new chamber; Butler decided that this should be in Lucknow. By dint of determination and bare-faced cheek Butler got his Council chamber built in Lucknow, setting off in the process both the protests of Allahabad and the doubts of the Government of India. Continuing to dissemble regarding his real aim, as he had told his brother-in-law in 1905 he would, he replied to petitioners from Allahabad 'that there is not and has not been question of transferring the capital' (Harcourt Butler Papers, 75, IOL). The Government of India was given precisely the same message. Nevertheless, that this had remained his purpose he confirmed in his autobiography. At that time he was overjoyed: 'I have exalted Lucknow and depressed "Allahabad", he told his mother, 'that will never be forgotten' (Harcourt Butler Papers, 12, IOL).

Crucial to the rise of Lucknow as a major political centre was the emergence of Muslim political activism. Up to the turn of the century north Indian Muslims followed the policies laid down by Sayyid Ahmad Khan: they were to steer clear of the nationalist politics, to concentrate on educational development, and to place their trust in the colonial government. But after 1900 UP Muslims found it increasingly hard to believe that such policies could adequately protect their interests. They began to protest in public, more frequently and loudly, and to organise politically to press forward their cause. Such developments drew increasingly on the large concentration of Muslim talent and wealth that lay in and around Lucknow. By doing so they brought the city to the centre of all-India politics.

Arguably the beginning of Lucknow's emergence as an all-India centre can be dated to the annual sessions of the Congress which were held there for the first time in 1899. It was a meeting notable only for the academic presidential address of Romesh Chandra Dutt, and the decision to define the organisation's primary objective as 'to promote by constitutional means the interests and the well-being of the people of the Indian Empire'. Yet Muslims found the presence of the Congress in the city extremely provocative, indeed, they were furious that government had allowed it to be there at all. They realised they must mobilise.

. . . the conviction was being forced upon them (they protested to government) that the activity of the Congress agitators cannot be adequately counteracted by following the lines of least resistance and that it is their duty as loyal citizens no longer to sit with folded hands, while agitators gain influence over the unthinking masses by monopolising Government appointments, and by getting themselves elected to Municipal Boards, the Legislative Councils and other public bodies.[2]

Muslims had come to feel under the rule of Sir Antony Macdonell, and they were right, that the aim was to shift the whole basis of government support in the UP more towards the Hindus (Curzon Papers, 201, IOL). The Muslim service classes had had plenty of evidence of the shift of emphasis: Persian had been removed from the curriculum of Allahabad university; a list of candidates for *tahsildar* and deputy collectorships had been rejected because it had too many Muslims; government had investigated why there were more Muslims than Hindus in the Police; orders had been issued that no more than three Muslims should be appointed for every five Hindus in all branches of the administration. After the Nagri resolution, which required all government documents to be in Nagri as well as the Persian script, Muslims realised that they must become politically active (Robinson, 1974: 134–5), and Lucknow swiftly emerged as the natural political centre. It was in Lucknow at a conference of August 1900 that a whole series of protests throughout northern India came to a head. It was here in October 1901 that Viqar-ul-Mulk called the first informal meeting to discuss political organisation in the house of the barrister, Hamid Ali Khan. It was here that Viquar ul Mulk's initiative reached its conclusion when delegates came on 22 October 1902 from Bihar and the Punjab as well as the UP to form a Central Muhammadan Political Association. The Association was still-born; a more emollient Lieutenant-governor seemed to make it less necessary. But the central role of Lucknow had been demonstrated.

The centrality of Lucknow was revealed again during the next phase of political activism, from 1906 to 1909. Here as Morley-Minto Council reforms were formulated, Muslims pressured government for separate electorates and special privileges. It was to the Qaisarbagh Baradari that delegates came from all over India on 15 and 16 September 1906 to draw up the Muslim Memorial to the Viceroy in which they set out their claims, the drafting being done, as Harcourt Butler's papers reveal, by Imad-ul-Mulk Sayyid Husayn, whose family came from Bilgram.

Admittedly, Lucknow seemed to lose its central role when Nawab Salimullah, furious at the way in which Bengali issues had been ignored in the memorial, led the move to establish the All-India Muslim League from Dacca. A significant group of Lucknavis travelled to East Bengal for the founding of the League. Also, effective control of this Muslim political organisation was first won by the Aligarh interest, and reinforced in the Aligarh session of the League in March 1908. But Lucknow came back into the picture when pressure was needed to achieve the objects of the memorial. Protest generated in Lucknow and its surrounding districts played a large part in April and May 1909, and again in July, in forcing the League leadership, most notably Ali Imam, not to compromise with the Government of India on its demand for exclusive separate electors and numbers of seats on legislative councils in excess of their numerical strength (Robinson, 1974: 175–94).

The key development responsible for the emergence of Lucknow was the shifting of the headquarters of the League to the city. The drive behind this shift came from Lieutenant-Governor Hewett. As patron of MAO College he had been humiliated when asked to intervene in one of the interminable squabbles between the European staff and the Aligarh trustees. His aim became to move the League away from what he considered a centre of Muslim protest. Ironically, by being moved to Lucknow it became linked to a veritable hotbed of Muslim political activism.

This outcome was not apparent in the spring of 1910 when, under secretary Aziz Mirza, the League offices opened in a bungalow on the Lal Bagh Road. But it quickly became apparent when, after Mirza's death, Sayyid Wazir Hasan became secretary in February 1912. Wazir Hasan, aged thirty-eight at the time, was a formidable organiser and one of the most gifted lawyers of his generation. He was a central figure in what came to be known as the 'Young Party', a loose grouping of lawyers, journalists and political aspirants mainly from petty zamindari backgrounds who differentiated themselves from the 'Old Party', an equally loose grouping of large landholders and successful men whose interests were often tied to government (Robinson, 1974, 174–95) . Nearly half the members of the 'Young Party' lived or worked in Lucknow, and for some at least the Raja of Mahmudabad was an important patron (Khaliquzzaman, 1961: 35). They were part of a world in which Muslims were often confident and successful; politics were less anti-Hindu than those of Muslims in, say, Allahabad. Wazir Hasan and his followers made possible the Congress-League pact of 1916 and the appearance of Lucknow at the forefront of national politics.

The context in which Wazir Hasan launched his campaign was propitious for a man seeking to transform League policy. Between 1911–16 Muslims received a series of severe blows: the repartition of Bengal in 1911, the rejection of their Muslim University scheme in 1912 and the Cawnpore mosque affair in 1913. Besides, Britain's failure to support the Ottomans against Italian aggression in Tripoli in 1911, her support for those Balkan states which invaded the Ottoman heartland in 1912 and her involvement in war against the Ottoman empire in 1914, all betokened a loss of sympathy for Muslims in the world at large. Viqar-ul-Mulk's response to the repartition of Bengal voiced the thoughts of many through these years:

It is now manifest like the midday sun that after seeing what has happened lately, it is futile to ask the Muslims to place their reliance on government. The days for such reliances are over. What we should rely on, after the Grace of God, is the strength of our right arm . . .' (Robinson, 1974: 204).

When the outbreak of World War One put constitutional reform on the agenda once more, Wazir Hasan had a clear use for this 'strong right arm'. The first step was to take effective control of the League. The opportunity came when the Calcutta session, which met in the aftermath of the repartition of Bengal, instructed Hasan to re-examine the League's constitution. He produced a draft constitution, apparently after consultation with branches of the Muslim League, which by reducing the annual subscription to Rs 6, lowering the educational qualification for membership to 'literate', and by increasing the size of the Council to 300, consolidated the 'Young Party's' control over the organisation. The draft constitution also gave the League the aim of working with other groups for 'a system of self-government suitable to India'. Thus it was to be stamped with the political objective of the 'Young Party'. Wazir Hasan got the League's Council to approve the new constitution in December 1912 and had it ratified in a full session of the organisation at Lucknow in March 1913. He had brought the 'Young Party' to power. That he had done so was demonstrated through 1913 and 1914 as the 'Old Party' set out both to form an alternative political organisation and to discredit the young leaders of the League. Wazir Hasan, wrote one critic, is the source of all evils and the man 'on whom is also primarily fixed the responsibility of formulating an ideal, which from the very nature of its being, is not only impossible of attainment but positively dangerous and ruinous to the cause of Islam.'[3]

Having seized control of the League and brought its aims into line with those of the Congress, Wazir Hasan's next move was to bring about joint political action. He worked at the local level with the Congress which was itself resolved to see rapprochment with the League wherever possible. He was quick, moreover, to see the opportunity provided by the World War; from February 1915 he set about preparing a scheme of political demands for the League to adopt. For these to succeed, it was crucial that League and Congress were seen to be working together. To this end Wazir Hasan in the face of bitter 'Old Party' opposition, fought for the League session to be held in Bombay alongside that of the Congress. This session resolved to frame a reform scheme and to confer with other organisations where necessary; the new political order was symbolised by the election of the Raja of Mahmudabad as president in place of the Aga Khan. All this had been arranged by the 'Lucknow gang', the Lieutant-Governor of the UP told the Viceroy, 'the small clique, which Wazir Hassan (sic) organises and Mahmudabad feeds. . . .' (Hardinge Papers, 90, Cambridge University Library).

Throughout 1916 Wazir Hasan steered his political strategy towards its climax. His 'gang' played a major role in the Reception Committee for the Congress which was to meet at Lucknow. He drafted the League's reforms scheme which was similar in all respects to that of the Congress except for the introduction of separate representation. His 'gang' dominated the League Council meeting at Mahmudabad House on 21 May which allowed his draft to go forward. They dominated the Council meeting of 12 October which decided that the League should meet at Lucknow alongside the Congress. They played a key part in creating the circumstances in which League and Congress could agree upon a joint scheme of council reforms at Lucknow and Mrs Besant, Bhupendranath Basu, Tilak and Jinnah could broker the final details of the compromise over separate representation for Muslims in the reforms which was to seal the 'Lucknow Pact' (Robinson, 1974: Chapter 6; Ahmad, 1988: 151–81).

It is still possible from some of the descriptions which remain to sense the flavour of this great political occasion in Lucknow. Enthusiasts cut the tyres of Tilak's car on his arrival so that he could be drawn into the city in an open carriage. On coming to the Congress *pandal* he was borne on the shoulders of the delegates from the floor to the platform. Swami Shraddhanand, who was also on the platform, speaks of the nature of the Muslim presence at the Congress session and how it was received.

The majority of Moslem delegates had donned gold, silver and silk embroidered chogas . . . Of some 133 Moslem delegates only some thirty had come from outside, the rest belonging to Lucknow City. And of these the majority were admitted free to delegate seats, board and lodging . . . A show was being made of the Moslem delegates. A Moslem delegate gets up to second a resolution in Urdu, He begins: Hozarat, I am a Mahomedan delegate. Some Hindu delegate gets up and calls for three cheers for Mahomedan delegates and the response is so enthusiastic as to be beyond description. (Ambedkar, 1946: 141).

By comparison as a government reporter noted, the League meeting was attended by few people, the delegates being carefully selected. There were not many from the Punjab, Bombay, Madras and Bengal; 'Old Party' men from the UP were not present. Lieutenant-Governor Meston, who visited the League meeting when 'the Home Rule Resolution was in full blast', told the Viceory that 'there were many empty benches. Very few of the audience were men of over 40, and I could see nobody of any position except the handful on the platform.'(Chelmsford Papers, 18, IOL). These descriptions underline the extent to which the Congress-League rapprochment and the Lucknow Pact were the creation of Wazir Hasan and his small group of followers.

From the point of view of Lucknow the achievement was remarkable. The name of the city had been given to one of the great icons of Indian nationalism. It had hosted what were arguably the most important sessions of the Congress since its foundation, in which not only had Hindus and Muslims come together in the cause of political progress but also the 'extremist' and 'moderate' wings, estranged since 1907. Present at the occasion, moreover, were many of the great figures of the nationalist era: Tilak, Khaparde, Rash Behari Ghosh, Motilal Nehru, Jawaharlal Nehru, Gandhi, Surendranath Banerjea, Mrs Besant, Sarojini Naidu, Jinnah, Mahmudabad, Mazhar-ul-Haq, Hakim Ajmal Khan, Dr Ansari. December 1916 in Lucknow was the moment when the focus of Indian politics began to swing decisively away from the maritime provinces towards the Hindustani heartland.

After the Lucknow Pact the political initiative moved away from Wazir Hasan. His main aim was to ensure that political reforms were carried out. But the 'Young Party' had a more radical agenda. He was attacked for his refusal to campaign for the release of the Ali Brothers, his support for the Montague-Chelmsford Report, his lack of interest in the fate of Turkey, and his dictatorial style. He and his patron, the Raja of Mahmudabad, had no course but to resign at the Delhi session of the League in 1918. The political initiative, however, did not move away from Lucknow. The fate of the Turkish Khilafat now became the great cause of Indian politics. Maulana Abdul Bari and the Farangi Mahal family now came to have something of the leading role that Wazir Hasan had had. Now when political leaders came to the city, they were as likely to visit the Farangi Mahal (in Pacha Wali Gali off the Chowk) as they were to visit Mahmudabad House in the Qaisarbagh.

As Wazir Hasan and Mahmudabad left the forefront of Muslim politics at the Delhi session, the ulama were on the platform, Abdul Bari at their head. The maulana was a man of immense potential influence, not only with family connections all over India, and a reputation built up since the early eighteenth century, but also as the spiritual guide of major political figures, among them Muhammad and Shaukat Ali, Hasrat Mohani and Mushir Husayn Qidvai. Indeed, such was his influence that in 1921 he was considered, along with Abul Kalam Azad, for the position of Shaikh-ul-Islam for the subcontinent. He and his family had a notable record in fighting for pan-Islamic causes. His grandfather had toured India in 1878 to raise funds for the defense of the Ottoman empire. He himself founded the Anjuman-e-Khuddam-e Kaaba in 1913 for the protection of the Holy Places. As World War One developed, he became more and more anxious about the fact of the Ottoman empire and Khilafat.

Throughout 1919 Abdul Bari tried to provoke India into action over the Khilafat. Early in the year he issued a fatwa enjoining jihad if there was any danger of infidels controlling the Khalifa or the Holy Places, tried to drum up support in the UP countryside and set up a newspaper to focus on Islamic issues, *Akhuwat*. In March Gandhi came to stay in Farangi Mahal and Abdul Bari set out on a campaign to win him for the Khilafat cause. This had succeeded by the autumn; 'I have made Mahatma Gandhi to follow us in the Khilafat question', he boasted later (Abdul Bari Papers, English File, Farangi Mahal). An All-India Muslim conference, the Maulana's idea, was held under the auspices of the All-India Muslim League at Lucknow's Rifah-i-Am Club in September 1919. Over 300 Muslims came from outside the city; the atmosphere was highly emotional. The most important resolution of the occasion, and one in which the Farangi Mahalis were involved, aimed to establish an All-India Central Khilafat Committee in Bombay, with branches throughout India. The Farangi Mahalis, with the help of Chaudhuri

Khaliquzzaman, drew up the Committee's constitution. Lucknow had seized the initiative once again.

In 1920 Abdul Bari was at the heart of the process which drew the Khilafat movement to adopt a policy of non-cooperation and then to capture the Congress. As matters unfolded, he was helped most notably by Shaukat Ali, who had just been released from internment, and to whom, along with Shaukat's brother Muhummad, he had given the title of maulana. He was also helped by a better organised and better mobil-ised ulama; in December 1919 he had taken the initiative in founding the Jamiyat ul-Ulama-e Hind. Abdul Bari's first problem was to per-suade the Central Khilafat Committee, which was dominated by Bombay merchants (who paid for its activities and were unwilling to risk the wrath of government), to adopt non-coperation. The first half of the year saw him in frenetic activity to this end: touring Sind twice, playing a leading role in Khilafat conferences at Bombay, Calcutta, Meerut and Madras, putting pressure on M.M. Chotani, who was his disciple and president of the Central Khilafat Committee, and using all his influence to ensure that the right people attended the Allahabad meeting of the Central Khilafat Committee (which voted on non-cooperation), and then using all his weight in the meeting, along with Shaukat Ali, to en-sure that the resolution on non-cooperation was not watered down. Subsequently he used his influence to ensure that Muslims attended the Special Congress at Calcutta in September which voted to support Gandhi's non-cooperation resolution. Abdul Bari's influence in 1919 and 1920 has come to be forgotten; the lives of the ulama have not been the favourite topics of the modern historical establishment. In 1929, however, his biographer (Inayatullah, 1929–30) asserted that Abdul Bari's correspondence from this period had to be studied to understand his significance and consultation of these papers proves him right (Robinson, 1974: 326–44).

After September 1920 Abdul Bari's political fortunes declined. His own influence was partially eclipsed by the rising star of Maulana Azad; that of Farangi Mahal by the entry of Deoband into the Khilafat move-ment. In 1921 and 1922 Abdul Bari and his followers drew away from the political aims of the Khilafat protest because they did not see why they should not have recourse to violence. In 1922 and 1923 they drew further apart as Hindu-Muslim communalism replaced cooperation. No new political or religious figure came forward to keep Lucknow in the forefront of politics. The city returned to being one of several major centres of political activity.

Thus the political fortunes of Lucknow were re-established. Many of her distinctive attributes had played their part in bringing about the change; the wealth of the taluqdars, the beauty of the city, the concentration of Muslim talent, the long-standing leadership in Islamic learning, the 'very perfect railway system'. Now she was set on the road to becoming the capital of the UP and ruling an extent of territory that she had not ruled since the days of Asaf-ud-Daulah. Moreover, her Muslim citizens had served notice of their ability to make a political contribution of all-India significance. For a moment between 1916 and 1920 Lucknow had been the capital of India's political movement against colonialism. Many felt, according to Harcourt Butler, that she deserved to be the capital of India in every respect (Awasthi, 1973: 144–5).

NOTES

1. Throughout this article this area which was known as the North-West Provinces and Oudh up to 1902 will be referred to as the UP.
2. 'The Humble Memorial of the Undersigned Residents of the City of Lucknow', enclosed in J.O. Miller, Chief Secretary to Government, NWP and O, to Secretary, Government of India, Home Department, 26 January 1900, L\P&J\6\712, India Office Records (IOR).
3. Article entitled, 'The All-India Muslim League and its Secretary' and signed 'A Muslim', 25 December 1913, enclosed in Nawab Fateh Ali Khan Qizilbash to Editor, *Civil and Military Gazette* (Lahore); the *Pioneer* (Allahabad); and *Morning Post* (Delhi), 25 December 1913, Meston Papers (6), IOL.

REFERENCES

Ahmad, Muhammad Saleem (1988), *The All-India Muslim League*, Bhawalpur, Ilham.

Ambedkar, B.R. (1946), *Pakistan or the Partition of India*, Bombay.

Ansari, Mufti Raza (1973), *Bani-e-Dars-e Nizami*, Lucknow, Nami Press.

Awasthi, D. (1973), *Administrative History of Modern India: Sir Spencer Harcourt Butler's Ideas, Policies and Activities in the United Provinces of Agra and Awadh 1918–1922*, Delhi, National.

Butler, S.H. (1906), *Oudh Policy: the Policy of Sympathy*, Allahabad, Pioneer Press.

Cole, J.R.I. (1984), *Roots of North Indian Shi'ism in Iran and Iraq: Religion and State in Awadh, 1722–1859*, Berkeley, University of California Press.

Husayn, Shah Muhammad (n.d.), *Bil Tanzim-i Nizam al-Ta'allum wal Talim*, Allahabad, Jalaluddin Ahmad.

Inayatullah, Muhammad (1938), *Risala-e Hasrat al-Afaq ba Wafat Majmu'at al-Akhlaq*, Lucknow.

Khaliquzzaman, Choudhry (1961), *Pathway to Pakistan*, London, Longmans Green and Co.

Kidwai, Riaz-ur-Rahman (1987), *Biographical Sketches of Kidwai's of Avadh (with special reference to Bara Banki Families)*, Aligarh, Kitab Ghar.

Metcalf, Barbara (1982), *Islamic Revival in British India: Deoband 1860–1900*, Berkeley, University of California Press.

Pirzada, S.S. (ed.) (n.d.), *Foundations of Pakistan: All-India Muslim League Documents, 1906–1947*, Karachi.

Reeves, Peter (1991), *Landlords and Governments in Uttar Pradesh: A Study of their Relations until Zamindari Abolition*, Delhi, Oxford University Press.

Robinson, Francis (1974), *Separatism among Indian Muslims: The Politics of the United Provinces' Muslims 1880–1923*, Cambridge, Cambridge University Press.

——— (1984), 'The 'Ulama of Farangi Mahal and their Adab', in Barbara Metcalf (ed.), *Moral Conduct and Authority: The Place of Adab in South Asian Islam*, Berkeley, University of California Press.

——— (1993), 'Scholarship and Mysticism in Early 18th Century Awadh', in A.L. Dallapiccola and A. Zingel-Ave Lalment (eds), *Islam and Indian Regions*, Stuttagart, Franz Steiner Verlag.

Sharar, Abdul Halim (1975), *Lucknow: The Last Phase of an Oriental Culture*, E.S. Harcourt and Fakhir Husain (trans. and eds), London, Paul Elek.

Sleeman, W.H. (1858), *Journey through the Kingdom of Oudh in 1849–1950*, 2 vols, London.

13

Lucknow Politics: 1920–47

PETER REEVES

In 1921 the UP Legislative Council voted to build its new Council House in Lucknow rather than in the capital of the province, Allahabad. This made Lucknow the capital of the province, even though it took until 1935 for the Secretariat to be moved fully to Lucknow and it was not until 1947 that Lucknow was formally recognised as the capital. At one level, recognition as the capital was merely a return to a status that Lucknow had lost in 1877, when the province of Awadh had been merged with the North-Western Provinces to form 'The North-Western Provinces and Oudh' and to the status that it had held from 1775 as the capital of the Nawabs of Awadh. However, given the political changes that had taken place since 1877—and the changes that would take place over the next three decades—the decision was much more important for Lucknow's political role than mere formal recognition as 'the capital'.

Two important results stand out. First, the decision to make Lucknow the capital brought a period of economic development to the city which had been stagnant, certainly since 1877 (Thomas 1982: 68–72) and probably from the time of the annexation in 1856. This economic development—like the new political importance of the city—meant great gains for some sectors of the population and an enhanced role for municipal government. For many others, however, economic development made living and working in the city very difficult. Second, and of more direct interest here, the decision made Lucknow the political centre of the province in the most important phase of India's movement towards independence and partition, as well as in the critical period of the transition of the province to provincial autonomy—and so gave the city a key role in those very significant shifts in political power.

This paper will look, firstly, at the way in which Lucknow became the *de facto* capital of the province, and will then examine the effects of that decision on the growth of the city. Against this background it will then analyse political life in the city: at the municipal level; in terms of its role as the political centre of the province; and in terms of the increased national prominence that the city attained in these years.

Making Lucknow the Capital

Lucknow became the *de facto* capital in 1921 as a result of the straight-out coercion of the members of the Legislative Council by representatives of the government of Sir Harcourt Butler. On 28 March 1921, the Government 'whip' in the UP Legislative Council, Kunwar Jagdish Prasad, ICS, the Education Secretary, sent a letter to MLCs thought likely to be Government supporters:

Dear—, A resolution will be brought forward on the 4th April that the Council Hall should be built in Allahabad and not in Lucknow. This will be opposed by Government. I trust you will see your way to be present on that date and give us your support. I need hardly point out how important the question is for the interests of the landowning classes generally. It is essential that none of our supporters should be absent. Yours sincerely, Jagdish Prasad (*Leader*, 20 Oct. 1921; UPLC, vol. IV, 306).

The move was successful and later, on 1 August 1921, the Government moved in the supplementary estimates that Rs 1 lakh be provided for the first stages of the construction of the Council House in Lucknow. The supporters of Allahabad as the site for the Council, attempted to defeat this by moving that the amount be reduced but, that was defeated by twenty-three votes (UPLC, vol. III: 446–98). This was reported to have also been the result of strong pressure from the 'chief whip', as well as senior official members of the Government:

The Financial Secretary wrote to such members of the Financial Committee as were known to be in favour of Lucknow asking them to attend the meeting of the Committee which was held in June last and vote the preliminary estimates in connection with the construction of the Council Chamber. The Finance Member himself wrote to some non-official members and took part in the cajoling and threatening of non-official members. It is even understood that a zamindar member who voted against Government was sharply taken to task in the highest quarters and was told that it was not proper behaviour on the part of a titled person to disregard the wishes of Government. (*Leader*, 23 Oct. 1921)

It was recognised, in fact, that it was not so much the 'Government' as the 'Governor'—the man who confessed to a *Taluqdari* reception on his return to the United Provinces in February 1915 that he had never been 'so gratified as when I saw myself described by a high authority some years ago as "Harcourt Butler of Oudh"!' The *Leader* of Allahabad had no doubt of it; in November it reported the opinion that Lucknow had been chosen on 'gubernatorial taste' rather than public interest (*Leader*, 13 Nov. 1921). Sir Harcourt Butler made no secret of his partiality for Lucknow and the taluqdars who dominated its social life (Butler 1923: 80–1) and this was widely recognised (Gilbert 1966: 42; Woodruff, 1963: 288). In his draft autobiography he admitted that he did his 'best to establish Lucknow as the de facto capital' and to 'dethrone' Allahabad—which he characterised as being tainted with Bengali and Maratha 'infusions' (Butler Papers: 8–9)

The battle between Lucknow and Allahabad, had a long history. Before the 1920s it was fought out in terms of the location of the High Court—which was at Allahabad—and its jurisdiction relative to that of the Judicial Commissioner's Court in Lucknow; but it was dubbed 'the capital controversy' in the local press because it was seen a 'battle for supremacy' (Buckee, 1972: 342).

The stakes were high because property owners in both cities were well aware of the importance of those who needed residences or other accommodation in the capital. In an earlier round of the controversy, in 1906, a memorial prepared by the British Indian Association (BIA) of Awadh— the association of the taluqdars, many of whom were owners of bungalows and other residential and commercial property in Lucknow—assured the Lieutenant-Governor that not only were there 'private capitalists (who) would willingly provide the necessary bungalows at Lucknow according to plans approved by the Municipal Board', but there was 'abundant room for over one hundred bungalows south of the river Gomati . . . while north of the river there is room for any expansion necessary' (*Indian People*, 15 July 1906).

Beyond the private housing, there were interests looking to the investment that would follow from the need for public buildings and amenities; the Rs 1 lakh voted to begin the Council House was only a fraction of what could be expected. In 1906 the BIA memorial had estimated that a complete shift of the High Court and Secretariat would cost Rs 15 lakhs, so it is not difficult to imagine that 15 years later expectations would be very much greater.

Others saw political influence as the prize. In an editorial entitled 'The Lucknow-Allahabad Controversy' in October, the *Leader* pointed to the political reasons why Butler was insistent on Lucknow. Pointing to the evidence of the Government 'whip' issued back in March, it argued that this indicated clearly

that the Government had made up its mind that the Chamber must be located at Lucknow and that the real reason for its decision was not that Lucknow was more centrally situated than Allahabad but that it wanted to prevent the Council being located at a place where it would be subjected to the liberalising influences of a democratic atmosphere. It desired to make the Legislative Council a bulwark of land-owning interests. It felt that the aristocratic and autocratic aroma of Lucknow was essential for protecting the Legislative Council from the pestilential influence of agitators and demagogues for whom despots have a holy horror . . . it is outrageous that in utter disregard of considerations of economy and of propriety and fairness, the Council Chamber should be located in the stifling and enervating atmosphere of taluqdar-ridden Lucknow (20 Oct. 1921).

The Rs 1,25,500 that the taluqdars subscribed for a statue of Butler that was unveiled as he left the province in December 1922 for his next posting (in Burma), and the 'shower' of Rs 5,000 that was dispersed at the unveiling by the leading maharanis and ranis, were a frank acknowledgement of this. 'Certain barons of Oudh', commented the *Leader*, 'must be feeling especially beholden to Sir Harcourt Butler' (25 May 1922, 23 Dec 1922).

The Development of the City

As a result of the decision to make Lucknow the *de facto* capital, there was a rapid and sustained growth of population (together with a qualitative change in population) because of the greater administrative, educational and political role which opened up for the city. The population of the city was 2,40,566 in 1921, of whom 2,13,494 resided in the municipal limits; by 1931 it had become 251,097 and by 1941 it had reached 3,87,177. (Census 1951: 169; Mukerjee and Singh 1961: 30–1). In the Census of 1951 the population was 4,96,861—a further increase of 28.3 per cent. This population growth was the result, primarily, of the transfer of officials to the city. The relocation of the Secretariat began in 1922, was speeded up from 1928 when the new Council Chamber was opened, and was complete by 1935 (Zaheer and Gupta, 1970: 5, 17,42; Mukerjee and Singh, 1961: 32). In addition, there was migration from rural districts of people looking for work and of 'capitalists' from surrounding areas looking for investment opportunities in, for example, rental property. Spate and Ahmad commented in 1950 that there were 'probably more people merely "living" in it than any other city of the plain' (1950: 273).

There was also a boost to the city's economy from increased trade, the development of industries such as printing and the significant building boom which the need for private housing as well as for official, educational and ancillary buildings produced. This meant construction activity which gave opportunities for 'contractors' as well as work for tradesmen and labourers. Construction was both large scale and residential. Among the largest public projects were the Council Chamber, the Civil Secretariat, and the new buildings to transform Canning College into Lucknow University—a project for which the Taluqdars alone contributed more than Rs 30 lakhs (Ganju 1980: 284). There was also a new Government House, as well as buildings to house the Chief Court which was inaugurated in 1925 following the upgrading of the Judicial Commissioner's Court. There were large private projects, also. There were, for instance, the newspaper offices for the *Pioneer* which moved to Lucknow in 1933 (which were designed by Walter Burley Griffin, a student of Frank Lloyd Wright; Young, 1963: 235–7) and for the newly-founded Congress paper, the *National Herald* which started in 1938. There were by the late 1920s seven Improvement Trust housing schemes, the building of official bungalows, and two blocks of model quarters and three development schemes for lower cost housing (Census, 1931: 149–50). All indicative of the push to develop residential accommodation, even before the major increase in population over the 1930s.

The city which emerged was dubbed 'essentially administrative and commercial' by Spate and Ahmad (1950: 272). The administrative functions followed from the shift of the capital; 'commercially', they argued, 'Lucknow probably ranks next to Cawnpore with important assembly markets for agricultural produce and with a provincial and even national market for its art and luxury products.'

There was relatively little heavy industry (certainly nothing to compare with Kanpur which was 60 miles away). The railway yards, the distillery-brewery, mills for the production of paper, sugar and cotton textiles, and printing and bookbinding establishments were the major industrial concerns. In 1937 the railway workshops, with ten thousand workers, had more than 50 per cent of the industrial workers of the city. The number of workers in the paper mills, sugar mills, cotton mills, and printing & bookbinding establishments were seven hundred and eleven, six hundred and ninety-three, nine hundred and thirty-two and six hundred and ninety respectively (Waheed 1937: 8). The workers in these industrial establishments came from some thirty villages around Lucknow in 1937; Waheed's survey at the time estimated that 15,000 workers came from those villages daily to Lucknow.

Workers in these industrial concerns at Lucknow were poorly paid. But in even more desperate straits were the workers involved in what Spate and Ahmed called (1950: 273) the 'more characteristic . . . craft industries: fine embroideries, jewelry, embroidery in gold and silver thread; and gold and silver wire and foil. Calico printing and the manufacture of chewing and smoking tobacco and perfumes'. These craft industries were, of course, Lucknow's traditional industries. A number of these industries, had declined by the 1920s. The once-famous calico printing industry for example, which had attracted English attention in the early seventeenth century was, by the 1930s, reduced to three workshops with just forty men (Bhattacharya, 1930: 401–2). And in virtually every area of the craft industries conditions of work, levels of wages and standards of living were appalling.

The 'development' of the city, therefore, was very uneven. At the start of the period, in 1921, some of the new, rural-based legislators found that it was a very expensive city in which to reside. 'It is a town meant for the Barons of Oudh and not for the ryots', complained Mr Shakir Ali, MLC from Basti, on 1 Aug 1921 (UPLC, III, 457) and conditions steadily worsened over the 1930s. The 'tenement census' conducted in conjunction with the Census of 1931 showed that half the Lucknow families lived in one room. The average density of Lucknow, excluding the Civil Lines, the Census Commissioner pointed out, was 23.2 persons per acre; but, 'in parts of (the industrially-important) Yahiaganj Ward the density reaches no less than 661 persons to the acre' (Census 1931: 135).

Waheed's report on housing conditions in Lucknow by 1937 highlighted 'congested slums' everywhere and 'appalling' conditions for labouring people: 'Industrial *mohallas* are slum areas where people crawl in for the night and creep out in the morning'. The poor—'petty shopkeepers, artisans, labourers, handycraftsmen (sic), ekka drivers and other transport workers', all faced 'severe problems'. Only the elite areas of Hazratganj and the Cantonment were free of the common problems of overcrowding and epidemic disease (Waheed, 1937: 8). Matters, moreover, were not improved by the population growth over the 1940s: a social survey of the city in 1954–56 reported that the Improvement Trust itself reckoned seven thousand two hundred and fifty-seven of the forty-one thousand houses in the city were 'not fit for habitation' (Mukerjee and Singh, 1961: 127). The survey reported further that density in many areas of the city was four hundred persons per acre—which Mukerjee and Singh regarded as being four times the norm! The conclusions of the survey underlined the great gulf that existed between the elite and the great majority of the population.

Some four per cent of the families have literally no roof over their heads. They simply live on pavements or under trees. Another fifteen per cent are huddled together in single room tenements and only eleven per cent of the families have four or more rooms per family.

As many as twenty-seven per cent of the families live in houses without a latrine, bathroom, kitchen, store and box-room, dining room, dressing room and verandah. Barely 14 per cent of the families have independent bathrooms available exclusively for their use and only fifty per cent have an exclusive latrine. As many as sixty-three per cent of the families have no independent kitchen and only one-fifth have electric supply available in the dwellings. (Mukerjee and Singh 1961: 143).

The Politics of the City

The development of the city had important repercussions for municipal politics both because of the opportunities it opened up in terms of trade, accommodation and building and because of the strengthening of particular social groups from migration to the city and its attractiveness to those with capital— merchants, entrepreneurs and retired officals with pension funds. For the stronger, propertied and capitalist elements in the city these changes were highly advantageous.

The Municipal Board and the Improvement Trust both became important political arenas, arenas which were made more open by the UP Municipal Boards Act of 1916 which provided for non-official (elected) chairpersons. Contests for control of the Board provided the major focus for municipal politics and this, from the outset, involved the balancing of communal interest—both Hindu-Muslim and Shi'a-Sunni—as well as class interests, since there was clearly competition between old capital and the new, *arriviste*, contractors given that the expansion of the city provided benefits for those who were in a position to exploit the expanded economic opportunities.

Political organisations were also not slow to see the importance of these developments and significant political figures, therefore, became key players in municipal politics; Khaliquzzaman was perhaps the key example. He presided over the Board for long periods; he was Chairman of the Board from 1923 to 1926, then from 1929 to 1932, and again from 1936 to 1945; indeed, he had both Board and Trust in his control simultaneously. This points to the assertion both of the older Muslim propertied classes and the connections increasingly made between nationalist political forces and municipal political institutions. Khaliquzzaman—who was a Congress organiser in the period before 1935 and a Muslim League leader after 1935—was very close to the Mahmudabad family and in 1930 he married, for the second time, the niece of Haji Istafa Khan, the proprietor of 'the well-known perfumery firm of Asghar Ali Muhammad Ali' (Khaliquzzaman 1961: 109).

More telling, however, was the role of those who benefitted from the expansion of the city. By the 1940s a third of the members of the Municipal Board were 'contractors' (Municipal Board 1942: 221) and clearly both the Board and the Improvement Trust were seen by many members as a means of furthering personal, family and clique interests.

An inquiry into the Improvement Trust was set up in October 1938 and reported in March 1941. Its brief was to investigate 'the serious financial and other irregularities in the administration of the Improvement Trust' and a series of specific complaints to do with Marris Market, conversion of lease-hold rights to freehold, delays and neglect in executing civil court decrees and the 'alleged failure to provide roads, drains, mains, sewers, light posts, before requiring allottees of plots to put up houses within a specified time' (Improvement Trust 1941: 1–2). The Committee found evidence of embezzlement, failure to collect *nazul* dues, confusion in the maintenance of records, favouritism in allocating land and failure to get houses built within the specified time. The Government had no difficulty in resolving 'that the administration of the Trust has been generally inefficient and unbusinesslike'.

The inquiry into the Municipal Board came after five years of criticism and complaint which culminated in the resignation of H.G. Walford and his claims that he could 'furnish details of malpractices and corruption prevalent in the Board'.

The reports revealed such manipulation of the situation that government would have been justified in intervening but this did not happen until after independence. In 1941–42, no action was taken by the provincial government. Roderick Church, who made a major study of municipal administration of post-independence Lucknow in the late 1960s believed that this was because it was not seen at the time as 'exceptional enough to require any special action' (Church, 1976: 216), although in Agra, where a similar investigation was made in 1941, action was taken to suspend the municipal board (Rosenthal, 1970: 19,21).

What that may suggest is that the wartime Government of 'advisers' were unwilling to upset the elite of the provincial capital, and even more that the interests of working people and of the poor—and they were largely synonymous in Lucknow in this period—counted for nothing. Moreover, it seems that either workers were distracted from a concern for political action in defence of their interests or they lacked an organised base from which to operate politically for those interests.

If one is looking for possible 'distractions' one could look at the increased nationalist activity of the period and at the upsurge of sectarian activity in Lucknow in the mid-to later-1930s as likely candidates. The period certainly was one of intense nationalist activity. Lucknow saw major instances of confrontations with the police: the anti-Simon demonstrations of November 1928, the civil disobedience *satyagraha* of May 1930, and the *kisan* rallies of 1938. Moreover, Mohurram may also have performed a function of releasing some of the potential political concern. It is possible also that, by the late 1930s, some of this potential was channelled into the Shi'a-Sunni conflicts which were an important element in Lucknow's 'sectarian' life (Freitag 1989: 258–60, 270–9). This would be to argue that the urban concerns may have been displaced onto the 'sectarian' because of the class position of Shi'i and Sunni groups and/or the nature of leadership within these segments of the Muslim population.

However, it seems more probable that the explanation lies in the lack of unions, of political organisations of workers—and the extreme difficulty that workers faced in attempting to organise because of a ready supply of unskilled labour in those industrial concerns that existed in the city and the oppressive nature of financial and craft relations within the artisanal workshops. Thomas claims to have evidence of 'strikes and periodic disturbances amongst many sections of the city's population' from 1900 onwards and considerable politicization of 'the city's educated elite' and 'the lower sections of the population' before 1920 (Thomas, 1982: 76–7). The evidence for the 1920–47 period suggests, however, that the odds were heavily against the workers.

Trade unions were slow to develop anywhere in UP. The first recognized union, which was formed in Kanpur, was established in 1928 and had initially about three thousand members and by the mid-1930s there were still only eight registered unions with less than nine thousand members (Mukhtar, 1935: 106; Rastogi, 1965: 190–1). By the end of the war (1939–45) there were eighty-one unions with sixty thousand members and then in the year of independence there was an unprecedented growth to two hundred and eleven unions with a hundred and forty thousand members (Rastogi, 1965: 191). Waheed's point that much of the labour in those industrial plants that operated in Lucknow came from the villages around the city, and on a daily basis, probably helps to explain the difficulties in developing labour organisations (Waheed 1937: 8).

Certainly strikes were risky. In 1921 there was a strike for higher wages involving five thousand workers in the railway workshop which lasted for two months and twenty days—but this does not seem to have been successful in getting the higher wages the workers sought (Mukhtar 1935: 28). In 1925 a strike at the paper mill showed the difficulties under which workers operated in strike action. 'The Mills dismissed the majority of the strikers and replaced them by new hands on lower rates of wages' (Mukhtar, 1935: 41).

Among the workers in the *karkhanas*—where increased wages were vital—there was a desperate need for organised union activity but Bhattacharya's account of the attempts that were made in the 1920s to combine and force the *mahajans* to increase wages by increasing the amount paid to the *karkhanadar,* points to the difficulties that they faced (Bhattacharya 1930: 409–10).

Lucknow as the Political Centre of the Province

Winning the 'battle' as the capital of the province had important political ramifications for the city; it gave a new status to the city as the arena for important aspects of provincial political life and it brought new political forces to the city. It also gave Lucknow a heightened national political recognition which threw the city's traditional characteristics into much sharper focus on a wider stage and also gave its political leaders expanded national roles.

The location and operation of the legislature—the Legislative Council (1921 to 1936) and the combination of the Legislative Assembly and Legislative Council (1937 to 1939 and 1946 onwards)—and the prolonged residence in the city of the legislators, provided the initial bases for strengthening the city's political role as the focus for political activity. The negotiations that surrounded legislation and the political bargaining or manipulation on which the province's political operations came to depend, constituted a new, vastly expanded, political life for the city.

Lucknow's own electoral field was highly significant, both as a test of the political control of particular individuals or—increasingly—of the political parties and also as an arena for the staging of direct, popular political conflict (a situation that both gained from, and had links to, the developing municipal electoral scene over the period). The rapid acquisition by Congress of control over the 'Non-Muhammadan'/'General' constituencies involving Lucknow; the longer-lived taluqdar influence in the Muslim seats; and the eventual Muslim League dominance of the Muslim constituencies were the key elements in Lucknow's electoral history in this period.

There was also the growing presence in the city of the political 'apparatus' and leadership of the main political parties. One development which underlines Lucknow's increasing political status in this period was the effective shift of control of Congress operations over the period from Allahabad to Lucknow (despite the continued operation of the Anand Bhavan/Swaraj Bhavan complex in Allahabad). In effect, this was the passing of the centre of the UP Congress factional system from Allahabad to Lucknow. At the beginning of the period, UP Congress politics revolved around the Allahabad-based faction leaders—Madan Mohan Malaviya and Motilal Nehru; and their influence continued through the period of Purushottamdas Tandon and Jawaharlal Nehru. But it is clear that in terms of the actual Congress operations from the later 1920s to the mid 1940s, the effective control moved into the hands of Lucknow-based organisers—especially Rafi Ahmed Kidwai and his 'Rafi-ans'—and, following him, Chandra Bhanu Gupta.

In the case of the Muslim League, Lucknow always was the important centre because of the importance of the Mahmudabad family and the energy and involvement of Lucknow Muslim politicians such as Khaliquzzaman and the Raja of Salempur. There certainly never was a period when Muslim League politics in UP did not contain a significant Lucknow organisational component. The Muslim League in the late 1930s—with Khaliquzzaman, Mahmudabad, Salempur—was central for the province and increasingly so for all-India Muslim League politics.

National Recognition

Lucknow, like other Indian cities, was the site for significant national events from time to time: the Congress and League sessions of 1916, which produced 'the Pact' on communal electorates and the similar parallel sessions of 1936 when electoral politics and 'Office Acceptance' were the key issues, are cases in point. The growing importance of Lucknow's political role in UP meant, however, that it became much more visible nationally and, over time, the basis for national-level attention and a possible stepping-stone to roles at the national level.

One major result of its national visibility was the wider recognition of Lucknow's own particular political features: greater awareness (although possibly not understanding or appreciation) of the intricacies of landlord political manoeuvring and of the complexities of Shi'a-Sunni intra-communal conflict are two key examples. On the landlord side, this recognition led to a greater utilisation of Lucknow as the arena for national-level landlord political agitation (as in the All-India Landlord Federation meeting of 1939) while in the case of the Shi'a-Sunni conflict it meant the conflict being played out before a national audience with an ever-widening (although not necessarily more helpful) circle of input.

National recognition led to a wider involvement of Lucknow-based politicians in the national-level affairs of political parties and of the translation of highly-skilled politicians from Lucknow to the national arena. The roles of Khaliquzzaman, the younger Raja of Mahmudabad and the Raja of Salempur in the crucial stages of the Pakistan movement are key examples of the first; but it is important to remember that during the war, both the All-India Muslim League and the Hindu Mahasabha were organised by Lucknow-based taluqdar landlords—Mahmudabad in the case of the League and Raja Maheshwar Dayal Seth in the case of the Mahasabha. Hindu nationalist interest in Lucknow had always been strong, in fact, and taluqdar-politicians like Raja Sir Rampal Singh of Kurri Sidhauli were never far from the centre of Hindu political activity and the activity in the 1940s of Raja Maheshwar Dayal Seth in the Mahasabha and Kunwar Guru Narain Seth in Aney's Hindu National League were a continuation of this interest.

Lucknow by 1947 was puzzling, even to those who lived and worked there. 'Magnus', a journalist in the 1940s tried to sum up the city in the *National Herald* in 1946. 'Lucknow', he wrote mockingly,

has remained a twentieth century Anglo-Indian suburb of Nabobic Oudh, with its insipid orgies and Haroun Al Raschid harems, with the bland expressionless statue of Harcourt Butler still riding his high horse, looking askance even at the Baradari, his spiritual home, with memories of buggy rides, Mahmudabad and insolvent nawabs.

REFERENCES

Bhattacharya, Ardhendhu (1930), 'Extracts from a survey of the small urban industries of Lucknow', *United Provinces' Provincial Banking Enquiry Committee, Report, vol. II, Evidence*, Allahabad, Superintendent, Government Press.

Buckee, G.F.M. (1972), *An Examination of the Development and Structure of the Legal*

Profession at Allahabad, 1866–1935, unpublished Ph.D. thesis, School of Oriental and African Studies, University of London.

Butler, Sir Spencer Harcourt (1923), *Speeches of His Excellency Sir Harcourt Butler, GCIE, KCSI*, Allahabad, UP Government Press.

Butler Papers, British Library, Oriental and India Office Collections, Papers of Sir Spencer Harcourt Butler, Mss. Eur. F116/58, 'First Chapters of an Autobiography'.

Census (1931), Census of India 1931, vol. XVIII, United Provinces of Agra and Oudh, Pt. l, *Report*, Allahabad, Superintendent, Printing and Stationery.

Census (1951), Census of India 1951, vol. II, Uttar Pradesh, Pt. I-A, *Report*, Allahabad, Superintendent, Printing and Stationery.

Church, Roderick (1976), 'Political Culture and Democratic Government in Urban India: The Case of Lucknow' in Donald B.Rosenthal (ed.), *The City in Indian Politics*, Faridabad, Thompson Press.

Freitag, Sandria (1989), *Collective Action and Community: Public Arenas and the Emergence of Communalism in North India*, Delhi, Oxford University Press.

Ganju, Sarojini (1980), 'The Muslims of Lucknow, 1919–39' in K. Ballhatchet and J. Harrison (eds), *The City in South Asia: Pre-Modern and Modern*, London, Curzon.

Gilbert, Martin (1966), *Servant of India, A Study of Imperial Rule from 1905–1910 through the Correspondence of Sir James Dunlop Smith*, London, Longmans.

Improvement Trust (1941), *Lucknow Improvement Trust Inquiry Committee, Report*, Allahabad, Superintendent, Printing and Stationery.

Khaliquzzaman, Choudhry (1961), *Pathway to Pakistan*, Lahore, Longmans Pakistan.

Mukherjee, Radhakamal and Baljit Singh (1961), *Social Profile of a Metropolis: Social and Economic Structure of Lucknow, Capital of Uttar Pradesh, 1954–56*, Bombay, Asia Publishing House.

Mukhtar, Ahmad (1935), *Labour Disputes and Trade Unions in India*, Bombay, Longmans Green.

Municipal Board (1942), *Lucknow Municipal Board Inquiry Committee, Report*, Allahabad, Superintendent, Printing and Stationery.

Pandey, Gyanendra (1978), *The Ascendancy of the Congress in Uttar Pradesh, 1926–34: A Study in Imperfect Mobilization*, Delhi, Oxford University Press.

'Rafi-an' (1972), 'Life and Times of a Gadfly: Story of Rafi Ahmed Kidwai', *Natonal Herald*, 24 Oct.–9 Nov.

Rastogi, J.L. (1965), *Industrial Relations in Uttar Pradesh*, Lucknow, The Author.

Reeves, Peter, Bruce Graham and John Goodman (1975), *A Handbook to Elections in Uttar Pradesh, 1920–1951*, Delhi, Manohar.

Reeves, Peter (1991), *Landlords and Governments in Uttar Pradesh: A Study of Their Relations Until Zamindari Abolition*, Bombay, Oxford University Press.

Rosenthal, Donald B. (1970), *The Limited Elite, Politics and Government in Two Indian Cities*, Chicago, University of Chicago Press.

Spate, O.H.K. and Ahmad, Enayat (1950), 'Five Cities of the Gangetic Plain: A Cross-Section of Indian Cultural History', *Geographical Review*, vol. XL, pp. 260–78.

Thomas, David A. (1982), 'Lucknow and Kanpur, 1880–1920: Stagnation and Development under the Raj', *South Asia*, new series, vol. V, no. 2.

UPDG (1959), *Uttar Pradesh District Gazetteers*, vol. XXXVII, *Lucknow*, by Vinod Chandra Sharma, Allahabad, Government of Uttar Pradesh.

UPLC, United Provinces of Agra and Oudh, Legislative Council, *Proceedings*, Allahabad, Superintendent, Printing and Stationery.

Waheed, A. (1937), 'Housing Conditions in Lucknow. Congested slums in all parts of the city', *Pioneer*, 7 July, p. 8.

Woodruff, Philip (1963), *The Men Who Ruled India*, vol. II, *The Guardians*, London, Cape, paperback, ed.

Young, Desmond (1963), *Try Anything Twice*, London, Hamish Hamilton.

Zaheer, M. and Gupta, Jagdeo (1970), *The Organization of the Government of Uttar Pradesh: A Study in State Administration*, Delhi, S. Chand.

14

A View from Lucknow: National, Communal and Caste Politics in Uttar Pradesh (1977–91)

VIOLETTE GRAFF

Few Indian State capitals, in the mid-seventies, looked as provincial and slow-moving as Lucknow; yet none was comparable in terms of political importance. The contrasts were striking: on the one hand, there was the middle-sized city where nawabi culture had not yet been entirely displaced by the more aggressive Punjabi ethos, and where one commuted at the pace of rickshawallas; on the other, there was the formidable Secretariat reminding every passer-by that, whatever the local circumstances, Lucknow was the seat of power from which a giant State was administered.

A crucial State indeed, Uttar Pradesh occupies a very special place on the Indian chess-board. Not only for obvious historical reasons, since it lies at the heart of the great empires of the past, but also because of its highly symbolic value. By 1977 the three Prime Ministers the country had known had been born here. By 1991 no fewer than seven of the nine Premiers had their political roots embedded deeply in one district or another of the State. Furthermore, as a result of the size of its population, UP sends 85 MPs (out of 540) to the Lok Sabha. This means that a swing in opinion here can make things difficult for the ruling party at the Centre and, of course, in the State itself when the majority in the Assembly differs from the majority in Delhi. It happened to be the case in 1969 and on several subsequent occasions, including 1992–93 when the 'Saffron wave' which swept the State culminated in the demolition of the Babri Masjid at Ayodhya, with the Centre helplessly watching the event. Each time the Centre was obliged to dismiss the State government and go in for fresh elections.

Assessing the mood and reactions of the people of Lucknow in the face of such ups and downs, along the years during which the city itself has changed beyond recognition (the population has doubled since 1981) is a difficult task. When I started work there with a view to writing the story of Lucknow and of UP as seen from the State capital itself, and not from Delhi, a number of eye-brows were raised. But Lucknow is hardly a State capital, people objected. It is just a satellite manipulated from the Centre. It is in Delhi that the Chief Ministers are selected and dismissed at will. Lucknow is just told to comply. Others went further, pointing out at the fact that Lucknow had little to do with UP politics as such. None of its Chief Ministers was born here, they said, except C.B. Gupta who had his political roots deeply entrenched in the city. Moreover none of these Chief Ministers, or hardly any, had ever understood the cherished nawabi culture and traditions of the city.

These arguments carried weight. However, what the Lacknavis do not seem to realize is that it is precisely the status of Lucknow as the State Capital, the importance of its *gaddi* (throne) and its special links with the Centre and national politics, that gives the city its peculiar colour and special composure to the people. They watch, they survive, they adjust. We shall try to see how, election after election, wave after wave, Chief Minister after Chief Minister, they have expressed themselves, more balanced and sober than many in the State when it comes to electing their own representatives, but fully in tune with the developments of the day.

Lucknow and UP

Writing in the sixties, an observer could refer to UP as one of the few States in India which was devoid of cataclysmic issues (Burger, 1969: Chapter 2). There were no groups trying to break away and form a separate State as had been the case in several States. Tensions pertaining to anti-Brahminism in South India, dominant caste rivalries characteristic of Andhra Pradesh, or hill-versus-plains frictions which had fractured Orissa, were unknown in UP. Linguistically, this Hindi-speaking state was homogeneous. By and large, the issues and emotions on which the opposition parties could capitalise were nowhere to be seen. The Congress ruled supreme. The upper castes were firmly entrenched.

Things could not be expected to stay this way for good. The upper castes (only twenty per cent of the population of UP, half of them being Brahmins) were unlikely to retain their hold over the administration and the political establishment. Indeed, the land reforms of the 1960s changed the power equations in the country-side (see Hasan, 1989). The backward castes who benefitted from the new measures started to claim a commensurate share of power. Further, the democratic process, however imperfect, instilled awareness and assertiveness among the downtrodden Harijans, who constituted twenty per cent of the population. It worked in the same way with the Muslim minority (fifteen per cent of the population) which had remained in UP after partition, when most of its elite had migrated to Pakistan. However, the Muslims adjusted to the political realities better than to the cultural and economic hardfacts. Soon their emerging leaders started concentrating on supposedly 'unreasonable' demands.

This is not to say that Muslims in the sixties had no cause for worrying. The Congress stalwarts who had strengthened their hold over the UP government in the 1950s had been paying only lip service to the secular policies of the Central government (Brass, 1974: Chapter 4). In Lucknow the consensus around the issue of secularism was quite different from that in Delhi. Moderate, not to say conservative, it reflected the views of the upper castes who were neither grieving over the lack of education among Muslims, nor prepared to fight for their emotional integration within India. True the minorities could feel secure. They were even courted during elections when their votes mattered—and they mattered enormously in a large number of constituencies—but no one really cared for what mattered most to them—Urdu, the language which at a time had been the epitome of the celebrated Lacknavi composite culture. And if anybody wanted to fight on this issue, he would have to think twice. On the extreme right of the political spectrum, the Jan Sangh, the nationalist organization which was championing Hindi, would seize any opportunity to enlarge its influence among the Congress base, the Brahmins and the Rajputs (Graham, 1990: 111–22).

All this changed gradually. The first salvo against the unquestioned supremacy of the Congress and the domination of the upper castes was fired by the formation, in 1967, of a Muslim co-ordination body (Muslim Majlis-e-Mushawarat) which spoke for the minorities. The second salvo was the open rebellion of Chaudhary Charan Singh against the Congress policies, marking the entry of the farmers on the political stage (Brass, 1985: Chapter 3). Other developments to follow since the late eighties and early nineties have been the dramatic mobilization of Hindu activist forces over the Babri Masjid–Ram Janambhoomi issue, conflict over the Mandal reservations for the OBCs (Other Backward Castes), rise of Dalit assertiveness, and crystallization of popular support for the creation of a Hill State of Uttarakhand. UP today is politically more volatile than any other State in the Union, and controversies and struggles that had been defused or pushed to the background have now surfaced with a vengeance.

Since castes and communities have come to play an increasing role in the life of the State, we would do well to take account of their distribution before proceeding further.

Geographically, it should be noted that, except in Uttarakhand where the Rajputs (Thakurs) are dominant, most castes from the Brahmins down to the Scheduled Castes tend to be State-wide rather than sub-regional in distribution (see Yadav and Banerjee, 1993). There is concentration, however, of the cultivating Jats (the only peasant caste not classified as 'backward') in the Western districts. And so is the case with the Gujjars. The Ahirs, a large caste, are strong everywhere except in the western districts and in the northern hills. The Lodhs are strong in the South-Central part of the State. The Scheduled Castes are numerically limited in Uttarakhand and especially strong in Awadh and Bundelkhand regions.

Caste is as important in the cities as in the countryside. Besides the Brahmins, the significant elite castes in the cities are the Banias and Kayasthas. The Brahmins are very much involved in politics. The Banias and Kayasthas continue to form a large part of the administration.

Muslims are concentrated in Rohilkhand and the Upper Doab. However, they are more urban than rural. A considerable number of Muslims comprises the artisans who continue to struggle to make a living in the many *qasba* (market) towns of the State.

This broad picture replicates itself within Lucknow. While the total population of Lucknow has almost doubled during the decade 1981–91, it is difficult to say how far the balance betweeen the different castes and communities has been affected. If we go by the estimates of the Lucknavis themselves, it would seem that the 'real city' (including Hasanganj with its prestigeous institutions and seminaries) has not changed much, and it has seemingly retained its traditional Muslim population (roughly 30 per cent of the local inhabitants). The atmosphere is tense at times but, until recently, it was not a hot-bed of communalism. Friction arose instead within the Muslim community, between the Shia's (about a third of the community) and Sunnis (see Hasan, Chapter 7). Brahmins and Kayasthas, though scattered all over, enjoy a large presence in the greener pastures of Lucknow East and the Cantonment, which also shelters the largest number of Punjabis. Equally scattered but with a concentration around Hazratganj are the Indian Christians of various denominations. Their number is not large and they are hardly well-off, but, because of the convents, colleges and institutions created by the Christian missionaries, they play an important role in the life of the city.

After years of stagnation, Lucknow has woken up. Increasing pollution notwithstanding, outsiders have come to realise the advantages of settling in this predominantly administrative city. Posh colonies have mushroomed and new constructions are appearing everywhere. Recent immigrants as well as a number of wealthy Lucknavis, eager to leave the congested and neglected parts of the old city, have settled in the fashionable new trans-Gomti area.

Given these recent trends, the social mosaic of Lucknow has changed. Estimates provided by local people indicate that Muslims now represent roughly 22 to 23 per cent of the population. Of the other castes and communities, estimates place Brahmins at about 6 to 7 per cent and Kayasthas at about 10 per cent. Banias are about 6 to 7 per cent also. While OBCs may constitute about 30 per cent, the Scheduled Castes are about 20 per cent.

Let us add that, within these categories, many different ethnic groups are represented. There are people from the hills who came to enter the services. There are a few Mahrashtrians, who are highly educated and respected. The same is true of the Kashmiri Pandits. As for the Bengalis, there has been a long tradition of coming to Lucknow. They served in the administration in British times and played a major role in the establishment of the University. It is the Punjabis and the Sindhis however, coming as refugees in 1947, who have called into question the romantic memories of the city and its leisured way of life. They quickened its pace. They may be behind its sudden leap forward.[1]

The 1977 Watershed and Janata Days

Let us now revert to the story of UP at a time when major changes were in the offing and let us remember briefly the difficult days of 1976, when the State, more than any other one, bore the brunt of the Emergency, with its load of rumors, fears or ominous silences. Especially in Lucknow, the seat of the government, distrust of the bureacracy was palpable. From elite circles down to rickshawallahs, caution was the order of the day.

No serious restrictions however, or so it seemed, had been placed on personalities who could prove dangerous to the regime. It was the case with Chaudhury Charan Singh who, once released from jail and back to his Mall Avenue residence, was at the centre of a large number of opponents. It was also the case with H.N. Bahuguna, who had not taken kindly to his dismissal as Chief Minister of UP in 1975. There were lesser known faces, who had in common the fact that they were deeply unhappy with the rise of Sanjay Gandhi. There were also those activists who had found in jail a common language with otherwise extremely hostile groups: the friendly links forged at the time by some Jan Sanghis with their Muslim co-detainees were hard to believe. They were to give a fantastic boost to the wave which was to sweep northern India when the elections were announced (Graff, 1980).

Inspite of his humiliating dismissal in 1975, H.N. Bahuguna had never severed his links with Lucknow. The news of his joining hands with Jagjivan Ram, together with the official launching of a Congress for Democracy (CFD) on 2 February 1977, were received with trepidation. In fact it changed the whole political scene (Weiner, 1983). While in Delhi Mrs Gandhi had to face the threat of widespread defections from the Congress Party, in UP as in most States of northern India, old foes set about the task of toning down their differences.

The Jan Sangh (JS), the Hindu right-wing party, had a number of committed supporters among the urban trading communities and the middle and rich peasantry in the Central districts of the State. It filled the gaps which were not taken care of by the Bharatiya Lok Dal (BLD), which represented peasant-Jat interests and was especially strong among the middle-level cultivating castes in central and eastern UP. Disadvantaged groups who had been won over by H.N. Bahuguna included the Muslims, who had been deeply antagonised by the family planning drive of Sanjay Gandhi, and who volunteered in thousands to canvass for their new heroes. The message from Jagjivan Ram being also clear, Harijans turned their back on Mrs Gandhi in large numbers.

By mid-March, the pattern was quite visible but the results went beyond the expectations. Especially in UP, where the Janata-CFD alliance made a clean sweep of the 85 Lok Sabha seats, with 68 per cent of the votes. In the constituency of Lucknow, it went even further. H.N. Bahuguna swept the polls with 73.0 per cent of the votes against the sitting MP, Mrs Sheila Kaul, a Congress stalwart (Weiner, 1983, chapters 3–5, Brass, 1985, also Wright, 1977).

The subsequent State elections were nearly as satisfying to the Janata which claimed 352 seats in a House of 425. However, the Congress had not fared that badly if one compares its vote-share of 31.9 per cent to its 1974 performance of 32.3 per cent, when it had won 215 seats.

This was the last show of combined strength and unity for the Janata. There were rifts and bickerings among the different components of the party, and the Chief Minister, Ram Naresh Yadav, found himself in an awkward dilemma over carrying out routine administration. The bureaucracy still remembers the lack of direction visible during the serious clashes between Sunni and Shia processions in Lucknow and in Kanpur (*Link*, 9 October 1977). Then, in Varanasi the celebration of Dusserah was marred by serious Hindu-Muslim rioting, the first intimation that communal harmony had to be nursed carefully if the JS and CFD constituencies were to be kept together (see Akbar, 1978).

But the situation was deteriorating rapidly. In December, the erosion of the Janata's popularity was obvious, and it showed in Lucknow when a Congress candidate, Swarup Kumari Bakshi, won the prestigious Lucknow East constituency, vacant since the June elections. Significant was the fact that H.N. Bahuguna who had garnered 50,160 votes from that very segment a few months earlier did not care to canvass for the Janata candidate, while the PCC President, Mrs Mohsina Kidwai, was extremely active. As a matter of fact, Mohsina Kidwai would win for herself, six months later, a superb by-election in Azamgarh, which would be considered as the first step in the Congress-I come-back in North India (Housego, 1979).

But in 1978 the days of Chief Minister Ram Naresh Yadav were far from over. He had been elected with some fanfare in December in Fatehpur. If Muslims and Scheduled Castes were showing signs of alienation, the Yadav electorate was kept happy. Most backward castes in fact were happy while, for the upper castes, the realisation was yet to come that the reservation policy for the backward castes so actively implemented in Bihar would soon be talked about in UP.

Strangely enough, the bitter power struggle which was already damaging the image of the Janata at the Centre was not repeated in UP (Jaffrelot, 1996: chapter 8). At least not inside the Jan Sangh—Bharatiya Lok Dal (BLD) combine, the main partners in UP, who were anxious to keep the CFD at bay and retain their hegemony.

Things changed drastically in October–November, with the protracted riots which played havoc in the old city of Aligarh (Graff, 1991), and with the controversy over the so-called 'dual membership'[2] taking a strident and disruptive character.

Then, in February 1979, Charan Singh reentered the Central Government after a protracted exile. It was at the instance of the former Jan Sangh ministers, L.K. Advani and A.B. Vajpayee, who were still extremely anxious to avoid a split within the Janata (Advani, 1979). This, however, did not deter the Choudhury from taking action, through Ram Naresh Yadav, against the Jan Sangh members of the Lucknow government. It was to cost Ram Naresh Yadav his Chief Ministership but the uneasy combination survived nonetheless. A new consensus man was found, Banarsi Das, acceptable to both the former Jan Sangh and to Charan Singh. He would not last more than a year because of the disintegration of the Janata Party.

The ultimate somersaults of the Janata, the power games at the Centre and in the States, and finally the death of the party at the hands of its own people, make sad reading.[3] They were watched with amazement and contempt from Lucknow. After all, most protagonists of the on-going drama hailed from the State. They were very well known in the city, whims and all. Some of them were never forgiven.

Indira Gandhi Returns

The way Mrs Gandhi brought about her second coming to power in January 1980 made history (see Weiner, 1983; Gould 1980 and Rudolph and Rudolph, 1980). She was greatly helped by her son Sanjay, whose initiative had precipitated the final split in the Janata Party and the emergence of its secular faction around Charan Singh. However, the talent and the conviction were undoubtedly her own. She paid more attention than anyone else to the poor and the minorities, and yet took care not to provoke a backlash from the high caste Hindus. She displayed equal cordiality towards religious leaders and to the renegades and dissidents who flocked to her.

This paid off in the 'Hindi Belt', though the outcome was not quite as convincing as it appeared at first glance, especially in UP, with 51 seats won out of 85 Lok Sabha seats.

On the opposition side, the share of votes was far from negligible: 29.2 per cent for the Janata (Secular)-Lok Dal and 22.6 per cent for the Janata. This prompted many observers to suggest that, with some understanding on the part of the opposition parties, the Congress could have been defeated. But this is less than certain. Many groups, castes and communities were no longer ready to listen to the people who had run the Janata Party. They would have gone back *en bloc* to Mrs Gandhi were it not for the haven Charan Singh promised to provide. He was listened to not only by the *kisans* but also by a large number of Muslims. The election results speak for themselves. The Lok Dal, which had put up 79 candidates of whom 30 belonged to the backward castes, won 29 seats and came second in another 29 constituencies. The Janata achieved a majority in only three constituencies despite a not insignificant number of votes.

It was a disaster that nobody in the party had anticipated. It carried a bitter lesson for the former Jan Sangh, the main component of the Janata in UP. It had relied on the assumed prestige of the Harijan leader, Jagjivan Ram. However, for all his experience as a minister, Jagjivan Ram was not a man to draw crowds. Worse, the party workers were not prepared to endorse his leadership. The lesson was hard to bear. Not only was it underlined that the high castes would never accept a Harijan as a Prime Minister, it was also made clear that the Scheduled Castes could not bring themselves to trust the Janata Party any more. Surprisingly enough the Chaudhury's party was extremely successful in the reserved constituencies, but this was not out of any love on the part of landless labourers (Weiner, 1983: 125–7). It was noted that wherever a Lok Dal candidate won in those constituencies, the turnout was much higher than elsewhere; second, there was a sharp polarisation between caste Hindus and Harijans.

The Muslims were divided. They knew that their votes had played a major role in 1977 and that they were just as important in 1980. This was evident from the promises made to the minority in party manifestoes, the care with which the candidates were chosen, and the ardour politicians displayed regarding their commitment to secularism. Their zeal did not fail to stimulate some unreasonable demands on the part of the religious leaders of the community .

The Muslim split was obvious in several constituencies, including Lucknow itself, where Mrs Gandhi's aunt, Mrs Sheila Kaul, was back on the scene. The choice was between her and a strong Janata candidate, Mahmood Butt. He was a Muslim. It is interesting that this did not deter the local RSS workers from supporting him fully. Even so, Mrs Kaul recovered her seat with a majority of 47.6 per cent, and Mahmood Butt won only 39.9 per cent of the votes.

When people went to the polls in early June the results were a foregone conclusion. Not only did the traditional electorate, minus some Muslims, come back to Mrs Gandhi in larger numbers, but the systematic bid made by her son to woo the Rajputs had paid off (see Rudolph and Rudolph, 1987b: 140–4). Gone were the days when Brahmins would dominate the UP scene. The stage was set for the Thakurs.

Now the question was: who would ascend the gaddi in Lucknow? The

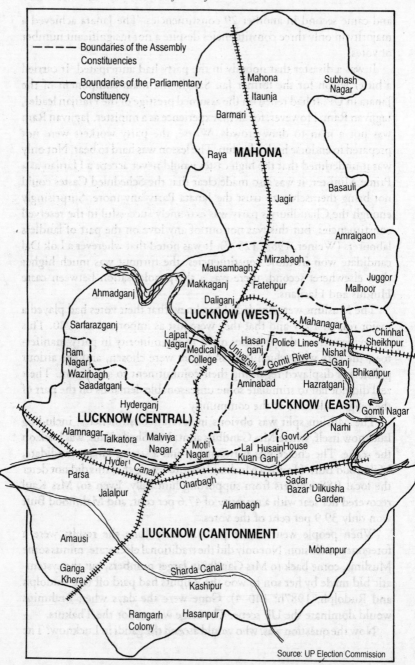

LUCKNOW 1991 PARLIAMENTARY AND ASSEMBLY CONSTITUENCIES

Boundaries of the Assembly Constituencies

Boundaries of the Parliamentary Constituency

Mahona

Subhash Nagar

Itaunja

Barmari

Raya

MAHONA

Basauli

Jagir

Amraigaon

Mirzabagh

Mausambagh

Juggor

Makkaganj   Fatehpur   Malhoor

Ahmadganj

Daliganj

LUCKNOW (WEST)

Mahanagar

Sarfarazganj

Chinhat
Sheikhpur

Lajpat
Nagar

Police Lines

Ram
Nagar

Medical
College

Hasan
ganj

Nishat
Ganj

University

Gomti River

Bhikanpur

Wazirbagh

Aminabad

Hazratganj

Saadatganj

LUCKNOW (EAST)

Hyderganj

Gomti Nagar

LUCKNOW (CENTRAL)

Narhi

Alamnagar   Talkatora

Malviya
Nagar

Govt.
House

Moti
Nagar

Lal   Husain
Kuan Ganj

Hyder Canal

Parsa

Jalalpur

Charbagh

Sadar
Bazar Dilkusha
Garden

Alambagh

LUCKNOW (CANTONMENT

Amausi

Mohanpur

Ganga
Khera

Sharda Canal

Kashipur

Ramgarh
Colony

Hasanpur

Source: UP Election Commission

answer was a man unknown, Visvanath Pratap Singh, former Chief Whip in the Vidhan Sabha, and later a Minister of State at the Centre.

On 23 June, the violent death of Sanjay Gandhi stunned India. Earlier questions had suddenly become irrelevant. Others came up. In Lucknow, from the very beginning, it was obvious that V.P. Singh's government was loaded with people he was not keen to work with (*The Statesman*, 20 July 1982). After Sanjay's death, these loyalists were certainly not prepared to disappear in the wilderness and, in any case, they were firmly entrenched in the Assembly. V.P. Singh had to carry on. He kept shuttling between Delhi and Lucknow as he was expected. Nevertheless, his personal crusades and moral integrity earned him respect and he was able to make his mark on regional developments.

On August 13, 1980, the last day of Ramzan (*Id*) in Moradabad, pigs were spotted wandering inside the *idgah* (the place for community prayers at Id). There was a furore and dramatic clashes between Muslim crowds and the police followed. These were echoed in other cities of Uttar Pradesh. It struck a deep note of alarm. Events in Iran and Afghanistan weighed heavily on the national scene and commentators detected a 'foreign hand'. (Jain 1980a and 1980b; also see Akbar, 1980 and Saberwal and Hasan, 1984). However, it was largely a case of administrative complacency and police prejudices and V.P. Singh owned full responsibility for the tragedy. He tendered his resignation. It was not accepted at this point. He would leave twenty months later, after a long, unsuccessful drive against *dacoits*, marked by a controversial policy of 'encounters' (planned police attacks), while repeated massacres of Harijans added to his sense of guilt.

When finally, all of a sudden, V.P. Singh resigned in March 1982, a successor had to be found. Given the prevailing practice in Delhi, he had to be brought to light by the Prime Minister. The man who fitted the bill was Sripat Misra: entirely loyal, without any base worth the name in the State, and yet with skills which would answer the need of the day. Moreover he was a Brahmin. Thakurs had to be shown their place. This, however, did not prevent them from remaining well entrenched in the government. Misra had to take them in his stride. His term was not an easy one and the gratest surprise was that he survived in office until August 1984.

It is true that UP was not at the time in the middle of a storm although, in September 1982, in Meerut, dramatic clashes had opposed Muslims and Balmikis (scavengers) for the first time, leaving the minority community with its questions and its anger in the face of a complacent administration (see Sharma, 1982; Chawla, 1982; and Chishti, 1982). Public opinion was soon diverted to other states where violence, in 1983, was to take an ugly turn: Assam where enforced elections led to ethnic and communal massacres, Punjab with its growing Sikh militancy, and Hyderabad with its religious festivals marred by recurrent bouts of communal fever.

Politically also the focus had shifted from the Ganga valley to other places. In the South, humiliating defeats in Karnataka and Andhra Pradesh caught the Congress unaware. In the North, it was the other way round: Congress proved resilient, and Mrs Gandhi managed convincing results in two BJP strongholds, Delhi and Jammu (see *Seminar*, January 1984; Hardgrave, 1984).

Religion Enters Politics

It is difficult to pin down the precise moment when, in UP, people came to ponder over the policy followed by the Prime Minister in the face of religious militancy. Since the Meenakshipuram conversion of untouchables to Islam in 1981, a Hindu backlash had been brewing. It started in 1983 with an uproar over reports that *vanaspati* (edible oil) was being adulterated by imported beef-tallow. Hindu right-wing activists led mass demonstrations, denounced the treachery of the authorities, and conjured up memories of the greased cartridges which had spurred the 1857 uprising (*India Today*, 30 November 1983: 22–5). The opposition joined in and, in this highly charged atmosphere, the Vishwa Hindu Parishad, a militant wing of the *Sangh parivar*, put into practice an earlier project: the organisation and launching of a series of marches or *Ekatmata Yagna Yatra* (integration rite). These marches crissed-crossed India during several weeks in November, presenting buckets of holy Ganga water to workshippers in some 300.000 villages (see Jaffrelot, 1996: 360–62). Needless to say, UP was at the core of the *Yatras* and fully involved emotionally. There were no serious incidents but Muslims understood the signals. They were to send their own ones at the first opportunity.

The Centre was in an aggressive mood. Over the last year, the electoral tests had not been encouraging. In December 1983, the ruling party had suffered defeat in Bulandshar, a prestigious Lok Sabha constituency, where the opposition had managed to exploit the beef-tallow rumours to the hilt. At the Assembly level too, the results for the Congress had not been good in the five bye-elections held simultaneously (see *India Today*, 31 December 1983: 18–19 and 15 January 1984: 28–32). The loss of the Pilibhit seat to the Rashtriya Sanjay Manch (RSM), the fledgling outfit of Indira Gandhi's estranged daughter-in-law, Maneka, the widow of Sanjay, who had joined hands with her husband's associate, 'Dumpy' Akbar Ahmad, was particularly humiliating to the Prime Minister (*India Today*, 15 April 1982: 8–17).

Pilibhit did not remain an isolated success. In May 1984, Maneka and 'Dumpy' managed to storm Malihabad, a constituency in the mango-belt near Lucknow (*India Today*, 15 June 1984: 18–19 and 52–3). This was much more than a warning. With Muslims and Thakurs turning their backs on the ruling party, the Congress had to remain content with a shrinking base of Brahmins and Scheduled Castes.

Hardly had the communal flames which had engulfed Bombay and Bhiwandi in 1984 died down, and hardly had the storming of the Golden Temple in Amritsar left the front pages of the newspapers, when state governments began to fall one after the other. It was as if the Centre could not bear dissent any longer. In Kashmir Dr Farooq Abdullah was dislodged unceremoniously to make room for his brother-in-law. In Hyderabad the charismatic film star, NT Rama Rao, was disposed off even more cynically, but protests and strikes were such throughout the country, that he had to be brought back. By comparison, events were proceeding smoothly in UP although, for the unfortunate Sripat Misra, it was the end of his political fortunes.

October 1984, which was to prove fatal with the assassination of Indira Gandhi, was marked by another event loaded with impending tragedies. It started with a gathering of sadhus on the bank of the river Saryu, in Ayodhya, on 6 October (Van der Veer, 1987). They were there to greet a religious procession coming from Sitamarhi in Bihar, which, with its few trucks, did not look very impressive. However, it bore an ambitious name: *Ram Janmabhumi Mukti Yajna*, 'a sacrifice to liberate the birth place of Ram', and the programme which was held the next day, with speeches and sacrifices, did not lack ambition either. Though carefully monitored by the Visva Hindu Parishad, it did not attract the kind of crowds which in 1983 had gathered around the *Ekatmata Yajna*. But the message vociferously expressed was: 'God is languishing in a Muslim jail (the Babri Masjid). He should be liberated'.

In Lucknow the meaning of the slogan was well understood. The sadhus had made it very clear that people were to give their votes only to those parties which promised explicitly to return to the Hindus their sacred places which had been desecrated. It is no surprise that the Chief Minister agreed to meet the procession before it wound its way to Delhi (Mustafa, 1984).

The seed was planted. It would take its own time to grow and be noticed. In Delhi and elsewhere, people could not spare even a fleeting thought for this kind of crusade: on 31 October tragedy had struck; Mrs Gandhi was assassinated and, if there was a villain on the Indian stage, it was no longer the Muslim. It was the Sikh.

The details of this tragic event are well known. So are those pertaining to the massacre of large numbers of Sikhs. It was not confined to Delhi. In UP, Kanpur was seriously affected. Lucknow remained quiet and soon braced itself to answer the call of Rajiv Gandhi, the successor.

People did not know much about him, but everybody was under the deep impression made by the young man on television. The self-control and dignity which he had shown during the days of mourning had won over many hearts. Everybody was grateful for the smooth succession and prepared to give him a chance. The electoral campaign for the Eighth Lok Sabha started within days, and the Congress showed its skill. Rajiv himself toured the country at an incredible pace, stressing everywhere he went that the very unity and integrity of India were at stake. However he carefully avoided saying anything which could be construed as a deviation from the cherished path of secularism. Indeed one had to read between the lines to understand that this India was a Hindu country and yet, every Hindu voter felt that he had been called upon and should come forward (Graff, 1987).

After the polls it was clear that, with 48.2 per cent of the votes and 415 seats out of 542 in the Lok Sabha, Rajiv Gandhi had won a mandate never accorded to his predecessors (Mirchandani and Murthi, 1985; Kothari, 1985). His victory gave a new colour to the political landscape, especially in UP. Here the tally was 82 out of 85 Lok Sabha seats with 51 per cent votes. The Bharatiya Janata Party, the Hindu party, was almost wiped out with just 6.4 per cent votes and not a single seat (in 1952 the newly-born Jan Sangh had managed 7.3 per cent). The Janata fared even worse with 3.6 per cent votes.

Most opposition leaders lost their deposits, including Maneka Gandhi who had persuaded herself that she could defy her brother-in-law in Amethi. The only party saved from disgrace was the Dalit Mazdoor and Kisan Party (formerly Lok Dal), which came second in most constituencies. True, it won only 2 seats, but it demonstrated that it was still a force to reckon with, and that it could retain a good percentage of the so-called Muslim vote (Graff, 1987).

When three months later India embarked upon what was a virtual mini-general election, with eleven States and one Union Territory going to the polls, the Congress party exuded confidence. In view of the unrelenting pace of the campaign that Rajiv had sustained, everybody expected the results to be as gratifying as at the time of the Lok Sabha elections. But they were not. First, as is always the case in State elections, local and caste issues came to the fore. Second, Rajiv and his aides had circulated very strict guidelines aiming at giving a cleaner image to the party. Half the sitting legislators were denied tickets. It amounted to letting loose an army of disgruntled men (*India Today*, 28 February 1985: 38–45 and 15 March 1985: 8–9). The miracle is that the results were not more disappointing. Except for Eastern UP where ten Thakur-dominated districts returned a large number of Janata and DMKP (Dalit, Mazdoor, Kisan Party) candidates, and Western UP where the DMKP improved its strength, the ruling party won convincingly in Central UP, Bundelkhand, Rohilkhand, and in the Hills.

If there was ever a smooth transition between two Chief Ministers in UP, it was in September 1985, when Narayan Dutt Tiwari, leaving for Delhi to retrieve his familiar Industry portfolio, passed on the post to a man who had for years dreamt of ascending the Lucknow gaddi (*India Today*, 15 October 1985: 32–5). He was Vir Bahadur Singh, a Thakur, a long-timer in the Government, but never a Chief Minister. He was welcome, if only because he was known as a protege of Arun Nehru whose influence at the Centre was by then formidable. He would leave 1000 days later, after the electoral defeat that the Congress party suffered in Allahabad in June 1988, at the hands of Visvanath Pratap Singh, the rebel former Finance Minister. V.B. Singh would not pay too dearly for that, and would be soon accomodated at the Centre. However, he was leaving behind him a sorry situation. The UP treasury was empty. The bureaucracy was more indisciplined than ever before. Tensions were surfacing at every level of the State, especially on the communal front. And, in the holy city of Ayodhya where things had been under control for decades, a major controversy had been brought to centre stage. Vir Bahadur would be remembered as the man who unlocked the gates of the Babri Masjid.

How far was he respnsible for this development? Let us remember the mood in high circles at the time. It was the end of Rajiv Gandhi's first year as Prime Minister. Those twelve months had been promising (Narain, 1986). The P.M. had reached an agreement in Punjab, another one in Assam. However, in December, disillusion set in. The Congress party had not visualized that it could be completely defeated at the hustings in Assam, where its candidates could not even garner the traditional Muslim votes. Worse, a bye-election in Bihar, in the remote constituency of Kishanganj, showed that even a westernized Muslim like the former diplomat Syed Shahabuddin, a strong Janata candidate, had a much greater appeal to minorities than the bearded Maulana that the Congress Party had set against him (*India Today*, 15 January 1986: 14–19). Conclusions were drawn. Muslims (whose vote had been neglected in 1984) had to be won over. A Muslim Union Minister, Z.R. Ansari (MP from Unnao, UP), was asked to undo the damage done by another Muslim Union Minister, Arif Mohammed Khan (also from UP, elected in Bahraich) who, at the instance of the Prime Minister, had seemed to signal in Parliament that the highly revered Muslim Personal Law could be reconsidered (see Gupta, Ahmed and Badhwar, 1986: 50–60). Muslims, including a number of secular Congress women, were up in arms, and it was all the more necessary to assuage their feelings that other moves were afoot which would hurt them deeply: Ayodhya, and the Hindu claim over the Babri Masjid, were on the Government agenda.

Was it absolutely urgent to take a decision? It is true that on 31 October 1985, a meeting organised by the Vishwa Hindu Parishad in Udipi had decided that the *Ramjanambhumi Mukti Yagya Samiti* (RMYS) should resume its activities. The *tala kholo* (open the locks) agitation was to lead to a major *Satyagraha* on Shivratri, on 9 March 1986. There were reasons to be anxious: twenty-five Ram-Janaki (Sita) *rath* (chariots) were criss-crossing UP, and the Bajrang Dal was in command.

The first step on the part of the UP Government that we know of and which was later directly connected with the RMYS claim, took place on 19 December at Ayodhya itself. Vir Bahadur was in the holy city to open the 'Ramayana *mela*'. It seems that he tried his best to pacify three dignitaries who were pleading forcefully against the 'illegal' closure of the Ramjanambhoomi. He would take necessary action, he said, but he needed a month's time to study the available facts. There are several versions of what happened next (Noorani, 1989). It seems that V.B.Singh was not unhappy with the decision which was taken. He is reported to have said: 'None of these Brahmin Chief Ministers ever had the guts to do it. I am a Thakur and I will . . .'

On 1 February 1986, the locks which had been rusting for nearly four decades, were opened. It was like opening the Pandora's box. Muslims were appalled, and even more so because of the aggressive and triumphant way Doordarshan, the national TV network, projected it. It was a great Hindu victory and sweet revenge for past slavery.

The developments of the Ayodhya crisis are too well known to need recalling in detail here. However, it is important to realize how deeply this abscess has festered and affected the political landscape of northern India and the mind of the common man. With militancy spiralling on both sides, everybody, except of course the *Sangh Parviar*, was trapped:

the Muslim leadership, the UP government and the administration, the Prime Minister and his men, and the contenders for power. Left to himself, the common man could have recovered his balance but he was not allowed to. From the very beginning he was led to react sharply, to answer indiscreet calls and boycotts, to take his defence in his own hands.

It remains a fact that, immediately after the unlocking of the Babri Masjid, there were no major incidents. However, tensions started simmering in Western UP (see Chowdhury, 1986) and violence erupted in various places, reaching Allahabad in June 1986. More disquieting than these local disturbances were the news regarding the circulation of arms and the mushrooming of *senas* (private armies) (*India Today*, 31 May 1986 and 15 October 1986). Mammoth rallies and *bandhs* considerably surcharged the communal atmosphere.[4] Then Meerut erupted in flames, with horrifying violence lasting for weeks (Engineer, 1987). The Chief Minister was lambasted for complacency. The attack was probably unfair, though it is clear that the man was more concerned with politics than with administration. Politically the situation was turning out to be difficult for him at the time. The first hiccup had already occured in October 1986 when the estrangement between Vir Bahadur Singh's patron, Arun Nehru, and Rajiv Gandhi took a bad turn. Not surprisingly the Chief Minister was not caught unawares. Commuting between Delhi and Lucknow, as he often did, he was able to discern the way the wind was blowing. Soon it became clear that he would back the Prime Minister to the hilt (Awasthi, 1988). His support would prove most useful when—precisely at the time of the Meerut riots—the Bofors scandal developed into a major crisis which shook the whole nation (see Wariavwalla, 1988). Local failures could be overlooked at a time when the principal aim of the Centre was to hold its ground in UP, UP which had always been the bulwark of Congress strength, and which was also the home-state of Vishwanath Pratap Singh, whose crusade for honesty around the Bofors scandal carried the potential for destabilising the Congress.

We cannot of course retrace the first hesitant steps of V.P. Singh during this eventful period. We are concerned here by the way he was perceived in UP. The fact is that his tenure as Chief Minister was remembered with respect, and his gauntlet thrown at the Prime Minister was greeted with tremendous enthusiasm in Lucknow and Allahabad (*India Today*, 31 May 1987: 24). Soon his crusades proved devastating. Throughout the State it was now rumoured that in high places there were thieves pocketing money. The Prime Minister was not spared.

Courtesy R.K. Laxman, 25 Jan. 1979

Courtesy R.K. Laxman, 19 Feb. 1980

Courtesy R.K. Laxman, 15 Nov. 1984

Courtesy R.K. Laxman, 6 June 1988

Courtesy R.K. Laxman, 7 Oct. 1990

Courtesy R.K. Laxman, 21 Dec. 1990

The famous Laxman cartoon, showing Rajiv dismissing godly monkeys once a much awaited bye-election in Allahabad was over, sums up the disquieting situation which prevailed in UP by mid 1988. In a desperate attempt to control a faltering image, the Prime Minister had to bring in a matinee-idol who played the role of Rama before an unconvinced electorate.[5] It was a pre-figuration of things to come. In 1989 religion finally entered politics with a bang. The central issue was not Ayodhya; it was the very future of the Prime Minister. Would he survive the Bofors scandal? Would the opposition parties settle for a kind of unity, that unity which had always eluded them except in times of crisis?

It would take many more months for the V.P. Singh-led Jan Morcha, the Janata, and the two Lok Dals to reach a shaky agreement. By then, in Lucknow, a new Chief Minister was trying to bring some order in the mess that was UP. Once more N.D. Tiwari had been called to the rescue. Time was running short indeed. With elections to be held before the end of 1989, there were, throughout UP, many under-currents to be taken care of. A powerful movement led by one peasant leader, Tikait, had revealed a deep resentment among farmers.[6] At a different level, Harijans had demonstrated a new awareness of their political weight. New leaders were emerging: Kanshi Ram and Mayawati of the Bahujan Samaj Party which had contested several by-elections and gathered a significant number of votes.

Last but not the least, the Bharatiya Janata Party was on the comeback trail. Two different strategies were at work, combining the different views of hawks and doves in the party, and it paid off. On the political front, the BJP had been able to impress upon V.P. Singh that it would be difficult to dislodge the Congress without its support, which claim was significantly reinforced by its electoral success in the February 1989 municipal elections (*The Indian Express*, 11 February 1989, *India Today*, 15 February 1989).

On the Ayodhya front, success was also at hand, if only because the growing instrumentalization of the Hindu symbols had caught the Muslim activists on the wrong foot. The Babri Masjid Action Committee (BMAC), literally playing into the hands of its adversaries, gave a call for a Muslim march on Ayodhya which could bring disaster.[8] Syed Shahabuddin saw reason, but not the hot-heads of the BMAC who gave in only when violence erupted in Muzaffarnagar, Khatauli and Aligarh, underlining the danger of the situation (Engineer, 1989). In the Hindu camp, there was jubilation. The bandh which the VHP had organised on 8 October as a counteroffensive to the BMAC march had been impressive. Now the Muslim activists were backing out, hurt and divided. It meant that, in Ayodhya, nobody would prevent the Hindu devotees, fifty thousand of them, from enjoying fully the on-going festivals. For the first time and as a sign of things to come, there were bricks, ready for worship and *darshan*. There were only five bricks but these were enough.

Churning of the Saffron Tide

Who was setting the country's political agenda in 1989? The government of India or the Sants and the Sadhus? And what was the margin of mano-euvre left to the government in Lucknow in the face of the approaching Lok Sabha elections, and the Ayodhya issue gaining in sharpness more than ever before? As so often in the recent past, the VHP had conjured up a most imaginative, or rather machiavellian, programme.[9] It had been launched at the confluence of the sacred rivers at Prayag (Allahabad), during the *Kumbh Mela* on 1 February. The holy men were by now fully convinced that the fate of *Bharat* was entirely in their hands. They met again in May in Hardwar, then in July in Ayodhya, and in August a carefully-laid plan for the construction of a magnificent temple dedi-cated to Lord Ram at Ayodhya was underway.

Meanwhile, on August 14, the High Court at Allahabad had directed the parties to the dispute not to take any steps to disturb the *status quo* at Ayodhya. Even so, the VHP and its satellites like the Bajrang Dal were not daunted by the ruling. What did this ruling matter in view of the giant programme which was afoot? The plan involved every village from every corner of the country to send a brick for the building of the Ram temple at Ayodhya. From 30 September onwards, *Ram Shila Yatras* (the convoys carrying bricks), would wind their way through the country to reach Ayodhya on 9 November. The *Shilanyas* would be performed, as it should be, with all the required rituals. As late as the first weeks of September, the Congress party, in Delhi, did not see the writing on the wall. On the other hand, in Lucknow, Chief Minister Tiwari was far from optimistic. He was too well aware of the risks inherent to the *Ram Shila pujas* (see *India Today*, 30 September 1989). He knew that the Bajrang Dal militants were already on the rampage, and that they would raise the communal tension to fever pitch. He knew also that Muslims had every reason to be mortally afraid. And yet he had to keep the coming elections in mind. [10] Especially where the minorities were concerned, he had now to think in terms of electoral gains and losses. How to make amends and compensate for the shock that the *millat* was bound to feel in November? The medicine, unfortunately, was to prove fatal.

Conventional belief has it that in Northern India, namely UP and Bihar, Muslims never stop grieving, never stop complaining. Never feeling guilty for the fact that their fathers divided Mother India, they are constantly mobilized by their leaders, religious or political, on issues which are largely irrelevant. They seem unable to adjust to modern realities, and would do anything to save their personal law, their way of life, their Koranic institutions; they are cut from the national mainstream and still, because of their numbers and their electoral weight in a large number of constituencies, they have to be 'appeased' . . .

The protracted struggle over the 'Minority' character of AMU (the Aligarh Muslim University) (Wright, 1966 and Graff, 1990) and, soon afterwards, the controversy over Shah Bano (Engineer (ed.), 1987 and Hasan, 1987) added grist to the mill. Even the fierce struggle in Lucknow in favour of the Urdu language, led by a well known personality of the city, Dr A.J. Faridi (a medical practitioner turned politician), looked suspicious (Brass, 1974). And yet, before Partition, Urdu had been the cherished language of North India, the very symbol of the composite culture which before independence was the pride of Brahmins, Kayasthas and Muslims alike.[11]

What led Narayan Dutt Tiwari, in 1989, to believe that the case of Urdu, which had been lying dormant for years (Mitra, 1989; Madan, 1989; Noorani, 1979) could be reopened without due preparation? In fact the news came as a bolt from the blue when, on 14 September 1989, it was announced that Urdu would be given the status of the second language of the State. The Bill would be introduced in the Vidhan Sabha on 27 September. But that very day Budaun in Western U.P. erupted in flames. This was the first communal riot to occur in a city where Hindus and Muslims had never clashed. It marked the beginning of a chain reaction that would eventually prove too costly for the ruling party. The *Ram Shilas Yatras* had started and were to leave a bloody trail. Alarming news came from distant places in Gujarat, Rajasthan, Madhya Pradesh, Bihar, all of them Congress-ruled States. Communal riots had returned with a vengeance and it was not just a coincidence. By now general elections were looming large. And, as if that were not enough, elections had also been announced at the Assembly level.

During that sinister period, the only party which seemed to know where it was really heading was the Bharatiya Janata Party. It had at long last reached an understanding with the opposition and, although not being party to the National Front which had been formed in 1988 by the Janata Dal and a host of regional parties, the BJP was well aware of the potentialities of such an agreement. It was therefore out of the question to whip up Hindu militancy. The Ramjamnabhoomi issue was not even referred to in the election manifesto of the party. Nor was it necessary. The job was carried on cleverly by the BJP's sister-organisation, the VHP. At one level, the slogans of the militants had undergone significant transformation (the smiling image of *Ram Lalla* itself had been changed into that of a warrior carrying a *trishul* and a bow ready for use) (see Kapur, 1993). At another level, talks were going on between Ashok Singhal, the General Secretary of the VHP, and Buta Singh, the Union Home Minister. And the conclusions were soon made known; the controversial *Shilanyas* would take place but court orders about maintenance of the *status quo* on the disputed site would also be respected.

For the Janata Dal, the situation was more than embarrassing. It could hardly behave like the BJP and use different strategies simultaneously to win over electoral support. Even less could it impose a single vision on the various leaders enrolled under its banner. Yet, the electorate had to be won over. As the Congress itself would soon discover, it was impossible to woo everybody. In the long run, in UP at least, it was expedient to remember that the minorities remained an important factor in a large number of constituencies. For Muslims, the JD President, Vishvanath Pratap Singh, had a clean personal image. However, he had become more and more entangled in his association with the Bharatiya Janata Party. A vicious campaign harped on his Hindu leanings and underlined his reluctance to speak out against the BJP communal politics. His dilly-dallying did not mean, however, that the JD Chief had not grasped the mounting anxiety of those who were now denigrated as the 'children of Babar'. By mid-October 1989, he was well aware of the problems on the ground (see Graff, 1992). When gory details started circulating about the recurrent massacres of Muslims in Bhagalpur (Bihar), he was ready to speak up and he found the right words. His rating shot up when he announced that he would start his electoral campaign from Bhagalpur. This contrasted sharply with the flamboyant promises of a *Ram Raj* made in Faizabad, less than three miles from Ayodhya, by Rajiv Gandhi on 3 November (see Chiriyankandath, 1992). When later on (14 November), V.P. Singh refused to share the rostrum and the flags of the BJP in Mathura, Hathras and Aligarh, he made history (Parthasarthy, 1989).

But the dice had been cast a few days earlier. Throughout India, on 9 November, the Urdu programme of the BBC had conveyed to every Muslim household that ultimately, in Ayodhya, officials and Congressmen had unrolled the Red carpet for the Vishva Hindu Parishad and its friends. The whole ceremony was broadcast (Mehta, 1989; *India Today*, 30 November 1989). A petrified minority missed no detail of the foundation of a 'Hindu Rashtra'.[12] Two days later the Shahi Imam issued an urgent call, strongly advising Muslims to vote for the Janata Dal.

The polls for the Ninth Lok Sabha were held on 24–6 November. They delivered an angry verdict. In the South, it was the established regional parties which were sent packing. In the Hindi heartland, it was the Congress, and its defeat looked ignominious. Its base had shrunk significantly although it remained important (39.5 per cent as against 34.5 per cent in 1977). In Parliament, with 193 seats, the former ruling party was still the largest single formation.

More serious was the fact that the actual winners had no national mandate (Padgaonkar 1989; Mitra, 1989). The much celebrated Janata Dal had less than one fifth of the total vote (17.8 per cent), with about one fourth of the Lok Sabha seats (142). The Bharatiya Janata Party had amazed the observers with its score of 88 seats (11.4 per cent votes), as against 2 in 1984. However, its base remained concentrated in a limited number of States. Last but not least, the CPI (M) had been the only 'regional' party which had survived the anti-establishment drive and of the 33 seats it had won, 27 were in West-Bengal.

With these three parties covering a large spectrum of ideologies and social forces, and with the significant emergence of the Bahujan Samaj Party, this victory was hailed as a triumph for Secularism, a triumph for Democracy. The National Front and its allies were however strange bedfellows, and the whole exercise was loaded with ambiguities. It would soon explode in the face of the people.

In UP, the crucial State, the situation was much more clear-cut than at the Centre. Here it was definitely V.P. Singh all the way, and the JD had every reason to feel elated (Brass, 1993a). It had cornered 35.9 per cent votes, 54 Lok Sabha seats, most of them being won very convincingly and not because of the adjustments arrived at with the BJP.

The visibility of the Congress rout was just as striking as was the JD victory. While the Prime Minister was never himself in danger (in spite of a serious local incident, he won handsomely in Amethi), his partymen were decimated.

If we now turn to the BJP, it is obvious that it had not made the inroads into the Hindu vote that its leaders had anticipated. In terms of seats won, the party had certainly improved its position, bagging now 8 Lok Sabha seats as compared to nil in 1984. However its candidates would have been nowhere without the seat adjustments arrived at with the Janata Dal and, in terms of votes, the party base remained hopelessly narrow, with 7.6 per cent of the votes. The situation was certainly more encouraging at the Assembly level but it was clear that the competition with the Congress party for the upper-caste vote and the Hindu-minded electorate had not paid off. Further, the Backward castes had shown much more interest for the JD promises concerning job reservations than in any 'Hindu' crusade (Brass, 1993a: 125–7). If anything, the traditional patterns of voting along caste lines had prevailed despite efforts to the contrary.

In Lucknow itself, an outsider almost succeeded in giving a fatal blow to the Janata Dal candidate. He was the formidable Balraj Madhok, the dissident leader of the former Jan Sangh. Most of the votes which would have gone to the BJP, had it been in the fray, went to him. Muslims took up the challenge. A glance at the results shows that they did not waste their ballots (hardly 7000 went to the numerous Muslim independents), and Mandhata Singh, the JD candidate, made his way through.

The Assembly results were just as chequered. The BJP candidates won in Lucknow West and Central, the Congress candidates in the Cantonment and Mahona, and it was only in Lucknow East that the JD managed to dethrone Mrs Swaroop Bakshi.

Mandir Obscures Mandal

When Mulayam Singh Yadav ascended the gaddi in December 1989, he was already well known. A Yadav, energetic and a self-made man, controversial also (there were rumors about a number of his friends having criminal records), and a proud disciple of Lohia, he was nobody's client. He had been duly elected as Chief Minister (a contest which had been lost by a bitter Ajit Singh) and, from the very beginning, it was clear that the relationship with the Centre would be very different. Lucknow would eventually call the shots in Delhi, not the other way round.

With the BJP, there was at first no obvious problem, only minor irritations which could have been avoided, like the inclusion of a member of the Babri Masjid Action Committee, Azam Khan, in the Government. It was still possible by then to entertain the hope that the Visva Hindu Parishad would not press its just released agenda concerning the construction of the Ram *mandir* in Ayodhya. It was a hope belied, although there was a benevolent postponement of the proposed action.

At the Centre the headaches of V.P. Singh were manifold. From Kashmir to Haryana, they took such proportions that, within months, he was led to believe that only a great *coup* could help him to retain the initiative within his party (see Sisson and Majumdar 1991; Sinha, 1991). The Janata Dal manifesto had made references to the recommendations of the Mandal Report.[13] Why not, then, implement them? The announcement, on August 7, had a stunning effect. More than anybody else, the BJP leaders foresaw the dramatic consequences of the move, the acceleration of the dreaded fragmentation of the Hindu society, when they were precisely trying to instill in it a fresh and exhilarating sense of unity. It was urgent to light a counter-fire, and it was L.K. Advani, the party President, who did the job. He took the lead of a *Ram Rath Yatra* which was to wind its way from Somnath, in Gujarat, to UP, through central and northern India, hammering *Hindutva* into the minds of the people, attracting devotees and *kar sevaks*, monitoring the journey in order to reach Ayodhya on 30 October, the day which had been irrevocably fixed by the holy men to start the construction.

The success of the *Ram Yatra* is well known. Although met at first with derision from many quarters ('Toyota Hinduism'), the movement was now seen as an irrepressible show of strength (*India Today*, 15 October 1990: 18–24). In UP the atmosphere was tense, to say the least. For weeks the Chief Minister had warned the population against the mounting communal challenge. Rally followed rally, speeches followed speeches—aggressive unfortunately, with a strong pro-Muslim bias, they soon became counter-productive (Das, 1990, Dasgupta, 1990). A major riot erupted in Colonelganj (Gonda district) during the *Durga Puja* festival. The toll was heavy, each political party ascribing the main responsibility to its adversary. Communal polarization increased. The Chief Minister was now labelled 'Mullah' Mulayam.

October 29, 1990. It was red alert in UP but Ashok Singhal, the VHP leader, had managed to reach Ayodhya. It was an achievement, if one remembers that the Rath Yatra had been stopped in Bihar six days earlier, and Advani arrested. But it goes also to show that militants cannot be stopped unless civil authorities are ready to use strong-arm tactics. When, on 30 October, kar sevaks managed to plant saffron flags on the domes of the Babri Masjid, the police (PAC) looked the other way. The Border Security Force (BSF) had to be called in and there was firing. On 2 November, a second assault was launched. Again the BSF was called in. On both occasions, there were casualties.

The situation in the State during the following months defies description. Hindu militancy had been whipped up to a dangerous level. In

Muslim *mohallas*, after the Colonelganj tragedy, there had been fear, anger, and clashes. Now it was much worse. Processions no longer carried lights but bones and ashes. *Asthi Kalash Yatras* were meticulously organized and, by December, they started winding their way from district to district, performing all the necessary rituals, dramatized by an impressive arsenal of videos and audio-cassettes which, at times, played havoc. It was especially the case in Aligarh during the second phase of the riots which shook the State to the core (*Frontline*, 22 December 1990). Agra had to be put under curfew. In Lucknow, the Chowk and Aminabad were not spared.

The Chief Minister was now a political pariah, with everybody crying for his blood. Yet, Mulayam Singh Yadav held his ground. On the one hand, he was fiercely demonstrating that he had the capacity to survive the fall of V.P. Singh although, at the tail end of October, the BJP had withdrawn its support to the Janata Dal. On the other hand, the UP Chief minister was able to convey the impression (which was not entirely untrue) that, at the Centre, he was a real king-maker. He had been fully involved in the 'conspiracy' which was to lead to the emergence of Chandra Shekhar as the leader of a dissident JD outfit, the Samajwadi Janata Dal, which was now relying on an extraordinary 'marriage of convenience' with Rajiv Gandhi.

It was, if anything, a precarious arrangement. For Chandra Shekhar, it meant that at long last he was Prime Minister: an old ambition too often thwarted by his rivals and which was now achieved, whatever the means. He managed somehow to cobble a Government together, though the number of his followers (58) was very limited.

In Lucknow the situation was just as confusing. Of the 206 JD MLAs, a bare 80 were firmly behind the Chief Minister. Congress supporters and BSP MLAs notwithstanding, Mulayam Singh Yadav was finding it difficult to retain a majority. Even his own constituency was turning hostile. The Yadavs had taken his high-handedness in Ayodhya badly and they had to be placated. On 12 November, an ordinance was promulgated, raising the reservation quota for the OBCs from 15 to 27 per cent. With regard to his Muslim friends, such manoeuvers and cajoling were hardly possible. His hands were tied. The Congress had made it very clear that he should soften his attitude towards the kar sevaks.

Five months of communal and casteist turmoils had set the country afire. Now, slowly, the heat was dying down. At least on the Ayodhya 'front', where the Prime Minister had managed to persuade the two warring camps (i.e. the VHP and the Babri Masjid Committee) to sit and talk (*India Today*, 15 December 1990: 40). On both sides there was agreement that they had to tread with caution. Enough damage had been done by irresponsible pronouncements earlier. It was time to cool down passions, and get ready for the State elections which could be called any day. In UP at least, by mid-December 1990, the BJP had already started the process of finalising its list of candidates for the 425 Vidhan Sabha seats.

At the national level also, the BJP was ready to face the electorate, which was certainly not the case with the other political parties. The Hindu leaders exuded confidence, and nobody could doubt their determination to carry on with their Hindutva line. And the agenda announced by the VHP was just as clear. A mammoth meeting was to be held in Delhi on 4 April. In UP, mass contacts and public meeting with religious heads would begin on 1 February, and gather momentum until 4 April. *Sri Ramnavmi* was to be celebrated throughout 'Hindudom'.

Meanwhile, in Delhi, the Chandra Shekhar 'interlude' was nearing its end. A minor, farcical incident provided the last straw.[14] The Prime Minister was not prepared to take it kindly. He recommended the dissolution of Parliament to the President, who agreed (13 March 1991), and was asked to continue in office until the next government was formed.

In UP, of course, Mulayam Singh Yadav was not caught napping. Ramnavmi had been difficult. Riots had erupted in many places and, in Saharanpur, it was especially serious. However, the Chief Minister was not prepared to resign because of a Congress diktat. On 4 April, the day when the Boat Club in New Delhi turned saffron (*Sunday*, 14 April 1991: 12–14), the day also when Narain Dutt Tiwari was to withdraw support to his government, the Chief Minister recommended the dissolution of the Assembly and launched what was to be a fight to the finish. The reconstitution of the UP Vidhan Sabha would coincide with the polls for the Tenth Lok Sabha. The two rounds would be held in May.

The outcome of these memorable elections is well known. A Ram hurricane swept Uttar Pradesh and, shocking as it was, the assassination of Rajiv Gandhi did not alter the results much (see Brass, 1993b). The Congress was routed, saving only 5 seats out of 85. Its traditional vote-banks, or what was left of them, had deserted. The Muslim vote, supposedly tactical with the single purpose of supporting any candidate who could defeat the BJP, went astray, or so it seemed, in many constituencies. Equally wasted were the votes of the Scheduled Castes who could not help a single BSP candidate to win (see Gould, 1993). The Rajputs had been lost earlier. This time the Brahmins, who had stayed all along with the Congress, crossed over to the BJP.

Less spectacular than the Congress rout but nonetheless serious, was the situation of the Janata Dal. It had to share its constituency with the SJD, and there was no way out of this dilemma: for a large number of Muslims, both VP Singh and Mulayam were 'messiahs'; the *millat* was not prepared to listen to indiscreet *fatwas* supporting the former or the latter; up to the last minute people hesitated.[14] This was not the case with the Jats or Yadavs. Caste solidarities were remembered—Ajit Singh representing the Jats (although, this time, a number of Jats crossed over to the BJP), Mulayam the Yadavs. For Kurmis and Lodhs, it was the other way round. The BJP leader, Kalyan Singh, was a Lodh. Both Lodhs and Kurmis joined the BJP herd. All in all this meant a poor score of 22 Lok Sabha seats for the JD, 4 for the SJD, though together they could have managed 37 seats with 31 per cent of the votes.

But was it possible in any case to neutralize the saffron wave? According to most observers, it was like a steam roller. Unstoppable. It carried the day, and it was, in fact, much more than a 'referendum for Ram'. It was a desperate wish of the people for something different. No Congress *Raj*. No corruption. No divisive mandalization. A chance given to an entirely new leadership whose commitment looked promising.

This enthusiasm of course varied from region to region. The Hindu consolidation was particularly convincing in Uttarkhand (for the first time), Rohilkhand (Muslim population, 28.9 per cent), Upper Doab (Muslim population, 19.6 per cent) and Awadh. It was less visible in Bundelkhand (SC population: 25.4 per cent) and in Lower Doab. All in all, going it alone and contesting as many as 82 Lok Sabha seats out of 85, the BJP bagged 50. Among winning candidates, many were well-known VHP activists.

If we turn now to Lucknow, the contrast in the local atmspheres between the Capital and most places in UP during this crucial period is striking. Not in terms of decibels. The noise was deafening. Nor in terms of *Jai Sri Ram*. It was Ram all the way. However, in Lucknow, the winning candidate was no brash VHP militant. He was the amicable Atal Bihari Vajpayee, the former President of the BJP, former Foreign Minister during the Janata days. He was known for his moderate, reasonable views. He was a forceful speaker, swaying crowds at will, but never forgetting his good manners. Moreover he was an old-timer. He had been a student on the Lucknow campus. He had contested twice (unsuccessfully) the Parliamentary seat (1957 and 1962). He knew the city well.[15] He was obviously an unassailable candidate, and his adversaries could not do much. Ranjit Singh (Congress) tried his best. He could count upon a large support from the Kayastha community. Surprisingly, for the first time since 1984, upon a welcome Sikh support. But the Muslims were uncertain. They were no longer enthused with the outgoing Mulayam, and with the results of his militant secularism. They would have been grateful for advice from the respected 'Ali Mian', the Rector of the *Nadwa*. It did not materialize. At the last minute they made up their mind in favour of the SJP candidate, Mrs Heeru Saxena, who stood no chance. Yet she garnered 16.3 per cent of the votes, leaving only 21.3 per cent to Ranjit Singh. The sitting JD MP, Mandata Singh, managed a poor 6.1 per cent. A.B. Vajpayee won handsomely with 53.5 per cent. So did his BJP companions in the five Assembly constituencies. The whole of Lucknow had turned saffron.[16]

And saffron also of course was the government which the BJP leader, M. Kalyan Singh, presented before the new Assembly on 22 June. Saffron was the whole team which went along on pilgrimage with the new Chief Minister to Ayodhya on 25 June (*India Today*, 31 July 1991). It is hardly necessary to underline the symbolic value of such a move.

Let us stop at that. Our purpose is not to bring back memories of a period which started on a rather sober note and concluded amidst violence and the dismissal of the Kalyan Singh government, in December 1992.

Since then, the political landscape of Uttar Pradesh has changed again and again. The future is unpredictable, and yet one thing is certain: the old UP order is gone, and the leaders who came up during the years tentatively described in this chapter, represent social forces which never had their say in the past history of the State. The backward castes are on the center stage. The Scheduled Castes want to be heard. The upper-castes are fighting fiercely to retain a power which is fast slipping from their hands. Muslims are slowly emerging from their stupor, and they are keen to find a place for themselves in the on-going process. But which process? Could it be that 'mandalization', which has been obscured by the Mandir movement, would now take precedence over religious militancy? Would communal harmony be remembered if the fight for power, is to shake the whole fabric of the State? Who knows?

Chief Ministers	Years of election (Lok Sabha and Vidhan Sabha)	Chronology of national events	(%) Votes polled by the leading parties (L.S.) in UP	(%) Votes polled by the leading parties (V.S.) in UP	(%) votes polled by the two main candidates in Lok Sabha Constituency
G.B. Pant (INC) (1946–52)	1945–46	Exodus of population (1947–48) Crisis in Kashmir (1947–49) Assassination of Gandhi (Jan. 1948) Integration of Hyderabad (Sept. 1948) Constitution in force (26 Jan. 1950) Death of Sardar Patel (Dec. 1950) Zamindari Abolition Act (1951) P.D. Tandon resigns from Congress Presidency (Sept. 1951)			
G.B. Pant (INC) (1952–54)	1952 (LS & VS)	Arrest of Sheikh Abdullah (1953) Birth of Andhra (1953) (1954) US-Pak Treaty (1955) Conference of Bandung	INC 52.99 PSP 17.8 JS 7.29	INC 47.9 PSP 17.8 JS 6.4	Vijaya L. Pandit (INC) 69.2 H.G. Dayal (JS) 23.6

Chief Minister	Year	Events					Candidate	
Dr Sampurnanand (INC) (1954–60)	1957 (LS & VS)	(1956) Linguistic States (1959) Flight of Dalai Lama (1960) Bifurcation of Bombay State	INC 46.3 PSP 15.3 JS 14.8		INC 42.4 PSP 14.5 JS 9.8		Pulin Banerji (INC) (INC) A.B. Vajpayee (JS)	40.8 33.4
C.B. Gupta (INC) (1960–63)	1962 (LS & VS)	Riot in Jabalpur (1961) War with China	INC 38.20 JS 17.57 PSP 10.35		INC 36.3 JS 16.5 PSP 11.5		B.K. Dhaon (INC) A.B. Vajpayee (JS)	50.5 37.5
Mrs S. Kripalani (INC) (1963–67)		Communal flare-up (Srinagar, Calcutta). The CPI splits Death of Nehru (1964) L.B. Shastri PM Indo Pak War (1965) Death of Shastri and Indira Gandhi PM (1966)						
C.B. Gupta (INC) (Mar–Apr. 1967)	1967 (LS & VS)	Congress is defeated in several states but retains a majority at the Centre	INC 33.4 JS 22.2 SSP 10.3		INC 32.2 JS 21.7 SSP 10.0		Anand Mulla (Ind.) V.R. Mohan (INC)	36.5 28.5
Charan Singh (diss) (Apr. 1967–Feb. 1968)								
C.B. Gupta (INC/INC(O)) (Feb. 1969–Feb. 1970)	1969 (VS)	Congress splits and is challenged by a Grand Alliance Dramatic riots in Ahmedabad (1969) and Bhiwandi (1970)	INC 33.7 BKD 21.2 JS 17.9					

Chief Ministers	Years of election (Lok Sabha and Vidhan Sabha)	Chronology of national events	(%) Votes polled by the leading parties (L.S.) in UP	(%) Votes polled by the leading parties (V.S.) in UP	(%) votes polled by the two main candidates in Lok Sabha Constituency
T.N. Singh (INC(O)) (Oct. 1970–Mar. 1971)		Naxalite violence in West-Bengal / Crucial elections in Pakistan			
K. Tripathi (INC) (Apr. 1971–June 1973)	(1971) (LS)	Ten millions of Bengali refugees in India / War with Pakistan / Birth of Bangladesh / Deterioration of the economic situation	INC 48.6 / BKD 12.7 / JS 12.3 / INC(O) 8.6		Sheila Kaul (INC) 71.6 / P.D. Kapoor 21.7
H.N. Bahuguna (INC) (Nov. 1973–Nov. 1975)	1974 (VS)	Railway strike / JP Movement / Emergency (June 1975)		INC 32.3 / BKD 21.2 / JS 17.9	
N.D. Tiwari (INC) (Jan. 1976–Apr. 1977)		Incidents at Turkman Gate (Delhi) and Muzaffarnagar (UP) / Rise of Sanjay Gandhi			
	(1977) (LS)	The Janata wave sweeps North India / Morarji Desai PM	Janata 68.0 / INC 25.0		H.N. Bahuguna (Janata) 73 / Sheila Kaul (INC) 23.2

Chief Minister (party, term)	Year	Events	Results	Lucknow candidate
Ram Naresh Yadav (Janata) June 1977–Feb. 1979	(VS)	Alarming riots in Aligarh (1978) and in Jamshedpur (1979) Split of the Janata (1979) Charan Singh PM	INC 31.9	
Banarsi Das (Janata) (Feb. 1979–June 1980)	1980 (LS)	Indira Gandhi returns to power	INC (1) 35.9 Janata(S) 29.0 Janata 22.6	Sheila Kaul (INC.1) 47.6 Mahmood Butt (Janata) 35.9
V.P. Singh (INC.I) (June 1980–June 1982)	1980 (VS)	Death of Sanjay Massacre in Moradabad Conversions to Islam in Meenakshipuram (1981)	INC(I) 37.7 Janata(S) 21.6 BJP 10.6	
Sripat Mishra (INC.I) (June 1982–Aug. 1984)		Violence in Punjab Operation Blue Star (1984) Assassination of Indira Gandhi		
N.D. Tiwari (INC.I) (Aug. 1984–Sept. 1985)	1984 (LS)	Rajiv PM. Congress sweeps the polls	INC(I) 51.0 LKD 21.6 BJP 6.4	Sheila Kaul (INC.I) 55.7 Yunus Saleem (LKD) 15.5
Vir Bhadur Singh (INC.I) (Sept. 1985–June 1988)	1985 (VS)	Electoral victory of the AGP in Assam Dangerous moves on the communal front. The Shah Bano case and the unlocking of the Babri Masjid (1986). Riots and violence in Meerut. VP Singh leaves the Congress (1987)	INC(I) 39.3 DMKP 21.3 JP 9.9	

Chief Ministers	Years of election (Lok Sabha and Vidhan Sabha)	Chronology of national events	(%) Votes polled by the leading parties (L.S.) in UP	(%) Votes polled by the leading parties (V.S.) in UP	(%) votes polled by the two main candidates in Lok Sabha Constituency
N.D. Tiwari (INC(I)) (June 1988– Dec. 1989)		Birth of the Janata Dal (1988) Massacre in Bhagalpur Rajiv opens the electoral campaign in Faizabad Shilanyas in Ayodhya (Sept.–Nov. 1989)			
Mulayam Singh Yadav (JD) (Dec. 1989– June 1991)	1989 (LS & VS)	Rout of the Congress, V.P. Singh PM Deterioration of the situation in Kashmir Mandal on the centre stage Ram Yatra of LK Advani Riots spread (Oct. 1990) Chandra Shekhar PM Congress withdraws support (March 1991)	JD 36.0 INC(I) 31.8 BSP 9.9 BJP 7.6	JD 29.8 INC(I) 28.0 BJP 11.8 BSP 9.3	Mandhata Singh (JD) 34.1 Dr Dauji Gupta (INC(II)) 29.4

Kalyan Singh (BJP) (June 1991– Dec. 1992)	1991 (LS & VS)	Assassination of Rajiv Gandhi (May). Saffron wave in Northern India but, at the Centre, the Congress is given another chance. P.V. Narasimha Rao PM. In UP, CM Kalyan Singh (BJP) defies Supreme Court orders concerning Ayodhya. Demolition of the Babri Masjid and President's Rule (Dec. 1992)	BJP 32.8 JD 21.3 INC(I) 18.7 SJP 11.0 BSP 8.7	BJP 31.6 JD 19.1 INC(I) 17.6 SJP 12.6 BSP 9.3	A.B. Vajpayee (BJP) 53.5 Ranjit Singh (INC(I)) 21.3
Mulayam Singh Yadav (SP) (Dec. 1993– June 1995)	1993 (VS)	Assembly election in the four former BJP-ruled states (Nov.). No come back however for the BJP in UP where SP and BSP join hands to form a government.	BJP 33.4 SP 17.9 INC 14.8 JD 11.5 BSP 10.8		
Ms Mayawati (June–Oct. 1995)		An uneasy SP-BSP relationship until Mayawati withdraws BSP support and ascends the gaddi for a few months at the discretion of the BJP BJP withdraws support in Oct. and the Governor dissolves the Assembly.			

Chief Ministers	Years of election (Lok Sabha and Vidhan Sabha)	Chronology of national events	(%) Votes polled by the leading parties (L.S.) in UP	(%) Votes polled by the leading parties (V.S.) in UP	(%) votes polled by the two main candidates in Lok Sabha Constituency
	1996	On the eve of the LS elections, the situation is not as tense as it was in 1991, but UP continues on the caste-community polarisation path. Regarding the political forces, the Congress is totally discredited and divided (N.D. Tiwari has left and leads a new outfit, the Congress (T). The 'secular vote' will have therefore to be shared between the Rao-led Congress, the SP, Janata Dal-Left combine and the BSP. The BJP is aiming at the Centre and does not try to revive the Saffron militancy.			
	(LS)	The LS elections in May bring no surprise. Votes are divided. Yet, in spite of a disappointing score, the BJP leader, A.B. Vajpayee (re-elected in Lucknow) tries to form a government but	BJP 33.4 SP 20.8 BSP 20.6 INC 8.14 JD 4.25 INC(T) 3		A.B. Vajpayee (BJP) 53.19 Raj Babar (SP) 37.2

fails. A JD man from
Karnataka, Deve Gowda,
takes over as PM, in the
name of a secular combine
(UF + LF) with the support
of the Congress

(VS)   Crucial legislative elections in UP (Oct.).
        Again a relative set back for
        the BJP, but such a fractured
        verdict that the non-BJP forces
        are unable to reach a compromise.

BJP + Samta	32.7
SP ⎫ JD + LF ⎬ + INC(T) ⎭	29.4
BSP ⎫ INC ⎭	27.8

SOURCES: Compiled from official reports of the Election Commission of India, and from David Butler, Ashok Lahiri, Prannoy Roy, *India 'decides'*, Delhi, Living Media, 1991. Since 1991, The Hindustan Times, Frontline, India Today, Muslim India.

Chart 1: Distribution of Caste and Communities in UP, 1931

Category	Name of caste	Percentge of total population
A. Upper castes	*brahman*	9.2
	thakur	7.2
	bania	2.5
	kayastha	1.0
	khatri	0.1
Total of sub-group A:		20.0
B. Middle castes	*jat*	1.6
	bhumihar	0.4
	tyagi	0.1
Total of sub-group B:		2.1
C. Backward castes	*yadav*	8.7
	kurmi	3.5
	lodh	2.2
	koeri	2.8
	gujar	0.7
	kahar	2.3
	gadaria	2.0
	teli	2.0
	barhai	1.5
	kachi	1.3
	kewat	1.1
	murao	1.3
	nai	1.8
	others	10.7
Total of sub-group C:		41.9
D. Scheduled Castes	*chamar*	12.7
	pasis	2.9
	dhobi	1.6
	bhangi	1.0
	others	2.8
Total of sub-group D:		21.0
E. Muslims	*shaikh*	3.2
	pathan	2.2
	julaha	2.0
	syed	0.7
	moghul	0.1
	others (*faqir, shunia, teli, nai, darzi, qasah*, etc.)	6.8
Total of sub-group E		15.0

SOURCE: 1931 Census. United Provinces of Agra and Awadh, Part 2, Provincial and Imperial Tables, 1933.

Chart 2: Figures at a glance (1991)

Region	S.C. population (in %)	Muslim population (in %)
Uttarakhand	17.5	8
Ruhelkhand	15.3	28.9
Upper Doab	19.3	19.6
Avadh	25.9	13.9
Lower Doab	20.7	10.9
Bundelkhand	25.4	6.3
Poorvanchal	20.4	12.6
State	21.1	15.9

SOURCE: Yogendra Yadav, *Frontline*, 3 Dec. 1993

Chart 3: Uttar Pradesh

	UP	India
Total population (in thousand)	1,39,031	8,43,930
Density per sq/km	471	267
Growth rate population (1981–91)	+ 25.16%	+ 23.50%
Sex ratio	882	929
Literacy	41.71%	52.11%
Urban population (in thousands)	27,653	2,17,177
(% of population)	(19.89)	(25.72)

SOURCE: *Census 1991*. Provisional population totals Series 1, Paper 1 of 1991.

Chart 4: Lucknow (population)

Population 1991, urban agglomeration (UA)	16,42,134
males	8,79,704
females	7,62,430
Sex ratio	867
Growth rate:	
1971–81	+ 23.79
1981–91	+ 62.97

SOURCE: *Census 1991* (Rural-urban distribution)

Religions (Lucknow)

	1971	1981
Population total (UA)	8,13,982	9,16,954
Hindus	5,63,964	7,03,453
(including S.C.)	77,241	
Muslims	2,30,107	2,79,890
Christians	5,927	7,674
Sikhs	12,210	14,386
Buddhists	201	236
Jains	1,560	1,768

SOURCE: *Census 1971*, Part II–C (Uttar Pradesh Social and Cultural Tables)
Census 1981, Paper 4, 1984

NOTES

1. I must here express my gratitude to the many friends and colleagues who, along the years, granted me long and fruitful interviews: Professor S.K. Narain, S.M. Jaffar, Ram Advani, the staff of the *Pioneer*, Sunita Charles, Principal I.T. College, and Dilip Awasthi, *India Today*. I benefited also from the rich experience of several Magistrates, MLAs and former MLAs, and from the personal knowledge of M. Lalji Tandon, BJP leader, who hails from the Chowk. Last but not least, I am deeply indebted to Professor Abha Awasti, Head, Department of Sociology, University of Lucknow, who helped me to decipher the maps of the city.

2. This refers to the demand that all Janata members severed their links with the Rashtriya Swayam Sevak Sangh (RSS), a demand which had been regularly put to the Jan Sangh leaders and no less regularly rejected (see Anderson and Damle, 1987: 216–22).

3. Excellent surveys of the Janata story and its last days are to be found in Narain (1978 and 1979) and Dasgupta (1980).

4. It is also during this extremely tense summer that the VHP announced that the next phase of its action would concern Kashi (Varanasi) and Mathura, to re-annex the Vishwanath Temple and the Shri Krishna Janambhoomi which had been desecrated by the Mughal emperors.

5. The matinee-idol was Arun Govil who, for millions of TV viewers, had embodied the mythical hero of Doordarshan's most popular serial, the Ramayana. However, the situation being what it was, the human being who embodied the hero was V.P. Singh himself, set out to rout the forces of evil.

6. The first and most impressive show of strength displayed by Tikait and his BKU (Bharatiya Kisan Union) took place in 1987. In 1988 it looked as if he were to don the mantle of Charan Singh (*India Today*, 15 March 1988: 44–6).

7. They were noticed for the first time during the Bijnor contest in December 1985, when Mayawati gave a real scare to the daughter of Jagjivan Ram, Meera Kumar. Afterwards, it was a meteoric rise.

8. Within the *millat* the opinion was not at all favourable to a 'long march' which, in concrete terms, looked suicidal (interviews in Lucknow in 1989; also see Nayar, 1988).

9. It was in evidence in Ayodhya, where the miniature-model of the proposed temple was displayed in a *pandal* facing the Babri Masjid, and VHP leaflets freely distributed.

10. Interviews with N.D. Tiwari in 1989–90.

11. Interviews along the years with personalities like Prof. Satish Chandra, Rajeshwar Dayal and his wife, née Srivastava, Prof. T.N. Madan, etc.

12. The role that the BBC broadcast played that day was to raise a furore in various circles (interviews with BBC journalists in 1990).

13. The report prepared by the Mandal Commission at the request of the Janata Party Government had been kept in cold storage since the Congress victory in 1980.

14. It was alleged that, at the instance of the Government, the residence of Rajiv Gandhi was under 'surveillance', and that two plainclothes constables from neighbouring Haryana had been spotted where they had no business to be.

15. Interview with A.B. Vajpayee in 1991 and 1992.

16. It is interesting to note in this context that, although in the sixties, in Lucknow, the Hindu party attracted a large chunk of votes and managed to secure the mayoral seat when Independents obliged, it was never able, however, to gain complete control of the Municipal Corporation. It is one of the reasons why, along the years, neither the Jan Sangh, nor the BJP, were able to play the role they had visualized for themselves in both the Legislative and the Parliamentary elections in the City (Graham, 1990: 241–7). In 1991 the pattern was entirely new: a Congress candidate as well entrenched as Mrs Premwati Tiwari, the sitting MLA in the Cantonment, had to bow out. In Lucknow-East the efforts made by the other Congress candidate, Mrs Bakshi, to win back her constituency failed miserably.

REFERENCES

Advani, L.K. (1979), *The People Betrayed*, Delhi, Vision Books.

Akbar, M.J. (1978), 'The Varanasi Riots', in Udayan Sharma (ed.), *Violence Erupts*, New Delhi, Radha Krishna.

———— (1980), 'Id, Day of Death', *Sunday*, 24 August.

Awasthi, Dilip (1988), 'A Skilful Survivor', *India Today*, 31 May 1988.

Anderson, Walter and Shridar D. Damle (1987), *The Brotherhood in Saffron*, New Delhi, Vistaar.

Brass, Paul R. (1974), *Language, Religion and Politics in North India*, Cambridge, Cambridge University Press.

———— (1985), *Caste, Faction and Party in Indian Politics*, vol. 2, Delhi, Chanakya Publications.

———— (1993a), 'Caste, Class and Community in the Ninth General Elections for the Lok Sabha in Uttar Pradesh', in Harold Gould and Sumit Ganguly (eds), *India Votes*, Part I, Westview.

———— (1993b), 'The Rise of the BJP and the future of Party Politics in Uttar Pradesh', in Harold Gould and Sumit Ganguly (eds), ibid., Part II.

Burger, Angela S. (1969), *Opposition in a Dominant Party System: A Study of the Jan Sangh, the Praja Socialist Party, and the Socialist Party in Uttar Pradesh, India*, Berkeley, University of California Press.

Chawla, Prabhu (1982), 'A Crisis of Faith', *India Today*, 31 October 1982.

Chiriyankandath, James (1992), 'Tricolour and Saffron: Congress and the New Hindu Challenge', in Subrata Mitra and James Chiryankandath (eds), *Electoral Politics in India*, Delhi, Segment.

Chishti, Anees (1982), 'Meerut: Anatomy of a Riot', *Economic and Political Weekly*, 30 October 1982.

Chowdhury, Neerja (1986), 'The Communal Divide', *The Statesman*, 18–20 April.

Das, Arvind (1990), 'Mandal-Mandir Tussle: Importance of Mulayam Singh Yadav', *Times of India*, 21 September.

Dasgupta, Jyotirinda (1980), 'India, 1979: The Prize Chair and the People's Share. Electoral Diversion and Economic Reversal, *Asian Survey*, February, pp. 176–87.

Dasgupta, Swapan (1990), 'Confrontation in UP: Logic of Mulayam Singh's Offensive', *Times of India*, 24 September.

Engineer, Ashgar Ali (1984), *Communal Riots in Post-Independence India*, Delhi, Sangam Books.

———— (ed.) (1987), *The Shah Bano Controversy*, Delhi, Orient Longman.

———— (ed.) (1987), *Delhi-Meerut Riots*, Delhi, Ajanta.

———— (1989), 'Communal Riots in Muzaffarnagar, Kathauli and Aligarh', *Economic and Political Weekly*, 1 January.

Gould, Harold (1980), 'The Second Coming: The 1980 Elections in India's Hindi Belt', *Asian Survey*, June 1980, pp. 575–95.

———— (1993), 'Mandal, Mandir and Dalits: Meddling class with Ethno-religions Conflict in Indias' Tenth General Election', in Harold Gould and Sumit Ganguly (eds), *The Ninth General Elections: The Hung Parliament: India Votes*, Part I, Westview.

Graff, Violette (1980), 'Communal Relations in Indian Politics, A Case Study: Chandni Chowk (1967–1977)', in Marc Gaborieau and Alice Thoruer (eds), *Asia du Sud: Traditions et Changements*, Paris, Fditions du CNRS.

———— (1987), 'The Muslim Vote', in Paul R. Brass and Francis Robinson (eds), *The Indian National Congress and Indian Society, 1885–1985*, Delhi, Chanakya Publications.

———— (1990), 'Aligarh's long quest for Minority Status', *Economic and Political Weekly*, 11 August, pp. 1771–81.

———— (1991), 'Religious Identities and Indian Politics: Elections in Aligarh, 1971–1989', in Andre Wink (ed.), *Islam, Politics and Society in South Asia*, New Delhi, Manohar.

———— (1992), 'The Muslim Vote', in Subrata K. Mitra and James Chiriyantadath (eds), *Electoral Politics in India* New Delhi, Segment Books.

Graham, B.D. (1990), *Hindu Nationalism and Indian Politics: The Origins and Development of the Bhartiya Jana Sangh* Cambridge, Cambridge University Press.

Gupta, Shekhar, Farzand Ahmed and Inderjit Badhwar (1986), 'A Community in Turmoil', *India Today*, 31 January, pp. 50–60.

Hardgrave, Robert L. (1984), 'India in 1983', *Asian Survey*, February.

Hasan, Zoya (1989), 'Power and Mobilization: Patterns of Resilience in Uttar Pradesh Politics', in Francine R. Frankel and M.S.A. Rao (eds), *Dominance and State Power in Modern India*, vol. 1, Delhi, Oxford University Press.

——— (1987), 'Minority Identity, Muslim Women Bill Campaign and the Political Process', *Economic and Political Weekly*, 7 January, pp. 44–9.

Housego, David (1979), 'A Woman MP with Winning Ways', *The Financial Times*, 5 February.

Jaffrelot, Christophe (1996), *The Hindu Nationalist Movement and Indian Politics*, New Delhi, Viking.

Jain, Girilal (1980a), *The Times of India*, 17 August.

——— (1980b), *The Times of India*, 3 September.

Kapur, Anuradha (1993), 'Deity to Crusader: The Changing Iconography of Ram', in Gyanendra Pandey (ed.), *Hindus and Others*, Delhi, Viking.

Kothari, Rajni (1985), 'Behind the Ballot: The Problem', Seminar, February.

Madan, T.N. (1989), 'Urdu in India', *Times of India*, 16 October.

Mehta, Vinod (1989) 'Thank you and Good Bye', *Sunday*, 26 November.

Mirchandani, G.G. and K.S.R. Murthi (1985), *Massive Mandate for Rajiv Gandhi*, Delhi, Sterling.

Mitra, Chandan (1989a), 'Eclipse of Urdu', *Times of India*, 4 October.

——— (1989b), 'The One-Fourth Mandate, *Times of India*, 30 November.

Mustafa, Seema (1984), 'UP Minorities cannot be taken for granted', *The Telegraph*, 26 October.

Narain, Iqbal (1978), 'India 1977: From Promise to Disenchantment', *Asian Survey*, February, pp. 103–16.

——— (1979), 'India 1978: Politics of Non-Issues', *Asian Survey*, February, pp. 165–72.

——— (1986), 'India in 1985, Triumph of Democracy', *Asian Survey*, February, pp. 253–69.

Nayar, Kuldeep (1988), 'The Need for Tolerance', *Sunday*, 24 July.

Noorani, A.G. (1979), 'Urdu: Victim of Deliberate Neglect', *The Indian Express*, 14 March.

——— (1989), 'The Babri Masjid-Ram Janambhoomi Question', *Economic and Political Weekly*, 4 November, pp. 2461–6.

Padgaonkar, Dileep (1989), 'Vote without Mandate', *Times of India*, 29 November.

Parthasarathy, Malini (1989), 'The Winning Strategy', *Frontline*, 9 December.

Rudolph, S.H. and Lloyd I. Rudolph (1980), 'The Centrist Future of Indian Politics',

——— (1987), *Pursuit of Lakshmi*, Chicago, Chicago University Press.

Saberwal, Satish and Mushirul Hasan (1984), 'Moradabad Riot 1980: Causes and Meanings', in Asghar Ali Engineer (ed.), *Communal Riots in Post-Independence India*, Delhi, Sangam Books.

Sharma, Udayan (1982), 'A Divided City', *Sunday*, 20 November.

Sinha, Dipankar (1991), 'V.P. Singh, Chandra Shekhar, and "Nowhere Politics" in India', *Asian Survey*, July, pp. 598–612.

Sisson, R. and M. Majumdar (1991), 'India in 1990', *Asian Survey*, February, pp. 103–12.

Van der Veer, P. (1987), 'God Must be Liberated', *Modern Asian Studies*, vol. 21, no. 2, pp. 283–301.

Wariavwalla, Bharat (1988), 'India in 1987, Democracy on Trial', *Asian Survey*, February, pp. 119–25.

Weiner, Myron (1983), *India at the Polls: The Parliamentary Elections of 1977*, Washington D.C., AEI.

Wright, Theodore P. (1966), 'Muslim Education in India at the Crossroads: The Case of Aligarh', *Pacific Affairs*, Spring-Summer.

——— (1977), 'Muslims and the Indian Elections: A Watershed?', *Asian Survey*, December.

Yadav, Yogendra and Ashish Banerjee (1993), 'Elections', *Frontline*, 3 December, pp. 20–7.

15

Through the Eye of a Street

IMTIAZ AHMAD

Cities the world over are believed by their inhabitants to have a distinct character of their own. What precisely this 'character' inheres in is, however, far from clear. Does it inhere in a city's monuments and buildings, its streets and alleys, its market places and restaurants? Or in its people, the diversity of social communities to which they belong, their various socio-cultural backgrounds, and the kinds of associations and institutions through which they order and enrich their daily lives? Or, is the character of a city linked to the kind of life style and pattern of living it allows for its inhabitants and occasional visitors?

There can probably be no settled answer. Everyone who has spent any length of time in Lucknow will, however, easily concede that the distinctiveness of that city has always consisted in its ability to provide for its inhabitants, both elites and commoners, wealthy and poor, the possibility of a leisured life. Precisely what constituted this leisured way of life changed over nearly a century and a half. Accounts of nawabi Lucknow detail at length the pleasurable pastimes of its populace (see Sharar, 1975), and has been captured precisely by Kippen. He writes:

A favourite pastime of Lucknowis was the preparation, presentation and tasting of food in all of which they are reported to have been skilled. The best cooks in India came from the kitchens of the Lucknow nobility.

The Nawabs developed a taste for animal combat, and tigers, cheetahs, leopards, camels, rhinoceroses, stags and rams were made to fight for the court's entertainment. Elephants, too, charged and butted each other with such terrific impact that it is said the noise could be heard for miles around. Cock-fighting was a particular favourite. In fact, almost any type of bird was made to fight not least the quail.

Contests of all kinds were invented in human combat too. Men expertly weilding the sword, spears and cudgels engaged in martial arts, almost all of which have become obsolete. The most famous form was called *bank* and could either be fought in contests or used purely for self-defense. It involved the use of knives, as well as holds and throws similar to those in a Japanese aikido. A small number of people still practice *bank* today.

Kite-flying and kite-fighting are diversions in which Lucknowis were, and still are, renowned for their expertise. Few people remain untouched by the passion displayed for a hobby. As a boy, my tabla teacher, when not found practising the instrument, would be out in the parks fighting with his kites. The evening skies over the old city are speckled with hundreds of entangled kites. The string is impregnated with secret compounds comprising substances like ground glass and crushed eggshell, and he who cuts his opponent's string, leaving his own kite flying aloft is the winner (Kippen, 1988: 15–16).

Cock-fighting, kite and pigeon flying or visiting the singing girls for a musical session (*mujra*) in the evening were the familiar pastimes of an era which virtually fell into decline after the British takeover of Lucknow. Thereafter, a new pastime acquired great popularity: a kind of idle and aimless dawdling after sunset in the fashionable shopping area of Hazratganj, which the British developed after the transfer of the provincial capital to Lucknow. It came to be described by a one-word expression, 'gunjing', which brings back happy memories to those who cherish Lucknow.

The emergence of Hazratganj as the setting for dawdling or lounging about in restaurants has to be seen against the background of the British concern to make their cities reflect their political authority (see King, 1976). Usually, the centre point of the part of the city developed by them was the residence of the Viceroy or his provincial representative, the Governor. From there, the parts of the city created by them radiated in different directions. Closest to the residence of the central or the provincial authority were the Secretariat and the bungalows of the senior bureaucrats. Further away were the bungalows of the maharajas, rajas or nawabs and members of the nobility. And, beyond these were built the shopping areas, banks, etc.

Hazratganj, the street of the respectable, refers to a part of a central vista which runs from the bungalows of the senior bureaucrats of the Secretariat (now housing the ministers) at one end, and Lucknow University and the Isabella Thobourn College, a prestigious women's college, at the other. On one side of this avenue, nearly a kilometre from the Governor's house, is the General Post Office, a stately building of white cement with a clock tower. On the other side is the Allahabad Bank, one of the oldest buildings of this part of the city. At the other end, approximately less than a kilometre, one finds a multi-storied shopping-cum-residential complex called Halwasiya Market adjoining the State Bank of India. Hazratganj is the name given to that stretch between the intersection facing the Allahabad Bank and the General Post Office, and the Halwasiya Market.

Hazratganj had been created as a posh shopping centre by the British. On both sides of the vista there were shops with a covered verandah running in front. The limits of Hazratganj in those days extended from the Capital Cinema directly facing the GPO to the Mayfair Cinema and the Lucknow Cathedral. There was no Halwasiya Market then as that building was constructed only in the fifties. There was also a huge life-like statue of King George VI in a park facing the GPO building. After a country-wide movement launched by the socialist leader Ram Manohar Lohia, during the sixties for the removal of symbols reminiscent of India's colonial and imperialist past this statue was removed. The canopy under which the statue stood is still there and is used by those who choose to sit and relax on a hot summer evening or by masseurs to cater to clients.

At the time that British glory was at its peak, Hazratganj was off limits to Indians. At certain hours of the evening, they were not allowed to enter the street. In case they did, they could only walk along a lane parallel to the main street. However, this ban could not have been continued for long. As a child growing up in Lucknow not far from Hazratganj, I have vivid memories of the celebrations marking the victory of the Allied forces in the Second World War. Huge crowds flocked to Hazratganj and greeted the British soldiers passing through the street. They were surrounded and cheered by crowds and could only make a quick escape by tossing chewing gum to the crowd.

Tea drinking was relatively unknown even around the end of the war. The Lipton Tea Company was trying to popularise its brand among Indians and Lipton's mobile vans were stationed at convenient locations in Hazratganj to distribute cups of free tea to Indians. Even if the entry of Indians was prohibited at some time in the past, it was no longer the case around the end of the Second World War. At any rate, the British left soon after and Hazratganj, which had started out as a shopping centre for the British and the landed aristocracy, many of whose members had their bungalows around it, underwent a tansformation.

The most fundamental change was in terms of its clientele. Increasingly this tended to consist, apart from a remnant of a highly modernised social elite which modelled its behaviour pattern and life style on that of the British and the landed aristocracy of the Rajas and Maharajas, of sections of the middle class dependent upon the Secretariat, and the sons and daughters of this class studying in Lucknow University. It was a familiar sight in the early years after Independence to see a class of Indians western in their taste and habit in felt hats patronising the exclusive stores of Hazratganj and boasting that their clothes had been tailored by Ram Lal, clothiers, tailors and drapers, their wrist watches bought from Whorra Bros, or their woolens drycleaned by Back In A Day. Each summer these western-looking gentlemen shifted to Nainital, the summer capital of the state, and there patronised the branches of the stores at which they shopped in Hazratganj. Gradually, however, this class of Indians was pushed out of their pre-eminent presence in Hazratganj by the more ordinary middle class: the junior bureaucracy, civil servants, and teachers and students of Lucknow University.

Lucknow had a small population of Anglo-Indians and Indian Christians, most of whom lived in the localities adjoining Hazragunj. The Anglo-Indians were largely dependent on the administration and worked as guards, drivers and ticket collectors in the railways. Their women worked as nurses or as secretarial assistants in the government offices. Their interactions with Indian were extremely limited. They usually kept to themselves or associated with British officials, with whom they identified closely. This invited a certain disdain and hostility from the local population which tended to keep them at a distance. There was an Anglo-Indian family living next to the college where I studied. All the boys used to have a great deal of curiosity about them. Each time they passed in front of the house, the women used to come out and scold them for making too much noise or being a nuisance, and asked them to disappear. The boys retaliated by breaking their flower pots and glass panes, and throwing stones from a distance. On the whole, therefore, the relationship between the Anglo-Indians and the local people was an uneasy one, devoid of interaction.

The Anglo-Indians had a visible presence in Hazratganj during the days of the British and for some time thereafter. The men, in dark suits, and bow-ties and girls dressed in flimsy blouses and dark skirts, converged daily on Hazratganj and paraded up and down the street demonstrating their somewhat stand-offish attitude towards Indians. Apart from the Railway Club close to Charbagh Railway Station, the Lucknow Cathedral right in the middle of Hazratganj and the Lucknow Club closeby were their principal meeting points. After the British left, the

Anglo-Indians were taunted and booed for their earlier stand-offish attitude and their proclivity to consider themselves the natural heirs and successors to the British. Gradually they stopped visiting Hazratganj. Many eventually left for England.

The Indian Christians did not have the liabilities of the Anglo-Indians. They were deeply embedded into the local population. Those who were well-off, were either professionals or worked in the government offices. This brought them in close contact with the local people. Poorer Indian Christians worked as nurses, midwives and wardboys, or as waiters and cooks. An average Hindu or Muslim might observe certain restrictions in visiting the homes of the Indian Christians, or sharing food with them, but this did not stand in the way of their having cordial relations with each other. Many of my college friends were Christians and each Christmas we visited them enthusiastically to partake of the excellent cakes and dry meats they prepared: On the occasion of Id, my family sent a portion of the vermicelli and sacrificial meat to their homes. Dr. F. Soloman, a practitioner of homeopathic medicine who had built up an impressive record of social work for himself, used to go about each Id and Diwali, visiting all the residents of the localities from where his patients came. This endeared him greatly to his associates and patients and created a vast network of social support from him so much so that he went on in the fifties to join politics along with Dr. A.J. Faridi, and contested elections from constituencies where Hindus and Muslims predominated.

Christian missions have had a remarkable presence in Lucknow since Nawabi times, probably because of the relatively tolerant and open attitude of the rulers. They had created a large number of educational and cultural institutions. This reinforced the close interaction between Indian Christians and the local people. Apart from the La Martiniere and Loreto Convent, created as relatively exclusive schools for the British as well as the Indian nobility, there were a host of other educational and social institutions patronized by a growing middle class. The same was true of the Young Men's Christian Association. Most of its activities such as games and sports and discussions, attracted others as much as Christian boys and girls. This gave the Christians a pre-eminence beyond what might be warranted by their numbers or their hold over economic resources, and softened popular attitudes towards them. Indeed, the model of the YMCA was later followed by the Bengali community which established the Bengali Club. Christian Missionary Schools are today among the most prestigious educational institutions in Lucknow, as elsewhere, and several of them are located in or around Hazratganj or are easily approachable from there.

The departure of the British was accompanied by the partition holocaust and the large-scale migration of Punjabi, Sindhi and Sikh refugees. Lucknow enjoyed a reputation as a city where peace prevailed even during the worst post-partition violence and rioting. A very large number of Punjabi refugees came to Lucknow and eventually made it their home. This had a most dramatic impact upon the city, including Hazratganj (see Saxena, 1973). On the one hand, the influx of a refugee population, which was seen by local inhabitants to be aggressive, boorish and unsophisticated, affected the polite forms of language which had been a treasured heritage of Lucknow. On the other hand, it brought about a significant shift in the makeup of the ownership of the shops in Hazratganj. A number of shops owned by Muslims who had left for Pakistan were given to refugees under the Evacuee's Property provision.

Another change which accompanied the influx of refugees was a steady increase in the number of restaurants and eating houses. There were only a few restaurants in Hazratganj during the British rule. After Independence, due largely to the changing clientele a number of restaurants of different types and ratings came up in Hazratganj. The Kwality restaurant housed in the Mayfair Cinema building (where English films are still screened), reminiscent of its colonial past, was exclusive. Then there was the Ranjana Restaurant which catered mainly to the middle class and was seen as a family place. This meant that if one went to Hazratganj accompanied by ladies one preferred to go to 'Ranjana', as it had separate cabins to seat women and families.

There was also Benbows Restaurant. It had been an exclusive pastry shop in earlier days, but with the change in Hazratganj's clientele, a section of the pastry shop had been converted into a restaurant. It was an exclusive tea shop and was patronised by senior politicians and journalists and renowned professors of the University who gathered there in the evenings to discuss current affairs and create networks of social relations. Leading socialist leaders like Acharya Narendra Dev, Ram Manohar Lohia, and Sucheta Kripalani, renowned academicians such as N.K. Sidhantha, D.P. Mukherji and D.N. Majumdar, and writers like Yashpal, Amrit Lal Nagar and Bhagwati Charan Varma, who dominated the political and cultural scene of Lucknow during the fifties, made it a point to come and spend a couple of hours at Benbows at least on Sundays.

Perhaps the most significant development in this sudden mushrooming of restaurants and eating places was the establishment, some years before Independence, of a Coffee House of the Indian Coffee Board. Coffee drinking had not been very popular in Lucknow. The new place was, to begin with, quite exclusive, where senior bureaucrats, journalists and University teachers dropped by. Within a few years, however, this exclusive character of the place was eroded. From being an exclusive place where one dropped in to have an aromatic cup of coffee, it soon acquired the character of a cafe where young journalists, junior teachers and students of the University came and spent long hours engaged in animated discussions about current affairs and academic subjects. Marxism being a major attraction for the younger people in the early fifties, a good many of the students subscribing to Marxist ideology also congregated here. There was a certain intellectualism, a sense of being a progressive, that went with being a regular at the Coffee House.

Indeed, spending a few hours here in the morning and again from early evening until the establishment closed at night had become such a habit amongst some, that those looking for them could be reasonably certain where to find them. Even if one were not a regular, and even if one had no money one could still be sure of finding a friend who would offer a welcome cup of coffee. This promoted a certain kind of parasitism. There were those who prowled around until one of their 'friends' or even a distant acquaintance showed up. As soon as he had taken a table and ordered coffee, they would come forward on the pretext of saying 'hello', pull up a chair, and sit down. Custom obliged the 'friend' to offer coffee even if friendship was superficial.

The third significant change which came over Hazratganj in the years following Independence was the growth of tiny kiosks in the verandah which ran right across the street in front of the impressive stores. This was largely a consequence of the shift in the clientele. As an increasing number from the middle class now flocked to Hazratganj not so much to shop as to enjoy a leisurely stroll, these kiosks did brisk business in cheap cosmetics, costume jewellery and similar items which this new clientele could afford. Thus, in effect, Hazratganj had within two decades after the departure of the British, become divided into two worlds. On the one hand, there were the exclusive stores where one peeped in or mustered up enough courage to enter and ask the price of a thing one could not afford, and on the other hand, there were the kiosks all along the verandah where cheaper and affordable items were on display.

The change in the clientele which now patronized Hazratganj had a particularly telling effect on its bookshops. There were three bookshops in Hazratganj. The British Book Depot and Universal Book Company had been established during the British period, and had a typical colonial ambience. They stored fiction, reference works and books on *shikar*, travel, interior decoration, hobbies, etc. The Universal Book Company also kept text-books for the University and Medical College. As the people who habitually read English fiction or books on shikar, travel and interior decoration, etc. gradually ceased frequenting Hazratganj, the types of books kept by both bookstories changed too. Both gradually ended up becoming outlets for text-books and stationery, first for the La Martiniere and the Loreto Convent and subsequently for the host of Christian and other public schools which started coming up around Hazratganj.

The third bookshop was Ram Advani. Established after Independence, Ram Advani was a specialized bookstore. Besides English fiction, it kept academic books on the social sciences and the humanities, particularly anthropology and sociology. It was air-conditioned (perhaps the only air-conditioned bookshop in the country at that time). A good many senior professors of the University used to visit the bookstore on their way home from the Benbows Restaurant or the Coffee House to see or browse through the new books that had arrived. Two easy chairs seated anyone wanting to browse through the books for sometime.

As browsing was possible and was in any case not frowned upon, this turned out to be a boon for keen students who wished to read the latest books but could not afford to buy them. There was one book on our courses, an anthropology text, of which only a single copy existed in the University Library. Since there was keen competition among the students to read it, I found it difficult to read the library copy. Nor could I afford to buy a personal copy. Accordingly, I periodically visited Ram Advani, picked up a copy of the book, sat down on one of the easy chairs in the corner and quietly read through the chapter which was to be the subject of the class lectures that week. As time passed, even Ram Advani had to adjust to the change in the clientele. and took to supplying books to outside libraries and scholars abroad. But it still remains a pleasant experience for anyone who had lived in Lucknow to drop in at Ram Advani on a visit to the city.

'Gunjing' as a word of common parlance came to acquire popularity in the context of these sea changes brought about by the democratisation of the clientele. Step by step, it came to denote a compulsive urge to go to Hazratganj for a couple of hours in the evening as an act of personal recreation. It was a common sight to see hordes of youngsters walking up and down, cracking jokes, chatting and engaging in mild taunts with similar other groups. The important point about 'gunjing' was that as the evening descended one felt impelled to don one's best attire and start moving towards Hazratganj. 'Gunjing' in this sense had an element of both the ceremonial and the mundane. Even in homes where boys and girls were brought up in strict discipline and denied the freedom to stay late out of doors, an allowance was made for them to spend a couple of hours dawdling around in Hazratganj. There is an interesting case of a friend who later went on to become a well-known film personality. Each evening, dressed in his immaculate suit he came to Hazratganj at sunset and walked up and down several times until the shops closed and the place was deserted. His friends jocularly observed that he suffered from a tremendous anxiety about Hazratganj and walked around each day to ensure that the place had not really shrunk.

The pressure of so many people flocking to Hazratganj each evening for a stroll necessitated that the street be kept as clear of traffic as possible. Traffic was allowed on the street but parking or stalling was discouraged. This rule was enforced particularly on the cycle rickshaws. Apart from cars which were few and far between, the horse-drawn *ikka* (a raised carriage where three people could sit, one in the middle with folded legs, and two on either side with feet resting on a platform) and *tonga* (a low carriage for four people, two up front and two at the back) the rickshaw was the ordinary mode of public transport in Lucknow. The ikka had become confined to carrying passengers between Aminabad, the traditional part of new Lucknow, and Chowk area, the nawabi Lucknow, and the tonga was primarily used to negotiate the distance to and from the railway station. Once the tonga ceased to be a popular mode of transportation, the *tongawallahs* started plying their tongas on a per person basis over short distances. It came to be used by people to reach Hazratganj, particularly from the old Lucknow areas. However, regulations required that the tongas let off their passengers at the point of entry to Hazratganj and were not generally allowed to go into the street. Under the circumstances cycle rickshaws were the common mode of transport inside Hazratganj. As soon as the passenger alighted, the traffic constable chased the rickshaw pullers away.

The processes of democratisation of the client population could not remain restricted at that level for long. Soon enough it extended itself to the rickshaw pullers as well. They no longer disappeared to their specified parking places after letting off their passengers, but stalled along the street waiting, looking for passengers. Quite by coincidence, this change was reinforced by another development in the old city, the nawabi Lucknow. This was the social devastation caused by the abolition of zamindaris among the Muslim aristocratic families.

As a Nawabi city, Lucknow could boast of a very sizeable aristocratic Muslim population which survived through exploitation of agricultural surplus. After the Mutiny these members of the Court aristocracy were displaced and in their place a new order of nobility was created from the ranks of the local rulers, the landowners and collectors, known as zamindars and taluqdars (Metcalf, 1979).

These new zamindars had been able to sustain a way of life marked by pomp and glory and indulgence in esoteric pastimes without having in any way to exert themselves. Unlike the intermediate landed aristocracy which had shifted to Lucknow from adjoining areas such as Sundila and Barabanki and established itself in the emerging legal and other elite professions, the traditional zamindars of Lucknow, most of whom were absentee landholders, had little need to develop skills, and continued to depend upon the surplus extracted from land in the form of land revenue.

The abolition of zamindaris in the post-Independence period dealt a severe blow to Muslim zamindars and the distant descendants of the former Nawab. Most of them had been absentee landlords, hardly ever having tried to establish any link with their zamindaris. Thus, zamindari abolition wrought widespread devastation, and took away all viable means of respectable social existence.

For some time respectability was maintained by sale of zamindari bonds issued by way of compensation for the land confiscated from them. This was followed by sale of such valuables as the household might have possessed, so as to maintain the facade of respectability and grandeur to which the families had become used. Once even this option had been exhausted, the only viable choice left was for the menfolk to wake up from their aristocratic slumber, take to work, and start earning. Unfortunately, used to an idle life style and given to enjoyment of pastimes, the men of these families had few skills. A false sense of prestige also prevented them from taking on gainful work or trade. One of the consequences was that women had to come forward and take up the responsibility of maintaining the families. As the intensity of poverty increased, Muslim women of the erstwhile aristocratic families began taking to clandestine prostitution.

Access to Hazratganj in a rickshaw which stalled around until a suitable client was found came in useful for the practice of clandestine prostitution. For one, it made it possible for these women to keep their family honour intact through the anonymity of a place where people of their own cultural environment were unlikely to be encountered. Further, it increased their chances of finding a customer who was likely to have the resources to pay, especially as the class that could afford the luxury of clandestine prostitution was much more likely to be found around Hazratganj. On the whole, therefore, around the late fifties and early sixties, the *burqa* clad woman sitting in a rickshaw, her veil slightly raised, was a pathetic sight.

Lucknow's face began to change rapidly after 1960. Until then Lucknow had persisted very largely as an administrative and cultural centre with little trade and commerce, which was virtually the monopoly of its Hindu trading communities and a small population of Muslim trading families. Around that time, Lucknow began experiencing industrial expansion through establishment of ancillary private industries along the highway to neighbouring Kanpur, and state-owned scooter and other industries eastward beyond the Gomti river. The one immediate consequence was the mushrooming of new residential colonies for a new skilled workforce. As these new migrants settled in residential colonies within reasonable distance from Hazratganj, they now began patronising the shopping area as a regular marketing place, and not a street where one came to spend a few leisurely hours strolling or interacting with friends.

This transformed the face of Hazratganj. Many of the old restaurants closed down, to be replaced by grocery stores. Old exclusive stores that so prominently displayed 'By Appointment to the Governor' converted themselves into sales depots holding 'exhibition-cum-sale' of cheap mill-made saris at reduced prices. A few exclusive shops were bought over by chain stores. Outside, the growth of kiosks and pavement shops multiplied, as did the number of hawkers and vendors. The construction of Janpath, a complex of retail stalls off the street, as well as the growth of small stalls selling cheap wares along the lanes leading away on the sides, has further eclipsed the grandeur of Hazratganj.

Outside, the volume of vehicles as well as people multiplied. To regulate traffic and to prevent the shoppers from spilling on to the street, the administration put up iron railings all along on both sides of the road which hampered free movement. As an old resident of Lucknow, who had in the past engaged in the familiar pastime of 'gunjing' with so many college and university mates, I went to Hazratganj every time I returned to Lucknow. I also visited the Coffee House and the Kwality Restaurant.

Each time, I felt deeply, that the Hazratganj I knew was lost forever. Nor were there the old friends I used to see. This does not mean that for old Lakhnavis, who cannot feel reconciled with the transformations of their city, nostalgia has to be nurtured for ever. Certainly not. A city has to grow and adjust to the processes of change and modernisation. The important thing is to remember that Lucknow was after all no ordinary city.

REFERENCES

King, A.D. (1976), *Colonial Urban Development: Culture, Social Power and Environment*, London, Routledge and Kegan Paul.

Kippen, James (1988), *The Tabla of Lucknow: A Cultural Analysis of a Musical Tradition*, Delhi, Manohar.

Metcalf, Thomas (1979), *Land, Landlords, and the British Raj: Northern India in the Nineteenth Century*, Berkeley, University of California Press.

Saxena, D.N. (1973), *Differential Urban Fertility: Lucknow*, Lucknow Demographic Research Centre, University of Lucknow.

Sharar, Abdul Halim (1975), *Lucknow: The Last Phase of an Oriental Culture*, E.S. Harcourt and Fakir Hussein (trans. and eds), London, Paul Elek.

Index